EUROPEAN
DEMOCRACIES

EUROPEAN DEMOCRACIES

FIFTH EDITION

Jürg Steiner
*University of North Carolina at Chapel Hill
and University of Bern, Switzerland*

Markus M.L. Crepaz
The University of Georgia

PEARSON

Longman

New York   San Francisco   Boston
London   Toronto   Sydney   Tokyo   Singapore   Madrid
Mexico City   Munich   Paris   Cape Town   Hong Kong   Montreal

Editor-in-Chief: Eric Stano
Senior Marketing Manager: Elizabeth Fogarty
Production Manager: Bob Ginsberg
Project Coordination, Text Design, and Electronic Page Makeup: Carlisle Publishing
    Services
Cover Design Manager/Cover Designer: Wendy Ann Fredericks
Visual Researcher: Rona Tuccillo
Manufacturing Manager: Mary Fischer
Printer and Binder: RR Donnelley & Sons Company/Harrisonburg
Cover Printer: Phoenix Color Corporation

Library of Congress Cataloging-in-Publication Data
Steiner, Jürg.
    European democracies / Jürg Steiner. — 5th ed.
        p. cm.
    Includes bibliographical references and index.
    ISBN 0-321-07773-3
    1. Europe—Politics and government—1945- 2. Democracy—Europe. I. Title.

JN94.A2S74 2006
320.94—dc22

                                                                2006040868

Visit us at www.ablongman.com

ISBN 0-321-07773-3

12345678910—DOH—09 08 07 06

CONTENTS

PREFACE

For this fifth edition Markus M. L. Crepaz has joined Jürg Steiner as coauthor. This collaboration was an incentive to rethink the substance and organization of the entire book. The biggest change since the fourth edition is that we now integrate Western and Central and Eastern Europe into a unified analysis. It is high time for such integration after the end of the cold war and the entry of most Central and Eastern European countries into the European Union.

Another big change is the addition of an introductory chapter, a systematic comparison of the history and politics of Europe and the United States. We have also added a new concluding chapter on Europe and globalization. A third important change is the stronger emphasis on historical depth of the analysis; we show more in detail, for example, on the historical origins of political parties and parliaments in the European context.

Much of the institutional material on political parties, election systems, cabinet formation, the courts, federalism, and the referendum remains in place but is, of course, thoroughly updated. For an overview of all the chapters, see the last section of Chapter 1, "Structure of the Book."

With regard to presentation, we have added many more graphs and updated photos. We also rely less on quotes and more on our own words to report new research findings from the literature, which should make the text more readable.

European Democracies is written by two European scholars with extensive experience in teaching European politics to American students. We use three pedagogical principles to make the material accessible. First, the material leads the student from known to unknown material, from easy to more difficult questions. If at all appropriate, for each new issue the text begins with the American situation and then asks how the European situation is both similar and different. Given this method, the organization of the text is by topic and not by country.

How can information about the individual countries be presented in a topical framework? This goal is accomplished by following a second pedagogical principle: A few carefully chosen in-depth discussions teach students more than broad surveys. Our goal is to teach students the major concepts of European politics. The text does not encourage students to memorize facts and names, but rather to understand the principles behind them. If a text tries to cover all European countries, the treatment of each country must necessarily be somewhat superficial. Limiting the discussion to the three or four largest European countries is also unsatisfactory, because some of the most exciting political questions arise in the smaller European countries. For example, Sweden in 1996 provides an excellent introduction to the concept of a minority cabinet with the rule of its small Liberal Party. This simple and instructive example is used to explain the general circumstances under which a party lacking a legislative majority might form a cabinet and govern.

As a third pedagogical principle, the text explicitly addresses why knowledge of other countries should matter to American students. When they have seen the many ways in which Europeans handle politics differently from Americans, they may ask: "So what? What does this mean for us? Should we act like Europeans, or should they act like us?"

The discussion of each topic ends with such normative questions without trying to answer them in any definitive way. In teaching on both sides of the Atlantic, it is striking to note the different responses of American and European students for many normative political questions. Although American and European students need not share the same values, they should become more aware of how their values differ. In studying these normative questions, students ultimately will learn more about themselves and their values.

Thus, our third pedagogical principle leads back to the first one: The study of European politics not only should start at home but should also end at home. Having seen how Europe is different, American students may change some of their ideas about how a good democracy should function, while at the same time some of their old ideas may be reinforced.

JÜRG STEINER
MARKUS M. L. CREPAZ

ABOUT THE AUTHORS

Jürg Steiner is professor emeritus at the University of North Carolina at Chapel Hill and the University of Bern in Switzerland. He held a 2003/2004 chair position at the European University Institute in Florence, Italy. He is the winner of several teaching awards. Earlier editions of *European Democracies* have been translated into Polish and Russian. His most recent publication is *Deliberative Politics in Action,* Cambridge University Press, 2004. Currently he works on the potential for deliberative politics in deeply divided societies such as Northern Ireland, the Ukraine, Bosnia-Herzegovina, Kosovo, and Turkey. Steiner is a Swiss citizen, dividing for more than 30 years his teaching time between the United States and Europe.

Markus M. L. Crepaz was born and raised in Austria. After attending the University of Salzburg from 1982 to 1986, he began his graduate study at the University of California, San Diego, where he completed his Ph.D. in 1992. He is currently an Associate Professor at the University of Georgia. He has published numerous articles on electoral engineering, European politics, corporatism, and the impact of political institutions on a host of policy outcomes. His current research focuses on the effects of increasing immigration on the willingness of European publics to continue funding the welfare state. His forthcoming book is entitled *Trust Beyond Borders: Immigration, Identity and the Welfare State in Modern Societies* and will be published by the University of Michigan Press in 2007. Having lived in both worlds, the Old and the New, gives him a unique perspective from which to teach and research European politics in the United States.

EUROPEAN DEMOCRACIES

CHAPTER 1

Becoming Modern in Europe and America: Different History, Different Politics

American tourists visiting European cities are invariably attracted to features in the landscape that Europeans take for granted, features utterly absent in the United States. Through the viewfinders and digital displays of their cameras they eagerly search for uniquely "European" features, and once they find them, they enthusiastically shoot away at the towering castles, impressive cathedrals, old town squares, and city walls. Much of contemporary European politics—such as the presence of Socialist parties, strong unions, secularism, and highly developed welfare states—is directly linked to these structures for they attest to a time of drastic status differences between the rulers and the ruled whose origins go back to the Middle Ages. In an attempt to overcome these status differences—for example, in making politics "the art of the possible" where virtually all adults can actively participate in the political process—European history became intimately intertwined with revolutions, upheavals of sudden and violent changes of power structures that ultimately manifested themselves in the presence of strong Socialist parties, powerful unions, mostly secular societies, and a highly influential state apparatus. The ultimate prize of these struggles was the development of extensive welfare states in Europe while the United States, lacking a "genuine revolutionary tradition,"[1] only developed a skeletal welfare state.

The absence of these architectural structures in the United States also helps to explain the deviant or exceptional nature of American politics. Although in every major modern country Socialist, Social Democratic, Labour, or Communist parties play a central role in the respective legislatures, in the United States Socialist parties are peculiarly absent, the welfare state is much less developed, unions are weak, and churches are strong. The consequences of these differences are that, "In comparative terms, the United States combines an extremely high standard of living with exceptionally low levels of taxation and social spending, and exceptionally high levels of income inequality and poverty."[2]

HOW DO WE KNOW THAT EUROPE IS DIFFERENT?

What exactly are the differences that set European and American politics and society apart? The following characteristics provide a place to begin:

- **Socialist Parties.** Socialist parties enjoy a massive presence in European legislatures, versus the total absence of Socialist parties in the American Congress.
- **The Welfare State.** The welfare state in Europe is extensively developed—for example, income replacement programs that protect people in case of accident, sickness, unemployment, and old age, but also programs that enable citizens to become active participants in the economic and social life of their country such as job training programs, stipends, subsidized transportation to work, educational subsidies and others—whereas the welfare state in the United States exists in only skeletal form.

1

10% more GDP on social .

In 2001, the 15 members of the European Union (Austria, Belgium, Denmark, Finland, France, Germany, Greece, Ireland, Italy, Luxembourg, the Netherlands, Spain, Sweden, Portugal, and the United Kingdom) spent on average around 24 percent of their GDP (gross domestic product) on such social expenditures while the United States spent about 14.8 percent,[3] as shown in Figure 1.1. Even countries with a long authoritarian past and that joined the European Union (EU) relatively recently such as Greece, Portugal, and Spain, and Central and Eastern European countries such as Hungary and Poland, spend a higher percentage of their GDP on social expenditures than the United States.

The goal of such programs is to make people's survival independent of the action of market forces. Redistribution is mainly achieved through taxes and transfer payments such as retirement, disability, and health-care payments. Welfare states have a high capacity to redistribute incomes. For example, the percent of households in poverty defined as living below 50 percent of median income *before* taxes and transfers in Sweden was 52 percent, whereas in the United States it was 37 percent

After taxes and transfer payments are taken into consideration, only 8 percent of Swedes lived in poverty whereas 24 percent of Americans lived in poverty in the mid-1990s. Taxes and transfer payments reduced poverty in Sweden by over 80 percent, but reduced poverty in the United States by only 34 percent.[4] The "redistributive capacity of the state" captures the degree to which taxes and transfer payments lift

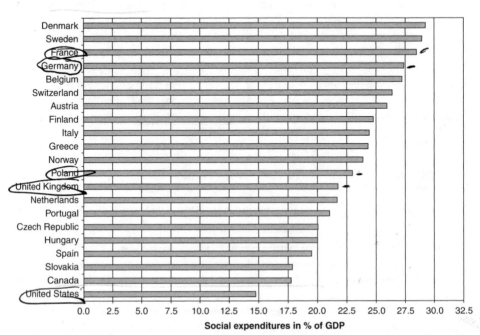

FIGURE 1.1 Social expenditures (old age, health, survivors, incapacity-related benefits, family benefits, and others) as percentage of gross domestic product. (*Source:* Organization for Economic Cooperation and Development. *OECD Social Expenditures Database,* 2005).

people out of poverty. Figure 1.2 shows that compared to all other European societies, the ability of taxes and transfer payments to lift Americans out of poverty is significantly smaller.

- **Unionization Rates.** Most European countries have a highly unionized workforce. Although union density—the percentage of workers who are also members of unions—is declining almost everywhere in industrialized democracies, the average union density in the 15 EU countries was around 43 percent, compared with 13 percent in the United States in 2003. There is tremendous variation in the union density rates in European democracies, ranging from a high of 88 percent in Denmark to a low of 9 percent in France. Still, union density in the "old" 15 countries of the EU before adding the 10 new countries in 2004 was more than three times higher than in the United States.[5]

- **Paternalism.** Europeans allow the state a much larger role to play in politics than Americans. The American proverb, attributed to Thomas Paine, sums it up quite succinctly: "That government is best that governs least." Europeans take the opposite view. They see government not as an obstacle, but as a facilitator that helps them achieve their goals and as a protector against misfortune. In public opinion polls, Europeans time and again are ready to grant government a bigger role than Americans. In the 1996 International Social Survey Program, the module "The Role of Government" revealed that about 32 percent of Americans either agree or strongly agree that "it is the

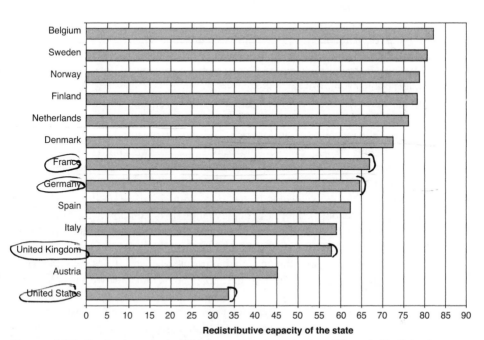

Figure 1.2 Redistributive capacity of the state (percent reduction of households living in poverty before taxes and transfers and after taxes and transfers) in the early 1990s. (*Source:* "Veto Players, Globalization and the Redistributive Capacity of the State: A Panel Study of 15 OECD countries," by Markus M.L. Crepaz, 2001, *Journal of Public Policy*, Vol. 21: 1–22).

responsibility of the government to reduce the differences in income between people with high incomes and those with low incomes." The respective percentage for West Germans who either agree or strongly agree is 49 percent, for Britons it is 54 percent, for Swedes it is 60 percent, and for the Italians and the Irish it is 65 percent. Similar numbers are obtained when question items deal with the "responsibility of government in providing decent housing," "providing a decent standard of living for the old," "providing a job for everyone who wants one," and even "controlling wages and prices."[6] In the 4th Wave of the World Values Survey in 2000, 70 percent of Austrians believed that "incomes should be made more equal" as opposed to "we need larger income differences as incentives." Sixty-percent of the Finns surveyed agreed with the fomer, and 62 percent of the French, while only 44 percent of Americans believed that incomes should be made more equal.[7]

It is not only in the perception of the public where the extensive role of the European state becomes evident. The constitutions of many European countries reveal a strong, perhaps even paternal role of the state. For instance, article 19 of the Dutch constitution states that "It shall be the concern of the authorities to promote the provision of sufficient employment". Or, article 20 which says that "It shall be the concern of the authorities to secure the means of subsistence of the population and to achieve the distribution of wealth." Similarly, article 22 argues that "The authorities shall take steps to ensure the health of the population. It shall be the concern of the authorities to provide sufficient living accommodation." Finally, article 23 argues that "Education shall be the constant concern of the government." To enshrine such "concerns of the government" into the American constitution when it was created would have been unthinkable. It may be even more unrealistic today to expect such articles could be incorporated into the American constitution through the amendment process, as individualistic beliefs and deep seated suspicions of the state are the predominant political attitudes in contemporary America.

- **Class Matters.** Another significant difference between Europe and America centers on the importance of class. Though waning, social class is still very important in Europe while much less so in America. The identity of an individual in Europe is very much connected to whether one belongs to the "working class" or not. In Europe, the school system channels pupils very early into various class-based categories, either toward vocational training or higher learning. Those who make it to the elite universities can expect to be rewarded with top-notch positions in government. One such school is the ENA (École Nationale d'Administration) in France. Seven of the past ten prime ministers went through that elite institution.[8] Education splits European society into the "working class" and the "upper class." To which class one belongs is clearly demonstrated in people's accents, titles, and lifestyles. There is a defined class consciousness in Europe, both among the working class and the privileged.

In the United States class does not play such a crucial role. Most people in America consider themselves to belong to the "middle class," a term that has utterly lost its meaning insofar as people who earn $30,000 and those who earn $500,000 annually count themselves among members of this group. It is more useful to think of "Americanism" as a creed. American identity is less a matter of material conditions or education and more a matter of ideology. The American creed includes liberty, egalitarianism (equality of opportunity), individualism, populism, and laissez-faire. When immigrants arrived in the New World they were a very disparate group whose identities were shaped by their primordial attachments—their nation, their "blood" relationships, their ethnic backgrounds. Until the middle of the 18th century there was very little awareness of an "American" ideology. However, as Great Britain started to put heavier loads on its colonies in the New World, such as with the Stamp Act of 1765, a new "Americanism" began to grow. The American creed developed as a necessary element to distinguish the American settlers from the British once the relationship between the settlers and their British government began to decline. America needed to develop its own identity vis-à-vis their British counterpart and in so doing constructed the American creed. Precisely because the multitude of races, nationalities, and ethnicities made it impossible to forge a common identity on such primordial building blocks, Americans invented an identity on the basis of ideological principles. It is for this very reason that some behavior can be called "un-American" while there is no such thing as behaving in an "un-Swedish" way.

- **Spirituality.** Religion plays a significant role in American society. Though European societies have become rather secular, religion in America is vibrant. As Figure 1.3 shows, in the 2000 World Values Survey, about 96 percent of Americans "believe in God" while only 53 percent of Swedes, 61 percent of French, and 64 percent of Germans

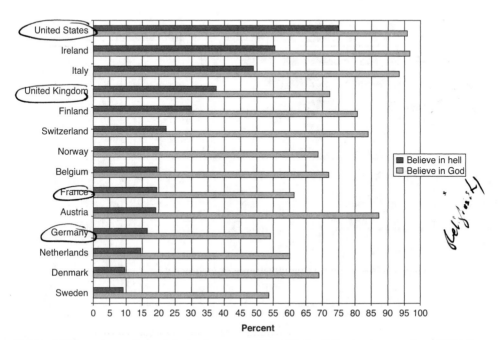

FIGURE 1.3 Percentages of respondents who answered "yes" to the following two questions: "Which, if any, of the following do you believe in? (a) Believe in hell. (b) Believe in God"(2000). (*Source: World Values Survey, 4th Wave*, International Consortium for Political Science Research. (Ann Arbor: The University of Michigan, 2000).

do the same. However, two European countries stand out quite dramatically: the strongly Catholic nations of Ireland and Italy. Ninety-seven percent of Irish "believe in God" along with 93 percent of Italians.

When asked whether people "believe in hell," the overwhelmingly strongest response comes from Americans, 75 percent of whom believe in hell, with only 9 percent of Swedes concurring. Again, people in the strongly Catholic countries of Ireland and Italy follow Americans in believing in hell, but with much reduced percentages of 56 and 48 percent, respectively.

The question item that reveals most dramatically the differences in the role of religion between Europe and America is the following statement: "Politicians who do not believe in God are unfit for public office." Remarkably, a majority of 53 percent of Americans either "strongly agreed" or "agreed" with that statement, while only 11 percent of the French, 16 percent of the Germans, 12 percent of the British, 10 percent of the Belgians, 4 percent of the Danes, and not even 2 percent of the Dutch either agreed or strongly agreed with that statement.[9]

As Figure 1.4 highlights, the response to this question, perhaps more than any other, reveals the important role that spirituality plays in American life in general but also in politics. When it comes to spirituality, a clear picture emerges: The United States is the most spiritual of the modern societies, followed, with some distance, by Italy and Ireland. Religion tends to be the least important in Sweden,

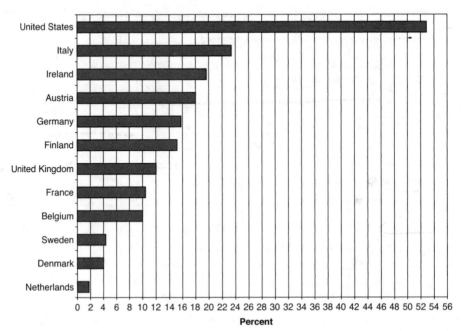

FIGURE 1.4 Percentages of respondents who either "strongly agreed" or "agreed" with the following statement: "Politicians who do not believe in God are unfit for public office". (2000). (*Source: World Values Survey, 4th Wave,* International Consortium for Political Science Research. Ann Arbor: The University of Michigan, 2000).

Box 1.1 Finn's Speed Fine Is a Bit Rich

One of Finland's richest men has been handed a record 170,000-euro (over 200,000 U.S. dollars) speeding ticket, thanks to the country's policy of relating the fine to your income. Jussi Salonoja, the 27-year-old heir to a family-owned sausage empire, was given the £116,000 ticket after being caught driving 80 km/h in a 40 km/h zone. Helsinki police came up with the figure after tax office data showed that Mr. Salonoja earned close to £7 million in 2002. If his penalty stands it will beat the previous record of almost 80,000 euros. That figure (£54,000) was paid in 2000 by Finnish Internet millionaire Jaakko Rytsola, when he was caught speeding. Yet Mr. Salonoja could get his penalty reduced, as was the case with Nokia executive Anssi Vanjoki. In 2002, Mr. Vanjoki's 116,000-euro fine was reduced by no less than 95 percent due to his drop in income following a downturn in the mobile phone maker's profits.

Source: *BBC News*, February 2, 2004.

Denmark, and the Netherlands. What is most fascinating is that when it comes to poverty reduction, social assistance programs, and the generosity of the welfare state in general, the Nordic countries tend to be in the lead while the United States is at the bottom. When it comes to religion, the United States is at the top of the league, but at the bottom when it comes to poverty reduction, social assistance, and welfare. The Nordic countries are generous with social programs and not very religious; the United States is very religious, but not generous with social programs. What is the explanation?

This last point highlights the massive differences between European and American politics. The burning question, of course, is how can these differences be explained? Where do they come from? How is it possible that someone who drives twice the speed limit can get a fine of over $200,000 in Finland, as shown in Box 1.1? Why is it that most European countries favor "equality" over "liberty" while the opposite is the case in America? We find the answers to these questions in the next section.

EXPLAINING DIFFERENCES: THE IMPACT OF HISTORY, GEOGRAPHY, AND CULTURE

It is actually quite remarkable that American politics is so different from European politics given that America was largely founded by European immigrants. Clues as to why European politics is different can partly be found in those monuments and features Americans love to visit when in Europe: the castles, cathedrals, city walls, and market squares that are conspicuously absent in America. These features significantly affected the process of what is called "modernization" or "nation building." It proved to be a wrenching process for all modern nations as major conflicts arose over the future identity of the nation, the legitimacy of rule, the capacity of the state to penetrate every nook and cranny of the new territory by its laws, and how to distribute the pieces of the economic pie. Many attempts have been made at explaining the "exceptional" nature of American politics. The following explanations highlight some of the most important, but definitely not all, reasons why there is such a remarkable difference between European and American politics.

- **Absence of Feudalism in America.** The castles, cathedrals, old town squares, and city walls that still dot the European landscape originated in the period of the Middle Ages when nobles controlled their realm from their castle, typically perched upon a hill. The motto of feudalism—the social relations between lords and vassals—could be described as "to serve and protect." The lord would protect his "objects" from attacks from neighboring lords; in turn, the peasants had to serve the lord by relinquishing a part of the fruits of their labor known as *tithe*, the root word for "tax," or through the widely despised *corvée, the* unpaid compulsory labor demanded by a lord or king. The respective social positions of peasants were "ascribed"; in other words, a peasant could never rise above his or her station. This established an extremely rigid class structure that continued throughout the Industrial Revolution, when many of the peasants became industrial workers and the nobility either morphed into captains of industry or became part of the landed aristocracy, such as the *Junkers* in Germany in the 19th and early 20th centuries. Even today in modern European democracies, obedience to political authority and deference to superiors is still observable.[10]

  America, on the other hand, has no feudal residues. It was born modern.[11] It was bourgeois from the beginning. When immigrants arrived on the shores of America,

PHOTO 1.1 Artist's rendering of Harlech Castle, Wales. (*Source:* Image Works)

they started with a clean slate. The sense of hierarchy that so permeated European society was significantly flattened when immigrants came to the New World. In America there was a much less developed social pecking order. As a result, class consciousness never developed to the same extent as in Europe. This meant that the sense of class, of exploitation over hundreds of years of peasants and workers upon which European Socialists and Marxists could build their revolutionary theory and practice, never had any traction in America. As so powerfully summed up by Werner Sombart: "No feudalism—no socialism."[12]

- **Relative Early Affluence.** Another explanation dealing with the American exception highlights the relative early affluence of American workers compared to their European counterparts. According to Karl Marx, immiseration and impoverishment of the working class is what kindles the fires of revolution. Comparing the fate of the workers in Germany with those in the United States, Sombart finds that American workers earned about two to three times more than German workers in the 19th century at roughly the same cost of living. Hence, American workers had less of a reason to storm the barricades. Again in the memorable words of Werner Sombart: "All socialist utopias come to grief with roast beef and apple pie."[13]

- **The Disintegrative Forces of Immigration.** The ethnic diversity of immigrants proved to be particularly corrosive when it came to establishing unions and Socialist parties in the United States. Different waves of immigrants of varying nationalities and religions coming into the United States created an extraordinarily diverse labor force. Socialists appealed to workers along class lines, while Democrats and Republicans exploited the ethnic differences in appealing to members. The craft unions in the American Federation of Labor (AFL) were organized along ethnic lines, which aggravated the problems faced by the Socialists—particularly after the 1890s when the largest streams of immigrants were no longer "old immigrants," British, Germans, and northern Europeans who were skilled and assimilated rather quickly into the larger society, but immigrants from Southern and Central and Eastern Europe, who had fewer skills, spoke poor English, and were discriminated against by the earlier immigrants who blended more easily with the native-born whites.[14]

In addition, immigrants themselves were ideologically quite distinct. The most radical immigrants were the Germans, who brought with them experiences of the failed democratic revolutions of 1848 and the persecution of Socialists under Bismarck in the 1870s. In addition, they had firsthand experience with the strains of industrial production. On the other hand, many immigrants were actually quite conservative and ready to absorb the reigning ideology of their new homeland. Because many experienced life to be so much better in the New World rather than their old homeland, they, ". . . with the enthusiasm of converts, praised the Republic and the material blessings it offered."[15] Moreover, given the sectarian, fundamentalist character of the Socialist Party, many Catholic immigrants could not find an ideological home in this party. In the words of Lipset and Marks: "Vigorous Catholic opposition to socialism can hardly be exaggerated as a reason for the failure of the Socialist party."[16] Finally, even the Socialists succumbed to racism allowing immigration only for Northern Europeans and excluding Catholics, and Southern and Central and Eastern Europeans. Obviously, the American experience in organizing for labor was very different from the European experience. Because European nations were relatively homogeneous, it was possible for "class" to become a salient issue. Only on the basis of ethnic homogeneity could class become a most powerful vector in European politics—a vector that ultimately pointed in the direction of the welfare state. In the American case, however, when it came to organizing for labor, blood proved to be thicker than water.

- **Frederick Jackson Turner's Frontier Thesis.** Turner, who was a historian, delivered a speech in Chicago in 1893 entitled "The Significance of the Frontier in American History." By "frontier" he meant the tip of the spear of westward expansion from the East Coast to the Pacific by settlers who claimed "free" land on which to build their livelihood. In Turner's words: "So long as free land exists, the opportunity for a competency exists, and economic power secures political power."[17] The opportunity to expand westward functioned very much like a safety valve insofar as it took the revolutionary winds out of the sails during periods of worker unrest in the industrial cities of New York, Boston, and Chicago. Many workers, instead of fighting it out with the industrial bosses, chose to move west, claim land, and in essence, become capitalists themselves. European workers did not have that option. European industrial cities were teeming with disgruntled workers who were ready to take on the fight with their bosses for fairer wages and better working conditions. According to Turner, however, the frontier, with its vast lands to the west, turned out to be ". . . the line of most rapid and effective Americanization"[18] while this very same process spelled doom for the Native Americans.

- **American Sectarianism.** Americans are some of the most religious people in the world while at the same time belonging to one of the most advanced nations in the world. This makes America quite distinct, as the typical pattern of development suggests that as economic development increases, adherence to traditional values (such as churchgoing) should decrease. This pattern clearly holds true in Europe, which is very secular. In the United States, most believers adhere to *sects*—such as the Babtists, Presbytarians, or Methodists, and many others—rather than *churches,* as is the case in Europe. European churches were always closely connected to the state. They were state financed, hierarchical, claimed to be the arbiter between the individual and God, and were actively engaged in political affairs, particularly as far as the alleviation of the plight of the poor was concerned. The close intertwining of God and politics can clearly be seen in such documents as *Rerum Novarum* (1891, Pope Leo XIII), *Quadragesimo Anno* (1931, Pius XI), and the *Catechism of the Catholic Church*. They speak to the wretched living conditions of the poor, the inhumane working conditions of laborers, and the need for a "just wage." The church presented itself as an agent of social reform and asked for active support from the people. In the view of the Catholic Church, the plight of the working class had to be seen as part of an organic whole where the whole community would be affected if workers were treated unjustly.

On the other hand, American sects never emphasized community. Rather, they highlighted individuality and the lone relation between God and the believer. Max Weber described powerfully the Protestant work ethic based on competitive, rational, individualistic behavior, which encouraged entrepreneurial achievement. The religious tradition of Protestant "dissent" has called on believers to follow their own interpretation of the scriptures, undiluted by formal religious institutions. In most Protestant sects, there is no agent or mediator between the believer and God as in Catholicism, where the church plays this role. In Weber's interpretation, responsibility for leading a virtuous life rests with the individual who stands alone before God, as committed sins cannot be absolved through confession. This puts a heavy burden upon a Protestant believer, for when the day of reckoning comes, all deeds will be added up cumulatively.[19] The consequence of this religious doctrine is that Americans are uniquely moralistic. They tend to see things in black and white—people or other countries are either "good" or "bad," behavior is either "right" or "wrong." In the words of Seymour Martin Lipset: "Americans are utopian moralists who press hard to institutionalize virtue, to destroy evil people, and eliminate wicked institutions and practices."[20] This dichotomous, almost fundamentalist worldview is revealed clearly in the rhetoric of foreign policymaking, from Ronald Reagan's aim to destroy the "evil empire" to George W. Bush's single-minded pursuit to smoke out the "evildoers" and the widespread references to scriptures that punctuate his speeches. "To endorse a war and call on people to kill others and die for the country, Americans must define their role in a conflict as being on God's side against Satan, for morality against evil."[21]

In addition, the congregational nature of American sects fostered egalitarian, individualistic, and populist values that located the purpose of religious organization not in arguing for social reform but for the spiritual satisfaction of the individual. This led to a shift in focus away from the community to the individual, from objective social conditions to the piety of the individual and what the individual could do to improve him- or herself. Indeed, Americans are workaholics. Statistics indicate that Americans are in the top three (together with Japan and Australia) in terms of hours worked per year.[22]

- **Racial Heterogeneity in America.** The creation and expansion of the welfare state in the 19th and 20th centuries in Europe was underpinned by a sense of community and social solidarity of citizens toward each other. The basic premise on which the state could extract large sums of money through taxation and distribute it in the form of benefits was that most people believed that the recipients of public funds were people like themselves, facing difficulties that they themselves might face one day.[23] This organicist notion of the welfare state was founded on widely held concepts of community and feelings of mutual obligation toward fellow citizens. In the classic study *Citizenship and Social Class*, T. H. Marshall explains the foundations on which social citizenship rests: "Citizenship requires . . . a direct sense of community membership based on loyalty to a civilization which is a common possession."[24]

In other words, the sacrifices citizens engage in by voluntarily giving up a significant portion of their income in order to finance the welfare state is easier to come by if the recipients of such assistance look and behave similarly to those who provide the assistance. If, however, there is a perception that taxes are paid by one type of people and received by another, the willingness to support such redistributive schemes is reduced. This is the major finding of a study by Alberto Alesina et al., who argue that the reason why the American welfare state is less developed is because ". . . racial animosity in the US makes redistribution to the poor, who are disproportionately black, unappealing to many voters."[25] In other words, people are more likely to support welfare if they see it received by people of their own race, but are less supportive if they see it received by people from another race.

Europe is not immune from such stereotypes as it confronts for the first time increased diversity as a result of massive immigration. As more and more immigrants stream to European countries, will Europeans be willing to continue funding the welfare state as the likely recipients of welfare become increasingly very different from them in terms of race, religion, ethnicity, and language? One of us (Markus M. L. Crepaz) has further researched this question and concludes that increased immigration will not lead to an Americanization of the European welfare state for two main reasons: First, the European welfare state became fully developed *before* widespread immigration occurred, in contrast to what took place in America. Second, the presence of an encompassing welfare state affects the levels of social trust in society, thus reducing resentment toward foreigners.[26]

This is not a complete list of explanations for the exceptional or deviant politics of America. However, this list can shed light on many differences between European and American politics. The attentive reader of this book will notice many such differences discussed in the following chapters, particularly in Chapters 2 through 8. These differences represent the ultimate causes as to why we observe variations in, for example, income inequality, voter turnout, poverty, and "life chances" between America and Europe.

STRUCTURE OF THE BOOK

Having seen in this first chapter how the history and politics in Europe are in important ways different from the United States, we turn in the following chapters to specific aspects of European democracies. However, we keep making comparisons with the United States in the individual chapters. We will also not limit ourselves to the present time, but, as in Chapter 1, we will give historical depth to our analysis.

We begin in Chapter 2 with political parties. In any democracy, political parties are of great importance because they compete in elections and thus allow citizens to select their leaders. Chapters 3 through 6 present the institutions within which political parties operate. We will show the great influence that institutions have on the behavior of political parties and individual politicians. We will also show that there is great variation in the institutional setting of European democracies, thus party systems vary greatly among European countries.

In Chapter 3 we will present how parliamentary elections are organized in Europe. American students will be surprised that there is only a single country, the United Kingdom, using the winner-take-all system as practiced for congressional elections in the United States. All other countries use proportionality or a mixture of winner-take-all and proportionality. Proportionality simply means that the percentage of parliamentary seats gained by a party corresponds to the percentage of its voter support.

Chapter 4 deals with the executive branch of government. In the United States, the head of the executive branch, the president, is elected by the people and the cabinet members serve at his pleasure. This is called a presidential system. By contrast, most European countries have a parliamentary system in which the head of the executive branch, called the prime minister or chancellor, is appointed by parliament. Cabinet members have a much stronger position than in the United States, and the prime minister or chancellor functions more like a captain of a team.

Chapter 5 addresses the courts, which are less powerful in European countries than in the United States. Europeans are often surprised by the great power exercised by the U.S. Supreme Court. Chapter 6 explains the use of federalism and the referendum in European democracies, and we will see that there is great variation in this respect. Some countries are very centralized, such as France, whereas other countries, such as Germany, have a federalist structure of government. The referendum is most heavily used in Switzerland; but other European countries also use increasingly the referendum.

Chapters 7 and 8 introduce more actors in European politics. Chapter 7 describes social movements such as environmental movements, and Chapter 8 discusses economic interest groups such as business associations and labor unions. Although political parties are the classical actors in any democracy, social movements and economic interest groups have sometimes an even greater influence on policymaking in Europe.

Having described the institutions and the actors operating within these institutions, Chapter 9 then presents data about the policy outcomes in European democracies, for example, the level of taxes or governmental health-care expenditures. Students are encouraged to explain variation in such policy outcomes among European democracies and also in comparison with the United States, using the material learned in the previous chapters. This will make for interesting term papers written by students.

Chapter 10 describes how in 1989 communism in the Soviet Union and Eastern Europe broke down, leading to the end of the cold war. In order to understand the current situation in Europe it is important to recall that the continent was divided by the Iron Curtain after 1945 for almost half a century. The enduring effect of this division is visible, for example, in the lesser economic development in Central and Eastern Europe.

Following up on Chapter 10, in Chapter 11 we explain how after 1989 the Central and Eastern European countries made the transition to democracy. In this chapter we will also see how Germany and Italy, after their defeat in World War II, made the transition to democracy. We will also cover the transition to democracy in Spain in the 1970s.

Despite the fact that fierce and extreme nationalism led to two world wars and all their devastating consequences, fierce nationalism is still a phenomenon to reckon with in Europe. It even led to a brutal war in the Balkans in the 1990s. We cover nationalism in Europe in Chapter12.

When there are deep divisions in a society, power sharing among the various societal groups may help to reach some level of stability. As we will see in Chapter 13 with regard to Northern Ireland and Bosnia-Herzegovina, for example, power sharing is not easily implemented in a successful way.

Chapter 14 addresses perhaps the most important development in European politics since World War II: the creation and development of the European Union. The goal is not to arrive at a United States of Europe after the model of the United States of America. It is a new form of government with political authority divided among the European, the national and the regional levels, with no level having ultimate priority. This new form of government may be called multilevel government.

Finally, in Chapter 15 we will put European politics in a global perspective and show to what extent European politics is influenced by what happens in the global setting, for example, with regard to international migration. Such migration, especially from third-world countries, has made Europe much more multicultural, which has led to challenging new problems, in particular with regard to the millions of immigrants of Muslim faith. What the United States has been learning for a long time, Europe now learns in a hard way—namely, that it is not easy for very different cultures to peacefully live together. As a typical immigration country, the United States has perhaps found it easier to accommodate different cultures than Europe, which has a much longer cultural tradition of its own. Thus, globalization is a great challenge for Europe, also in other aspects such as the increased amount of economic competition on a global scale.

Discussion Questions

1. What other differences than those highlighted above exist between American and European politics?

2. For those of you who have traveled to Europe, what places have you visited and why?

3. In most European countries, "equality" is considered to be prior to "freedom," whereas the opposite is the case in the United States. Is it possible to have both a highly egalitarian and a highly free society?

4. Is "class" an important concept in America? If yes, what "classes" can you identify and how do you draw the lines between them?

5. How does religion influence American and European politics? In which of the two places is the influence of religion on politics more extensive?

6. Does "freedom" include the right to organize in the form of unions?

7. As mentioned earlier, in international statistics on hours worked per person, the United States tends to be at the top. Why do Europeans work less?

8. How do these differences in American and European politics and society manifest themselves in policy outcomes?

---

[1]Louis Hartz. *Liberal Tradition in America. An interpretation of American Political Thought Since the Revolution.* (New York: Harcourt Brace, 1955).

[2]Seymour Martin Lipset and Gary Marks. *It Didn't Happen Here. Why Socialism Failed in the United States.* (New York: Norton and Company, 2000, 284).

[3]Organization for Economic Cooperation and Development (OECD). *Total Public Expenditures as % of GDP.* (Author, 2005).

[4]Markus M. L. Crepaz. Veto Players, Globalization and the Redistributive Capacity of the State: A Panel Study of 15 OECD countries. *Journal of Public Policy,* Vol. 21, 2000: 1–22.

[5]European Industrial Relations Observatory (EIROnline). Available online at http://www.eiro.eurofound.eu.int/2004/01/feature/tn0401101f.html.

[6]ISSP (International Social Survey Program). *The Role of Government.* (Zentralarchiv für Empirische Sozialforschung, Köln, 1996).

[7]*World Values Survey,* 4th Wave. International Consortium of Political Science Research (ICPSR). (Ann Arbor: The University of Michigan, 2000).

[8]The French Elite. In ENA we trust. *The Economist* July 21, 2005.

[9]*World Values Survey.* International Consortium for Political Science Research (ICPSR). (Ann Arbor: The University of Michigan, 2000).

[10]Seymour Martin Lipset. *American Exceptionalism: A Double Edged Sword.* (New York: Norton, 1996).

[11]Barrington Moore. *Social Origins of Dictatorship and Democracy. Lord and Peasant in the Making of the Modern World.* (Boston: Beacon Press, 1966).

[12]Werner Sombart. *Why Is There No Socialism in the United States?* (White Plains, NY: International Arts and Sciences Press, 1976). First published in German in 1906.

[13]Ibid., 26.

[14]Lipset and Marks, 2000.

[15]M. L. Hansen. *The Immigrant in American History.* (New York: Harper Publishers, 1964, 96).

[16]Lipset and Marks, 154.

[17]Frederick Jackson Turner. *The Frontier in American History.* (New York: Henry Holt and Company, 1920, 13).

[18]Ibid., 3.

[19]Max Weber. *The Protestant Ethic and the Spirit of Capitalism.* (New York: Routledge, 1999). Originally published 1904/1905.

[20]Lipset 1996, 63.

[21]Ibid., 20.

[22]For statistics, see: http://www.nationmaster.com/graph-T/lab_hou_wor.

[23]David Willets guotedin: " Discomfort of Strangers," by David Goodhart. *The Guardian:* February 24, 2004.

[24]T. H. Marshall. *Citizenship and Social Class.* (London: Pluto Press, 1950, 24).

[25]A. Alesina, E. Glaeser, and B. Sacerdote. *Why Doesn't the US Have a European Style Welfare State?* (Cambridge, MA: Institute of Economic Research, 2001, 1).

[26]Markus M. L. Crepaz. *Trust Without Borders. Immigration, the Welfare State and Identity in Modern Societies.* (Ann Arbor: The University of Michigan Press, In press).

CHAPTER 2

Political Parties

In any democracy, political parties are essential because they compete in elections, allowing citizens to elect their leaders. Without political parties, democracy is not possible. Therefore, it seems appropriate to begin our study with political parties. At the beginning of the chapter, we discuss the role of political parties in democracies in general, and then turn to the specific parties in European democracies. We begin with the Socialist party, which is difficult to explain to an American audience because Americans often identify European socialism with the old Soviet Union. This is a misguided comparison, as European Socialists are very much democratically oriented. We then turn to the Liberals, a term that is used very differently in Europe than in the United States; European Liberals are strongly free-market oriented. Next come Conservatives, Christian Democrats, the New Radical Right, Greens, and country-specific regional parties. We will see that a simple dimension from left to right is not sufficient to locate European parties in a meaningful way. Rather, we need a multidimensional space to locate European political parties. Understanding the concept of multidimensional space is crucial to understanding this chapter.

The United States has only two viable political parties, although sometimes efforts are made to create a third party. European democracies, by contrast, have a multitude of political parties. Another difference is that political parties play a much bigger role in Europe than in the United States. This is true, in particular, for parliamentary elections and the formation of cabinets, as we will see in Chapter 3 and Chapter 4. Thus, it is appropriate to devote this second chapter to the description of the political parties in European politics. They do not simply differ on a dimension from left to right, and one may even ask whether the terms *left* and *right* have not become too vague to describe clearly enough the political parties in Europe. As noted, we will see that the European political parties are located in a multidimensional political space, which is the key concept of the chapter. As we go along, we will show the relationships among the various parties, making it increasingly clear what is meant by a multidimensional political space. But before we do this we need to examine the origins of political parties, the functions they serve, the difference between parties and interest groups, and how parties change over time.

POLITICAL PARTIES—THE "CHILDREN OF DEMOCRACY"

The development of political parties is closely linked with the process of democratization, particularly with the extension of mass suffrage. Most European countries completed this process by the early 1920s. Before the establishment of general voting rights, there existed only groups of notables who congregated in small "clubs" or "caucuses." They used their means and influence to make themselves, or their protegés, available as candidates to be elected. Membership in such "clubs" was tightly controlled and kept at very low numbers.

16

Such clubs, cliques, or caucuses did not seek expansion of their members like modern parties. They did not open their doors to anyone who wanted to become a member. Only "qualified" members of society—that is, those who could bring influence to bear on the interests of the groups—could join these illustrious caucuses. For conservative groupings in late-19th-century Europe, this meant that the members of such cliques or clubs were made up of aristocrats, industrial magnates, bankers, wealthy businessmen, and even influential clerics. For liberal "clubs" this meant membership included servants of the state, teachers, journalists, and a few intellectuals.[1] This system of privileged access became outmoded once mass suffrage was extended.

The introduction of universal or near universal suffrage in the early 20th century had two significant consequences. It led to the rise of Socialist parties and it expanded the role of parliaments. At the beginning of World War I, membership in the German Social Democratic Party numbered more than a million, and the party enjoyed an annual budget of more than 2 million German marks.[2] The universal right to vote combined with an explosive membership turned Socialist parties into the first mass political parties. Mass membership in the Socialist parties also led to an equalization vis-à-vis the much smaller but well-endowed conservative caucuses, which were made up of few wealthy individuals. Socialist parties relying on collective financing could field candidates for election to parliaments without needing the support of conservative-leaning capitalists. With a strong party structure and public financing, Socialist parties could now afford to print their own newspapers and support political campaigns, thus opening the door for the development of mass parties as we understand them today. The contrast between the highly disciplined, publicly financed, and tightly organized mass parties and the "cliques" made up of men of privilege is stark. As explained by Max Weber: "Now then, the most modern forms of party organizations stand in sharp contrast to this idyllic state in which circles of notables and, above all, members of parliament rule. These modern forms are the children of democracy, of mass franchise, of the necessity to woo and organize the masses and develop the utmost unity of direction and strictest discipline."[3]

FUNCTIONS OF POLITICAL PARTIES

What do political parties do? It seems difficult to conceive of politics without reference to political parties. Yet, for the public, the term *political party* generally has negative connotations, in the sense that parties are simply vehicles for individuals to rise to power, or that they are the realm in which corruption unfolds, as exemplified by the party machines in the United States at the turn of the century. The German term *Parteibuchwirtschaft* and the Italian term *Partitocrazia* highlight the corrosive character of political parties. Both terms refer to the tendency of political parties to act as patrons and individuals as clients. There are numerous examples of such behaviors—for example, when citizens attempt to get access to public housing, having the right "party book" might help them be selected over others without such an affiliation. In addition, party affiliation may aid in getting a job as a civil servants, receiving public contracts, and so on. As a result, people, particularly in tough economic times, will join political parties not out of conviction, but out of necessity. The acronym of Mussolini's fascist party was PNF (*Partito Nazionale Fascista*). Many people joined that party not for reasons of conviction, but for what the Italians called *per necessità famigliare*, (for family reasons), which carries, of course, the same acronym. Today commentators often urge politicians to rise above "party politics."

Political scientists, on the other hand, have a much more positive view of political parties. They argue that the modern representative democracy is not possible without political parties. The main functions of political parties are as follows:

- **Parties Structure the Popular Vote:** Political parties are the crystallization point of the multitude of political demands. They reduce the people's varied standpoints to a few manageable ones, thereby aggregating diverse interests. Parties represent the main cleavages in society—the main lines of political contention, such as socioeconomic, regional, linguistic, or religious differences. The party labels function in most cases as signals for citizens that indicate where the various parties stand and help reduce the complexity of the issues at hand.

- **Parties Recruit Leaders for Public Office:** In premodern times, leaders inherited their positions as kings, dukes, or barons, for example. With political parties in place, leaders emerge in such structures as a result of what amounts to an apprenticeship, which unfolds over long periods of time. Many leaders of parties start out at the lowest political rungs and work their way up to the top. Parties thus act as a recruiting vessel in which activists develop over time the skills necessary to take on leadership positions.

- **Parties Formulate Public Policy:** The perennial question in politics of "what is to be done" is generally spelled out in so-called party platforms. Parties usually spend a large amount of effort and time on the creation of these platforms because they represent the codified convictions and intentions of the respective political parties. Public policy typically emerges from these platforms, oftentimes as a result of compromises with other parties that share political power through coalitions.

- **Parties Organize the Flow of Power:** In most parliamentary democracies, people vote for parties, not for individuals. Thus, parties act as an intermediary between the public and the state. Parties connect voters to the political world. Also, across most European democracies, the party with the highest popular vote is asked to form a government. Members of European parties in the legislature tend to display stronger coherence, with less wiggle room to vote differently than what their party advocates, compared to their American counterparts. Thus, political power is inseparably connected to political parties.

The American political scientist Elmer Schattschneider remarked in 1942: "It should be flatly stated that the political parties created democracy and that modern democracy is unthinkable, save in terms of parties."[4]

DIFFERENCES BETWEEN POLITICAL PARTIES AND INTEREST GROUPS

In modern polities based on popular sovereignty and mass suffrage, two paths—one formal and the other informal—toward making policy exist. The formal path is via political parties and other constitutionally recognized methods, such as referenda and plebiscites. The informal path is through interest groups, sometimes referred to as "pressure groups," which lobby lawmakers to engage in policies that are favorable to their cause. While at first glance political parties and private interest groups may look similar, they are in fact quite different. There are three main differences between political parties and interest groups, as follows:

- **Political Parties' Concerns are Public in Nature:** This stands in stark contrast to private interest groups, which tend to approach the state in order to gain advantage for their generally small numbers of supporters. This is typically the case for economic interest groups such as the labor unions in the United Kingdom (e.g., TUC—Trades Union Congress) or the American Medical Association (AMA) in the United States. The large-scale public concern of political parties is evident in the so-called "catch-all" parties, that is, parties that appeal to basically every strata in society. The advantages that accrue as a result of interest group activity, on the other hand, tend to flow to only a very small slice of society.

- **Political Parties' Candidates Stand for Election:** This is another significant difference between political parties and interest groups. Although it is true that in many countries voters vote for parties rather than individuals, it is very clear in each circumstance who the party leader will be, even before the election. Each party will offer a clear choice as to who would become prime minister, the leader of the opposition, or who would head various ministries, even before the election. Interest group politics is much less transparent; much happens in the lobbies of parliaments or Congress that is not exposed to public scrutiny, and lobbyists do not have to face the public in the same way as party leaders. Party leaders must mobilize enough people to vote or not vote for them, while this check of accountability is completely absent in the realm of interest groups. Interest groups do not attempt to achieve their goals by electing leaders from among their own ranks to government office.

- **Parties are Publicly Financed; Interest Groups are Not:** This statement is not entirely true. Parties do receive some support from members just as interest groups do. Parties also receive support from interest groups, but both of these sources of income are significantly smaller than what parties receive through public financing. Most European parties receive benefits in kind, such as free broadcasting time before elections, free mass mailings, and even grants to parliamentary groups to cover their operating expenses. Many European countries receive public funds in proportion of the share of votes received. Financing of interest groups is a wholly private affair and is mostly generated by member contributions.

SOCIALISTS

The term *Socialist* is derived from the Latin root word *socius*—a comrade or fellow. Socialists claim that they want to extend help to all needy members of society as if they were comrades or fellows. In the United States, *Socialist* tends to have a very negative connotation, which goes back to the time of the cold war. The official name of the Soviet Union at that time was the Union of Soviet Socialist Republics (USSR). But in that instance, the term *Socialist* referred to the dictatorial phase following the proletarian revolution, as we will see in Chapter 10. The Soviets claimed they were still in this phase because capitalism had not yet been defeated worldwide. In European democracies, however, Socialist parties are firmly committed to democracy. Nonetheless, after the Soviet Union began to crumble, Socialist leaders were worried that the name of their party would be tainted. Thus,

---

Box 2.1 Socialists Ponder a Changed World

NEW YORK—Buoyed by the collapse of one of its oldest foes, the Communist movement, but uncertain about its own role in the post-cold-war world, the Socialist International gathered in New York this week to set a course for the future. Willy Brandt, the former West German Chancellor who has been president of the Socialist International since 1976, chaired the two-day meeting at the Waldorf-Astoria. Mr. Brandt suggested that Socialism is a victim of semantics. "Let's face it," he said, "Socialism has been discredited by the mess created in the so-called 'socialist countries.'" "Our traditional role has not changed," said Pierre Mauroy, former Prime Minister of France and First Secretary of the French Socialist Party. "As the countries of Eastern Europe move towards a market economy, Social Democracy will continue to serve as a strong counter-balance to the excesses of laissez-faire."

Source: *New York Times*, October 11, 1990.

---

the late Willy Brandt, former West German chancellor, addressing the Socialist International in October 1990, said: "Let's face it. Socialism has been discredited by the mess created in the so-called 'socialist countries'" (see Box 2.1).

We will describe the rise and fall of communism in Chapter 10. There we will see that since the end of the cold war, the Communist parties in both Western and Central and Eastern Europe have changed greatly. They now claim to be Socialist in orientation. In order to emphasize this change, many of the old Communist parties took on a new name; the Italian Communist Party, for example, now calls itself the Democratic Party of the Left. In France, however, Communists kept their old name, although the French party has greatly changed too.

In Box 2.1, reference is made to social democracy. Is there a difference between a Socialist and a Social Democrat? Yes and no. The difference is certainly not in the sense that Social Democrats support democracy more than Socialists do. The precise party label depends on the country and is relatively inconsequential. In France the party is called Socialist, and in Germany it is called Social Democratic, but this difference in name does not mean the French party supports democratic principles any less so than does the German party. Particular national circumstances also explain why in Great Britain and the Netherlands, for example, the Socialists are called the Labour Party.

A distinction between Socialists and Social Democrats is sometimes made in internal party discussions between leftists and moderates. In Spain, for example, leftists sometimes criticized the former Socialist prime minister Felipe González for taking a Social Democratic route, by which they meant that he was too accommodating to the interests of the business community. These questions of terminology are tedious but necessary to prevent misunderstanding. For the remainder of the book, the term *Socialist* is used unless there is a need to make a differentiation.

How do Socialists view the world? What are their goals and strategies? Essentially, they see the gap between rich and poor as too great. A major goal of Socialist policy is to narrow this gap. Socialists argue that the fruits of democracy can be enjoyed only by people who have a sufficient level of economic security. As the German dramatist Bertolt

Photo 2.1 Bertolt Brecht: "Your prior obligation is to feed us." (*Source:* Getty Images)

Brecht (Photo 2.1) wrote in the famous *Threepenny Opera*, people first must eat.[5] Individuals who must worry constantly about what to eat, where to find shelter, and what to do in case of illness and in old age are not truly free. They are unable to participate in political life, which therefore tends to be dominated by the more affluent and, as a result, is not really democratic.

According to Socialist thinking, the state must intervene in the economy if more equality in society is to be achieved. If market forces have free play, the gap between rich and poor will only widen. It is only the state that has the necessary authority to redistribute income from the rich to the poor. For Socialists, state intervention in the economy is not an obstacle but a precondition for an effective democracy. Thus, what we see here are fundamentally different definitions of democracy. From the perspective of a free market, a democracy should give everyone the freedom to profit from given opportunities. From a Socialist perspective, a democracy can function only if the state corrects the distribution of wealth arrived at by market forces.

Although Socialists agree among themselves on the necessity for the state to redistribute income, there is wide disagreement in the Socialist ranks about the specifics of this intervention. One option is to nationalize private companies. If business belonged to the state, the rich could not get richer through the accumulation of profits, because the profits would go to the community as a whole. Nationalization was, for a long time, popular among many Socialists. When Socialist François Mitterrand became president of France in 1981, key sectors of the economy—including almost all banks and large pharmaceutical companies—were nationalized. These measures, however, were less dramatic than they may appear to an

American observer. First, prior to the emergence of the Socialist movement there was a century-long French tradition of a strong state role in the economy. Thus, long before Mitterrand took office, many banks already belonged to the state. Second, the state under Mitterrand did not take over small businesses such as the corner bakery. Socialists, too, believed that the quality of the famous French bread would be better if a multitude of private bakers competed with one another. Thus, French Socialists were not, in principle, against competition. In fact, part of their justification for nationalizing big companies was that under state control, these companies could compete more successfully in the world market.

During their time in office, French Socialists became more critical of nationalization, and they even began a program of denationalization. A key reason for this change in policy was that the Socialists had to accept the fact that financial investors were worried about nationalization and withdrew large amounts of capital from France during the time Socialists were in office. At about the same time, the British Labour Party, too, moved away from a policy of nationalization. It had been the opposition party for a long time and feared that continuing to insist on nationalization would frighten investors, which, in turn, would make voters reluctant to support the Labour Party.

Socialists in other countries had turned away earlier from the concept of nationalization. Thus, Helmut Schmidt, the Social Democratic West German chancellor from 1974 to 1982, never tried to implement a program of nationalization. Socialists such as Schmidt preferred more indirect state intervention through tax laws, social programs, and so forth. They accepted private ownership of big companies, as long as the companies' power was sufficiently checked through governmental regulation. This has now become the general policy among European Socialists.

Until recently, European Socialists agreed that economic growth was good, provided that the fruits of this growth were not unfairly distributed in society. The main controversy concerned the question of whether the state should intervene directly, through nationalization, or whether redistribution of income could be achieved better through more indirect state measures. Today, a more fundamental question is discussed among Socialists, namely, whether the side effects of economic growth are so negative that, ultimately, they may place the survival of the human race in jeopardy. Such side effects often are referred to by the technical economic term *external costs*. The debate about the external costs of economic growth has split the Socialists severely. On one side are blue-collar workers who wish to profit through higher wages from continued economic growth. They tend to support, for example, the expansion of nuclear power to prevent energy shortages. On the other side is a new breed of more intellectually oriented Socialists—teachers, social workers, and so on. For them, limits must be imposed on economic growth; otherwise, our natural environment eventually will be destroyed. As a prime example, these new Socialists cite the death of the forests caused by acid rain. They also point out that current economic life puts too much stress on working people, leading to all sorts of health problems. These Socialists see dangers not only in an unrestricted free market but also in large and often anonymous state bureaucracies. They advocate a much simpler lifestyle and a more decentralized government structure with extensive self-administration at the local level. Instead of producing more cars to commute to increasingly distant workplaces, people should bicycle to work in their own, relatively self-sustained, small communities.

Such an interpretation of Socialist thought leads to a search for new political allies. Traditionally, the Socialist parties were confronted only with the choice of alliances to the left or to the middle. They could try to forge a coalition with the Communists—the strategy chosen in France by Mitterrand from 1981 to 1984—or they could keep their distance from the Communists and seek partners from the middle of the party spectrum, which is what Schmidt and his predecessor, Willy Brandt, achieved in Germany through their coalition with the Free Democratic Party (Chapter 3). The new breed of Socialists sees political life less in terms of left and right. For them, the important question is whether someone uncritically supports more economic growth or whether one is willing to reconsider the concept of growth and seek alternative lifestyles. Here Socialists find allies among environmentalists and, in particular, the Green Party, which is described later in this chapter. Members of the women's movement, the youth movement, the peace movement, and oppressed minorities such as foreign workers and homosexuals also are seen as potential allies. As a consequence of these developments, the Socialists are less and less a predominantly blue-collar, working-class party. As political scientist Herbert Kitschelt states, "in most countries the class structuring of the (Socialist) vote has progressively declined over time, though with a different pace and rhythm."[6] Increasingly, the Socialists get their support from people working in education, health care, social work, counseling, communication, and the arts.

As a result, at the end of the millennium Socialist parties were scrambling to find a new identity. The three most vocal proponents of this new orientation were Prime Minister Tony Blair of the UK, Chancellor Gerhard Schröder of Germany, and President Bill Clinton, who proclaimed in the 1998 State of the Union address: "My fellow Americans, we have found a third way." On June 8, 1999, Tony Blair and Gerhard Schröder signed a document entitled "Europe: The Third Way." On June 3, 2000, Chancellor Schröder invited the leaders of about a dozen countries, including the United Kingdom and the United States, to Berlin for a meeting entitled "Progressive Governance in the 21st Century." What does "third way" mean, and how has it changed the policies of Social Democratic parties?

In the perception of Clinton, Blair, and Schröder, the latter of whom coined the term *Neue Mitte* (new middle) meaning essentially the same thing as the "third way," it meant to come to grips with some of the excesses of state intervention. For example, the document highlighted that in the past, "the promotion of social justice was sometimes confused with the imposition of equality of outcome," that the "means of achieving social justice became identified with ever higher levels of public spending regardless of what they achieved," that "rights were elevated above responsibilities," that the "balance between the individual and the collective was distorted. Values that are important to citizens, such as personal achievement and success, entrepreneurial spirit, individual responsibility and community spirit, were too often subordinated to universal social safeguards," and that "the ability of national governments to fine-tune the economy in order to secure growth and jobs has been exaggerated."[7]

These are remarkable admissions of the failures of social democracy in the past and read more like a critique by conservatives who are shouting "I told you so." Nevertheless, the policies of the "third way" include, among others, the following:

- Embracing globalization and scientific changes by establishing an environment in which businesses can prosper and adapt and new businesses can be set up and grow.
- Flexible adaptation of workers to changing demands in the workplace, meaning that wages should move up or down in proportion to demand and making it easier for workers to be hired and fired.

- Reconciling environmental responsibility with a modern, market-based approach. Public expenditures as a proportion of national income have reached their limits of acceptability. The public sector needs to be radically modernized and public services need to be reformed to achieve better value for the money. Concepts of efficiency, competition, and high performance must be emphasized.
- Tax policies to promote sustainable growth by cutting corporate tax rates, rewarding "hard work" through a reduction of personal and corporate tax rates, and simplifying the tax code.
- Establishing an active labor market policy for the Left by ensuring that the state is an active agent for change. This means reforming welfare systems that put limits on an individual's ability to find a job by transforming the safety net of entitlements into a springboard to personal responsibility.

"Third way" policies have influenced major legislation such as the North American Free Trade Agreement (NAFTA, signed into law in the fall of 1993—Bill Clinton has been talking about the "third way" since 1992) in the United States, in which President Clinton was able to form coalitions with business-oriented leaders against organized labor and representatives in his own party to push through legislation that acknowledged the increasing importance of globalization, free markets, and the attendant efficiencies that are supposed to come along with them. Another example of "third way" policies is Bill Clinton's welfare bill, signed into law in August 1996, which replaced a long-standing entitlement program (AFDC—Aid to Families with Dependent Children) with a new law that was intended to end "welfare as we know it" by requiring recipients to work and limiting benefits to five years.

The leader who probably went the furthest in implementing elements of the "third way" is the Social Democratic Chancellor of Germany Gerhard Schröder. Facing high unemployment rates in excess of 10 percent and intent on making the German economy more competitive by reducing the tax rates on businesses, Schröder engaged in what some describe as a major attack on the generous German welfare system. Germany has some of the highest labor costs of the European countries. The total labor costs per worker in Germany amount to about 33 dollars per hour, whereas in the United States this number is closer to 22.[8] The social security contributions that are paid by employers are almost as high as the actual wages paid to workers.

Why would reducing the welfare state be advantageous for the German economy? The argument is as follows: In order to maintain the extensive German welfare state, high taxation levels are necessary, making it difficult for German companies to compete against countries with more limited welfare states and lower taxes. By cutting back the welfare state, taxes can be lowered, which in turn should make Germany economically more competitive by creating higher profits that could then be plowed back into human and investment capital.

This argument was not well received by members within Schröder's own party and certainly not among the German unions. The architect of the cutback to the German welfare state was Peter Hartz, former head of personnel at Volkswagen, the German car giant. Fittingly, the new law became known as HARTZ IV, and came into effect in January of 2005. According to the new law, receivers of social benefits (*Sozialhilfeempfänger*) are now counted as unemployed and will receive the so-called *Arbeitslosengeld II*

Box 2.2 Schröder Plans Early German Poll

Opposition Christian Democrats were jubilant after beating his Social Democrats in North-Rhine Westphalia (NRW) . . . The Social Democrats had ruled the state for 39 years; high unemployment was a key factor in their defeat . . . Mr. Schröder's Social Democrat-led government not only lost its traditional powerbase on Sunday, but it now has so few seats in upper house of parliament that its ability to actively govern is massively diminished. The Social Democratic Party's setback in NRW - Germany's most populous state, was even bigger than the Social Democrats had expected, and the worst for the party in half a century. Official results showed them taking 37.1 % - with the Christian Democrats comfortably ahead with 44.8 %. . . . Some 13 million people were eligible to vote in Germany's most industrialized state. NRW includes the Ruhr Valley, known for its steel production. But, of Germany's five million unemployed, more than one million live in NRW. For nearly four decades, the Social Democrats have ruled there, benefitting from the solid working class electorate.

Source: *BBC News*, May 23, 2005.

(unemployment benefits II), which is 345 euros (around $420.00 at current exchange rates) a month. Beneficiaries must be ready to accept a wide range of jobs, such as the so-called "1-euro jobs," jobs that are paid less than the collectively agreed-upon wage agreements (*Tariflohn*), and "mini-jobs," which do not provide encompassing insurance. HARTZ IV will involve stringent means testing, including the size of an apartment and the amount of people's savings. People who have not worked for at least 12 months over a period of two years do not get any support.

For a Social Democrat such policies are difficult to swallow. Indeed, largely as a result of these policies, Schröder lost a Land (state) election in what used to be a social democratic stronghold, North-Rhine Westphalia, in the spring of 2005. In the German bicameral legislature this also meant that he lost a majority in the Bundesrat (the equivalent of the Senate in the United States), prompting him to ask for a vote of no-confidence and calling for early elections.

The German case highlights the boundaries to which political leaders can push their parties before voters will reign them in. Parties do change, but they are also "sticky" in the sense that parties have, over time, built up constituencies who expect various goodies from their parties. Leaders who attempt to engage in change too quickly and too radically will be punished at the ballot box—a tough lesson Chancellor Schröder had to learn the hard way (see Box 2.2).

LIBERALS

For Americans it must be surprising to learn that in European countries there are political parties that call themselves Liberal parties but are in important aspects the very opposite of American liberals. European Liberals are the most free-market-oriented among European political parties, whereas in the American political spectrum, liberals are the most critical of market forces. As in the previous section, we have here another case where political labels have very different meanings in Europe and the United States. The term *liberal* is derived from the Latin root word *libertas,* meaning freedom. Thus, it is natural that in some European countries the Liberals include the term *free* as part of their official name. In Germany, for example, the Liberals are called Free Democrats. In the United States, *liberal* designates a position to the Left and *freedom* a position to the Right—for example, the conservative organization Young Americans for Freedom. In Europe, *liberal* and *free* are used as synonyms.

European Liberals emphasize the importance of individual freedom in every aspect of life. Economically, this leads to a strong preference for free markets, both domestically and internationally. But European Liberals advocate a "free market" for moral issues, too. They wish to leave the choice on issues such as abortion and divorce primarily to the individual, who should take personal responsibility. They don't like the state and its bureaucrats to intrude into the private life of citizens. The free and autonomous decisions of individuals are at the core of liberal thinking. Large organizations are viewed with skepticism because Liberals believe that they tend to limit individual freedom. This applies not only to the state but also to other large organizations, such as trade unions and churches.

The historical roots of European liberalism go back to early modern Europe—the 15th to 18th centuries. In medieval times, the individual was seen primarily as member of a group or community. People were strongly embedded in their towns, guilds, monasteries, universities, and so on. They defined themselves, to a large extent, as members of such groups, and these definitions gave meaning to their lives. Individuals were like members of a body. As a leg has meaning only as a part of the entire body; a medieval baker, for example, had meaning only as a member of his guild.

Given this medieval perception of the individual, it was a true revolution when the individual emerged as a private human being with his or her own worth independent of all group memberships. In early modern Europe, the individual began to stand for him- or herself. The individual was allowed and even encouraged to think for him- or herself, to make his or her own life plans. This stress on the individual was linked with the emerging industrial and commercial capitalism, which in turn caused individualism to grow further. Migration, urbanization, and technological change opened a new range of occupational choice, and these new opportunities required new skills. The capacity to achieve and perform in new roles acquired great importance. The individual stood much more for him- or herself than in medieval times. Individual self-fulfillment and individual happiness became goals in themselves. These are, in a nutshell, the historical roots of the Liberal parties in Europe. They emphasize individual autonomy and individual freedom above all—both in economic and moral aspects. The individual should make his or her own choices and live with the consequences, for better or for worse.

According to Liberal thinking in the European sense, the less state intervention, the better. This does not mean, however, that Liberals do not see some useful role for the state. Thus, European Liberals believe the state has certain responsibilities for helping the unemployed, the handicapped, and the old, although Liberal social programs are more limited than those advocated by Socialists. Liberals in Europe also acknowledge that some regulations for moral behavior are necessary, in particular for adolescents. They also support governmental programs to fight drug abuse, although many Liberals are willing to legalize "soft" drugs.

The exact role European Liberals see for the state is a constant topic for internal party discussion, and great differences usually exist among the varying positions within each party. Internal differences are, indeed, a major characteristic of European Liberals, which is understandable given their heavy emphasis on individual autonomy. In parliamentary debates, the Liberals are usually those with the least amount of voting discipline. The German Free Democrats are a good example of a Liberal party with much internal dissent. Some in the party stress individual freedom with regard to social issues, whereas other German Free Democrats put the emphasis on unleashing market forces in the economy. Depending on which side has the upper hand, the party enters different cabinet coalitions, either more to the left or more to the right (see Chapter 3).

Returning to the United States, it is interesting to ponder who in American politics is liberal in the European sense. In the United States one tends to call such politicians conservative on economic issues and liberal on social issues.

CONSERVATIVES

The meaning of European liberalism can be further clarified by comparing it to European conservatism. The term *conservative* is derived from the verb *conserve*, which, according to the *Oxford English Dictionary*, means "keep from decay or change or destruction." What do Conservatives wish to keep from decay, change, or destruction? Above all, the structure of authority in society. Conservatives believe that individuals are lost if they are not embedded in a firm structure of authority. Conservatives have a very different view of the individual than Liberals. According to Conservative thinking, individuals are by nature weak and need guidance. If left alone, they are likely to mess up. They must be guided by authorities such as the state, the church, the family, and so forth. Conservatives worry that these authorities may decay. Therefore, it is the primary goal of Conservative policy to preserve the structure of authority in society. This does not mean Conservatives object to all change, but change should not be sudden and abrupt.

The major difference between Conservatives and Liberals concerns the extent to which moral decisions should be left to the individual. Unlike Liberals, Conservatives advocate relatively strict guidance in such matters as abortion and drug use. This guidance can come through governmental regulation, as well as from such institutions as the church and the family. Thus, it is only logical that Conservatives support measures to strengthen the church and the family. Another difference between Conservatives and Liberals concerns attachment to symbols of the state. For Liberals, state symbols—such as the national flag and the national anthem—are not rejected, but they do not have great emotional value. Liberals are too individualistic to enjoy marching with others behind a flag. Conservatives, on the other hand, claim that the state needs strong symbols to maintain its authority. According to Conservative thinking, the state must be based not only on rational utility but also on emotions. Therefore, Conservatives revere state symbols and are offended when others do not.

In economic questions, both parties share a preference for free-market solutions and are therefore natural allies in this respect. If differences between the two parties occur, it is usually because Liberals defend the principle of free competition even more consistently than Conservatives. This can be explained by the different ways Conservatives and Liberals justify the free market. For Liberals, free-market competition encourages individuals to develop their potential to the fullest extent. Thus, the free market finds its justification in the needs of the individual. Conservatives share this view to a large extent, but they also refer to the natural order of society to justify the free market. According to Conservative thinking, a hierarchical structure of society corresponds to a law of nature. As in the animal world, among human beings there are always some who are naturally stronger and more successful than others. Conservatives applaud biologists such as Konrad Lorenz, who have discovered that there are natural leaders in the animal world and believe that analogies can be made with the human race. Some people will always be economically more successful than others, and this should be considered as natural. To try to redistribute income to achieve economic equality goes against nature. The economically successful should be allowed to keep most of the fruits of their success. Given their emphasis on order, it becomes understandable why Conservatives are sometimes afraid of too much competition. To be sure, in their rhetoric Conservatives are always very much for the free market. But if bankruptcy of a large company threatens the economic and political stability of an entire region, Conservatives are likely to be more willing than Liberals to bail out the company with governmental monies.

If we rely only on the terms of the political Left and the political Right, it is virtually impossible to differentiate Liberals and Conservatives in the European context. But if we use the two-dimensional space shown in Figure 2.1, the two parties become quite distinct. In this figure we avoid the terms *left* and *right* altogether because they are too vague. They were introduced into the political vocabulary during the French Revolution. When the French National Assembly gathered in 1789, the deputies advocating change happened to sit to the left of the chairman, and those defending the status quo sat to his right. The chairman began to refer to them as the "left" and the "right." Thus, the two terms emerged in an accidental way. Still, they were quite useful because European history after the French Revolution was for a long time a battle between the forces of the old privileges and those advocating change. In today's Europe, however, politics has become so complex that we need more than a single dimension of differentiation.

In Figure 2.1, the horizontal axis goes from a state-controlled to a free-market economy. The farther left a party is located, the more it supports state intervention to redistribute income from rich to poor. The farther right it is located, the more it supports free play for market forces. The figure indicates a position toward the right for both Liberals and Conservatives. Liberals support free economic competition somewhat more consistently than Conservatives, for the reasons just noted. But, overall, the two parties are very close together on the horizontal axis. The vertical axis goes from authoritarian to individualistic. An authoritarian position emphasizes the importance of authority in society, whereas an individualistic position stresses individual autonomy. Here Conservatives and Liberals are much more clearly distinguished, although some overlap also exists on this dimension. More so than Socialists and Liberals, Conservatives vary a great deal from country to country, which is clearly visible in the variety of labels used for Conservative parties. In Great Britain the party with the conservative orientation is simply called the Conservative Party. In most other European countries, however, Conservatives carry other party labels; in Sweden, for example, they are called the Moderate Unity party; in Greece, New Democracy; in Spain, Popular Alliance.

Why does such variety exist among Conservatives from country to country? By their very nature, Conservatives stress the importance of national identity. As a consequence,

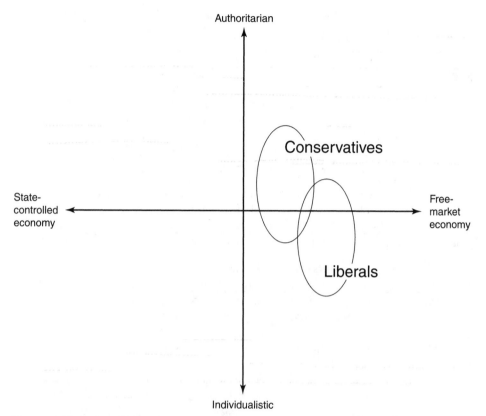

FIGURE 2.1 Location of Liberals and Conservatives on a dimension from state-controlled economy to free-market economy and on a dimension from authoritarian to individualistic.

each party has emerged from its specific national context without much international influence. Socialists and Liberals, on the other hand, have more universal messages, so it was more natural for them to cooperate at an international level. The lack of international unity among Conservatives is shown in their difficulty in organizing as a single party in the European parliament (Chapter 13).

To illustrate the complexity of describing the Conservative parties in Europe, we will first discuss the British Conservatives, often also called Tories. Political scientists Paul F. Whiteley, Patrick Seyd, Jeremy Richardson, and Paul Bissell carried out a sample survey of Conservative Party members just prior to the general election of 1992.[9] The interviewees had to respond to a battery of items like the following:

- The death penalty should be reintroduced for murder.
- The consumer needs much stronger protection from the effects of the free market.
- Government should encourage private education.

To examine whether there were ideological divisions within the party, the authors of the study submitted the responses to a statistical technique called factor analysis. The findings revealed three broad ideological categories among the party members: traditionalism, progressivism, and individualism. Traditionalism is described as:

> Perhaps the oldest ideological tendency in the party, being rooted in the values of the land-owning aristocracy. It stresses patriotism and authority but often takes an antimodern attitude to social and political change such as the emancipation of women, racial integration and the availability of abortion and easy divorce . . . . It tends to be rather anti-European, and covertly, if not occasionally overtly, racist. Traditionalists are also strong supporters of the idea of social "discipline" and law and order; they tend to favor capital punishment and emphasize the importance of punishment as a means of dealing with crime.[10]

The traditionalists in the Conservative Party are sometimes referred to as Tories. Thus, the name *Tory* may refer to the party as a whole or only to a subgroup of the party. Besides the Tories, the subgroup of the Whigs, which is characterized by progressivism, is also prominent. The authors of the study describe the progressive Conservatives as follows:

> Progressive Conservatism also has a long pedigree, originally associated with [19th-century prime minister Benjamin] Disraeli. . . . It was, however, revitalized by the post–World War II election defeat and the perception that the party needed to adapt to the changes introduced by the post-war settlement and the 1945–50 Labour Government. Progressives support the . . . welfare state and up to the 1980s this also went with the acceptance of Keynesian methods of macroeconomic management. These ideas . . . stress the importance of a social safety net to deal with poverty, limited redistribution of income and wealth, and a paternalistic commitment to caring for all members of the community. Along with support for limited redistribution goes agreement with government intervention to regulate markets in the interests of both consumers and producers.[11]

The progressive Conservatives in Great Britain are relatively close to the Labour Party in stressing the importance of government intervention to help the poor. But contrary to Labourites, the progressive Conservatives pursue such policies out of paternalistic attitudes, which have a long tradition in Conservative ranks all over Europe. It was at the end of the 19th century that conservative German chancellor Otto Bismarck introduced broad-ranging governmental social programs in order to help the poor. His motive was not a more egalitarian society but more societal stability, which might be endangered were the poor to riot. The third subgroup in the British Conservative Party is described by Whiteley and his colleagues as follows:

> Individualism has its origin in nineteenth century . . . market liberalism which emerged within the Liberal party but migrated to the Tories after the Liberal split over Irish home rule in 1885. Individualism is pre-occupied with petit-bourgeois concerns about private property and the interests of the small businessman. It supports the ideal of laissez-faire and reduced government intervention in the economy. The most enthusiastic supporters of the Thatcher government's privatization programmes can be found among this group. Individualists believe that the welfare state undermines self-reliance and enterprise, and that government should cut taxes and de-regulate business. They tend to be anti-welfare and are

inclined to blame the victim when it comes to explaining the origins of poverty or unemployment.[12]

It is interesting to note that the British Conservatives have a Liberal element in their ranks and that this addition occurred for historical reasons that go back to the 19th century. This is a good illustration of how political parties often evolve in a haphazard way. In thinking about political parties one should keep this aspect in mind: Political parties are not simply the creation of men and women who share the same political ideas. Often, one has to consider particular historical circumstances to explain why different sets of ideas are united in the same political party.

CHRISTIAN DEMOCRATS

In some countries, such as Germany, for example, there are parties with the label Christian Democrat. These parties are usually quite Conservative in orientation, but also emphasize social programs based on Christian doctrines. According to Christian thinking, it has always been important to help the poor. Great emphasis is also put on the need to help families. Thus, although Christian Democrats are often lumped together with Conservative parties, with regard to social and family programs they have distinctive features. In other countries, such as the Netherlands, Christian Democrats stress the need for social and family programs so much that they are not considered to be parties of the political right but are thought of as center parties.

NEW RADICAL RIGHT

The New Radical Right has a much less coherent program than the Socialists, Liberals, Conservatives, or Christian Democrats. Each of the latter parties is based on ideas that can be traced to a particular philosophical tradition. One can identify the philosophers who laid the groundwork for the ideologies of these parties. The New Radical Right, by contrast, is much more amorphous in its ideas. It is primarily defined by what it is against; in this sense, it is to a large extent a protest party. Given this orientation, the New Radical Right is able to attract a great variety of voters who mainly have in common the fact that they are dissatisfied with the established political parties.

The New Radical Right is in some ways a continuation of the fascism of the first part of the 20th century. To emphasize this element of continuity, the New Radical Right is sometimes called Neofascist. There are, however, important differences between fascism and the New Radical Right, so it may be better to reserve the term *fascism* for the earlier historical period. Parties that cling to the old Fascist traditions are not very successful. On the other hand, parties of the New Radical Right that use the parliament as their arena to point out shortcomings of the "old parties," unleash tirades against immigrants and the parties that support them, highlight the scandals in which established parties are involved, and identify abusers of the welfare state and politicians who enrich themselves at the public trough have found some resonance with this populist message.

Fascism was introduced by Benito Mussolini in Italy during the early 1920s. The term is derived from the Latin *fasces, which* means a bundle of sticks tightly held together—a symbol of strength in ancient Rome. In Germany, Adolf Hitler founded the National Socialist Party, which was also Fascist in orientation. The main characteristic of Fascism was its extreme nationalism and militarism. The total identification with one's own nation had, as a corollary, the rejection of everything that was alien to that nation. Under Hitler, this led to the atrocious attempt to exterminate Jews in concentration camps. Other groups, such as Gypsies, also were considered undesirable and suffered the same fate.

With regard to the role of the state in the economy, Hitler and Mussolini had an ambivalent attitude. Mussolini was a militant Socialist before founding his Fascist movement, and Hitler included the term *Socialist* in the name of his party. The Fascists' main objection to the political Left was its international orientation. Fascists found it unpatriotic that Communists and Socialists looked for allies in other countries. The call for workers of all countries to unite was diametrically opposed to Fascist thinking, which saw one's own nation as the sacred community to which all allegiance was owed. In this context, it is an interesting historical detail that Mussolini was expelled from the Socialist Party because of his vehement support for the entry of Italy into World War I. Rejecting Communists and Socialists for their lack of nationalistic feeling did not mean that Fascists had no reservations about the free market, however. The notion of competition was too disorderly for them. Fascists advocated a strong state that would show leadership in economic matters. Simply working for profits was not proper for Fascists, who deep down felt only disdain for the capitalist mentality. Hitler had a very stormy relationship with the business community. On the one hand, he needed its support, but on the other hand, he hated the business world.

How different is the New Radical Right of today from the fascism of Hitler and Mussolini? First, the New Radical Right has chosen other party labels, such as Freedom Party in Austria, National Front in France, Republicans in Germany, Progress Party in Norway, New Democracy in Sweden. Second, the New Radical Right claims that its distinction from fascism is not only in labels, but also in democratic orientation. It is true that in contrast to Hitler and Mussolini, the leaders of the New Radical Right in their speeches support the notion of democracy. But in today's Europe, the value of democracy is so commonly accepted that it would be political suicide to take an antidemocratic position. Thus, the leaders of the New Radical Right do not object to democracy at all; on the contrary, they often criticize the ruling political elites for not being sufficiently democratic in listening to the voice of the common people. Whether the New Radical Right itself would behave in a democratic way if in power is untested and remains an open question. Third, economically the New Radical Right is more for the free market than the Fascists were. It argues in particular against high taxes, wasteful welfare programs, and arrogant state bureaucrats.

In Figure 2.2, we locate the New Radical Right on the same two dimensions used in Figure 2.1. On the vertical dimension, the New Radical Right is at the authoritarian pole. Strength and discipline are emphasized in its ranks. Typically, parties of the New Radical Right have a strong leader, for example, Jean-Marie Le Pen of the National Front in France and Jörg Haider of the Freedom Party in Austria. Law and order are important values for supporters of the New Radical Right. Part of authoritarianism is also nationalism, and the voters of the New Radical Right are very nationalistic, which is particularly expressed by their demand that the number of foreign workers and refugees be kept as low as possible. With regard to the horizontal economic dimension, we have already seen that the New Radical Right takes a strong position against wasteful government spending; it

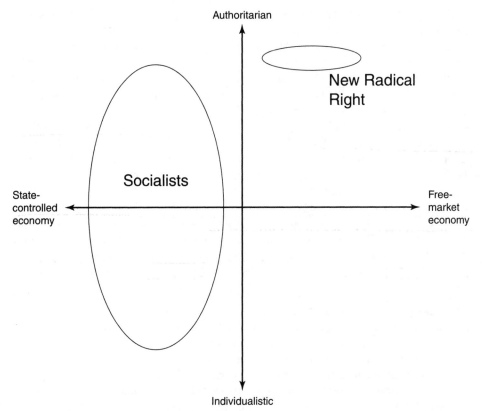

FIGURE 2.2 Location of the New Radical Right and Socialists on a dimension from state-controlled economy to free-market economy and on a dimension from authoritarian to individualistic.

objects, in particular, to welfare benefits for "outsiders" in society, such as immigrants, the homeless, drug addicts, homosexuals, unwed mothers, and abstract modern artists. The free-market position of the New Radical Right is not derived from broad economic and philosophical principles but from the wish not to pay high taxes. Hans-George Betz emphasizes the same point:

> The radical populist right's neo-liberal program is only secondarily an economic program. Primarily, it is a political weapon against the established political institutions and their alleged monopolization of political power which hampers economic progress and suppresses true democracy.[13]

Why the name *New Radical Right*? The terms *new* and *radical* help to differentiate the New Radical Right from the Old Moderate Right. If we refer back to Figure 2.1, the Old Moderate Right is the authoritarian wing of the Conservatives. When we compare Figures 2.1 and 2.2, we see how the line between the New Radical Right and the Old Moderate Right is blurred. It is therefore easy for the New Radical Right to pull support from dissatisfied voters of the Old Moderate Right, particularly during hard economic times. The voters floating between Conservatives and the New Radical Right are mostly middle class. On the one hand, there are people of the old middle class—shopkeepers, craftspeople, farmers—who fear for their economic future and are attracted by the anti-tax rhetoric of the New Radical Right. On the other hand, there are also voters of the new middle class—computer experts, media consultants, financial analysts, and so on—who find the government-off-your-back message of the New Radical Right appealing. As Betz puts it, these highly educated people "accept the market as the ultimate arbiter over individual life chances and . . . are well-prepared to play the game of individual effort, self-promotion, and self-advertisement."[14] Figure 2.2 shows that the New Radical Right may pull support also from Socialists, who are widely dispersed on the individualistic–authoritarian dimension. Toward the authoritarian pole one finds mainly blue-collar, working-class Socialists who may be attracted by the antiwelfare message of the New Radical Right, because they tend to resent welfare programs for people whom they consider unworthy.

We now have identified the two core groups from which the New Radical Right pulls its support: the middle class and blue-collar workers. As Herbert Kitschelt puts it: "[T]he secret of the New Right's success is the combination of the two electorates in a single right-authoritarian message . . . . Racism serves as glue between the economic and social agenda of the authoritarian Right."[15] Betz summarizes the essence of the New Radical Right as follows:

> Radical right-wing populist parties are radical in their rejection of the established sociocultural and sociopolitical system and their advocacy of individual achievement, a free marketplace, and a drastic reduction of the role of the state. They are right-wing in their rejection of individual and social equality, in their opposition to the social integration of marginalized groups, and in their appeal to xenophobia, if not overt racism. They are populist in their instrumentalization of sentiments of anxiety and disenchantment and their appeal to the common man and his allegedly superior common sense.[16]

The National Front in France, with its leader Jean-Marie Le Pen, perhaps typifies best the phenomenon of the New Radical Right. Le Pen is a populist who knows how to mobilize the masses. As described by Pierre Bréchon and Subrata Kumar Mitra, Le Pen criticizes the ruling political elites of France as being too soft to provide effective solutions for contemporary problems, in particular with regard to immigration:

> The National Front has risen to national prominence because it has succeeded in giving concrete political expression to a latent xenophobia, reinforced by the problem of immigration. It has succeeded in placing this latent xenophobic fear in the context of a general ideology of the extreme right, based on a rejection of established political parties and distrust of democracy. Essentially an able populist politician, Le Pen mobilizes opinion against the political elite, whom he presents as far too soft to provide effective solutions for contemporary problems. By expressing it politically, the National Front has given both reinforcement and legitimacy to xenophobia.[17]

Le Pen is shrewd in how he chooses his words. He claims not to be anti-Semitic, but at the same time he trivializes the Nazi gas chambers, he claims not to have any ill feelings against foreigners, but warns that "France will become an Islamic republic" (Box 2.3). He speaks of "inequality of the races" but puts this statement in seemingly scientific terms in

Box 2.3 On the Right, Le Pen Talks of Deluge

AMIENS—Like the stand-up comic he sometimes resembles, Jean-Marie Le Pen, attired in a double-breasted blue blazer and gray slacks, strode the stage, a microphone pinned to his lapel. For two hours, without notes, he announced the apocalypse that awaits France if it does not reverse an "invasion" of third-world immigrants.

"This vanguard of millions of foreigners will turn itself into an army and then into a flood," warned the tribune of the ultra-right National Front. "France will become an Islamic republic!"

As Mr. Pen's silky, sarcastic oratory swept over a rapt audience of 1,200 or so that had paid $5 a seat, all of France's problems were revealed to be the fault of freeloading immigrants: unemployment, crime, housing shortages, an overburdened social security system, crowded hospitals and schools where too many children do not speak French.

"France," said the National Front's presidential candidate, bending down at the knees, twisting his face grotesquely and spreading his arms forlornly, "is like an old drunken lady whose purse is wide open and who gives money to whoever passes by." Laughter and applause exploded in appreciation for the gifted mimic on the stage.

Source: *New York Times*, March 29, 1988.

claiming that history has demonstrated that the races "do not have the same evolutionary capacity."[18] In the first round of the French presidential elections on April 21, 2002, Le Pen scored his biggest victory by serving a humiliating defeat to Socialist Lionel Jospin and coming in second behind Jacques Chirac. Chirac received 20 percent of the vote, Le Pen a little over 17 percent, and Jospin a little over 16 percent. This result sent shockwaves through France and Europe and virtually guaranteed victory to Jacques Chirac a week later in the second round of elections, which consists of a run-off between the two leading candidates. For the overwhelming number of French voters Le Pen was an unacceptable candidate, thus virtually ensuring Chirac's victory.

In Austria, the leader of the Freedom Party, Jörg Haider, is even shrewder in hiding a xenophobic message behind relatively moderate language. As he exclaimed in one of his speeches, "We have not led wars in past centuries against the Turks so that they now fill our school classes."[19] His audience understood the message and exploded in frenetic applause. With this strategy, Haider's Freedom Party became the most successful of all the parties of the New Radical Right; in the 1996 elections for the European parliament, the Freedom party received a stunning 28 percent of the Austrian vote.[20] In October of 1999 during national elections, Haider's Freedom Party polled 27 percent of the popular vote and became the second largest party in Austria, beating the conservative Austrian People's Party (ÖVP) by around 700 votes. After lengthy negotiations among the other political parties, it became clear that the Freedom Party would actually become part of a governing coalition together with the ÖVP. Once the new coalition government was sworn in, the other 14 members of the European Union imposed unilateral diplomatic sanctions against

Austria. Eventually the sanctions were lifted after Haider gave up his party leadership position and retired to Carinthia and a council of "wise men" declared that the diplomatic sanctions on Austria were counterproductive.

What are the prospects for the parties of the New Radical Right in Europe? It seems that they are greatly helped by high levels of unemployment. This can most clearly be seen in the unsettling successes of two radical right-wing parties in Germany in the September 2004 Land elections in Saxony and Brandenburg, both of which are located in the former East Germany. In Saxony, the NPD (*Nationaldemokratische Partei Deutschlands*— National Democratic Party of Germany) gained 9.2 percent of the popular vote and placed 12 members in Saxony's parliament. In Brandenburg, another radical right-wing party, the DVU (*Deutsche Volksunion*—German People's Union) gained 6.1 percent of the popular vote, translating into six parlimentary seats.

The political success of these parties is directly related to the government's attempts at cutting back the welfare state. One of the central planks on which both parties campaigned was against cutbacks of the welfare state. In some areas of Saxony, unemployment reaches 25 percent and more. Much of the support for the radical right-wing parties came from workers who did not want to see their social benefits reduced. "For us the social question is closely connected to the national question," says Holger Apfel, the leader of the NPD, "the solution for Germany's unemployment problem is to first create jobs for Germans, and later create a foreigner re-patriation policy, so we can free up jobs for Germans, and especially sending home foreigners who are on the dole and who are criminals." [21]

It appears that cutting back the welfare state in Germany, a policy espoused by the Social Democrats, is directly connected to the rise of radical right-wing parties that agitate toward the maintenance of such benefits. Such parties would resolve the problem of high unemployment by severely restricting immigration or even deporting foreigners. We are highlighting this connection to emphasize that the policies of any given party can directly affect the policies of other parties. What parties stand for is in reality an interactive process shaped by long-standing ideologies, personalities, political institutions, and sheer political expediency.

In this section, we have seen that the New Radical Right has a very amorphous message that is nevertheless well understood by its supporters. They may not agree among themselves on many issues, but they find something in the message of the New Radical Right that appeals to them—be it the call for tax cuts and the expulsion of foreign workers, the criticism of state bureaucrats, the demand for law and order, the antifeminist position, and so on.

GREENS

The environmental Green Party made its appearance on the European political scene during the late 1970s and early 1980s. A third dimension is necessary to define the political position of the Greens. This dimension ranges from material to postmaterial and was introduced by political scientist Ronald Inglehart.[22] The material end of the dimension means a conventional support for economic growth. This position is based on the assumption that bigger is better: The more goods and services a society produces, the better off are the members of that society. At the postmaterial end of the dimension, limits to economic growth are advocated in order to save the environment and increase the quality of life. We encountered this postmaterial position earlier in this chapter when discussing the emergence of a new wing in the Socialist Party.

A postmaterial orientation means that material goods no longer have first priority and that people seek fulfillment primarily of their spiritual, ethical, and aesthetic needs. Self-actualization is a key postmaterial concept. Great emphasis is also put on cooperation and communal living. According to the Greens, it is time for Western societies to move from a material to a postmaterial stage. In their view, this is the only way to save our souls and our natural environment. The implication of this thinking is a completely new orientation toward work. We must again find fulfillment in our daily work. This is impossible if we are merely small wheels in large bureaucratic organizations, whether public or private. The desired situation is work in a small commune: Some people can bake bread or care for the elderly, others can repair bikes or computers, and these occupational positions can easily be exchanged. The Greens acknowledge that this is not the most efficient way to organize the economy, but they challenge the usual definition of economic efficiency measured in the increase of the gross domestic product (GDP). The GDP does not reflect, for example, stress on human beings and the destruction of nature. According to the Greens, the crucial criterion for work must be how much it contributes to the quality of life for human beings, as well as for animals and plants. Nature must be brought back into equilibrium. With this philosophy, the Greens also have developed a strong interest in world peace and the fate of third-world countries.

In Figure 2.3 the horizontal dimension from state-controlled economy to free-market economy remains the same as in Figures 2.1 and 2.2. The vertical dimension now goes from postmaterial to material. If we were to add the dimension from individualistic to authoritarian, we would arrive at a three-dimensional political space. As we remember from geometry, it is possible to plot three dimensions on a two-dimensional sheet of paper, although the graph may lose clarity. In the current context, the depicted two dimensions in Figure 2.3 are sufficient, as the dimension from individualistic to authoritarian is relatively unimportant for the location of the Greens.

Although Greens are united in their emphasis on postmaterial values, they are more dispersed on economic questions. Generally, they tend toward the Left, and many Greens, indeed, come from a Socialist or even a Communist background. Other Greens, however, see more merits in market mechanisms. Disagreements about the relative importance of the free market and state intervention have led to a great deal of tension among the Greens and, occasionally, even to splits into separate parties.

Figure 2.3 also shows the position of the Swiss Automobile Party, which is the pure opposite of the Greens and helps clarify further the Green perspective. The Automobile Party has recently changed its name to the Freedom Party, but colloquially it is still mostly referred to by its original name. It takes the material position to an extreme. The car is considered to be the ultimate material good, which has to be protected against government interventions by all means. A slogan of the Automobile Party is "Unrestricted Driving for the Free Citizen." The supporters of the party protest whenever efforts are made to limit driving for environmental reasons. Such limiting measures include higher gasoline taxes, lower speed limits on highways, traffic-free streets in the inner cities, more stoplights, and less parking space. The Freedom Party considers such measures to be unnecessary restraints on the enjoyment of driving a car. This view is diametrically opposed to what is

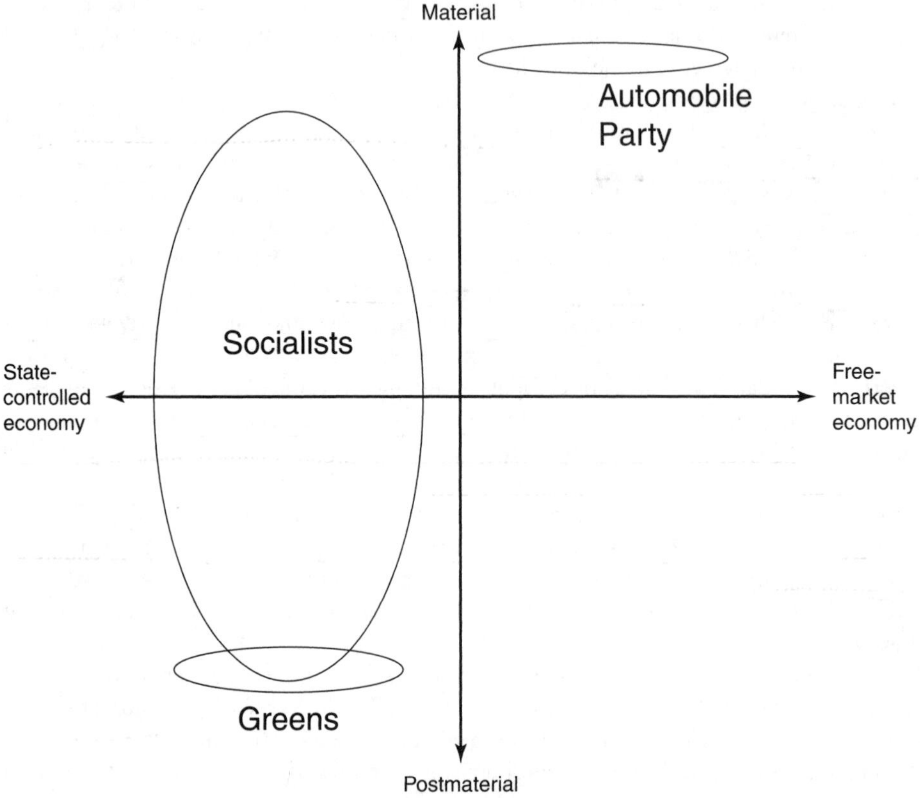

FIGURE 2.3 Location of Greens, Socialists, and Automobile Party on a dimension from state-controlled economy to free-market economy and on a dimension from material to postmaterial.

dear to Green supporters. Emotions are high between the two sets of values; as an illustration one may think of a chaotic traffic situation in which a Green supporter on a bike and a supporter of the Automobile Party in a car begin to argue with each other.

The Greens are unusual not only because they do not fit the traditional patterns of party conflict in Europe, but also in the sense that they wish to be a completely different type of party. According to their views, the leaders of the established parties form an oligarchy and have lost touch with ordinary citizens. The Greens demand a fundamental democratization of political life and try to implement this principle first in their own ranks. Ideally, the Greens would like to have no leadership, but equal participation by all members. To move toward this ideal, the Greens initially developed unusual party rules, particularly in Germany. There, the Greens at first did not allow their members of parliament to have incomes higher than those of blue-collar workers; the surplus had to be contributed to the party. After two years in office, Green members of parliament also were expected to rotate their seats to others in the party. These rules led to a great deal of acrimony in the German Green Party; they have often been violated, and in the meantime many of the rules have been abolished or at least relaxed.

Who are the Green supporters? Much research has focused on this question, resulting in a high consensus on who votes for the Greens. According to the succinct summary by

Herbert Kitschelt they are "younger, educated, urban, secular members of the new middle classes."[23] They tend to work overproportionally in the public service sector—in particular, in education, health, and social work. The Greens also attract many feminists, gays, and lesbians.

What specific policies do the Greens propose? A good illustration is the policy program decided by the German Greens at their party convention in March 1996. It is entitled "Alliance for Work and the Environment" and contains a new energy tax and cuts in the work week.[24] According to the Greens, these two proposals offer the best hope for protecting the environment and reducing the country's persistent high unemployment. A so-called eco-tax would be imposed on atomic and hydroelectric power, as well as on fossil fuels—but not on renewable energy sources such as solar power. This eco-tax would be so stiff that energy consumption would significantly drop, which in turn would substantially cut pollution. The revenue produced by the eco-tax would be used to strengthen the welfare system. Job creation would be spurred by cutting the work week to 30 hours and abolishing overtime. As the spokesperson of the Greens claimed, these policies are meant as an alternative to what is called in German an *Ellbogengesellschaft*—literally an "elbow society," where everyone is aggressively using his or her elbows to get ahead.

Are the Greens likely to be a short-term phenomenon, or are they likely to endure as a political party? This is a widely discussed question that is addressed in a sophisticated way by political scientists Mark N. Franklin and Wolfgang Rüdig.[25] In their view, a necessary condition for the Greens to endure is "their ability to maintain a functioning and well-resourced party organization."[26] On these grounds, there were initially many doubts because the organization of the party was very chaotic, which made a bad impression on many potential supporters. But in recent times, this has greatly improved. As a leading German Green put it after a successfully organized election campaign in one of the German states: "Now you can invite us into your homes. We don't wear purple mesh stockings any more, and our hair doesn't look like exploding steel wool. We no longer live off shrill slogans."[27] (See Box 2.4)

With regard to the social base of the Greens, Franklin and Rüdig arrive at the conclusion that it is very volatile. There is not yet much party loyalty, so that the Greens must "mobilize many of their supporters afresh for each election."[28] The environment as the major issue of the Greens is also taken up by the Socialists, as we have seen earlier in the chapter. Environmentalists may also vote for a variety of other parties, as Oddbjørn Knutsen found out in a study of the party systems in the Scandinavian countries.[29] Thus, the Greens have no monopoly on environmental issues; voters with environmental concerns may easily move among several parties. The social base of the Greens may become more stable if a broadly based network of Green supporters develops.

In the United States the environmental movement is quite strong, but the Green Party hardly exists. Why is this so? In Chapter 3, we will see that it may have to do with the particular American election system, which disadvantages smaller parties.

REGIONAL PARTIES

To locate regional parties, we have to introduce still another dimension of party space, the center–periphery dimension. If we take a typical regional party, such as the Scottish National

> ### Box 2.4 Happy 25th Birthday Greens. What's the Plan Now?
>
> Twenty-five years ago, on the 13th of January 1980, the German Green Party was officially born. Since then, they have strayed from their sunflower-laced ideals, which over the years included pulling Germany out of NATO and instigating super high gas prices. Thank God. Today, Germany's Greens — now the strongest Green Party in the world — turn 25. There won't be any grand parties or brouhaha. They did a bit of that last year to fete the unofficial 25-year anniversary. Still, it is worth taking a moment to raise a glass to a party that began as a scruffy band of pacifist idealists and has evolved into one of the nation's biggest power players. Many of the Greens' early devotees were members of the famous '68 generation, a group of left-wing radicals who wanted to change the world. Others were Trotskyites and Maoists. They sailed into the German conscience on the wave of post-World War II memories and experiences. That wave remains powerful even today and continues to influence the Greens' and other parties' policies.
>
> Source: Spiegel ONLINE, January 13, 2005.

Party, it is not possible to locate it on a left–right dimension, nor are the authoritarian–individualistic and material–postmaterial dimensions of much help. Regional parties defend the interests of a periphery against the interests of the center of a country. Most political parties look at political life from the perspective of the national capital, where they have their headquarters and the focus of their daily activities. From this center perspective, the interests of peripheral regions often are neglected. It is against such neglect that regional parties try to fight. They look at politics from the vantage point of their regions. This center–periphery dimension was introduced into the literature by the late and highly respected Norwegian political scientist Stein Rokkan.[30]

In recent years, the importance of regional parties in Europe has increased rather than decreased. With more modernity, one may perhaps have expected the opposite trend: With fewer people in farming, higher levels of education, more geographical mobility, more travel, and more exposure to mass media, one might have thought that attachment to one's region would become less important. But there is obviously a need in the modern world for roots, and the region is, for many, an entity that gives roots to the past and a feeling of solidarity to people with similar traditions and values. We will deal further with the question of regionalism in Chapter 6 on federalism, in Chapter 12 on nationalism and ethnicity, and in Chapter 14 on the European Union. This extensive treatment of the issue will show how important regionalism is in today's Europe. In addition to the Scottish National Party, the United Kingdom also has regional parties in Wales and Northern Ireland. In Spain, there are parties representing, in particular, the Basque, Catalan, Andalusian, Galician, Aragonese, and Valencian regions. Belgium is the European country where regionalism is most strongly expressed in the party system. Not only are there special regional parties for the Flemish and Walloon regions, more important, some of the major parties have special organizations for the two regions. Thus, there is a Francophone Socialist Party for Wallonia and a Flemish Socialist Party.

Currently, the most successful of the regional parties is the Northern League in Italy. Its appeal has also to do with the fact that it expresses views close to the New Radical Right. This is another example showing how European political parties are often hard to classify in mutually exclusive categories. At the core of the Northern League is the Lombardy League (Lega Lombarda), which was founded during the early 1980s by the charismatic leader Umberto Bossi. For electoral purposes, the Lombardy League united with other regional leagues in northern Italy to form the Northern League. Some of Bossi's rhetoric is quite close to that of the New Radical Right; for example, when he accuses the established parties of wanting to transform Italy into a "multiracial, multiethnic, and multireligious society" that "comes closer to hell than to paradise."[31] Bossi exploits resentment not only against foreigners, but also against the economically less-developed Italians from the south. He promotes nationalism within the north of Italy, even playing with the idea that one day northern Italy could form a nation of its own. In September 1996, Bossi organized a three-day independence rally along the banks of the Po River and ending at the sea in Venice. Arriving in Venice, he delivered a tirade against the "colonialists" in Rome who, he said, have robbed the north of Italy of its hard-earned money and its cultural identity.[32]

Belen Couceiro has compared the French National Front, the German Republicans, and the Lombardy League and has found many similarities.[33] Other scholars, such as Stefano Bartolini,[34] stress more the unique Italian character of the Northern League, so that it seems problematic to them to put it in the same category as the National Front and the German Republicans. The United States has also strong regional identities, but no regional parties have emerged.

A MULTIDIMENSIONAL POLITICAL SPACE

We have now located the political parties of Europe in a complex multidimensional political space, using four different dimensions. One may add still other dimensions; for example, a religious–secular or an urban–rural dimension. The reader should be aware that these dimensions are theoretical constructs that were developed so that we can better understand the ideological position of the various parties—but these constructs should not be seen as representing in any way an objective reality. As any other construct, these constructs have a subjective character rooted in the cognitive frameworks of the researchers who have proposed them. Reality can always be constructed in different ways, and there are certainly other ways to categorize the ideologies of the political parties in Europe. The four-dimensional space presented here is merely one possibility to make sense of the variations among the parties. In research about American politics, a multidimensional space is often used for the location of presidential candidates.

However we categorize the European political parties, there is no doubt that it has become more complicated to categorize them in an adequate way. This is true not only for foreign observers but also for Europeans themselves. The labels of the various political parties can no longer easily be identified with specific policy positions. This is different from traditional European politics, which was largely dominated by a single left–right dimension defined in economic terms. Now, other dimensions have equal and sometimes even more importance. To be sure, economic issues are still salient, such as taxes, social security, unemployment compensation, and financing of health care. But these economic issues are often of a very technical nature, so they do not raise much emotion in the general public. Other issues often create more controversy, such as how to regulate or deregulate drugs or whether to limit private automobile traffic. Such issues have little to do with the traditional left–right dimension.

Party competition may take place along specific dimensions, but in a multidimensional space there are many other possibilities of party competition. Let us call axes the battle lines among the political parties. As an illustration, Figure 2.4 presents a new and important axis of party competition that cuts across two dimensions: the authoritarian–individualistic and the material–postmaterial. Of the four quadrants, only two are heavily populated in current European politics: the authoritarian–material and the individualistic–postmaterial quadrants. The battles on this axis are very emotional, the issues clear-cut and highly visible. Either one legalizes drugs, or one does not; either private automobiles are blocked from the inner city, or they are not; either refugees are accepted, or they are not; and so on.

The three traditional European parties—the Socialists, the Liberals, and the Conservatives—have difficulties in defining their positions on this axis. If the Socialists move too much toward the individualistic–postmaterial end, they risk losing their blue-collar, working-class supporters to the New Radical Right. If the Socialists move too much away

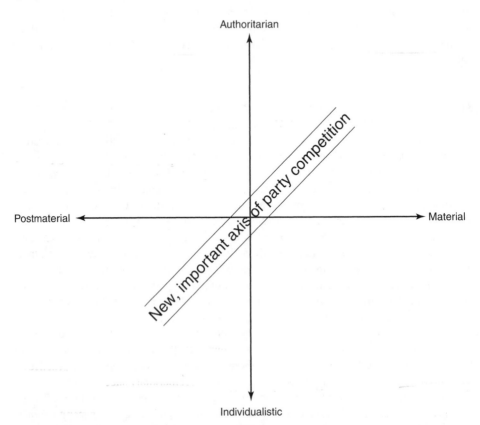

Figure 2.4 New, important axis of party competition.

from the individualistic–postmaterial end, they risk losing their newly gained supporters in the service sector to the Greens and other left-libertarian parties. The situation is no better for the Conservatives. If they move too far away from the authoritarian–material end, they lose voters to the New Radical Right; if they move too close in this direction, they lose voters at the center of the axis. The Liberals feel most comfortable in the individualistic–material quadrant; many of their supporters are upper-middle-class people who are individualistic on matters such as abortion but wish to enjoy their material consumer goods. If the political battles rage on the new axis, Liberals can either stay away, making their party irrelevant, or they can take a position on the new axis and risk being internally torn apart, with some of their supporters going to the Conservatives and others to the Socialists. Most comfortable on the new axis are the New Radical Right and the Greens. Being at both ends, they can easily define the nature of the political game, putting the other parties in an uncomfortable defensive position. This discussion illustrates the importance of how the battle lines are defined in a multidimensional space. To be successful, a party has to be able to define the political axes in such a way that it is located at a strategically advantageous location. The Free Democrats, for example, are well off if party competition in Figure 2.4 takes place either along the horizontal or the vertical axes because then they can take a clear offensive position.

Have the terms *left* and *right* become useless if one wishes to understand party competition in Europe? Yes and no. For scholarly analyses in political science, the two terms have become so vague that scholars are better off not using them at all and relying instead on more clearly defined terms, such as *postmaterial* and *individualistic*. But European politicians and voters still think in terms of left and right, and because we as political scientists need to understand their thinking, we still have to be concerned with the terms *left* and *right*. What is meant by these two terms in current European politics? Oddbjorn Knutsen has studied this question for the voters in several European countries and has come up with a double conclusion.[35] On the one hand, the terms *left* and *right* continue to be identified by the public with the traditional economic dimension of state-controlled economy versus the free market. But on the other hand, to be at the Left increasingly is also identified with postmaterial values, to be at the Right with material values. As Knutsen writes, "the new meanings of left and right are added to the old meanings." Therefore, we have now a left–right dimension "incorporating many types of conflict lines, and with different meanings to different people."[36] As argued earlier, such a broad dimension has lost its usefulness for analytical purposes, but it continues to be used by European voters and politicians to understand political life. In this sense the left–right dimension remains important in European politics.

A spatial term often used in European politics is the term *center*, and one speaks frequently of center parties. In Scandinavia there are political parties that explicitly call themselves center parties. Whatever their specific names, center parties are located at the median or close to it on all important dimensions. New research on center parties stems from Hans Keman[37] and Reuven Y. Hazan.[38] Keman calls the center parties "pivot parties in West European party systems . . . the linchpin for parliamentary democratic practice in multiparty systems . . . many of these parties have been remarkably successful in electoral terms as well as in gaining and keeping office."[39] Hazan agrees with Keman that center parties have great political influence in many European democracies; he goes a step further in also researching "the effect that the center has on the other parties in the system."[40]His conclusion is that a strong center party causes other parties to take more extreme positions than they otherwise would.

Downplaying the electoral appeal of the center, George Rabinowitz and Stuart Elaine Macdonald point out that center parties may be perceived to be wishy-washy in not taking a clear stand on issues and therefore may not be very successful among voters.[41] Rabinowitz and Macdonald argue that in the mind of voters most issues are reduced to two sides: either you are for public transportation, or you are not; either you are for stricter measures against drugs, or you are not. In order to be successful, parties should take a clear stand on either side; the only qualification is that they must make sure not to be seen as extremists but as responsible, as Rabinowitz and Macdonald put it, to stay within a region of acceptibility. The research reported here about center parties is a good example of how lively and controversial political science research can be. Who is right in the present case? Is the center a good location to run, or not?

MEMBERSHIP IN POLITICAL PARTIES

Membership in a European political party is quite different from party membership in the United States. Americans reveal their party identification by registering, voting in general elections, and answering opinion surveys, but they do not formally join a party as they would a professional association or a service club, by paying annual dues and carrying a membership card. Europeans do precisely that when they join a political party: Membership in a political party is applied for, and the party has the right to reject applicants, although this happens rarely.

What percentage of European voters are members of a political party? Figures vary strongly from country to country; usually membership is below 10 percent, and in some places as low as 5 percent or even less. There is also quite a bit of rotation, with many people moving in and out of parties. In Norway, for example, Per Selle and Lars Svasand found that in each of two 4-year periods they studied, "more people moved in or out of parties than were stable members."[42] Although it is common in Europe to give up membership in a political party, it is rare to change membership from one party to another. In the Norwegian study by Selle and Svasand, only 3 percent and 1 percent, respectively, did so in each of the two 4-year periods. It is one thing to quit a party but quite another thing to join another party. The latter is considered by many Europeans as disloyal.

There is much debate about whether party membership in Europe is in decline, and there are, indeed, some countries and individual parties where such a decline has been registered. But in their careful study, Selle and Svasand come to a more nuanced conclusion. They find that in Great Britain, the Netherlands, and Denmark, party membership has decreased, but that it has increased in Belgium, Austria, Ireland, Germany, and Finland. In other countries, they find no clear trend. It is also interesting that the same party may gain members in one country but lose members in another country.

What are party members doing in their parties? For many, the answer is "not much." Various studies have found that merely about 10 to 20 percent of members are really active in their party organizations. Even for many of these members, the emphasis of their party activities is less on political discussions than on leisure and entertainment. To attract members, political parties organize all kinds of nonpolitical activities such as dances, hikes, picnics, and so on. The single most important political function of parties is to nominate candidates for political offices, an aspect to which we turn in the next chapter.

People outside a political party still may display party loyalty, but for some reason they decide against becoming formal party members. For Great Britain, the Netherlands, and Germany, Bradley M. Richardson has found that between 50 and 70 percent of all the voters are "stable psychological partisans." His analysis demonstrates that "many voters' long-term party ties are buttressed by stable views toward long-term party principles and/or stable party images; many voters' loyalties are further fortified by negative views of opposing parties. This constrained structure of responses to parties makes European partisanship resemble an affect-laden schema."[43]Thus, we should distinguish carefully between party membership and party loyalty. Although, in general, party members show higher party loyalty than nonmembers, there is also some overlap in the sense that party loyalty may be higher among some nonmembers than among some members. Such members may simply forget to cancel their party membership but are no longer emotionally attached to the party. In this context, it is important to note that membership dues are not very high, and in most cases are well below $100 annually.

STABILITY AND CHANGE OF PARTIES AND PARTY SYSTEMS

So far we have in detail described individual parties. The term party system, however, does not refer to any individual party, but rather to a set of parties and their relationship to each other. In the previous section we argued that the origins of parties were directly connected to establishment of the mass franchise achieved in most countries by the early 1920s. As a result, once voters were allowed to give expression to their political desires by voting for their preferred party, the party system became "frozen" in time.[44] Indeed, party systems remained relatively stable until the late 1970s and early 1980s. However, in the 1960s social movements began to stir, which would manifest themselves eventually as new parties in the 1980s.

The rise of new parties, such as the Greens, can partly be explained as a result of increased education, the satisfaction of material demands and socialization during a period of economic well-being. Other parties, such as radical right-wing parties, emerge as a result of new political issues such as immigration; yet other parties form partly as a result of splitting off from established parties, such as Jörg Haider's Freedom Party in Austria (FPÖ). As a result of intraparty fights between Haider and others members of the party, in April of 2005 Haider formed a new party, the so-called Bündnis Zukunft Österreich (BZÖ), which managed to not only become a new party but also to become part of a governing coalition together with the Austrian People's Party, even though nobody ever voted for this party! Similarly, the German general election of 2005 was contested by a new left-wing party, the so-called Linkspartei (Left Party), which consisted of a fraction of the old Sozialdemokratische Partei Deutschlands (SPD) led by Oskar Lafontaine and Gregor Gysi, the head of the Partei des Deutschen Sozialismus (PDS), the successor party to the Communist Party in the former German Democratic Republic. This, in effect, meant that the German election was contested by two parties on the left, the traditional SPD and a newcomer the Linkspartei, which, true to its name, is to the left of the SPD.

The perhaps most disconcerting development over the last two decades has been the degree to which voter turnout has declined in many European democracies. The party of "nonvoters" has become one of the largest parties in many European countries, such as in France where in the 2002 presidential election more than 40 percent of the voting-age population did not participate. Similar tendencies can be found in Austria, the United Kingdom, and Germany, where the percentage of the party of "nonvoters" in the most recent elections reached 25, 39, and 21 percent, respectively.

Despite these changes to the party-landscape over the last two decades, it is also true that the basic Socialist/Conservative divide has remained rather stable with core blocs of voters providing continued support. Though there is certainly change occurring in European party systems, there are also continuities observable, particularly as far as the established parties are concerned.

We are now familiar with the wide range of political parties in Europe. We have learned that we need to think in terms of a multidimensional space in order to understand the location of the various political parties. In the following chapters, Chapter 3 through 6, we will learn about the institutions in which European political parties operate. In these chapters we will also see how the number and the kind of parties depend very much on the institutional setting of the respective country.

Discussion Questions

1. Why does the term "liberal" mean something very different in the European political context as compared to the American political context?

2. Why are parties crucial for modern, democratic politics?

3. Why are there no Socialist parties in the United States?

4. Many European countries have postmaterial parties represented in their legislatures. Why are there no postmaterial parties in the American House of Representatives?

5. Are European Social Democratic parties such as the German SPD comparable to the American Democratic party?

6. Many European countries, such as the UK or Germany, have regional parties. Why does the United States not have regional parties, i.e., why is there not, for example, a Texan party or a Southern party?

7. Are there politicians in the United States who would fit into the New Radical Right in Europe? Who are they?

8. What is the advantage of perceiving the political space in a multidimensional fashion as opposed to the traditional left right spectrum?

---

[1]Maurice Duverger. *Caucus and branch cadre parties and mass parties* in Peter Mair (ed). The west European party system Oxford University Press 1990. [Excerpted from *political parties their organization and activity in the modern state* originally published in 1954]

[2]Ibid.

[3]Max Weber. [1919]. Politics as a Vocation. In H. H. Gerth and C. Wright Mills (eds.), *From Max Weber. Essays in Sociology.* (New York: Oxford University Press, 1946, 102).

[4]Elmer E. Schattschneider. *Party Government.* (New York: Rinehart, 1942, 1).

[5]Bertolt Brecht, *Threepenny Opera.* (New York: Grove, 1949, 66–67).

[6]Herbert Kitschelt. Class Structure and Social Democratic Party Strategy. *British Journal of Political Science* (July 1993): 319. See also Herbert Kitschelt. *The Transformation of European Social Democracy.* (New York: Cambridge University Press, 1994).

[7]The complete document can accessed online at: http://www.socialdemocrats.org/blairandschroeder6-8-99.html.

[8]*Economist,* June 26, 2004, p. 100.

[9]Paul F. Whiteley, Patrick Seyd, Jeremy Richardson, and Paul Bissell. Thatcherism and the Conservative Party. *Political Studies* 42 (1994): 185–203.

[10]Ibid., 190.

[11]Ibid., 190.

[12]Ibid., 190–191.

[13]Hans-George Betz. The New Politics of Resentment: Radical Right-Wing Populist Parties in Western Europe. *Comparative Politics* 25 (July 1993): 418.

[14]Ibid., 423.

[15]Herbert Kitschelt. Left-Libertarians and Right-Authoritarians: Is the New Right a Response to the New Left in European Politics? (Paper presented at the Western European Area Studies Center, University of Minnesota, November 1991), 15, 23.

[16]Betz, The New Politics of Resentment, 413.

[17]Pierre Bréchon and Subrata Kumar Mitra. The National Front in France: The Emergence of an Extreme Right Protest Movement. *Comparative Politics* 25 (October 1992): 80.

[18]*New York Times,* October 2, 1996.

[19]*Tages-Anzeiger,* Fernausgabe, February 2, 1993 (translation J. S.).

[20]*Neue Zürcher Zeitung,* October 14, 1996.

[21]National Public Radio, November 23, 2004.

[22]Ronald Inglehart. *The Silent Revolution: Changing Values and Political Styles Among Western Publics.* (Princeton, NJ: Princeton University Press, 1977).

[23]Herbert Kitschelt. Left-Libertarian Parties: Explaining Innovation in Competitive Party Systems. *World Politics* 40 (January 1988): 194–234.

[24]*The Week in Germany, A Weekly Publication of the German Information Center, New York,* March 8, 1996.

[25]Mark N. Franklin and Wolfgang Rüdig. On the Durability of Green Politics. *Comparative Political Studies* 28 (October 1995): 409–439.

[26]Ibid., 434.

[27]*New York Times,* September 20, 1993.

[28]Franklin and Rüdig, On the Durability of Green Politics, 434.

[29]Oddbjorn Knutsen. The Materialist/Postmaterialist Value Dimension as a Party Cleavage in the Nordic Countries. *West European Politics* 13 (April 1990): 258–274.

[30]Stein Rokkan. *Citizens, Elections, Parties: Approaches to the Comparative Study of the Process of Development* (Oslo: Universitetsforlaget, 1970). See also special issue on Stein Rokkan, *Historical Social Research* 20 (No. 2, 1995).

[31]Quoted in Betz, The New Politics of Resentment, 417.

[32]*New York Times,* September 16, 1996.

[33]Belen Couceiro. Analyse rechtspopulistischer Parteien in Westeuropa mit besonderer Berücksichtigung der "Front National," der "Partei der Republikaner," und der Lega Lombarda. (Seminararbeit, Universität Bern, 1993).

[34]Personal communication, June 1993.

[35]Oddbjorn Knutsen. Value Orientation, Political Conflicts and Left-Right Identification: A Comparative Study. *European Journal of Political Research* 28 (1995): 63–93.

[36]Ibid., 87.

[37]Hans Keman. The Search for the Center: Pivot Parties in West European Party Systems. *West European Politics* 17 (October 1994): 124–148.

[38]Reuven Y. Hazan. Center Parties and Systemic Polarization. An Exploration of Recent Trends in Western Europe. *Journal of Theoretical Politics* 7 (4, 1995): 421–445.

[39]Keman, The Search for the Center, 124, 145–146.

[40]Hazan, Center Parties and Systemic Polarization, 436.

[41]George Rabinowitz and Stuart Elaine Macdonald. An Illusory Rescue of the Proximity Theory of Electoral Choice. *American Political Science Review* (forthcoming).

[42]Per Selle and Lars Svasand. Membership in Party Organizations and the Problem of Decline of Parties. *Comparative Political Studies* 23 (January 1991): 463.

[43]Bradley M. Richardson. European Party Loyalties Revisited. *American Political Science Review* 85 (September 1991): 751, 766.

[44]Seymour Martin Lipse and Stein Rokkan. *Party Systems and Voter Alignments. Cross-National Perspectives* (New York: The Free Press, 1967).

CHAPTER 3

Parliamentary Election Systems

Our discussion now turns to the institutions within which political parties operate, and in the current chapter we deal with parliamentary election systems. By this we mean the formal rules according to which elections of parliament are organized, which vary widely among European democracies. Students should learn how election rules affect the success of political parties, both positively and negatively. Election rules, like any rules, are never neutral. We discuss in detail Great Britain, the Netherlands, Switzerland, Ireland, Germany, France, and Italy. Each of these countries has special features in its election rules, thus illustrating the wide range of possibilities available for organizing parliamentary elections.

Americans are accustomed to simple rules for parliamentary elections. For the U.S. Senate, whoever receives the most votes in his or her state is elected. The same rule applies to the U.S. House of Representatives: Whoever wins the most votes in his or her congressional district is elected. In Europe, the simple winner-take-all system in its pure form is used only in Great Britain, where it is called "first-past-the-post." This system may also be called single-member-district/plurality, meaning that only one member of parliament is elected per district and that it is sufficient to reach a plurality of the votes (not a majority) in order to get the seat. The other European countries use a wide variety of rules to elect their parliaments. Election rules are not interesting for their own sake, but because they influence the way the political game is played. The connection between the rules of the game and the game itself is well known from sports. Changes in the rules of a sport often influence the kinds of players who are able to make the team. As we see in this chapter, the same holds true for politics. A politician who is successful under one set of rules may not be successful under another set of rules. We will illustrate this argument with cases where the electoral rules have been changed.

Like the U.S. Congress, most European parliaments have two chambers (bicameral systems). There are, however, some exceptions. Sweden, for example, has a single chamber of parliament (unicameral). In the U.S. Congress, the Senate and the House have roughly equal power overall. In most European countries, the pattern is different, with one chamber having a dominant position. The more important chamber is often called the lower house, the less important chamber the upper house. These two terms originated from Great Britain. The House of Lords formerly consisted of hundreds of members of the hereditary nobility and some members who received titles merely for their lifetime. However, the House of Lords Act (1999) fundamentally changed the character of the House of Lords by removing hereditary peerage. The first line of the new law is very explicit: "No-one shall be a member of the House of Lords by virtue of hereditary peerage." However, to make this fundamental constitutional change possible, a compromise was reached, allowing 90 hereditary peers to remain in the House of Lords on a temporary basis. The House of Commons is democratically elected on the basis of one person, one vote. In former times, the House of Lords had more prestige and power, hence the term *upper house*. But over the centuries, the House of Commons, the "lower" house, became more and more important, and today it is the dominant chamber. Thus, contrary to what one may logically expect, the term *lower* connotes more power than *upper.*

WINNER-TAKE-ALL: GREAT BRITAIN

Both the House of Commons and the House of Lords meet in Westminster Palace on the river Thames (Photo 3.1). From about 1340, Parliament began to meet in Westminster, which can be considered the birthplace of modern parliaments. In 1941, during World War II, the chamber of the House of Commons was destroyed by German air attacks. After the war, the chamber was rebuilt based on the old designs. Buildings can be an important part of the tradition of institutions, and this was well understood when Westminster was rebuilt according to the old plans.

For the election of the members of the House of Commons, the country is divided into as many electoral districts as there are parliamentary seats—currently 646—and in each district the candidate who has the most votes wins the seat. As in the United States, there is no requirement that the winner reach an absolute majority of 50 percent +1; a mere plurality of the votes is sufficient. Thus, with three candidates in a district, the winner may receive only 40 percent of the vote, with perhaps the two other candidates each getting 30 percent.

The winner-take-all system is strongly biased in favor of the two largest parties in a country. In the U.S. Congress, no third parties have been represented to any significant extent in recent times. Is this due to the electoral system? Yes, most likely. But U.S. third parties get so few votes in congressional elections that, at first glance, it may not be clear how their lack of success could possibly be due to the electoral system. This chapter should

Photo 3.1 Great Britain's House of Parliament, Westminister, London. (*Source:* Royalty Free/Corbis)

make clear that under a different electoral system, U.S. third parties would have a better chance of representation in Congress. In presidential elections circumstances are somewhat different, so third-party candidates have a better chance, as the candidacy of Ross Perot in the 1992 election illustrates. In this chapter, however, we are concerned only with parliamentary, not presidential, elections.

In British parliamentary elections, third parties are numerically much stronger than in American congressional elections. As a consequence, and paradoxically, it is easier to demonstrate with the British case how a winner-take-all system works against third parties. If third parties get a fair amount of voter support, it is easier to see how this support fails to translate into parliamentary representation. The discrimination against third parties can best be illustrated with the 1983 general election, in which third parties received particularly high voter support but little parliamentary representation. The information is presented graphically to highlight the tendency of winner-take-all systems to create large disparities between popular support and actual allocation of seats in parliaments.

Inspection of Figure 3.1 clearly demonstrates the disparity between the percentage of popular votes and the percentage of seats allocated. The Conservatives, while only winning a plurality of the vote (42.4 percent), won a landslide 61.1 percent of parliamentary seats, as shown in the much larger bar for the percentage of seats.

This large victory occured because the opposition was badly divided. Shortly before the election, moderate Labour members had split from their party to form their own centrist Social Democratic Party (SDP). The SDP entered into the so-called Alliance with the Liberals, which meant the two parties agreed to have only one candidate in each district, either a Social Democrat or a Liberal. Before the 1983 election, the Liberals were the perennial third party in British electoral history. They achieved sizable voter support but hardly any seats because they were first-past-the-post in only a very few districts. In the 1974 election, for example, the Liberals won a substantial share of voter support (18.6 percent) but managed to win only 13 seats (2.0 percent). Uniting their forces in 1983 in the Alliance, Liberals and Social Democrats hoped to win not only voters but also seats. But this hope was disappointed; their voter support of 25.4 percent translated into a mere 3.5 percent of the

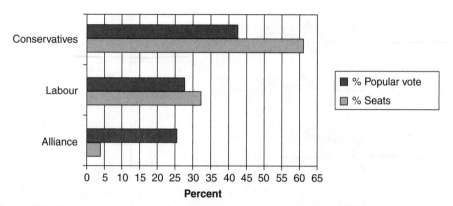

FIGURE 3.1 Voter support and percent of parliamentary seats in 1983 general election to the British House of Commons. (*Source: European Journal of Political Research* 12 (September 1984): 342.)

seats. The Alliance was punished by an electoral system where only winning matters, and a good showing in second or third place counts for nothing.

With only a slightly higher voter support of 27.6 percent, Labour won nearly ten times as many parliamentary seats (32.3 percent) as the Alliance. The reason was that Labour voters were concentrated in working-class districts where, in many cases, the party was able to come in first. The Alliance voters, in contrast, were spread more evenly over all districts. This distribution made for a good showing overall in the country but resulted in very few district victories. And with the winner-take-all system, only victories count.

To understand fully the winner-take-all system, we also must consider anticipatory effects. Many voters do not like to "waste" their vote on a party that is expected to have no chance of victory. In the 1983 election, this mechanism worked strongly against the Alliance. Many voters seriously considered voting for it but, according to a study by Ivor Crewe, eventually did not, because they anticipated that the Alliance candidates had no chance of winning their district.[1] The British case also should help us understand that election rules are not simply a given but are themselves an outcome of the political game. Because it was at a serious disadvantage under the winner-take-all system, the Alliance advocated a change to proportional representation. But Conservatives and Labour, which both greatly profited from the existing system, were opposed to such a change, and, given the distribution of the seats in the House of Commons, the Alliance had no chance to have its way.

The same fate for small parties in the United Kingdom was repeated in the 1992 election. This time it was the Liberal Democrats, a merger between the Liberal Party and the Social Democratic Party, which ran against the other two large, established parties. And again, the logic of the winner-take-all system took its toll: Even though the Liberal Democrats polled 17.9 percent of the vote, they ended up with only 3 percent of the seats in the British House of Commons (see Figure 3.2).

The reason why neither of the two large parties in Great Britain want to change the electoral system is shown in the results of the 2005 elections to the British House of Commons. This time it was the Labour Party that profited from the distortionary effects of the electoral system.

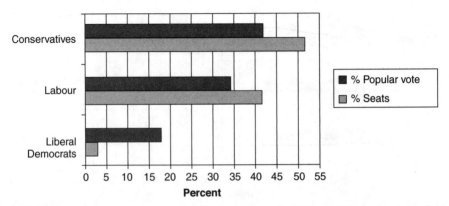

FIGURE 3.2 Voter support and percent of parliamentary seats in 1992 general election to the British House of Commons. (*Source: Keesing's Record of World Events* 38 (London: Longman, 1992), p. 38868.)

Figure 3.3 indicates that while only three percentage points in the popular vote separated Labour from the Conservatives, this small margin in popular votes translated into 25 percent more seats for Labour than for the Conservatives! With only a little over 35 percent of the voters choosing Labour, the lowest percentage of popular votes for a winning party ever, Labour can still claim a majority in the House of Commons of over 55 percent of seats. Voter turnout in the 2005 election was 61.3 percent, two percentage points higher than in the 2001 election.

The winner-take-all electoral system demonstrates even stronger disparities between seats and votes when the electoral fortunes of small parties are examined. As shown in Figure 3.3, the Liberal Democrats received over 22 percent of public support, yet this translated only into 9.6 percent of all seats (62).

Until now, we have focused on the negative effects on smaller parties of the winner-take-all system. On a more positive note, one also could argue that this type of electoral system helps to prevent the entry of extremist parties to Parliament, thus making governance easier. The American and British cases seem to support this argument, as extremist parties are not represented in either country's legislature. This moderating effect, however, is likely to occur only for a unimodal distribution of voter preferences, where most voters are in the middle and few are at the extremes so that their distribution looks like a bell-shape curve. The United States and Great Britain have, by and large, such unimodal distributions of voter preferences on most important dimensions, and therefore approximate the situation depicted in Figure 3.4. Under these conditions, we would indeed expect a moderating effect, because, to win, an extreme would lead nowhere. After all, most voters are located in the middle. (For a discussion of where exactly in the middle parties should locate themselves, see the section on a multidimensional political space in Chapter 2.)

Figure 3.5 represents an extremist distribution of voter preferences, with the highest number of voters at the two extremes. We can easily see that in such a situation a moderate position has little appeal. Let us assume that the voters at the left of our political dimension in Figure 3.5 are Catholics and those at the right are Protestants, with the two groups far apart on all important issues. With a winner-take-all system, one candidate is

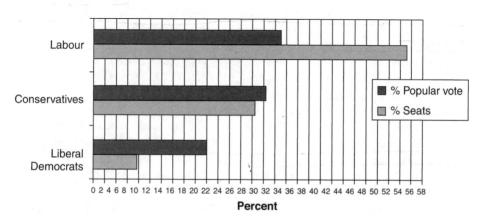

FIGURE 3.3 Voter support and percent of parliamentary seats in 2005 general election to the British House of Commons. (*Source:* BBC News, "Election 2005.")

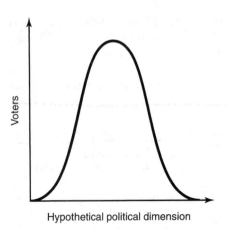

FIGURE 3.4 Unimodal distribution of voter preferences on a hypothetical political dimension.

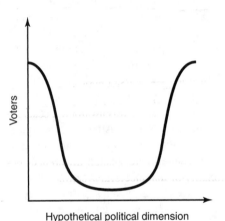

FIGURE 3.5 Extremist distribution of voter preferences on a hypothetical political dimension.

likely to appeal to Catholics, the other, to Protestants. The election then corresponds more to a census, in the sense that the size of the two groups is counted. The campaign will have a polarizing effect, because each candidate will do everything to *mobilize* the members of his or her group. This is basically the situation in Northern Ireland. The only difference between that situation and the situation represented in Figure 3.5 is that one group in Northern Ireland, the Protestants, is numerically stronger than Catholics, which further exacerbates the problem, because in most districts Catholics have no chance of winning. London is slowly beginning to recognize the unfairness of the winner-take-all system under these circumstances and has imposed proportionality rules for local elections in Northern Ireland and for elections of Northern Ireland representatives to the European parliament. For the crucial elections to the House of Commons, however, Northern Ireland continues to use the winner-take-all system (more on the troubles in Northern Ireland in Chapters 12 and 13). The difficulties that the winner-take-all system encounters in Northern Ireland also can be seen in many third-world countries. If, for example, the electorate comprises two historically hostile ethnic groups, under a winner-take-all system each group will be highly motivated to use all legal—and, sometimes, illegal—means to turn out more voters than the other group, and elections will tend to be polarizing.

PARTY LIST PROPORTIONAL REPRESENTATION: THE NETHERLANDS

The basic principle of party list proportional representation (hereafter, PR) is simple: A party receives parliamentary seats in proportion to its share of the total vote. If a parliament has 100 members and a party wins 10 percent of the total vote, then that party will be awarded 10 parliamentary seats. If the party wins 1 percent of the vote, it receives 1 seat. What if a party in this situation wins 1.5 percent of the vote? Will it receive 1 or 2 seats? This will depend on what fractions of seats the other parties get. Mathematically this is not an easy problem, and there are different formulas to find a solution. Together with the mathematician Hans Riedwyl, one of us (Steiner) has dealt with this problem at the crossroads of political science and mathematics in the journal *Comparative Politics*.[2]

The Netherlands uses party list PR in its most simple form. The Dutch parliament has 150 members, who are elected from a single, nationwide electoral district. The political parties submit lists of their candidates, and the voters simply choose one of these lists.[3] The votes are tallied in a two-step process. First, the number of votes nationwide for each party is counted and then converted into a percentage of the total vote cast. In the 2003 election, the Christian Democratic Appeal received the most votes (28.6 percent), the Labour Party came in second (27.3 percent), and the Liberals finished third (17.9 percent). According to the PR system, the Christian Democrats were awarded 44 seats; Labour, 42; and the Liberals, 28. The other 36 seats were awarded to six smaller parties. The smallest party receiving parliamentary representation, the Political Reform Party, was awarded 2 seats for its 1.6 percent of votes cast.

Figure 3.6 clearly shows how closely the percentage of popular votes per party and its corresponding percentage of seats track each other. There are very small differences between the two bars, indicating the high proportionality of that electoral system.

We now know how the first step of the Dutch electoral system—the distribution of parliamentary seats to the political parties—works. The second step is to consider how the individual parties determine which of their candidates will be elected. Each party lists its candidates in the order in which they will be awarded the seats won by the party. For example, the Labour Party's first 42 ranked candidates became its parliamentary representatives. This system of having the parties rank their own candidates provides an important means of controlling the behavior of party members.

How is the ranking done? Who gets the favorable ranks at the top? Who would be so foolish as to enter the race last on a list? The ranking is done by the party organizations, without the help of primaries. A small group, such as the party's executive committee, usually prepares the party list. A party convention then approves the list, usually without making major changes. A young party member beginning his or her career would feel honored just to be placed on the list, even if the actual rank gave absolutely no chance of election. By working hard for the party, a candidate expects to move up the list to finally receive a rank that assures him or her of election to a parliamentary seat. Prominent party leaders and successful members of Parliament are usually given places on the list that virtually guarantee reelection to Parliament. This system strengthens the parties by giving them the opportunity to reward loyal party members with good rankings and punish less loyal ones with bad rankings.

The Dutch system of party ranking stands in sharp contrast to American practice. An American candidate need only receive the most votes in a district. This voter support often

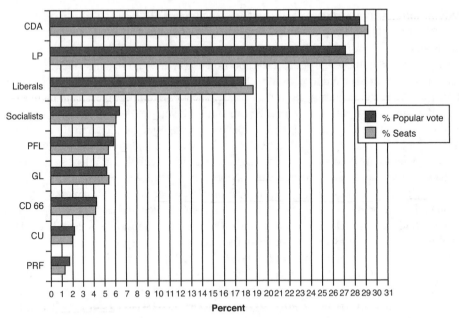

CDA = Christian Democratic Appeal; LP = Labor Party; PFL = Pim Fortuyn List; GL = Green Left;
CD 66 = Center Democrats; CU = Christian Union; PRF = Political Reform Party

Figure 3.6 Voter support and percent of parliamentary seats in 2003 general election to the parliament of the Netherlands. (*Source:* De Telegraaf, January 23, 2003.)

depends only slightly on the candidate's party loyalty, and sometimes it is even advantageous for an American candidate to demonstrate some independence from the official platform of his or her party.

The lack of party discipline in the United States, however, cannot be due solely to the system of election, because Great Britain combines the same winner-take-all system with a fairly high party discipline. Although it is certainly true that party list PR as practiced in the Netherlands contributes to strong party discipline, it is not true that strong party discipline is impossible under a winner-take-all system. Whether party discipline is strong or weak in a winner-take-all system also depends on other factors—in particular, on whether a country has a presidential or a parliamentary system of government. As noted, Great Britain has a parliamentary system, and in such systems the formation of a government and the vote of confidence in parliament strengthen party discipline. In the absence of a parliamentary system, the United States can afford low party discipline. Thus, the winner-take-all electoral system, in combination with the absence of a parliamentary system, explains to a large extent why American political parties have low party discipline.

In the Netherlands, party list PR has contributed to a diverse multiparty system, because small fringe parties have a chance of winning parliamentary representation. As we will see in Chapter 11, Transitions to Democracy, the first free Polish election organized according to pure proportionality led to an even more diverse party system than in the Netherlands.

With an electoral system of pure proportionality, in the United States any group receiving as little as 0.25 percent of votes cast would win a seat in the U.S. House of Representatives (1 out of 435 seats). How many groups could receive at least so much support? How many votes could a party win stressing environmental issues, as the Green Party does?

The introduction of party list PR in the United States might allow the election of representatives from a great variety of parties. Under such a system, congressional membership would more closely reflect the diversity of the American population, and many voters would find a party closer to their preferences than under the current two-party system of Democrats and Republicans. What would be the major disadvantages of using a proportional representation system for American congressional elections? Americans often say they would miss voting for a particular candidate whom they know personally and consider their own representative. This weakness, however, can be remedied without abandoning the principle of proportionality. Party list PR as practiced in the Netherlands is not the only way to implement the principle of proportionality. More personalized forms of proportionality are also feasible. We turn next to Switzerland, Ireland, and Germany as illustrations of more personalized systems of proportional representation.

PERSONALIZED PROPORTIONAL REPRESENTATION: SWITZERLAND, IRELAND, AND GERMANY

Switzerland

For the election of the National Council, the lower house of Parliament, the Swiss modify party list PR in two important ways. Both modifications have the consequence of personalizing relations between voters and candidates. The first Swiss modification is that rather than a single, national electoral district, they have 26 electoral districts, corresponding to the 26 Swiss cantons. The 200 National Council seats are divided among the cantons according to population. The largest canton, Zürich, elects 34 representatives, and the smallest cantons, only 1. The parties submit candidate lists in each canton containing the names of their candidates for that canton's seats. The results are counted separately for each canton.

Having 26 electoral districts instead of a single national district works against the smaller parties. If Switzerland were treated as a single electoral district, only one-half of 1 percent of the vote would be needed to win 1 of the 200 National Council seats. With elections taking place in 26 separate districts, however, a higher percentage of votes is needed to win. In Zürich, a party must win about 3 percent of the vote to win 1 of the canton's 34 seats. In a canton with 10 seats, 10 percent is necessary to receive 1 seat. In the small cantons with only 1 seat, the party with the most votes wins the seat. Thus, if the number of seats per district is reduced to 1, the proportionality system becomes a system of winner-take-all.

If this system were applied to the United States, the 50 states could be the electoral districts, and within each state the congressional delegation would be elected according to proportional representation. In this way, some of the disadvantages of pure proportional representation could be alleviated. Very small parties would be able to win seats only in the largest states, such as California and New York.

The second Swiss modification is that the voters, not the parties, rank the candidates. The parties merely submit a list of names without rank, usually in alphabetical order. The voters do not actually rank the candidates in the sense of first rank, second rank, third rank, and so on. They can merely decide for each candidate whether (1) to leave the candidate unchanged a single time on the list, (2) to put the candidate on the list a second time, or (3) to drop the candidate from the list. The only condition is that the overall number of names is not greater than the number of seats to be elected from the canton. A voter also can decide to make no changes at all on the list. In this case, no preference is given to any of the candidates, but the ballot counts for the number of seats attributed to the party.

Voters may further complicate their list by writing in candidates from other parties. Thus, a Socialist voter may put a Free Democratic candidate on his or her list, either once or twice. With this write-in possibility, computation of the results becomes very complicated. In the previous example, the Free Democratic write-in candidate counts for the Free Democratic Party and detracts from the Socialist Party's strength; the voter has split his or her vote between the two parties. Voters can go even further and write in candidates from as many parties as they wish, but, again, the total number of names is not allowed to exceed the number of seats in the canton.

The computation of the results proceeds, in principle, in the same manner as in the Netherlands. First, for each canton, the number of seats each party receives is determined. Second, candidates win these seats in order of their ranking. This ranking is based on the number of times a candidate's name appears on all the lists, including write-ins on other parties' lists.

The freedom of choice that the voter has in Swiss system weakens the party's control over its candidates, and thus party discipline is as low as in the United States. Although a Swiss party still controls whether or not a candidate gets listed, it cannot influence a candidate's

PHOTO 3.2 Late 19th century cartoon showing the effects of proportional representation in Switzerland which introduced proportional representation in 1918.

chances of election through rank on the list. Once candidates are listed, they are on their own and must try to get a maximum number of voters to write them in twice and a minimum to cross them out. Although this system gives great power to the electorate, it also increases the influence of interest groups. These groups inform their members about the candidates who favor their interests and for whom two votes should be cast, as well as about candidates who should be crossed out because they do not favor the group's interests. A teachers' group, for example, will inform its members which candidates are sympathetic to teachers' needs and which are not. Letters are sent out by a large number of groups ranging from businesspeople to fishing workers. Candidates depend on political parties only for getting listed on the ballot; to be elected, they must obtain the support of a large number of different interest groups.

The Swiss still vote for party lists, but their electoral system allows them to express preferences for and against particular candidates. The election also takes place in relatively small districts, where voters feel more at home than in a single national district. These factors together personalize the relations between voters and candidates. With this electoral system the Swiss currently have 13 parties in the National Council. We discuss the party structure in the Swiss parliament in the next chapter in connection with cabinet formation in Switzerland.

Ireland

Personalized proportional representation also can be attained through the single transferable vote (STV) system, as practiced in the Republic of Ireland. Although Ireland is the only European country using this system, it is worth discussing because some local U.S. communities use the system and there are efforts to use it more widely in the United States (see the end of this section).The reason this electoral system is called STV should become clear as we proceed. Ireland's parliament, with a total of 166 seats, is elected from 41 districts, with the number of seats per district ranging from three to five. In each district, voters rank the candidates in order of preference, for example candidate A rank number 1, candidate B rank number 2, and so on. To be elected, a candidate needs a quota of the total votes according to the so-called Droop formula:

$$\frac{\text{total valid votes}}{\text{seats} + 1} + 1 = \text{quota}$$

With four seats in a district and 100,000, votes, the required quota is 100,000 divided by $5 + 1 = 20,001$. When the counting of the ballots begins, at first only the first rankings on the ballots are considered. Let us assume that based on these first rankings candidate A reaches the quota. He or she is therefore declared as elected. What happens in the further counting with the ballots where candidate A ranks number 1? Obviously he or she does not need these ballots anymore, so they can be transferred to the second-ranked candidates on the respective ballots. Let us now assume that candidate B reached the quota, too, and is declared elected. In the further counting there are ballots where candidates A and B take the first two ranks and, of course, they do not need these ballots anymore. According to the logic of STV these ballots are transferred to the third-ranked candidates. As the counting further continues, candidate C also reaches the quota and is declared elected. If the district has four seats to allocate, the counting still continues and the ballots with candidates A, B, and C in the top positions go to the fourth-ranked candidate, and this procedure goes on until all seats are filled.

The system works like runoffs, in which voters are called to the ballot a second time. With STV, however, voters make their choices in a single ballot, hence the term *single transferable vote*. One problem still remains—namely, the potential for abuse in the sense that the election officials could count the ballots in the order in which votes are transferred to their liking. If they like, for example, candidate B, ballots would be counted early on that could be transferred to B. Different rules exist to prevent such abuse and to make the system work as randomly as possible, but the potential for abuse nevertheless exists.

What are the optimal strategies for candidates within an STV system? The electoral game is certainly much more complex and subtle than with winner-take-all, where you simply need more votes than any other candidate. With STV you may do well even if you are not the first choice of many voters but are ranked second or third—perhaps even fourth or fifth—by a large number of people. On the other hand, you are likely to attain a bad election result if, other than a core of dedicated supporters, you do not have many other voters willing to rank you. As Michael Gallagher summarizes, "a candidate with relatively little first-preference support but with wide acceptability to many voters may fare better in terms of seats than one with more hard-core support but with little ability to attract lower preferences from supporters of other parties or candidates."[4]

Figure 3.7 showing results for the 2002 election is based not only on the first rankings but also on the transferred votes. The figure shows that STV had a proportional effect on the distribution of seats, in the sense that the smaller parties also received representation. Thus, although candidate-centered, STV does not work as much against smaller parties as the winner-take-all system. The two large parties in the figure, Fianna Fáil and Fine Gael, have both grown out of the Irish struggle for independence. The STV has strong supporters. Election expert Enid Lakeman states, "STV will force [the voter] to recognize that there are degrees of excellence among the candidates of his preferred party and will further invite him to consider candidates of other parties and indicate any with whom he has a measure of agreement."[5]

With regard to the United States, experts on electoral systems agree that a change from the current winner-take-all system to the principle of proportionality would only be possible if the new system were based not on party lists but on the STV. An advocate of

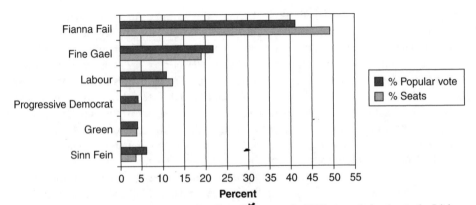

Figure 3.7 Voter support and percent of parliamentary seats in 2002 general election to the Irish parliament (DÁil). (*Source:* Irish Online Election Database.)

STV for America, George H. Hallett, Jr., argues that "it can transform our legislative elections from contests to win all the spoils of victory for one group and keep other people out to invitations to all citizens to come in and take part in a great cooperative democracy."[6] Hallett even expects that STV eventually may be required by the courts in the United States, because it gives adequate representation to such minorities as Hispanics and African Americans. The STV system is not unknown in the United States. In New York City, for example, the local school boards are elected according to this system; in Cambridge, Massachusetts, the city council is elected in this manner.

Germany

Germany uses yet another system of personalized proportional representation. Its main feature is that each German voter has two votes on his or her ballot—the so-called first and second vote. The first vote is according to winner-take-all in single districts, the second for party list proportionality. Surveys indicate that most German voters do not fully understand how their complicated electoral system operates. Whether or not it is understood, however, the system's results have been reasonable compared to the extreme party fragmentation of the pre-Hitler Weimar Republic. In the Bundestag, the lower house of Parliament, there are two major parties, the Christian Democrats and the Social Democrats, but some smaller parties also have representation. Very tiny parties, however, are excluded from parliamentary representation. As we will see in Chapter 11, Transitions to Democracy, Hungarian voters have also two votes, as in Germany, one according to winner-take-all in single districts and the other for party list proportionality. In Hungary the votes are counted independently of each other, whereas in Germany the counting of the two votes is linked in a complex way.

When the constitution of the Federal Republic of Germany—then West Germany— was written in 1949, the Western powers, especially Great Britain and the United States, urged the adoption of a winner-take-all system that they hoped would prevent severe party fragmentation. Many German leaders argued, however, that a winner-take-all system could not adequately represent the political diversity of the country. As political scientist Kathleen Bawn argues, there were also strong domestic political pressures against a winner-take-all system.[7] The Social Democrats had, at the time, slightly less voter support than the Christian Democrats and feared that a winner-take-all system would allow the Christian Democrats to win an absolute majority in parliament and to govern alone. To prevent such an outcome, the Social Democrats enlisted the support of the Free Democrats and other smaller parties, which, out of self-interest, were also against the winner-take-all system. In the crucial vote in the body enacting the electoral law, the winner-take-all system was defeated 36:28 against the opposition of the Christian Democrats. As Bawn comments, the selection of the German election system shows "that the political aspect of institutional choice is important. . . . Electoral systems can be explained as a social choice, affected by the interests of the participants and by the institutions that structure the choice"[8]

The solution enacted was to elect one-half of the Bundestag by the winner-take-all system and the other half by proportional representation. Each voter votes twice, once in the winner-take-all election and once in the proportional representation election. The former is called the voter's first vote; the latter, his or her second vote. Both votes are cast the same day, on the same ballot. For the first, or winner-take-all, vote the country is divided into small electoral districts that correspond in number to half of the parliamentary seats.

In each district the candidate with the most votes is elected. For the proportional part of the election, the Germans use party list PR, with the candidate ranking done by the parties. The electoral districts are the individual German *Länder* (states), such as Hamburg, Bavaria, Saxony, and so on.

Voters are allowed to split their two votes. In the winner-take-all election, they may vote for one party and in the party list PR election, for another. This provision creates the opportunity for some highly sophisticated voting behavior. Supporters of the small Free Democratic Party might cast their first vote for a candidate of one of the two large parties, knowing that their own candidate has virtually no chance of winning the winner-take-all election, but they can still cast their second vote for their own *party* list. The crucial point of the system is that only the second vote determines the total number of seats a party gets in parliament. Each party receives the same proportion of seats as its nationwide proportion of second votes placing the German system a very proportional on as show in Figure 3.8. With the first vote, the voters merely determine which candidate should represent their specific district. The candidates elected in this way are then subtracted from the total number of seats a party has gained, and the remaining seats are filled from the top of the party lists in the individual states. A hypothetical example is as follows: A party gains 33 percent of the second votes nationwide and therefore receives 33 percent of the 672 seats in the Bundestag—224 seats. The party wins 100 single districts, and the remaining 124 seats are filled from the top of the party lists in the individual states.

The fact that German voters are allowed to split their votes has the consequence that a party may win more single-district seats in a state (*Land*) than it is entitled to in this state on the basis of its support in the second votes. In such cases, the strict principle of proportionality is broken, in the sense that the party can keep as surplus mandates (*Überhangmandate*) the additional seats won in single districts. In the electoral history of Germany, the number of surplus mandates has ranged from 1 to 16, so the issue may appear to be a technicality with little significance. Max Kaase, however, makes the interesting

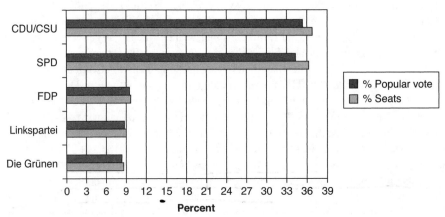

CDU/CSU = Christian Democratic Union/Christian Socialist Union
SPD = Social Democratic Party of Germany
FDP = Free Democratic Party of Germany

FIGURE 3.8 Voter support and percent of parliamentary seats (Second votes) in 2005 general election to the German parliament (Bundestag). (*Source: Der Spiegel. Wahl 2005.*)

comment that "if two parties in a coalition advise their supporters to strategically split their ballots between the two partners, or if one large party were to formally split into two parties, then a large number of surplus mandates could be artificially created." For Kaase, the issue of surplus seats "points to a definite deficiency, a fault in the present electoral system that could be used for a manipulation of the electoral outcome because it allows for different weights of individual voters."[9]

The German system also contains a provision for a threshold against tiny parties. This threshold denies parliamentary representation to parties that win less than 5 percent of the second votes nationwide and are also unable to win three single districts. To get any parliamentary seats, one of these two criteria must be met. The threshold is defended on the grounds that parties failing to cross it are so tiny that they have no real parliamentary legitimacy. The actual electoral disadvantage for tiny parties is even greater, because voters do not expect them to cross the threshold and, therefore, tend to vote for other parties that they know will win seats. In the 2005 election, radical right-wing parties attained only 1.8 percent of the second votes and were unable to win any single district, and therefore received no parliamentary representation. Tiny parties may still get representation if they are regionally concentrated. This happened to the Party of Democratic Socialism, the former Communists in East Germany, who got their support mostly in Eastern Germany. Although they never received 5 percent nationwide, they got at least three direct seats qualifying them for parliamentary representation.

CHANGING THE ELECTORAL SYSTEM: FRANCE AND ITALY

As Kathleen Bawn has argued with the German example, electoral systems "are bargained over by parties and individuals with conflicting interests."[10] The logic of this argument is that parties and individuals may attempt to change electoral systems that no longer serve their interests. In the United States, there is occasionally talk of changing the way Congress is elected, but, practically speaking, no changes are likely to occur any time soon. So it is interesting for American readers to see how electoral systems are actually changed. We use France and Italy as illustrations.

France

In 1985 the French changed their double-ballot system to the principle of proportionality, but in 1986 they changed back to the double-ballot system. Before the 1993 election, there was talk of a renewed change to proportionality, although this time no change occurred. These events illustrate that electoral systems are not a given but are the result of the political game.

France practiced proportional representation under its Fourth Republic (1946–1958). With the change to the Fifth Republic in 1958, General Charles de Gaulle and his supporters introduced a system whose most visible feature is that two separate elections take place a week apart; hence it is called the two-ballot system. For the purpose of parliamentary elections, France is divided into the same number of electoral districts as there are seats in the National Assembly, the lower house of the French parliament, which meets in the Palais Bourbon on the left bank of the river Seine. To be elected on the first ballot, a candidate has to receive an absolute majority (50 percent plus 1) of votes cast in his or her district. In addition, a candidate's share of the vote has to constitute no less than one-fourth of registered voters. Because the first ballot usually lists candidates from several parties, there are relatively few districts where a candidate receives the votes necessary to win the election at that point. Only candidates who appear on the first ballot can be listed on the second ballot, and all candidates who receive less than 12.5 percent of the first ballot are eliminated.

At the time of the two changes of the electoral system in 1985 and 1986, the main parties of the Left were the Socialists and the Communists, and the parties of the Right the Union for French Democracy (UDF) and the Rally for the Republic (RPR). The normal pattern in the first ballot was that candidates from all four major parties plus, in many districts, those from several minor parties also enter the competition. The main function of the first ballot is to check the voting strength of each individual party. Thus, the first ballot functions in some ways like an American primary. The main competition occurs on the one hand within the Left and on the other hand within the Right. On the Left, the question was whether the Socialist or the Communist candidate received more votes. Similarly, UDF and RPR candidates competed for the first place on the Right.

For the second ballot, the usual situation is that the weaker candidates on both the Left and the Right withdraw. The purpose of withdrawing is to increase the chance that one's side of the spectrum will win. If, for example, the UDF candidate in a district received 30 percent on the first ballot and the RPR candidate 25 percent, the chance of the Right to win could be increased if their forces were combined so that only the stronger candidate remained in competition. If the Right united behind the UDF candidate, it would be suicidal for the Left to continue the race with both a Communist and a Socialist candidate. The logic of the electoral system is for the Left, too, to withdraw its weaker candidate.

This device of voluntary withdrawals works best if, in the country as a whole, both parties on either side have about equal strength. Thus, if the RPR candidate withdrew in the previous example, this could easily be compensated for by the withdrawal of a UDF candidate in another district. The situation is more complicated when one party is clearly stronger than the other party of the same side. In the history of the Fifth Republic, this was often the situation of the Socialists vis-à-vis the Communists. In the 1981 parliamentary election, for example, the Socialists received nationally 37.8 percent voter support on the first ballot; the Communists received merely 16.1 percent. If the Communist candidate had been required to withdraw in every district where the Socialist candidate was stronger on the first ballot, there would have been very few districts where the Communist candidate could have represented the Left on the second ballot. Recognizing this difficulty, and in an effort to ensure maximum Communist voter turnout on the second ballot, the Socialists withdrew some of their own first-ballot candidates, even though these candidates ran ahead of the Communist candidates. With the support of the Socialist voters, the Communist candidates in these districts then had a chance to win the second ballot. Which candidate withdrew in a particular district was decided in negotiations between national and local party headquarters. The goal of this political maneuvering was to ensure that both sides got parliamentary seats in approximately the same proportion as their national strength on the first ballot.

Sometimes, however, this goal is not attained because voters do not follow the recommendations of their party leaders. This is especially a problem for the Communist Party, which is considered by many Socialist voters as too extreme. As a consequence, such voters often do not follow their party leaders' recommendations and abstain on the second ballot or even vote for the candidate of the Right. This mechanism can be demonstrated by comparing the seats received by the Communist Party in the 1981 election with its voter support. Although the voter support was 16.1 percent, the party received only 9.1 percent of the seats. For Domenico Fisichella, "the general conclusion that emerges from the French experience is that its Communist party is always—and almost always to a marked extent—underrepresented under the double-ballot system."[11] The Socialists, on the other hand, profited from the Communist support in the second ballot and received 59.3 percent of the seats, although their voter support in the first ballot was "only" 37.8 percent (see Table 3.1).

This discussion shows that the French double-ballot system demands a great amount of skill on the part of the political parties and their leaders. The game has to be played very differently in the two ballots. On the first ballot, the main competition is within the coalition of the Left and within the coalition of the Right; on the second ballot, the competition changes to the battle between the Left and the Right.

Why did the French change in 1985 from the double-ballot system to proportionality? It was the Socialist Party—in particular its leader, François Mitterrand—who pushed for the change. Why did the Socialists replace an electoral system from which they so obviously had benefited? The answer is that the electoral situation had greatly changed since 1981, and the Socialists feared that they would be hurt by the double-ballot system in the 1986 election. Opinion surveys and local elections had revealed such a loss of voter support for both Socialists and Communists that the parties of the Right were expected to take over control of the National Assembly. This situation would be difficult for Mitterrand, whose first term as president did not end until 1988. As we will see, a French president under the Fifth Republic has much power, and Mitterrand used this power to pass the change in the electoral system in Parliament.

Mitterrand hoped that proportional representation would increase the number of parties in the National Assembly, thus making the parliamentary situation more fluid and allowing him and his party more room to maneuver. This is exactly what happened in the March 1986 election. Splinter parties of the Right distracted so much voter strength from the RPR and the UDF that the two parties' combined seats fell short of an absolute majority in the National

TABLE 3.1 Voter support and parliamentary seats in the 1981 election for the French National Assembly

Parties	Voter Support (%)	Seats %	Seats N
Socialists	37.8	59.3	281
Communists	16.1	9.1	43
Rally for the Republic (RPR)	20.8	16.9	80
Union for French Democracy (UDF)	19.3	13.3	63
Others	6.0	1.4	7
Total	100.0	100.0	474

Source: European Journal of Political Research 10 (1982): 334.

Assembly. The two parties were particularly hurt by the entry of 35 members of the National Front to Parliament (see Table 3.2).

Immediately after the 1986 election, the newly elected Parliament changed the electoral rules back to the double-ballot system. This time, the push came from the RPR and the UDF. They did not like the fact that the National Front could challenge them at the extreme Right. Returning to the double-ballot system was anticipated to weaken the National Front, which indeed it did. When, after the 1988 presidential election, early parliamentary elections were called, the National Front virtually disappeared from Parliament, although it remained at about the same level in voter strength (Table 3.3).

TABLE 3.2 Voter support and parliamentary seats in the 1986 election for the French National Assembly

Parties	Voter Support (%)	Seats	
		%	N
Socialists	31.4	36.6	211
Communists	9.8	6.1	35
Rally for the Republic (RPR) Union for French Democracy (UDF)	41.0	48.0	277
National Front	9.7	6.1	35
Others	8.1	3.2	19
Total	100.0	100.0	577

Note: In addition to RPR and UDF lists, there were also joint RPR–UDF lists.
Source: European Journal of Political Research 15 (1987): 719.

TABLE 3.3 Voter support and parliamentary seats in the 1988 election for the French National Assembly

Parties	Voter Support (%)	Seats	
		%	N
Socialists	37.6	48.5	280
Communists	11.3	4.7	27
Rally for the Republic (RPR)	19.2	22.2	128
Union for French Democracy (UDF)	18.5	22.4	129
National Front	9.6	0.2	1
Others	3.8	2.0	12
Total	100.0	100.0	577

Source: European Journal of Political Research 17 (1989): 749.

In the 1988 election, the Socialists had recovered their 1981 voter strength, but before the 1993 election they were back in deep electoral trouble. Once again, there was talk that Mitterrand might change the electoral system back to proportionality.

But this time no change occurred, mainly because, contrary to 1985, the Socialists had no majority in the National Assembly to ram through a change in the electoral law (compare Tables 3.3 and 3.4). The 1993 elections were then a real catastrophe for the Socialists. Not only did their voter support drop from 37.6 percent to 17.6 percent (Table 3.4.), but their parliamentary representation had nearly a free fall from 280 to 53 seats. This severe drop in seats was clearly a result of the double-ballot system. Had the electoral system been changed to proportionality, the Socialists also would have lost many seats, but with a 17.6 percent voter support they still would have kept about 100 seats (17.6 percent of 577 seats).

The next parliamentary elections were held in 2002. Figure 3.9 shows the disproportional character of the two-round system for all political parties. Even though the National Front received 11.3 percent of the vote, it did not gain any seats. The reason for this is simple: Even if an extreme party makes it to the second round, it is very unlikely that it will win any seats against a more centrist party. On the other hand, the Communists managed to gain 21 seats on the basis of 4.8 percent of the vote, which was concentrated in very few districts.

The disproportional character of the electoral system also becomes apparent for large parties. Figure 3.9 shows that with only a third (33.7 percent) of the popular votes, the Union for the Presidential Majority received an almost two-thirds (61.9 percent) majority in the National Assembly. This is an even larger distortion than in the British winner-take-all system, in which the ruling Labour party received 35.3 percent of the vote, which translated into 55.1 percent of the seats in the British House of Commons.

A useful measure of "electoral distortion" might be simply the difference between the percentages of seats minus the popular vote percentages. The larger that number, the larger the electoral distortion. If this measure were applied to the case of the United Kingdom,

TABLE 3.4 Voter support and parliamentary seats in the 1993 general election for the French National Assembly

Party	Voter Support (%)	Seats %	Seats N
Rally for the Republic (RPR)	20.4	41.9	242
Union for French Democracy (UDF)	19.2	35.9	207
Socialists	17.6	9.2	53
Communists	9.2	4.2	24
Front National	12.5	0.0	0
Others	21.1	8.8	51
Total	100.0	100.0	577

Source: Le Monde, March 23, 1993.

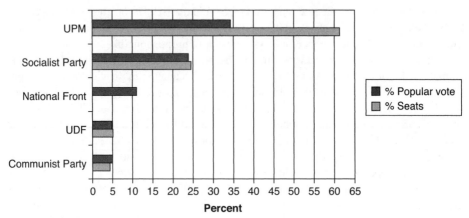

UPM = Union for Presidential Majority
UDF = Union for French Democracy

Figure 3.9 Voter support and percent of parliamentary seats in the 2002 general election for the French National Assembly. (*Source:* Elections in France. Electionworld.org/Elections around the World.)

the "electoral distortion index" would show 19.8 (55.1 − 35.3), and for France it would show 28.2 (61.9 − 33.7) for the two victorious parties.

Using the political fortunes of the National Front as an example, it becomes clear how strongly electoral rules can affect the fate of political parties. In 1993 the National Front gained 12.5 percent. Yet the National Front won not a single district, neither on the first nor on the second ballot. In 1986, by contrast, its electoral support was only 9.7 percent, but with proportionality then in force, it gained 35 seats in the National Assembly. However, in 1997 the National Front received 15.3 percent of the vote, its best showing ever, but with proportionality absent, gained only one seat. And in 2002, with 11.3 percent of the vote and proportionality absent again, the National Front did not win a single seat. France of the Fifth Republic is a classical example that demonstrates how changes in electoral rules can strongly influence the strength of various parties in Parliament. This precisely is the reason why Giovanni Sartori described the electoral system as "the most manipulative instrument of politics."[12]

Italy

Italy changed its electoral system in 1993 from party list proportionality to a mixed system, with 75 percent of the members of Parliament being elected by winner-take-all in single districts and 25 percent by party list proportionality in regional districts. After the Fascist dictatorship under Benito Mussolini (Chapter 11), Italy established a democracy but did not manage to arrive at much governmental stability, as we will see in Chapter 4. Part of the problem was the large number of parties that emerged under the electoral system of proportional representation. In the last election before the end of the cold war, 14 parties were represented in the Chamber of Deputies, the lower house of Parliament (Table 3.5).

The end of the cold war changed Italian politics in a fundamental way. Gone was the fear of a Soviet-inspired Communist takeover. The Italian Communist Party changed its name to Democratic Party of the Left, but a faction split and created its own Reform Com-

TABLE 3.5 Voter support and parliamentary seats in the 1987 election to the Italian Chamber of Deputies

Party	Voter Suport (%)	Seats	
		%	N
Christian Democrats	34.3	37.0	234
Communists	26.6	28.1	177
Socialists	14.3	14.9	94
Italian Social Movement	5.9	5.6	35
Republicans	3.7	3.3	21
Social Democrats	3.0	2.7	17
Radicals	2.6	2.1	13
Greens	2.5	2.1	13
Liberals	2.1	1.7	11
Proletarian Democracy	1.7	1.3	8
Venetian League	0.8	0.0	0
South Tirol People's party	0.5	0.5	3
Lombard League	0.5	0.2	1
Sardinian Action party	0.4	0.3	2
Piedmont Regional Autonomy	0.2	0.0	0
Piedmont	0.2	0.0	0
Val d'Aosta Union	0.1	0.2	1
Others	0.6	0.0	0
Total	100.0	100.0	630

Source: European Journal of Political Research 16 (September 1988): 580.

munist Party. In the 1992 parliamentary election, the Democratic Party of the Left received 16.1 percent of the votes, and the Reform Communists received 5.6 percent (Figure 3.10). Combined, this was 21.7 percent, down from the 26.6 percent that the old Communist Party received in the 1987 election. The Christian Democrats were also down from 34.3 to 29.7 percent. Down also were the Socialists as the third largest party, from 14.3 to 13.6 percent. The great winner of 1992 was the Northern League, which increased its voter support from 0.5 to 8.7 percent. Although a regional party of the north, it is also a protest party with some closeness to the New Radical Right (discussed in Chapter 2).

After the 1992 elections, government instability continued in the usual manner. This lack of positive change, combined with the discovery of several bribery scandals involving the highest levels of Italian politics, began to shake up the situation. In this shake-up the instrument of the popular referendum was of key importance. Reform-minded men and

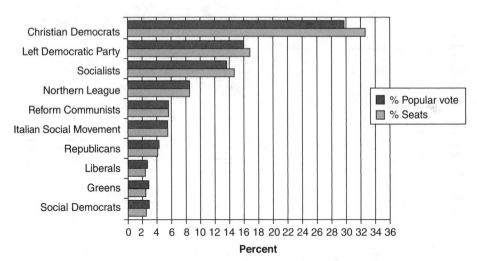

Figure 3.10 Voter support and percent of parliamentary seats in the 1992 election to the Italian Chamber of Deputies. (*Source: Keesing's Record of World Events* 38 (London: Longman, 1992, p. 38870).

women, under the leadership of Mario Segni, who had left his Christian Democratic Party, collected enough signatures to put several changes in the Italian political system to a popular vote. The most important proposal was to change the electoral rules for the Senate, the upper house of Parliament. Seventy-five percent of the senators would be elected by winner-take-all, while for the remaining 25 percent, party list proportionality would continue to be used. The expectation was that linking the senators closer to the voters would cut down corruption because voters could more easily vote corrupt politicians out of office. It was also hoped that the new electoral system would cut down on the number of parties in the Senate. The change in the electoral rules was overwhelmingly accepted in the referendum, with 82 percent voting yes. After the results were in, there were celebrations in the streets. Commentators spoke of a new beginning, the end of the old Italian Republic, and the beginning of a Second Republic (Box 3.1).

After the referendum, Parliament extended the new electoral system also to the Chamber of Deputies, and new elections for both houses of Parliament were held in March 1994. Each voter had two votes, one for the winner-take-all part of the election, the other vote for the proportionality part. A first test for this system was the local elections held in November and December 1993. These local elections were characterized by a sweeping defeat of the parties that had ruled Italy for so long. The Christian Democrats dropped in their support from around 30 percent in the preceding local elections to less than 10 percent. The other parties of the old ruling coalitions suffered even bigger losses. Big winners were the former Communists, the Democratic Party of the Left, who won in major cities including Rome and Naples. Big gains were also made by the Northern League and the Italian Social Movement, which had changed its name to the National Alliance.

In the weeks before the national elections, the Italian party system was in real turmoil. The Christian Democrats changed their name to Italian Popular Party. New parties were created, some parties merged, and others split. Mario Segni, the key organizer of the referenda on political reforms, initiated a party called Pact for Italy. Silvio Berlusconi, a wealthy busi-

---

Box 3.1 Italians Give Big Support to New Way of Politics

ROME—In a striking repudiation of the political order, Italy's voters gave over-whelming support Monday to plans to dismantle the postwar electoral system that many Italians blame for chronic corruption and a succession of weak and unstable governments. After two days of voting in a landmark referendum, Italians demon-strated their desire for profound change by approving the direct election of most senators and a ban on government financing of political parties. They also voted to abolish ministries for state industry, tourism and agriculture, which in recent years had become notorious havens of patronage.... "This result shows the coun-try's enormous will for change," said Mario Segni, the maverick Christian Democ-rat who broke with his party and organized the referendum.

Source: *International Herald Tribune*, April 20, 1993.

---

nessman and owner of the famous soccer club A.C. Milano, founded the party Forza Italia, the expression used to cheer up Italian national sports teams ("go Italy, go"). Among all par-ties there was great uncertainty about how best to compete under the new election system. For the winner-take-all part, electoral alliances had to be formed in order to increase the chances of winning districts. But with whom and with what exact commitments? And then there was still one-quarter of the seats to be filled by proportionality, and for this part of the election, strategies other than those used for the winner-take-all part had to be used.

Let us begin the analysis of the election results with the proportionality part for the Chamber of Deputies. Here a threshold of 4 percent of the votes had been introduced as nec-essary in order to receive any representation at all. Seven parties were able to cross this threshold: Forza Italia with 21 percent, Democratic Party of the Left with 20.4 percent, National Alliance with 13.5 percent, Popular Party with 11.1 percent, Northern League with 8.4 percent, Reform Communists with 6 percent, and Pact for Italy with 4.6 percent. So the newcomer Forza Italia, only two months old, was the big winner. Another big winner was the National Alliance, which increased its voter share since the previous election from 5.6 to 13.5 percent. The Democratic Party of the Left and the Reform Communists, the two descendants of the Communist Party, both slightly increased their share of the votes—the Democratic Party of the Left from 16.1 to 20.4 percent, the Reform Communists from 5.6 to 6.0 percent. Thus, together the former Communists reached 26.4 percent, again coming close to their best results in the past. The Northern League stagnated and dropped slightly from 8.7 to 8.4 percent. The Pact for Italy of Mario Segni attained a disappointing 4.6 percent of the votes. The big losers were the former Christian Democrats who, despite their name change to Popular Party, dropped from 29.7 to 11.1 percent. The Socialists of former prime minister Bettino Craxi, now under indictment, did not even reach the threshold of 4 percent.

If the elections had been held according to proportionality entirely, as in all previous elections since World War II, the story would end here. But under the new election law, three-quarters of the deputies were elected in single districts according to the winner-take-all principle. And for this part of the elections quite a different game was played. Whereas each party campaigned for itself in the proportionality part, the winner-take-all part ne-cessitated electoral alliances. Because in single districts only winning counts and there are no rewards for being second, third, and so on, the Italian parties tried to form broad-based electoral alliances. Three such alliances emerged, one each at the Left, the Center, and the Right. The electoral alliance of the Left consisted of the Democratic Party of the Left, the Reform Communists, the Greens, and some other leftist parties. The electoral alliance of the Center brought together the Popular Party and Pact for Italy. At the Right, an electoral alliance was forged among Forza Italia, the Northern League, the National Alliance, and some other rightist parties.

The purpose of the electoral alliances was to unite behind a single candidate in each district and thus increase the chances of winning the district. The Right, for example, would have a candidate of Forza Italia in one district, of the Northern League in another district, of the National Alliance in a third district. The distribution of the districts within each electoral alliance led to much bickering. The electoral alliances were also unable or unwilling to establish common programs. So it is important to understand that the three alliances were formed for purely tactical electoral purposes and lacked internal unity.

In Table 3.6, the results of the proportionality and the winner-take-all parts of the election are added. Column 1 gives the seats won according to proportionality, column 2 according to winner-take-all, and column 3 gives the total number of seats. It is clear that the new electoral system did not have the desired effect to reduce the number of parties in parliament. As a columnist for the Italian newspaper *La Stampa* put it the day after the elections: "Behind the great change, there was to be seen the usual Italian political uncertainty, unstable if not ungovernable, seeking only cease-fires or revenge."[13]

The second elections under the new rules took place in 1996. This time, only two electoral alliances were formed: the Olive Tree alliance at the Left and the Freedom alliance at the Right. The latter included Forza Italia, the National Alliance, and some smaller rightist parties; contrary to the 1994 election, the Northern League did not take part in the Freedom alliance and preferred to enter the election on its own. The Olive Tree alliance included the Popular Party, the Democratic Party of the Left, the Greens, and some other smaller parties of the Center Left. The Reform Communists were not part of the Olive Tree but collaborated with it to some extent. The clear loser was the Freedom alliance, which gained only 246 of the 630 seats in the Chamber of Deputies.[14] The Olive Tree had a better result, with 284 seats, but remained short of the absolute majority of 316. Together with the 35 seats of the Reform Communists, however, the Olive Tree had an absolute majority, which led the leftist Italian newspaper *L'Unitá* to set the headline "La Vittoria Dell'Ulivo" (The Victory of the Olive Tree).[15]

A closer look at the election results reveals that even after the 1996 elections the Italian party system has not become much simpler. To be sure, the Olive Tree, together with the Reform Communists, had an absolute majority in the Chamber of Deputies. But the Reform Communists were still Marxist in ideological orientation and continued to have the hammer and sickle in their party emblem. Thus, collaboration between the Olive Tree and the Reform Communists would be difficult. Furthermore, one has to consider that the Olive Tree contained parties with quite different ideological orientations. This was also true for the Freedom alliance. The continued fragmentation of the Italian party system is most clearly visible when we look at the results for the proportionality part of the elections. This time, the following parties could cross the threshold of 4 percent: Democratic Party of the Left, 21.1 percent; Forza Italia, 20.6 percent; National Alliance, 15.7 percent; Northern League, 10.1 percent; Reform Communists, 8.6 percent; Popular Party, 6.8 percent; Chris-

TABLE 3.6   Parliamentary seats in the 1994 election to the Italian Chamber of Deputies

Party	Seats		
	Proportionality	Winner-Take-All	Total
Northern League	10	107	117
Party of the Democratic Left	37	72	109
Nationale Alliance	22	87	109
Forza Italia	32	67	99
Reform Communists	12	27	39
Popular Party	29	4	33
Christian Democratic Center	0	29	29
Democratic Alliance	0	18	18
Socialist Party	0	14	14
Greens	0	11	11
Pannella Reformers	0	6	6
The Network	0	6	6
Social Christians	0	5	5
Union of the Center	0	4	4
Others	0	31	31

Source: European Journal of Political Research 28 (1995): 393–405.

tian Democratic Center,[16] 5.8 percent; and List Dini,[17] 4.3 percent. Compared with the previous election, none of the parties could pull away from the pack. If we make a comparison with the proportionality figures for the 1994 elections, we see that the Democratic Party of the Left and Forza Italia have changed their places at the top of the list, but that the relative size of the two parties has changed little. After both elections, Italy had no party with much more than 20 percent voter support. If we count the number of parties crossing the threshold of 4 percent, there is even an increase from seven to eight from the 1994 to the 1996 elections.

In the wake of the 2001 elections two moderate blocs emerged. On the Center Right is the "House of Freedoms" consisting of Go Italy, the National Alliance, the Christian Democratic Center, and the Northern League. The Center Left, the Olive Tree coalition, consists of the Democrats of the Left, the Daisy Democracy, the Italian Democratic Socialists and Greens, the Party of the Italian Communists, and the New Socialist Party of Italy (Table 3.7).

If the intent of changing the electoral law was to reduce the number of parties, that goal was only partly achieved. The number of parties winning more than 4 percent in the 2001 election was indeed reduced to five as compared to eight in the 1996 election. Nevertheless, given that 75 percent of the seats are allocated on the basis of winner-take-all, combined

TABLE 3.7 Parliamentary seats in the 2001 election to the Italian Chamber of Deputies

Party	Seats		
	Proportionality	Winner-Take-All	Total
House of Freedoms alliance		·	
Forza Italia	62	116	
National Alliance	24	75	
United Christian Democratic Center	0	40	
Northern League	0	30	
Total:	86	261	347
Olive Tree alliance			
Democrats of the Left	31	107	
Daisy Democracy	27	53	
Italian Democratic Socialists and Greens	0	17	
New Socialist Party of Italy	0	3	
Party of the Italian Communists	0	9	
Total:	58	189	247
Refounded Communists	11	0·	11
South Tyrolese People's Party	0	3	3
Val D'Aosta List	0	1	1
Total:	155	454	609

Note: The reason why the total number of seats does not add up to 630, which is the traditional number of seats in the Italian parliament, is that some seats in the winner-take-all part have not been assigned yet due to various interpretations on how to proceed in cases when a list does not have enough candidates to fill all the seats gained in that constituency.
Source: European Journal of Political Research, Vol. 41 (2002): 992–1000.

with the introduction of an electoral threshold to 4 percent it is remarkable that there are still 12 parties represented in the Italian National Assembly. Four of the 12 gained seats on the basis of proportionality *and* winner-take-all, (Go Italy, National Alliance, Left Democrats, The Daisy), one party gained access to Parliament on proportionality votes alone (Communist Refoundation), and seven parties gained access on the basis of the winner-take-all rule (Christian Democratic Center, Northern League, New Socialist Party of Italy, Italian Democratic Socialists, Party of the Italian Communists, the South Tyrolese People's Party, and the Val D'Aosta List). Of the eight parties that did not win seats on the basis of proportionality *and* winner-take-all, seven parties managed to get access to Parliament on the basis of winner-take-all alone (mostly regional parties and "ideological" parties that have strong concentrated support in certain regions), while the principle of proportionality has given life to only one party: the refounded Communists.

This highlights another important issue: The number of parties, while oftentimes driven by the electoral system, is not necessarily *only* driven by it. It also depends on the number of cleavages in a society. A society with many cleavages might have many parties in parliament even though the electoral system is winner-take-all. Conversely, it is possible that a country with proportional representation might be divided only along one dimension. As a result, there might only be two or three parties represented even though proportional representation is in force. A prime example of such a society is Austria after World War II and throughout the middle 1980s.

In the French case we have seen how politicians attempt to change the electoral system in order to maximize their chances to win the next election. Italy can now also be added to this list. In the fall of 2005, seven months before the next general election, the ruling Center–Right coalition, under the leadership of Silvio Berlusconi, pushed through a plan to change the current electoral system (75 percent of seats based on single-member district, and 25 percent based on proportional representation). On October 14, the lower house of Parliament, in which the Center-Right coalition has an absolute majority, overwhelmingly supported Berlusconi's bill to introduce an electoral system where 100 percent of the seats are allocated on the basis of proportional representation. With passage of this bill into law, Italy comes full circle from having an electoral system based on 100 percent proportional representation for all seats until 1994, when the first national elections were held under the then-new electoral system (75 percent of seats based on single-member district, 25 percent on proportionality). Today, 11 years later, Berlusconi has managed to change the electoral system back to 100 percent proportional representation, to the bitter dismay of opposition parties, in an obvious attempt to win the next election. The cases of France and Italy have raised the question of whether it is proper for politicians to change electoral rules in their favor. In sports it is certainly not allowed to change rules during a game.

Box 3.2 Silvio Berlusconi's Parliamentary Games

What to do when polls show you might lose the next election? If you're Italian Prime Minister Silvio Berlusconi, you just change the rules. He's on a legislative rampage and more changes are just around the corner.... On October 13, his coalition passed a major electoral reform which critics say was intended to improve Berlusconi's chances in April [2006]. Under the bill, the next elections, slated for next spring, would be based on a system of proportional representation. This would mean voters would choose party lists rather than individual candidates. Essentially, it reverses a 1993 change to the electoral system which sought to fix an Italian democratic state which saw 51 government changes in 47 postwar years. . . . Berlusconi was lukewarm about the legislation at first, agreeing to it only to save his coalition. But then the prime minister had his market researchers check out their computer programs and data bases. After testing various models, they concluded that Berlusconi's only chance to capture a majority in next year's elections would be under electoral laws heavily based on proportional representation.

Source: Spiegel ONLINE. October 21, 2005.

VOTER TURNOUT

Voter turnout in Europe is generally much higher than in the United States, usually in the 70, 80, or even 90 percent range. Why is there so much more interest in parliamentary elections in Europe than in the United States? Many factors come into play, such as differences in the system for voter registration, size of the countries, and education. In the context of the present chapter, it is interesting to discuss the possible influence of electoral rules on voter turnout. Generally speaking, electoral rules as used in Europe give the voter more influence on the outcome of parliamentary elections than in the United States. In many U.S. congressional districts, the incumbent is so firmly established that a challenger has little chance. Often, competition works only when there is no incumbent or for a first-term incumbent. Even if a district is truly contested, voters with somewhat extreme views may feel left out because both the Democratic and Republican candidates tend to run on a platform that is pretty much in the middle. If a voter has a Green preference, for example, he or she may not feel represented by either candidate and may stay home.

In parliamentary elections in Europe, it is not so unrealistic that a few votes may make a difference. In a proportional election system, just a few more votes may secure an additional seat for a party. Why do the British have a much higher turnout than the Americans, although both practice the winner-take-all system in single districts? Contrary to the United States, Great Britain has a parliamentary, not presidential, system for selecting its executive. As a consequence, as we see in the next chapter, party discipline in Parliament is much more important, and this, in turn, helps to mobilize voters on election day. In this chapter we have seen how voter preferences are translated into parliamentary seats, and we have encountered a wide variety of electoral rules. Such variation does not occur randomly but has to be seen in a historical context. Those who make the rules have the power. Rules are also important once a parliament is elected and begins to operate. In the next chapter, we turn to these internal operations of European parliaments and, in particular, to the selection of cabinets out of their midst.

This chapter contained a lot of technical information about parliamentary election systems in Europe. This information should not be memorized for its own sake. Students should be challenged to understand how election systems are man-made and can be changed with different impacts on the party systems.

Discussion Questions

1. Calculate the index of "electoral distortion" (percent of popular votes minus percent of seats) for the largest parties in the Netherlands. Is it higher or lower than in the UK or France? Why?

2. Designing electoral rules raises the crucial question of what "representation" should mean? What do you think "representation" actually means?

3. Which system, proportional representation (PR) or single member district (SMD) is more "representative"?

4. In SMD, how can a voter's view be represented if he or she does not share the ideology of the lone incumbent?

5. Who should have the authority to change electoral rules—parliament, the voters, the courts, a combination of these?

6. Is a political game ever over, so one can change the rules for future games?

7. Should the new rules come into effect only when the politicians making the new rules have left office?

8. Or should there be a waiting period of, say, ten years until the new rules take effect?

9. Why is the electoral system described as the "most manipulative instrument of politics"?

Calculate the index of "electoral distortion" (percent of popular votes minus percent of seats) for the largest parties in the Netherlands. Is it higher or lower than in the UK or France? Why? Electoral rules such as the difference between proportional representation and winner-take-all raise fundamental issues of what "representation" actually means. Which of the two systems do you think is more representative? In single-member districts, how can a voter's views be represented if he or she does not share the ideology of the lone representative? Conversely, how can somebody in a proportional representation system be responsive to the needs of individuals in a particular area if that individual ended up in parliament by virtue of having been listed high on the party list?

[1]Ivor Crewe: Why Labour Lost the British Election. *Public Opinion* 6 (June/July 1983): 60.

[2]Hans Riedwyl and Jürg Steiner: What Is Proportionality Anyhow? *Comparative Politics* 27 (April 1995): 357–369.

[3]Parties submit different lists in different administrative districts. These lists are then linked at the national level.

[4]Michael Gallagher: Comparing Proportional Representation Electoral Systems: Quotas, Thresholds, Paradoxes and Majorities. *British Journal of Political Science* 22 (October 1992): 480.

[5]Enid Lakeman: The Case for Proportional Representation. In Arend Lijphart and Bernard Grofman (eds.), *Choosing an Electoral System: Issues and Alternatives.* (New York: Praeger, 1984, 49).

[6]George H. Hallett, Jr. Proportional Representation with the Single Transferable Vote: A Basic Requirement for Legislative Elections. In Arend Lijphart and Bernard Grofman (eds.), *Choosing an Electoral System.* (New York: Praeger, 1984, 125).

[7]Kathleen Bawn: The Logic of Institutional Preferences: German Electoral Law as a Social Choice Outcome. *American Journal of Political Science* 37 (November 1993): 965–989.

[8]Ibid., 987–988.

[9]Ibid., 163–164.

[10]Kathleen Bawn. The Logic of Institutional Preferences: German Electrical Law as a Social Science outcome. *American Journal of Political Science* 37 November 1993): 965.

[11]Domenico Fisichella: The Double-Ballot System as a Weapon Against Anti-System Parties. In Arend Lijphart and Bernard Grofman (eds.), *Choosing an Electoral System.* (New York: Praeger, 1984, 183).

[12]Giovanni Sartori. *Parties and Party Systems.* (Cambridge: Cambridge University Press, 1976).

[13]Quoted in *New York Times,* March 30, 1994.

[14]*Neue Zürcher Zeitung,* April 23, 1996.

[15]*L'Unità,* April 23, 1996.

[16]When the old Christian Democratic Party changed its name to Popular Party, the Christian Democratic Center split to the Right.

[17]List of the outgoing Prime Minister Dini, see Chapter 4.

Cabinet Formation and Heads of State

Our discussion of the institutions within which political parties operate continues in this chapter. Having described in Chapter 3 the rules for parliamentary elections, we turn now to the rules for cabinet formation. We need to understand that most European democracies have a pure parliamentary system in which the cabinet with a prime minister or chancellor at its head is appointed by the parliament. Sometimes parliamentary systems are unstable, but we will show that this is by far not always the case. In fact, cabinet formation may take many different forms, and we will illustrate this with examples from Great Britain, Germany, Switzerland, Sweden, Italy, and France. In the United States, the president as head of the executive branch holds also the symbolic role of head of state. In Europe this is different—the prime minister or chancellor is not head of state; this role belongs to a monarch or a civilian president.

In the United States, the relationship between the legislative and executive branches of government is characterized by a system of checks and balances. The president, as chief executive, is elected not by Congress but directly by the people—if we disregard the aspect of the electoral college. Congress cannot oust the president with a vote of no-confidence. The only exception, impeachment, is very different from a vote of no-confidence. On the other hand, the president cannot dissolve Congress and call for early elections.

Most European democracies have a parliamentary system with rules fundamentally different from those of the American presidential system. (The major exception is France, which combines a presidential and a parliamentary system under the constitution of the Fifth Republic, discussed later in the chapter.) The most important characteristic of the parliamentary system is that the executive is selected by the parliament and depends on the confidence of parliament for survival. The voters elect their parliament, which is therefore the sole body that can claim to represent the will of the people in a direct way. The ways in which presidential and parliamentary systems relate voters to the legislative and executive branches of government are presented in Figure 4.1.

The executive branch in a European parliamentary system is the cabinet, which is headed by a prime minister whose role is very different from that of the U.S. president. (Depending on the country, the prime minister may have the title of *chancellor.*) In the United States, cabinet members are appointed by the president and serve at his pleasure. Some cabinet members may come from the Congress; however, if they accept a cabinet position, they must give up their seat in Congress.

In a parliamentary system, leading members of parliament form the cabinet. The prime minister is merely the first of the team—hence the term *prime minister,* or in Latin *primus inter pares* (first among equals). The rule is that the prime minister and the other ministers retain their seats and voting rights in parliament while serving in the cabinet. There are, however, a few exceptions to this rule. In Switzerland, Norway, and the Netherlands, cabinet members are required to give up their parliamentary seats. There are also exceptions to the rule that cabinet members are selected from the parliament. Especially in crisis situations,

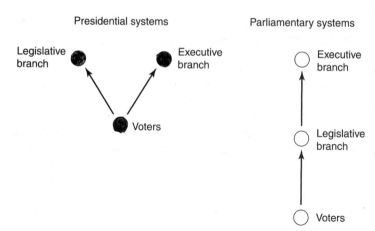

Presidential systems   Parliamentary systems

FIGURE 4.1 Relations between voters and the legislative and executive branches of government in presidential and parliamentary systems.

it may happen that persons with high reputations from outside parliament are asked to serve in the cabinet. This was, for example, the case in Italy during a severe crisis in 1993, when the president of Italy's Central Bank was called in as prime minister.

Within any particular cabinet, the prime minister's role may be stronger or weaker, depending on the individual's personality and the overall political circumstances. Legal authority also plays a role. In Germany, for example, the prime minister (called the chancellor) is particularly strong because he has the legal authority to give directives to other cabinet members. This authority is not available in many other countries, where the prime minister must rely on more informal means to exert influence.

A new cabinet must win a vote of confidence in parliament. In some countries an explicit vote of confidence is not necessary. In such cases, the cabinet is formally appointed by the head of state—for example, by the queen in Great Britain—and it is assumed that the cabinet has the confidence of parliament unless the latter explicitly expresses its lack of confidence. But this technicality does not change the basic fact that the cabinet depends on the confidence of parliament. In a vote of confidence, party discipline is imposed. If a member of parliament breaks party discipline in a vote of confidence, this is likely to lead to severe sanctions and, in some cases, even expulsion from the party. To understand the vote of confidence, we must understand that the relevant actors are not individual members of parliament, but the parties. The question is not how individual X, but how party X, will vote.

Just as parliament gives its confidence to the cabinet, it may withdraw this confidence at any time. The only formality required is a vote of no-confidence, which is a political act and does not imply that the cabinet has done something improper or illegal. Thus, a vote of no-confidence is very different from impeachment in the United States. An impeached and convicted U.S. president leaves political life in disgrace, whereas a prime minister whose cabinet loses a vote of confidence usually stays on as a member of parliament. He or she even may continue to play a leadership role, for example, as head of the opposition. How parliaments handle votes of confidence and no-confidence varies greatly from country to country. The most influential factor is whether a single party controls a majority in parliament and is thus able to form a cabinet of its own.

Before we begin our overview, a clarification is necessary for Americans who wish to read European newspapers. In Europe the cabinet is often called the "government"; in Great Britain, for example, one speaks of the government of Tony Blair. In French the term is *gouvernement*. In the United States, by contrast, the term *government* has a much broader meaning, referring not only to the executive branch, but also to all three branches together. When Americans mean "government" in the European sense, they often speak of the administration, such as the Bush administration. When Europeans speak of the administration, they mean the state bureaucracy. These semantic differences show that often it is not easy for either Americans or Europeans to read newspapers from the other side of the Atlantic.

SINGLE-PARTY MAJORITY CABINETS

In this section we discuss situations where a single party possesses a majority (50 percent $+1$) in parliament and forms the cabinet alone. Great Britain is the classic example of this situation, and we use it as our illustration. In Great Britain, general elections usually give an absolute majority of seats in the House of Commons to either the Labour Party or the Conservative Party. Since 1945, there have been only two brief exceptions to this rule, both in the 1970s. The upper house of Parliament, the House of Lords, can be largely disregarded in the process of cabinet formation.

If one party has a majority in the House of Commons, cabinet formation is straightforward because party discipline is imposed: The majority party simply forms a cabinet. This can be well illustrated with the events following the 2005 election, when Labour won 356 of the 646 seats. After this victory, it was clear that Labour would form the cabinet. Who would be the prime minister and the other cabinet members? For this question, we must distinguish between two situations: Either the winning party was already in power before the election, or it was in opposition. In 2005, Labour had been in power since 1997. In accordance with the idea of never changing a winning team, most members of the old cabinet, including Prime Minister Tony Blair, retained their positions. The second situation was illustrated in 1979, when the Conservatives, under the leadership of Margaret Thatcher, won the elections as the opposition party. In such cases, the concept of a shadow cabinet is important. During the period of opposition, a party announces the names of members who would fill the various cabinet positions in the case of electoral victory. This cabinet-in-waiting is called the shadow cabinet. Its members act as spokespersons of their party in parliamentary debates. The shadow foreign minister, for example, confronts the actual foreign minister in debates on foreign affairs. This is a good training ground, giving the shadow foreign minister experience in foreign affairs should his or her party win the next election.

How can a member of Parliament advance in the party to become a member of the cabinet or the shadow cabinet? Because the House of Commons is very large, with more than 600 members, there will always be many more ordinary members than leaders. The leaders sit on the front benches at either side of the aisle—the government on the right side of the speaker, the opposition on the left side. The distance between the front benches is two swords plus one foot, a reminder of the long tradition of the House of Commons. The nonleaders must sit at the back and are therefore called backbenchers. How do backbenchers become leaders? They must prove themselves to their peers in Parliament. If this is done successfully, they may one day rise to a cabinet position and, ultimately, perhaps even to the prime ministership.

If we compare the career path of a British prime minister with the usual path to the American White House, the differences are striking. Of the last five presidents, four became presidents without any prior Washington experience: Jimmy Carter, Ronald Reagan, Bill Clinton, and George W. Bush. All four, in fact, made beneficial use of the argument that they were not part of the Washington establishment. The elder Bush had much Washington experience before becoming president—for example, as head of the Central Intelligence Agency (CIA)—but he had been in Congress for only a short period of time. British prime ministers complete a long apprenticeship in the House of Commons before entering office. Which career path is preferable? An American president who comes from outside may have the advantage of bringing a "fresh wind" and a new outlook, but this advantage is countered by a lack of experience, which can be seen as a real disadvantage. As former German chancellor Helmut Schmidt notes:

> It remains a pity that the process of nominating and electing [an American] President does not pay any attention to their foreign political expertise or experience or ability. They have never been tested in it, whereas in a parliamentary system, people who make it to the top have been tested first.[1]

Differences between Great Britain and the United States are also striking with regard to the role of the opposition. In Great Britain, as long as the government party does not lose its majority through defections or losses in elections for vacant seats (by-elections), it can pursue whatever policies it chooses. In the Falkland Islands crisis of 1982, for example, the Labour Party had no means of impeding the war policy of the governing Conservatives. When the government decided to send warships to liberate the Falkland Islands from Argentine occupation, there was nothing the opposition could do about it. Under the British system, the majority cabinet governs with an absolute mandate. This mandate is buttressed by the norm of "collective responsibility," which is a uniquely British doctrine. It states that all members of the cabinet must support the official government line. If not, they must be willing to resign their posts. The purpose of this doctrine is to signal to the people the unity of the government. One of the most spectacular resignations occurred during the buildup to the Iraq war when the leader of the House of Commons, Robin Cook, resigned from the cabinet on March 17, 2003, stating that he "cannot accept collective responsibility for the decision to commit Britain now to military action in Iraq without international agreement or military support."[2]

The function of a motion of no-confidence submitted by the opposition needs clarification. As long as the governing party controls a majority of the parliamentary seats, such a motion has no chance of success. The governing party has enough votes to defeat such a motion, which will be supported only by the opposition. So why submit a motion of no-confidence to begin with? The purpose is not to topple the government but to give the opposition the opportunity to say what it finds wrong with the policies of the government and what it would do instead. The government, in turn, has the opportunity to defend its policies. In this way, the voters see the differences between the governing and the opposition parties. On election day the choices are thus clear: The voters can opt either for a continuation of the existing policies or for a change to the policies advocated by the opposition.

In order to understand why, in a vote of no-confidence, members of Parliament vote strictly along party lines, one has to understand the role of the so-called whips. They are members of Parliament who exercise supervisory functions. Headed by a chief whip, the whips must make sure all their colleagues are present for an important vote, particularly for a motion of no-confidence. Because voting is public, they also see to it that everyone is following the party line. Both the governing party and the opposition have whips. The expression entered into the parliamentary vocabulary during the 18th century. It was taken from fox hunting, which was very popular at the time in the British upper class, but is now illegal. The "whipper-in" had the task of keeping the hounds in the pack. The highest level of required party discipline is the three-line-whip, where the agenda point to be voted on in the House of Commons is, in a literal sense, underlined three times. Members of Parliament (MPs) rarely deviate from the party line, mostly in order to take a position on an issue that is particularly popular in their district. However, during the second Blair government (2001–2005), 218 Labour MPs voted against their whip at least once. There is a hard-core group of about 60 who have voted against the whip on ten or more occasions. Given the reduced majority of 66 seats of the third Blair government, "it would only take just over half of these sixty to vote against the government to defeat it."[3]

And indeed, this happened for the first time during Tony Blair's tenure in November 2005 when he lost a crucial vote on his much favored antiterror bill. Blair's bill would have allowed to hold terror suspects for 90 days without charge, up significantly from the current 14 days, and it would also outlaw training in terrorist camps, encouraging acts of violence and glorifying terrorism. Forty members of his own Labour Party voted against his bill, striking a serious blow to his authority. Despite having a majority of 66 seats in the House of Commons, Blair lost the terror bill by 322 to 291, indicating that sometimes even the toughest whips can't keep the MPs in check. In most cases, however, party loyalty combined with the whips' ability to persuade, makes MPs to trot the party line.

By contrast, in the United States, a congressperson's first interest is his or her constituency, not his or her party. It is electoral success in the constituency that ensures political viability, not party loyalty. As a result, congresspersons have a tendency to first ensure the support of their constituency, oftentimes through inefficient, so called "pork barrel" projects (e.g., when a congressperson attaches a rider consisting of a post-office, or a bridge, or a highway to be built in her constituency to an omnibus bill) rather than by displaying party loyalty.

In the United States the distinction between governing and opposition parties is much less clear than in Great Britain. Prior to the 1996 American presidential elections, the Democrats controlled the White House and the Republicans controlled the Congress, so that in the election campaign it was often unclear who could take credit and who was to blame for governmental policies. In Great Britain, the governing party must take full responsibility for all government policies. As a consequence, the voters have a clear choice: Continue with the governing party or oust it. Americans prefer to check and balance governmental power. Which system is more democratic, and what is the meaning of the term *democratic* in this context?

Although the executive branch in Great Britain, when compared to that in the United States, has more leeway to pursue long-term policies, its power should not be exaggerated. First, it must contend with powerful interest groups outside the House of Commons. Second, the British cabinet also must consider the wishes of its backbenchers; otherwise it might suddenly be faced with serious internal party rebellion. A good illustration is the ousting of Margaret Thatcher as prime minister in November 1990 after having been in

---

Box 4.1 Thatcher Resigns as Prime Minister

LONDON—Margaret R. Thatcher, faced with the prospect of a humiliating defeat in a contest for leadership of her bitterly divided Conservative Party, called an end to a remarkable era in British politics Thursday by announcing her resignation as prime minister. Mrs. Thatcher, who had insisted adamantly Wednesday that she would run again in a second round of voting against party rival Michael Heseltine, changed her mind overnight after a parade of cabinet ministers told her in individual meetings that they thought she would lose. Some even told her they would oppose her, according to party sources.

Source: *Washington Post,* November 23, 1990.

---

office since 1979. Thatcher was increasingly seen in her own party as arrogant and autocratic. As prime minister, she was also leader of her party. For this position, there is a yearly vote among all MPs of the party, although this is usually a formality for a sitting prime minister. In November 1990, however, Thatcher was challenged by her former defense minister Michael Heseltine, who had been dismissed by Thatcher from his job in the cabinet and forced to take a seat on the back benches. From there he began to organize an effective campaign against the leadership of Margaret Thatcher. In the vote for the leadership position, Heseltine stood as candidate against Thatcher. In the first ballot he lost, but only narrowly, so that Thatcher did not reach the votes required by the party rules. She was still confident that she would win the second ballot, for which fewer votes were necessary to win. But when important cabinet members told her that she might not have the necessary votes or even that they would personally vote against her, she withdrew her candidacy (Box 4.1). In the second ballot, two other powerful party members entered the race, Foreign Minister Douglas Hurd and Finance Minister (Chancellor of the Exchequer) John Major. Again there was no winner, but Major was very close, so that the two other candidates withdrew in his favor, and no third ballot was necessary. Thatcher was bitter, accepted from the queen the title of nobility "Lady," and moved to the House of Lords.

This episode shows that the power of a British prime minister is not unlimited, even if she or he has a majority in Parliament. The real challenge comes not from the opposition party but from within her or his own party. It is interesting to note that during the November 1990 crisis, the Labour opposition submitted a motion of no-confidence against the government. As expected, according to the British rules of the game, party discipline among the Conservatives worked, and the motion was defeated. Submitting the motion gave Labour the chance to criticize the disarray of the government. Labour did not, however, expect to win the motion of no-confidence.

How Are Cabinet Decisions Usually Made in Great Britain?

Typically in the British cabinet, there is an open and frank discussion concerning decisions to be made, in which every cabinet member is heard, but the prime minister has the right to sum up the discussion. Votes are virtually never taken. Patrick Gordon Walker, a former member of the cabinet, describes an imaginary cabinet meeting. After a lengthy discussion, the prime minister sums up and concludes as follows: "Is the cabinet agreed with my summing up and the additional points made by the chancellor? (Silence, with a few muttered 'agreed')."[4] This summing up gives quite a bit of power to the prime minister.

Finally, we must address the question of how the government party and the opposition party compete with each other in the British system. The normal pattern is that they both take a moderate position in the middle, where there are the most voters, as Great Britain has a unimodal distribution of the electorate, as depicted in Figure 3.1 in Chapter 3. Margaret Thatcher was a notable exception to this rule, as she pursued very conservative policies. She had the ambition not simply to appeal to the preferences of the voters but to change these preferences. As we remember from Chapter 3, she was never able to attract a majority of the voters; she became prime minister only because the opposition was so badly split.

The Labour Party, too, at times tried not simply to appeal to the existing preferences of the voters but to change these preferences. When in opposition after 1979, Labour advocated very leftist policies, insisting in particular on a strongly state-controlled economy. However, the party came to acknowledge that the financial "markets remained nervous about the possibility of a Labour victory ... Labour did moderate its policies in an attempt to reassure markets."[5] At the forefront of these changes was Tony Blair, who in 1994 took over as leader of the party. Under his leadership, Labour abandoned its commitments to nationalization and dropped from its program the demand for "common ownership of the means of production, distribution and exchange." Blair hailed the day of this decision as "a day of destiny for our party and our country."[6] Blair also took up traditional conservative values such as fighting crime. After his speech at the party convention in September 1996, the British Union Jack was projected on the wall behind him, which emphasized that Labour was no longer willing to leave the theme of patriotism to the Conservatives.

The change to the middle paid off for Tony Blair. On May 1, 1997, three years after he took over as leader of Labour, he won an overwhelming victory in the parliamentary elections. As Table 4.1 shows, Labour won 418 seats against only 165 for the Conservatives. The very next day, Prime Minister John Major moved out of his official residence at

TABLE 4.1 Voter support and parliamentary seats in 2005 general election to the British House of Commons

Party	Voter Support (%)	Seats	
		%	N
Labour	35.3	55.1	356
Conservatives	32.3	30.6	198
Liberal Democrats	22.1	9.6	62
Others	10.3	4.7	30
Total	100.0	100.0	646

Source: BBC News, Election 2005.

Box 4.2 Labour Takes over as "Curtain Falls" on Tories

LONDON—As the last results of the general election straggled in Friday afternoon, as the vanquished left No. 10 Downing Street and the victor accepted the queen's "kind offer" to move in, as the simple majesty of this nation's transfer of power unfolded, Britain surveyed with amazement the near obliteration of the Conservative Party, once the political juggernaut of Europe. A modest British-style motorcade—three cars and some motorcycles—escorted the Labour Leader, Tony Blair, from his home to Buckingham Palace, where he was asked, and agreed to form a government, ending 18 years of Conservative rule. Earlier, Mr. Blair's defeated rival, John Major, submitted his resignation to the queen. He also announced that he would resign as leader of the Conservative Party, setting off a battle among survivors to take his place. "When the curtain falls, it's time to get off the stage," said Mr. Major, who looked relieved as he left the prime minister's official residence.

Source: *International Herald Tribune*, May 3, 1997.

---

10 Downing Street, and Tony Blair and his family moved in (Box 4.2). As noted in Chapter 3 for earlier British elections, this time, too, the winner-take-all system exaggerated the size of the victory of the winning party; Labour won 43.1 percent of the popular vote, but 63.4 percent of the parliamentary seats. Under Margaret Thatcher, the Conservatives had their greatest success in 1983, when they won 42.4 percent of the popular vote and 61.1 percent of the parliamentary seats (Table 4.1). Thus, Blair's triumph was even greater than Thatcher's at the height of her career.

However, as shown in Chapter 3, Tony Blair, while still winning the 2005 election, emerged with a diminished majority and diminished status. Only slightly over 35 percent of the people voted for Labour, giving him a majority of barely over 55 percent of seats in the House of Commons. Nevertheless, he is the only Labour leader in history who won three elections in a row.

One advantage of a parliamentary system, particularly of the British type where government consists mostly of bare majority cabinets, is accountability. Because of the principle of "fusion" of powers between the executive and legislative branch it is very easy to affix praise or blame for whatever outcomes a government generates. Over the last decade, Great Britain experienced the most sustained economic growth on record, with low unemployment (4.7 percent), low inflation (1.6 percent), low interest rates (4.7 percent), and a forecast economic growth rate of 2.5 percent at the time of the election. Tony Blair made sure voters understood that his policies were responsible for such a good economic record. But why was he not more successful at the 2005 elections?

The answer again lies in the direct accountability of the prime minister in parliamentary systems. Many British citizens, even members of his own cabinet, as noted earlier, did not agree with his stance on whether Iraq possessed weapons of mass destruction and his unwavering support for war in Iraq. These issues deeply divided the Labour Party, even more so after the Special Advisor to the Director of Central Intelligence, Charles

Duelfer, failed to uncover weapons of mass destruction in Iraq. Blair's image "was severely tarnished, with critics branding him as a lying lapdog of a warmongering American president."[7] Responsibility in a parliamentary system based on single-party, bare majority cabinets rests ultimately with the prime minister, a lesson Tony Blair learned the hard way.

MINIMAL-WINNING CABINETS

In a parliamentary system, when no party controls a majority in parliament, the process of cabinet formation is very different from that in Great Britain. One possibility is the formation of minimal-winning cabinets, where as many political parties as are necessary form a coalition to attain a majority in parliament. In other words, all coalition partners are necessary to form the cabinet; there are no surplus members in the coalition. Should we not expect all cabinet coalitions to be of a minimal-winning size? What is a rationale for adding more parties than are necessary to win?[8] Why include, say, a third party in a coalition if two parties have enough votes for a majority in parliament? As we will see in the next section, such oversized coalitions can and do occur. Germany since 1969 is a good illustration of how minimal-winning cabinets are formed. In the 1969 election to the Bundestag, the Christian Democrats (CDU)[9] received 242 seats, the Social Democrats (SPD) 224, and the Free Democrats (FDP) 30. The Christian Democrats felt they had won the election, and they pondered the question of whether they should enter a coalition with the Social Democrats or with the Free Democrats. They were shocked when, late in the election night, SPD and FDP announced they had made a deal. With 254 seats together, they were just above the necessary majority of 249, so they could, indeed, win a vote of confidence in Parliament. Legally, everything was in order, but a public debate began over whether the procedure followed on election night was in accordance with the spirit of basic democratic principles. The question was raised whether excluding the party with the most votes from the cabinet violated the will of the electorate. The counterargument was that more voters had supported SPD and FDP together than CDU alone, so the new cabinet was, in fact, based on the majority will of the people. What emerged from this debate was the informal rule that the voters should be informed of the coalition intentions of the various parties before the election. It should not be left to a few leaders to decide on election night what coalition is to be formed. In many other European democracies, however, such an informal rule does not exist, thus the composition of the cabinet may still be decided by a few key leaders on the election night.

In Germany, with the Greens emerging in the 1980s and maturing in the 1990s, it has not only become more difficult to say with whom a coalition will be formed but also what the election outcome is going to be. For example, it was widely assumed that for the 1998 election, the Conservatives and Social Democrats would form a grand coalition, until the actual results were in and the Social Democrats and the Greens proved to be stronger than expected. This election result led to a rethinking of possible coalition partners and, having a numerical majority for a possible "red-green" coalition, momentum grew for the formation of such a coalition *after* the election. Indeed, such a coalition was promptly installed.

Similarly, during the short campaign in the summer of 2005, and particularly after the formation of the *Linkspartei* (Left Party), which consisted of a more leftist part that split off from the SPD and combined with the PDS (the Communist Party of former East Germany), it was assumed that the CDU/CSU would form a coalition with the FDP. Again, actual election results interfered with coalition plans before the election: The CDU/CSU disappointed bitterly and even together with the FDP would not have a majority of seats in the German Bundestag, obliterating all promises to form a CDU/CSU and FDP coalition. Finally, a grand coalition of CDU/CSU and SPD formed, and because CDU/CSU was slightly larger than SPD the chancellorship went to the former, with Angela Merkel of the CDU as chancellor. Since the late 1960s the German party landscape has become much more variegated, making it very difficult to tell voters before an election takes place with whom large parties will form a coalition.

Another informal rule regarding cabinet formation developed from an episode in the fall of 1982 in the middle of a legislative period. The coalition of Social Democrats and Free Democrats was still in office, but there were increasing strains between the two coalition partners, especially over economic matters. Under the strong influence of its economics minister, the FDP advocated more free-market solutions, broke its coalition with the SPD, and entered into a coalition with the CDU. Social Democrat Helmut Schmidt was thus replaced as chancellor[10] by Christian Democrat Helmut Kohl in a parliamentary vote. The reason Schmidt was ousted was not his unpopularity; on the contrary, opinion surveys indicated that Schmidt was more popular than Kohl at that time. The reason was that the FDP changed coalition partners. A public debate began as to whether a small party should have the power to replace the chancellor in this way; after all, the Free Democrats had campaigned in the parliamentary election of 1980 with the promise to continue their coalition with the Social Democrats. Was this promise valid for the entire legislative period? Was it a betrayal of the voters to change coalitions midcourse? The argument was made that a cabinet had been formed without due input by the voters. Early elections were demanded for such situations so the voters could decide. Kohl took this demand seriously, and in the spring of 1983, early elections took place. The coalition of CDU and FDP won, and thus had a direct mandate from the voters. It seems likely that in the future, changes of coalitions will no longer occur without a prior election. This would be an informal rule supplanting the formal rule of the "constructive vote of no-confidence." This is a special German feature that we do not find in any of the other countries discussed in this chapter. The constructive vote of no-confidence means a cabinet can be overthrown only if, with the same vote, a new cabinet is selected. Thus, a vote of no-confidence cannot merely be negative regarding the current cabinet, but also must be "constructive" in forming a new cabinet. This rule was applied in the 1982 change from the Schmidt to the Kohl cabinet. What the new informal rule seems to say is that for a change in cabinet, new parliamentary elections are preferred to the instrument of the constructive vote of no-confidence. This happened again in 2005 when the coalition of SPD and Greens was so weakened by the emergence of the Left Party that the coalition was no longer viable to govern in an effective way. The SPD/Green coalition was replaced, as noted, by a coalition of CDU/CSU and SPD—not with a constructive vote of no-confidence, but rather after early elections. The development of a set of widely accepted, informal rules for the process of cabinet formation was important for the stability of Germany. This contrasts with the Weimar Republic, before Hitler's takeover, when deep disagreements existed about the very rules for cabinet formation. Today, the political elites by and large agree on how the game should be played.

One of the central features of parliamentary systems is that executive authority not only emerges from legislative authority but that executive authority is also responsible to it.

The vehicle by which this responsibility is carried out is enshrined in Article 68 of the German Basic Law (Grundgesetz), which allows for the chancellor to call for a vote of confidence. If it fails, the president can dissolve Parliament and call for new elections. This article was used by Chancellor Gerhard Schröder in the spring of 2005 to dissolve his government and call for new elections one year ahead of the regularly scheduled general elections in 2006. The reason why he asked members of his own party and the members of the Green Party to withdraw their support for his government was occasioned by a defeat of the SPD in the Land elections of North-Rhine Westphalia. Losing this election also meant that he lost majority support in the German upper house, the Bundesrat. He lost this election due to the unwillingness of many voters in that region to go along with his plans to revamp the German welfare system, known as Agenda 2010, which would involve painful cuts in Germany's hitherto generous welfare system. Using Article 68 of the Basic Law raised serious constitutional issues insofar as it was argued that losing a Land election does not constitute a sufficient reason to force a dissolution of Parliament. After all, his government still had a majority in the Bundestag, Germany's lower house. In effect, Schröder asked members of his own ruling coalition to vote against him to ensure losing the vote of no-confidence, and thereby forcing new elections. Some constitutional theorists were concerned about this "insincere" use of Article 68. Nevertheless, the German Supreme Court eventually concurred with the decision of Parliament, and the German President also gave a green light for new elections to take place on September 18, 2005 (see Box 4.3).

Box 4.3 Gerhard Schroeder, the Great Manipulator

German Chancellor Gerhard Schroeder is engaging in elaborate tricks and a real abuse of the German consitution in order to force new elections. It would be much easier if he just hung up his hat and stepped aside. On Friday, German Chancellor Gerhard Schroeder will ask the German parliament, the Bundestag, to take a vote expressing its confidence in his government. In actuality, however, the chancellor is asking the parliamentarians—a majority of whom belong to his governing coalition—to do exactly the opposite: they should vote against him, or at least abstain. Only then would the chancellor lose the vote of confidence and only then can German President Horst Koehler dissolve the parliament. And finally, only then can the new general elections be held that Schroeder has called for this autumn. It would be the third time in the history of the Federal Republic of Germany that a chancellor was able to force new elections by using the vote-of-no-confidence tool. Both Chancellor Willy Brandt in 1972 and Chancellor Helmut Kohl 10 years later had their governments called into question by the parliament. The German constitution does not allow the chancellor to dissolve parliament himself—an effort to prevent a repeat of Adolf Hitler's manipulation of the interwar Weimar Republic to cement his hold on Germany's government. Just like his political grandson Schroeder, Brandt wanted to achieve a clear mandate for his policies. But in contrast to today's situation, Brandt at the time really did lack a reliable majority in parliament.

Source: Spiegel ONLINE, June 29, 2005.

TABLE 4.2 Voter support and parliamentary seats in 2005 general election to the German Bundestag

Party	Voter Support (%)	Seats %	Seats N
Conservatives (CDU/CSU)	35.2	36.8	226
Social Democrats	34.2	36.2	222
Free Democrats	9.8	9.9	61
The Left Party	8.7	8.8	54
The Greens	8.1	8.3	51
Others	4.0	0	0
Total:	100.0	100.0	614

Source: Der Spiegel. Die Wahl, 2005.

Once the seats were tallied, it was clear that five parties gained representation in the German parliament (Table 4.2). None of the "expected" combinations such as an SPD/Greens or a CSU/CSU and FDP gained enough seats to form a coalition based on a majority of seats. In addition, Germany does not have a tradition of minority governments, making this one of the most challenging government formations after World War II. In the ensuing coalition negotiations, various options were entertained, such as a "traffic light" coalition (Red, Yellow [FDP], Greens), or a "Jamaica" coalition (Black [CDU/CSU], Yellow, Green—the colors of the flag of Jamaica). The central problem of such negotiations is not only the need to find a combination that ensures a majority, but also a majority of parties that can actually work together. Oftentimes, this automatically excludes particular combinations, such as a red-red-green combination. Neither of the two "red" parties (the SPD and the Linkspartei) was willing to share executive power with the other, as they had split up over major policy differences just a few months before the election.

Eventually, on October 10, 2005, three weeks after the election, negotiations over the formation of a grand coalition with the first female chancellor in German history, Angela Merkel, were initiated. In the tradition of parliamentary systems that the party with the highest vote share also gets to determine who becomes chancellor, for the Conservatives this meant yielding many important ministries to the Social Democrats. But because the vote was so close, with Merkel performing much worse than expected and Schröder performing much better, the Social Democrats exacted a high price from the Conservatives. In turn for accepting Merkel as chancellor, the Social Democrats gained control over the ministry of finance, foreign affairs, health, justice, labor, environment, and transport.[11]

Ultimately, cabinet formation is more challenging in systems that have forms of proportional representation systems. As we have seen, in the British case, cabinet formation is straightforward. However, with a higher number of parties gaining representation, even "traditional" coalition combinations may not reach a majority. They will try to keep the number of coalition partners as small as possible because fewer compromises will have to be made in such a type of coalition.

OVERSIZED CABINETS

Though they do not occur often, certain circumstances encourage the formation of oversized coalition cabinets. Oversized cabinets include more coalition partners than are necessary to attain a majority in parliament. Switzerland is a unique case in two ways. First, it is an extreme illustration for oversized cabinets. Second, it is not even clear whether Switzerland is indeed an example of a parliamentary form of government. Switzerland is the only system where once a government is set up by the legislature, the legislature cannot dissolve it. The members of the government are elected by the legislature for the entire legislative period of four years. Thus, in Switzerland, unlike in a regular parliamentary system, the government is *not* responsible to the legislature, at least not in a formal way. Thus, the term of responsible government as previously explained does not apply to Switzerland. Of course, in order to pass legislation, the government still depends on the support of the legislature, but the legislature has no way to withdraw the confidence from the government and thus topple it.

In 2003, the proportional electoral system led to the results shown in Table 4.3 for the National Council, Switzerland's lower house of Parliament. Some of the parties listed in Table 4.3 require brief comments. The Swiss People's Party, which is the largest party in the Swiss National Council, is a radical right-wing party known for tougher immigration laws, law and order, and for keeping Switzerland out of international organizations such as the European Union (EU) and the United Nations (UN). Its supporters are mostly German speakers. The Free Democratic Party is a classical liberal party that favors as little state intervention as possible and is supportive of free-market ideas. It is liberal along certain issues such as drug use and same-sex marriage. The Freedom Party is very closely associated with the Free Democratic Party and appeals mostly to French-speaking voters.

The cabinet is elected in a joint session of both houses of Parliament. The upper house, the Council of States, has 46 members, 2 from each canton.[12] The relative strengths of the various parties are not very different in the joint session from those in the lower house shown in Table 4.3. The size of the Swiss cabinet—seven members—is unusually small.

TABLE 4.3 Voter support and parliamentary seats in the 2003 general election for the Swiss National Council

Party	Voter Support (%)	Seats
Swiss People's Party (SVP)	26.7	55
Social Democratic Party (SPS)	23.3	52
Free Democratic Party (FDP)	17.3	36
Christian Democratic Party (CVP)	14.4	28
Green Party (GPS)	7.4	13
Freedom Party (LPS)	2.2	4
Others	8.7	12
Total	100.0	200

Source: Electionworld.org. Elections Around the World. Switzerland 2003.

That size is fixed by the Swiss constitution. Another specifically Swiss feature is that all seven cabinet members are of equal rank, and no one carries the title of prime minister. There is merely a rotating chair on a yearly basis according to seniority. After the 1959 election, the Social Democrats had two seats in the cabinet, the Free Democrats two seats, the Christian Democrats two seats, and the Swiss People's party one seat. The 2003 election changed this seat distribution for the first time after 44 years, with the Christian Democrats having to cede one seat to the right-wing Swiss People's Party that was now the strongest party, while the Christian Democrats had fallen to fourth place. The Federal Councillor who occupies this seat is Christoph Blocher, who has used populist strategies with a nationalistic orientation to attract voters.

The principle of proportionality limits competition among the parties. To be sure, they try to win as many parliamentary seats as possible. But, once parliament is elected, it is mutually agreed that each party will receive its fair share of cabinet seats, with fair being defined as proportionate. In this way, cabinet formation is indeed simple. Once the results of the parliamentary election are known, it is a question of simple arithmetic as to how the cabinet seats will be distributed among the parties. No complicated maneuvers are made to change coalitions, and, unlike the situation in Germany, small parties are unable to play a pivotal role. In Switzerland, the process of cabinet formation does not lead to clear winners and losers.

Are the Swiss, by nature, more cooperative than others? This hypothesis must be rejected, because there was a time when the Swiss played the game of cabinet formation very competitively. For many centuries after its foundation in 1291, Switzerland was a loose, mainly military federation of independent cantons. The country lacked a common executive at the national level. During the first half of the 19th century, Switzerland experienced a bitter fight over the issue of centralization of power. The Free Democrats advocated more centralization, while the Christian Democrats, at that time called Conservatives, fought any attempt to create a central executive. This conflict led to a short civil war in 1847, won by the Free Democrats. As the winners, the Free Democrats established a constitution in 1848 that provided for a national executive: the seven-member cabinet. For parliamentary elections, the winner-take-all system was chosen. In the first elections, the Free Democrats received a parliamentary majority and used this majority to form a cabinet consisting only of members from their own party, a single-party majority cabinet as is the custom in Great Britain. Election after election, they renewed their majority in Parliament and each time filled the cabinet posts with their own people.

A turning point came in 1891, after nearly a half-century, when the Free Democrats still had a majority in Parliament but offered one of the seven seats to the Conservatives. In 1918, the Conservatives received a second seat, with the Free Democrats still controlling the other five seats. In the same year, the winner-take-all system for parliamentary elections was changed to the current system of proportionality. The same development— from confrontation to cooperation—happened with regard to the Social Democrats, who began to gain parliamentary strength early in the 20th century. Initially, the Social Democrats had been treated as outcasts. When they organized a general strike in 1918, the cabinet intervened with troops. This resulted in bloody clashes, and on several subsequent occasions Parliament refused to accept any Social Democrats in the cabinet. The turning point here came during World War II, when the first Social Democrat was allowed to join the cabinet. In 1959, the Social Democrats received a second seat, and thus had representation corresponding to their electoral strength. The principle of proportionality is applied not only to political parties but also to the linguistic groups in Switzerland. The country has four official languages, with 63.7 percent of the population speaking German, 20.4 percent

French, 6.5 percent Italian, and 0.5 percent Romansh—a language spoken only in Switzerland. A variety of other languages are spoken in Switzerland, mainly by foreigners, but none of them has official status. The French and Italian speakers together always have two or three seats in the cabinet, corresponding to their proportion in the population. These rules of proportionality in cabinet formation are not written down in the constitution or in special laws but are based on informal, mutual understandings.

Oversized coalitions are not unique to Switzerland. Even Great Britain, the classic example of a competitive democracy, went through a period of an oversized coalition during World War II, when Conservatives, Labour, and Liberals together formed the cabinet. If an oversized coalition includes all major groups of a country, one also uses the concept of power sharing. This concept is often discussed as a solution for multicultural societies, and we will come back to this concept in Chapter 13.

MINORITY CABINETS

We speak of minority cabinets when the party (or parties) forming the cabinet does not possess a majority of the seats in parliament. Sweden offers good illustrations of why minority cabinets form and how they operate. An episode in April 1996 illustrates how the Social Democratic cabinet managed to govern despite its minority status. It negotiated with the Center Party a package of measures to reduce the budget deficit. This package included, among others, cuts in the aid for developing countries and an increase in energy taxes. But as the leader of the Center Party emphasized, his party is not part of the cabinet and wishes to keep its independence for other parts of the budget.[13] In the same way, the Social Democratic minority cabinet seeks, on a case-by-case basis, support from other parties.

The Social Democrats again formed a minority cabinet after the 2002 election. As Table 4.4 shows, they only had 144 out of 349 seats (41.2 percent). After some initial

TABLE 4.4   Voter support and parliamentary seats in the 2002 election for the Swedish Parliament[a]

Party	Voter support (%)	Seats
Social Democrats	39.8	144
Moderates	15.2	55
Liberal People's Party	13.3	48
Christian Democrats	9.1	33
Left Party	8.3	30
Center Party	6.1	22
Green Party	4.6	17
Others	4.6	0
Total	100.0	349

[a]Sweden has a single house of parliament.
Source: Electionworld.org. Elections Around the World. Sweden 2002.

> ## Box 4.4 Sweden: Social Democratic Government Propped up by Greens and Lefts
>
> After weeks of bartering following the September 15 general elections, Goran Persson's Social Democrats (SAP) have negotiated a new arrangement with the Green and Left parties. This will continue the arrangement in the last parliament, where both parties supported the SAP despite being denied ministerial posts. Prime Minister Persson again intends to rely on the Lefts and Greens on budgetary and social policies and on the opposition Moderates on international issues. Persson's SAP won 144 of the 349 seats in parliament, against 158 taken by the four centre right parties led by the Moderates. Counting on the support of the 30 seats of the Left Party, this meant that the SAP was one seat short of a majority in the single chamber *Riksdag*. With 17 seats the Greens held the balance of power, which they used to try to extract ministerial posts by threatening to support a right wing vote of no confidence in Persson. Eventually, however, the Greens came to terms with the SAP on a similar basis to that agreed after the latter's weak showing in the 1998 elections but with expanded influence within government ministries. This guarantees that the SAP can muster enough votes to survive any no-confidence vote and pass its annual budget. Persson welcomed the Greens' renewed cooperation by calling for the development of a "green welfare statex." Green Party spokesman Peter Eriksson agreed ecstatically, proclaiming, "This is the best deal the Green Party has ever made."
>
> Source: World Socialist website, October 17, 2002.

wrangling they secured the cooperation of the Left Party and the Greens to support their policies on a case-by-case basis. Such arrangements may be described as "contract parliamentarism," which regulates the roles and functions between the governing parties and the support parties. Such a contract is typically of a written nature, is public, extends beyond any specific legislative deal, and includes members of the support parties to serve at high levels, but not cabinet-level positions.[14] The two support parties, the Left Party and the Greens, were allowed to place functionaries into several ministries, but were not able to secure any ministries for themselves. (See Box 4.4)

Minority cabinets are not unique to Sweden. In the next section we encounter minority cabinets in Italy, in a much more complex context. Even Great Britain, where normally one party wins a majority and forms a single-party majority cabinet, occasionally has minority cabinets—for example, during two brief periods in the mid-1970s (discussed earlier in the chapter). It should be clear by now that chaos will not necessarily result if a majority coalition cannot be formed in a parliamentary system. With minority cabinets, governmental life can continue in an orderly way for quite a while.[15] Minority cabinets are not rare at all. For the period 1945 to 1995 over one-third of all cabinets in Sweden were of the minority type. Besides Sweden, minority cabinets were particularly frequent in Denmark and Norway.

CABINET INSTABILITY

We have now discussed four European democracies in which the executive cabinet is selected by the parliament: Great Britain, Germany, Switzerland, and Sweden. In each of these countries different rules govern the process of cabinet formation, yet all four countries have relatively stable executives. This finding should lead us to reject the hypothesis that selection of the executive by parliament necessarily leads to instability. Indeed, it seems that stability is possible under widely differing circumstances. By the same token, there is no guarantee that a parliamentary system leads to cabinet stability. Italy offers the prototypical example of high cabinet instability under a parliamentary system.

Ever since the end of World War II, the Italian parliament has had a large number of parties, but so does the Swiss parliament, and we have seen how much cabinet stability Switzerland enjoys. In contrast to Switzerland, however, Italy always had strong parties at the extremes, the Neofascist Italian Social Movement at the Right and the Communists at the Left. Until the end of the cold war these two parties were always excluded from cabinet positions. The argument for their exclusion was that they did not accept basic democratic principles. Cabinet formation, therefore, was always limited to the moderate parties in the middle: Christian Democrats, Liberals, Republicans, Social Democrats, and Socialists. At first it was easy to form a cabinet from among this set of parties. Immediately after World War II, the Christian Democrats had close to, and at one time even slightly above, a majority in parliament. They developed into *the* governing party: Without their participation, no cabinet could be formed. The prime minister and other key ministers were always selected from the ranks of the Christian Democrats.

The dominant position of the Christian Democrats turned out to be a basic weakness of the system. In a democracy, the voters should have a realistic possibility of ousting a party from power. But in Italy, there was simply no numerical alternative to a cabinet led by the Christian Democrats, because cabinet participation of Communists and Neofascists was out of the question. Whatever the election results, until the early 1980s, the prime minister was always a Christian Democrat. It might be expected that the dominant position of the Christian Democrats at least had the advantage of leading to cabinet stability, but the opposite was true. Cabinets were usually short-lived, and Christian Democratic prime ministers succeeded one another at brief intervals. This occurred in part because the Christian Democratic party was in fact a loose federation of several independent factions. Each faction was identified with a particular leader and had a strong organization of its own.

During the time of Christian Democratic dominance, cabinet formation was mainly a result of infighting among these various factions. If a faction was excluded from important cabinet posts, it maneuvered to overthrow the cabinet and replace it with a cabinet dominated by its own people. As a consequence, Italy had frequent cabinet crises, despite the fact that the prime minister was always a Christian Democrat. The composition of the cabinet constantly changed, but the game was always played among the same few politicians. They were mostly Christian Democrats but included also some members of the smaller parties of the middle. A key actor might have been prime minister in one cabinet, absent from the next one, then foreign minister, and prime minister again in still another cabinet. An extreme case was Christian Democrat Giulio Andreotti, who held posts in 36 cabinets, including seven turns as prime minister. As Carol Mershon characterizes the situation aptly, "cabinets in Italy both changed and remained the same."[16] Because of this basic stability it was not costly to overthrow a cabinet because the politicians responsible for a cabinet crisis could be surely predicted to participate again in future cabinets. The end of the cold war changed Italian politics in a fundamental way, but cabinet instability continued. As we have seen in Chapter 3, the fear of a Communist takeover in Italy had gone; the Communist Party changed its name to Democratic Party of the Left and, hence, became a potential coalition partner to form a cabinet. Another important development was the discovery of major political corruption scandals involving virtually all political parties and key sectors of the business community. We have also seen in Chapter 3 how the electoral system was changed through a popular referendum from proportionality to a mixed system, where three-quarters of the members of parliament are elected by winner-take-all and the remaining quarter by proportionality. In March 1994, the first election under the new system brought great changes among the political parties (Table 3.6 in Chapter 3). The Christian Democrats suffered heavy losses although they had changed their name to Popular Party; the Northern League was greatly strengthened; the Italian Social Movement changed its name to National Alliance and also had a great electoral success; and finally, a new party, Forza Italia founded by Silvio Berlusconi, immediately became an important player in Italian politics.

Forza Italia, the National Alliance, and the Northern League together had a majority in Parliament, and they tried to form a cabinet. But there were great ideological differences among the three parties. The Northern League wanted to decentralize the country, whereas the National Alliance favored a strong central authority. Umberto Bossi, the leader of the Northern League, raised questions of whether the National Alliance was too authoritarian to participate in the government. The leader of the National Alliance, Gianfranco Fini, made every effort to project the image of a modern and respectable party. He repeatedly described the Holocaust as an error that led to horror. But for many this was too weak a condemnation of the Fascist past. It was also disturbing that at the victory celebration of the National Alliance at Rome's Piazza del Popolo, hundreds of youth in the crowd gave straight-arm Fascist salutes and chanted "Duce! Duce!" as was the custom during the regime of Benito Mussolini. It was also a worrisome sign that one of the seats of the National Alliance was won by Alessandra Mussolini, the dictator's granddaughter. She declared before the elections: "Fascism was a very important part of history that can no longer be demonized or canceled out. But it's history, and no one is thinking of introducing it again."[17] After the elections, many newspapers in other European countries expressed great worries that the Neofascists would participate in a future Italian government.[18]

But what about Forza Italia and its leader Silvio Berlusconi, who was to be prime minister of the new cabinet? Would he be able to hold the parties of the Right together and to make sure that the National Alliance would not gain too much influence? What was his program? He attracted the voters mainly by his smooth personality and much less by any specific program. To be sure, he advocated tax cuts and more free-market policies, but when, after the elections, he described the goals of the future government, it all sounded very vague. He postulated, "all types of freedom: the family, the individual, business, the free market, competition, profit, solidarity, Christian traditions, respect and tolerance toward all, even our adversaries."[19] The *New York Times* called Berlusconi "Italy's Knight in Teflon. With his business empire and his 70-room villa outside Milan, and with his sense of personal style, Mr. Berlusconi has packaged himself as the Italian dream."[20]

It was only after six weeks of arduous negotiations that, in May 1994, Berlusconi was able to put together a cabinet of his Forza Italia, the National Alliance, and the Northern League. But in December of the same year Berlusconi resigned. There were major defections in his coalition; furthermore, his brother received a suspended jail sentence for corruption charges, and Silvio Berlusconi himself was interrogated about his business dealings. Because it was not possible to put together a new coalition among the parties represented in parliament, a banker without political affiliation, Lamberto Dini, formed a caretaker cabinet of so-called technicians. This cabinet was able to survive for about a year, but then early parliamentary elections were called for April 1996.

As we have seen in Chapter 3, these elections ended with a victory of the Center Left. The Democratic Party of the Left, the Popular Party, the Greens, and some smaller Center-Left parties had put together an electoral alliance called Olive Tree, which gained the most parliamentary seats, although not quite an absolute majority. But in the vote of confidence, the Reform Communists supported the government of the Olive Tree, which was headed by Romano Prodi of the Popular Party, a respected university professor of economics. Despite their support of the vote of confidence, the Reform Communists refused to be represented in the government, which therefore had a minority status. It was an indication of the delicate position of the Reform Communists that one of their members voted against the government and in protest left the party. The Prodi government was the fifty-fifth since World War II, but Prodi promised that it would be an exceptional government in the sense that it would survive the entire legislative period. It did not.

In 1998 the Reform Communists withdrew their support from the Prodi government, considering it not enough to the Left. Then Massimo D'Alema of the Democratic Party of the Left could again get the support of the Reform Communists although not their entry into the government. D'Alema was prime minister for two years but resigned in 2000 after a severe defeat of the Left in regional elections. For the remainder of the legislative period in 2001, Socialist Giuliano Amato headed still another cabinet of the Left. In the legislative elections of 2001, the Right won a majority and it was once again Berlusconi who became prime minister. He stayed in office the entire legislative period from 2001 to 2006, a first in Italy since World War II. But this did not mean that Italy was no longer plagued by instability—there was constant infighting among the coalition partners of the Right. At one point Berlusconi was even forced to resign as prime minister, only to succeed himself. (See Box 4.5.)

For the April 2006 general elections, Berlusconi, a master of staging a political spectacle, vowed to stay in power. In February of that year he declared himself to be the "Jesus Christ of Italian politics" who sacrifices himself for everyone. Earlier, he also compared himself to Napoleon in describing his achievements during the past five years in office.[21] Berlusconi, the richest man in Italy, controls significant elements of the Italian media. He directly controls two private television channels and, as prime minister, indirectly controls three public TV channels. In addition, as explained in chapter 3, he pushed through a change in the electoral law, making it 100 percent proportional in the hope that would help him win the election.

Berlusconi's challenger was Romano Prodi again, an economics professor, former Italian prime minister, and former president of the European commission. In terms of personality, Berlusconi, and Prodi could not have been any more different. Berlusconi, the flashy populist, showman, and former cruise ship crooner, and Prodi the bookish, dull, technocratic professor. Predictably, the campaign leading up the April 10 election was one of most bitter ones in recent Italian history.

Box 4.5 Berlusconi Wins Confidence Vote. Bid to Bring Squabbling Coalition into Line

ROME, Italy—Italian Prime Minister Silvio Berlusconi has survived yet another vote of confidence in his government, successfully gambling on a bid to bring his bickering coalition into line.

The vote—won by 333 to 148 in the Chamber of Deputies—was focused on the government's plans for pension reform, which Berlusconi says are vital to kick start Italy's fragile economy.

Since coming to power in 2001 the Berlusconi government has faced more than 30 confidence votes and had it lost the latest one, it would have been forced to resign.

The government coalition comprises four main members. Berlusconi conservative Forza Italia; the far-right National Alliance; the Northern League, headed by Umberto Bossi, which wants devolution for northern regions; and the centralist Christian Democrat party, the Democratic Union of the Center (UDC).

The crisis engulfing Berlusconi's government was sparked by European elections in June when his Forza Italia party lost ground to its three coalition partners. Buoyed by the result, they began demanding a greater say in policy-making.

The Northern League and the UDC have been at odds over devolution, and have been trading tit-for-tat political blows.

Analysts see the Berlusconi "back me or sack me" vote as designed to stop individual disgruntled Northern League parliamentarians breaking ranks and embarrassing the government by voting against single articles.

Source: CNN.com, July 29, 2005

It also proved to be one of the closest ones. It took two days to finalize what the exact election outcome was, with Berlusconi, at the time of this writing (April 12, 2006) still not conceding defeat, arguing that irregularities in the counting of the votes of Italian expatriates have given unfair advantage to Prodi. Italians voted for both houses, the lower house (Camera dei Deputati) and the upper house (Senato) over two days, Sunday and Monday (April 9 and 10).

For the lower house Prodi's center-left Union coalition won 49.8 percent of the popular vote while Berlusconi's center-right House of Freedom coalition won 49.7 percent, a difference of only 25,000 votes compared to the 38 million votes cast. In the upper house, it first appeared that Berlusconi had won, but after the votes of the Italian expatriates were counted, the Prodi coalition also won a wafer thin majority in the upper house of 158 seats over 156 seats for the Berlusconi coalition. Both, the center left, as well as the center right coalitions range from their centrist "anchor parties" (Forza Italia on the right and L'Ulivo on the left) to the extremes of their respective partisan coloration. Prodi's Union party encompasses the center-left L'Ulivo, as well as the refounded communists, socialists, greens, communists and radicals while Berlusconi's coalition consists of the center-right Forza Italia in addition to right wing populist, and former fascist parties.

What is ironic is that despite the extremely close election outcome, based on proportional representation, Prodi will have a comfortable majority in terms of seats. How can this be? The

TABLE 4.5 Voter support and parliamentary seats for the 2006 general election in Italy (lower house)

	Voter Support	Seats
L'Unione (Prodi)		
L'Ulivo	31.3	220
Rifondazione Comunista	5.7	41
La Rosa nel Pugno	2.6	18
Comunisti Italiani	2.3	16
Italia dei Valori (incl. 1 abroad)	2.2	17
Verdi	2.1	15
Others	3.6	15
Seats won abroad for L'Unione		6
Total:	49.8	348
La Casa della Liberta (CDL) (Berlusconi)		
Forza Italia	23.7	137
Alleanza Nazionale	12.3	71
UDC	6.8	39
Lega Nord	4.6	26
Democrazia Cristiana-Nuovo PSI	.6	4
Seats won abroad for CDL		4
Total:	49.7	281

Note: L'Ulivo (olive tree—main "anchor party" on the center left); Rifondazione Comunista (Refounded communists); La Rosa nel pugno (Rose in your fist—socialists and radicals); Comunisti Italiani (Italian communists); Italia dei valori (Italy of values); Verdi (Greens); Forza Italia (Go Italy—main "anchor party" on the center right); Alleanza Nazionale (National Alliance—radical right wing, fascists); UCD (Union of Christian Democrats); Lega Nord (Northern League—right wing populists); Democrazia Cristiana—Nuovo PSI (New Socialist Party).
Source: Der Standard, April 11, 2006.

distribution of votes for the lower house was based on a single, nationwide district, with the proviso that the party coalition which wins a plurality in terms of votes will get at least 340 out of 630 seats (54 percent), the so called "majority bonus." Similarly, for the upper house, any coalition which wins a plurality will receive at least 55 percent of the seats in each respective region guaranteeing Prodi a substantial majority in terms of seats over Berlusconi particularly in the lower house. The idea of this quirky law was to ensure solid majorities, thus increasing the effectiveness of law makers to pass legislation. Even more ironic is that the author of this law was Silvio Berlusconi himself.

The majority bonus ensured that while only 25,000 votes separated the two major coalitions, Table 4.5 shows Prodi's L'Unione will have 74 seats more than Berlusconi injecting a large dose of disproportionality. Another change that backfired for Berlusconi was to allow

Italian expatriots to vote in these elections for the first time assuming they voted for him. However, not only did they not vote for him, but it appears that the expatriot's votes were the ones that broke his political back. Six Senate seats were allocated for Italian expatriots in four gigantic global districts: Europe (2 seats), Asia/Africa, Oceania, Antarctica (1 seat), North/Central America (1 seat), and South America (2 seats). Of the six, four went to Prodi's coalition, one to Berlusconi's and one to an independent party.

Italy represents another example where changing the electoral system, or wealth, or controlling the media does not ensure victory. Italian voters grew tired of Berlusconi's antics and, more importantly, became concerned about the weak economic growth, high unemployment, and its incapacity to adjust to a globalizing world, thereby attracting the dubious title of the "new sick man of Europe."[22]

THE SEMIPRESIDENTIAL SYSTEM OF FRANCE

France is unique among European countries in having a semipresidential system. Like the United States, France has a president elected by the people, but it has also a prime minister. This system was established with a new constitution in 1958 at the beginning of the Fifth Republic. (France numbers each new democratic period in its history; the First Republic was during the French Revolution). The Fourth Republic (1946–1958) had a parliamentary form of government, and—much like Italy today—was very unstable and had frequent cabinet crises. The country also suffered from internal conflict over its involvement in colonial wars in Indochina and Algeria. In 1958, the turmoil was so great that the parties in Parliament were no longer able to form a viable cabinet. Charles de Gaulle stepped in; in 1940, he had escaped the German occupation by going to London, where he organized the Resistance movement. Returning to France in triumph in 1944, he served briefly as head of the government, but soon, disgusted by the bickering among the many parties, he retreated to his rural hometown to await the hour when he could emerge as the savior of France.

Unlike other strong leaders in French history, de Gaulle did not establish a dictatorship. However, he changed the political institutions so much that his coming to power in 1958 was counted as the beginning of another Republic. He built a political system that was a combination of a presidential and a parliamentary system, with both a president and a prime minister. Since the retirement of de Gaulle, the relation between president and prime minister has changed greatly. But let us first see what the relation was under de Gaulle himself. As president, he liked to handle the big questions, leaving the routine day-to-day work to the prime minister. The president was elected by an electoral college and, after 1962, directly by the people. To be elected directly by the people corresponded to de Gaulle's leadership style. He did not want to depend on the goodwill of professional politicians, whom he detested for their selfish maneuvers. De Gaulle liked to enter into a dialogue directly with the French people, who in his view had more common sense than the politicians. De Gaulle saw himself as France's father figure. If he explained what had to be done in the higher national interest to the men and women of France, he was sure they would trust and follow him. De Gaulle believed that his personal mission was to restore the historical greatness of France. At the end of his speeches he used to intone the national anthem and exclaim with a grandiose gesture of his arms, "Vive la France!"

De Gaulle held office from 1958 to 1969, and, during those years, he acted in many ways like a powerful monarch. Many important decisions were made by him alone, and critics raised the question of whether France was still a genuine democracy. A bothersome issue was the fact that the president was elected for a very long term—seven years—and could run for reelection as many times as he wished. Another distinguishing characteristic was the importance attached to the popular referendum. At first sight, this seems to have increased the democratic quality of the regime. Indeed, in Chapter 6 we see how, in some European countries, the referendum is used to strengthen the political role of the people. But, under the rules of the Fifth Republic, the referendum strengthens the president by allowing him to bypass Parliament and appeal directly to the people.

Still another issue that raised questions about the democratic nature of the Fifth Republic was that in its early years Parliament had virtually no power. In contrast to the system of the Fourth Republic, the prime minister was not selected by Parliament but was appointed by the president. Under de Gaulle, the prime minister served completely at the pleasure of the president, who could dismiss him at any time. The role of Parliament was very limited. Sometimes a new cabinet sought the approval of Parliament, but such approval was not necessary. Under de Gaulle, Parliament also had few legislative powers, because the president often ruled by executive decrees. With regard to the relationship between the president and the prime minister, all essential power lay with the former. The prime minister had to do whatever the president did not wish to do himself. This system was tailored to the personal needs of de Gaulle, who saw himself as a world leader and liked to concentrate his attention on the big questions of foreign policy and defense. He left the day-to-day business, and especially contact with Parliament, to the prime minister.

During the first years of the Fifth Republic, de Gaulle was very popular and much admired. The French people were grateful that he saved the country from the chaos of the Fourth Republic and restored order. De Gaulle fulfilled the longing for a strong leader—as had Napoléon I after the French Revolution, Napoléon III after the revolution of 1848, and Marshal Pétain after France's defeat in 1940. But unlike his predecessors, de Gaulle was ultimately not a dictator. To be sure, he eliminated many checks and balances from the political system of France. He felt responsible only to his beloved French people. Some feared that this was empty rhetoric and that de Gaulle would secure his reelection by manipulation, but this fear was unjustified. When his first term was over, de Gaulle sought reelection in a free and open competition. His main adversary was Socialist François Mitterrand, later himself president of France.

Mitterrand forced de Gaulle into a runoff, which de Gaulle won only narrowly; afterwards, much of his charismatic attraction was lost. In May 1968, he was challenged by a massive student revolt. In the following year, he tried to restore his prestige with a referendum on regional reform and reorganization of the Senate, the upper house of Parliament. De Gaulle hoped that these reforms would be popular and that an overwhelming approval by the people would again enhance the legitimacy of his regime. But he was disappointed when the referendum was defeated by a majority of 53 percent. De Gaulle had seen enough and, although he legally was not required to do so, he resigned from the presidency and retired to his small hometown, deeply hurt.

The United States had a stormy relationship with de Gaulle, who took no orders at all from Washington. He withdrew French troops from the North Atlantic Treaty Organization (NATO) command and kicked NATO headquarters out of Paris; the headquarters had to be relocated to Brussels. Since then, American opinion has become more positive toward de Gaulle. In the early 1990s, a survey among political scientists at American universities showed strong support for the view that de Gaulle was a figure of great historical consequence and that he brought "authority and stability" back to France.[23] This positive evaluation in retrospect is due to the fact that the institutions of the Fifth Republic were able to survive de Gaulle. Initially, it was feared that the constitution of the Fifth Republic was tailored too much to the personal needs of de Gaulle. But since 1969, France has had four presidents, and the Fifth Republic is still intact. The presidency is still the most powerful institution in France, although not as much as in the early years of de Gaulle. Since de Gaulle's resignation, other institutions, in particular Parliament and the prime ministership, have been strengthened, so that today the system has more checks and balances than when de Gaulle was at the height of his power.

A major constitutional change came into effect in 2000 that limits the term for president to five years. The first term of current President Jacques Chirac lasted from 1995 to 2002, but his second term will be up in 2007. What has been reduced also since the time of de Gaulle is the plebiscitary nature of the presidency. The immediate successor of de Gaulle, Georges Pompidou, organized a referendum in 1972. But then there was no referendum for 20 years, and it was only in 1992 that Mitterrand used the referendum in the hope of strengthening his political standing. The issue was the ratification of the Treaty of Maastricht for further European integration (see Chapter 14). Opinion surveys indicated strong public support, and Mitterrand hoped to reverse his decreasing popularity with a clear victory in the referendum. But as the day of the referendum approached, public support dwindled and the referendum passed only by the narrowest margin. As in the case of de Gaulle in 1969, Mitterrand learned that the French president could no longer use the referendum for his own purposes, as was the case in the early years of the Fifth Republic. In 2005 President Chirac submitted the new constitution of the EU (see Chapter 14) to a referendum, and to the embarrassment of Chirac the people voted against the constitution.

The most ambivalent feature of the Fifth Republic is the status of the prime minister. What happens if Parliament is of a different political orientation than the president? To whom is the prime minister responsible? To Parliament or to the president? This was no problem up to 1981 because both the president and the majority in Parliament were always of the Right.

Therefore, the selection of the prime minister by presidents de Gaulle, Pompidou, and Valéry Giscard d'Estaing, who were all of the Right, did not encounter opposition in Parliament. In 1981, Socialist Mitterrand won the presidency. Confronted with a Parliament dominated by the Right, he immediately called early parliamentary elections, which the Socialists won (Table 3.1, Chapter 3). It was no problem, therefore, for Mitterrand to appoint a Socialist as prime minister. The dominance of the Socialists came to an end with their defeat in the parliamentary election of March 1986. Confronted with this situation, Mitterrand chose to invite Jacques Chirac, a leader of the Right, to form the new cabinet. This was the first time in the history of the Fifth Republic that the president and the prime minister had come from opposite ends of the party spectrum. This system of a president of one side of the political spectrum and a prime minister of the other side is called *cohabitation.* Although there were fears of a constitutional crisis and even of a breakdown of the Fifth Republic, cohabitation worked relatively smoothly. It came to an end in 1988 when Mitterrand was reelected to a second term as president. He immediately called early parliamentary elections, which brought losses to the Right but not enough gains to the Left to reach a majority.

In this situation Mitterrand selected Socialist Michel Rocard as prime minister, who formed a minority cabinet. We have already dealt with the concept of a minority cabinet in the Swedish and Italian contexts; the Rocard cabinet serves as another illustration of how minority cabinets can survive. Robert Elgie and Moshe Maor have studied the survival tactics of the Rocard cabinet.[24] By the spring of 1991, as a result of defeats in elections for vacant seats, the Socialists were down to 274 seats in the National Assembly, 15 short of an absolute majority. Where could they find the necessary votes? There were 21 deputies who belonged to no party; the Rocard government could rely on, at most, 14 of these independents to support its policies. Thus, in the best of cases, it still needed at least 1 defection from either the Communists on the Left or the Christian Democratic Union at the Center. A good illustration of how Rocard could put together a winning coalition was the bill to reform local government that came to a vote in April 1991. One deputy of the Christian Democratic Union voted with the government; of the independent deputies, 11 did likewise, and 3 abstained. Because not all deputies were present, the bill could pass by 1 vote. Sometimes, however, the Rocard government was unable to put together such winning coalitions. But in such cases it could resort to Article 49–3 of the French constitution, which allows the government to engage its survival to depend on the passage of a bill. This constitutional article is formulated in such a way that for the government to fall, the opposition needs a majority of the *total* membership of the National Assembly—not only of those voting. This is a more difficult requirement for the opposition than in Sweden and Italy, where a majority of those voting is sufficient to bring down a government. At first sight such nuances in voting rules may seem trivial and dull. But the case of the Rocard government shows that details of voting rules may be of crucial importance for the survival of a government.

In the 1993 parliamentary elections the Socialists suffered heavy losses (Table 3.4, Chapter 3). Once again, as from 1986 to 1988, Mitterrand had to live in cohabitation with a prime minister from the Right. This time, it was Edouard Balladur. With everyone having learned from the earlier period of cohabitation, a relatively smooth relationship developed between the president and the prime minister. As a leading newspaper put it, relations between President Mitterrand and Prime Minister Balladur "are not idyllic, but correct and polite."[25] After the expiration of his second seven-year term in 1995, Mitterrand retired, and Chirac was elected president. Once again, president and parliament were of the same political side, so Chirac could elect a prime minister of his side. In 1997, the left won the parliamentary elections and it was back to cohabitation.

The 2002 presidential elections represented a watershed event in the history of French politics when Le Pen's National Front received more votes (16.86 percent) than the Socialists (16.18 percent) in the first round, relegating them to third place. This meant that in the second round Le Pen would square off with Jacques Chirac, who received 19.88 percent of the first-round vote. Not only were many French ashamed that a candidate running on an antiimmigrant and anti-Semitic platform could reach second place in the first round, many were shocked that the Socialists' candidate, Lionel Jospin, was beaten by Le Pen. This was not only due to the fact that Jospin was a uninspiring campaigner, but even more so by the inability of the Left to present a more coherent party platform. As the Left splintered, the Right was able to just barely top the Socialists and relegate them to third place.

However, weeks after the presidential elections, the French went to the polls again—this time for parliamentary elections. Cohabitation ended in the wake of the 2002 election when the Right gained nearly 63 percent of the seats in the National Assembly and Chirac installed someone of the Right as prime minister.

In conclusion, we can say that the institutions of the Fifth Republic allowed France to get out of the instability of the Fourth Republic. To be sure, there are still some remaining ambiguities. In particular, it is not clear what exactly the powers of the president are when he belongs to a party that is in opposition to the majority in the National Assembly. What is most important for the democratic vitality of the institutions of the Fifth Republic is that the National Assembly has again become the place for the big political debates of the country. The vitaliy of this debate is aided by the system of checks and balances between the Palais Bourbon, the seat of parliament, and the Palais de l'Elysée, the seat of the president.

ADVANTAGES AND DISADVANTAGES OF PARLIAMENTARY AND PRESIDENTIAL SYSTEMS

In Chapter 13 on power sharing, we will argue that in divided societies particular constitutional features may have a higher chance of achieving social peace than others. With the breakdown of the Soviet Union and the formation of many new and independent Central and Eastern European countries in the 1990s, questions of "constitutional engineering" have emerged. In other words, what advantages and disadvantages do various forms of political institutions have? Is it possible that some institutions can make a tense political situation even worse by systematically excluding particular groups, while others allow for the inclusion of a variety of such groups into government and thus alleviate potential problems?

One can think of constitutions very much like architectural structures. Architects and urban studies specialists have uncovered that it is possible to literally build aggression into some structures. High-density buildings with little greenspace, few trees, and no areas for children and adolescents to play tend to generate aggression among the inhabitants of such structures. The same logic can be applied to constitutions: If they systematically disadvantage particular groups, limit their opportunities to voice their opinions, either underrepresent them or not represent them at all, and provide privileged access to some and not to others, it is possible to build political upheaval into particular constitutions. In this chapter we have highlighted cabinet formation, which speaks directly to the relations between the executive and legislative powers. What are the advantages and disadvantages of presidential systems and parliamentary systems?[26] In the European context, there are of course no pure presidential systems. The semipresidential systems of France and Finland are the only exceptions. However, American students will appreciate the direct comparison between European parliamentary systems and the American presidential system.

Advantages and Disadvantages of Presidentialism

The main advantages of presidential systems are threefold. First, legislative terms are fixed. Americans are used to very "regular" election intervals. Every four years, like clockwork, there is a presidential election. This regularity provides executive stability that allows for predictable policy planning. The president cannot be removed, save via the impeachment clause.

Second, the chief executive is popularly elected. This enables the American president to claim to speak for the majority of the people. In parliamentary systems the chief executive, the prime minister, cannot claim to have the same kind of popular mandate as an American president, although in systems with two major parties it is very clear to voters who will be their prime minister depending on which party they vote for. This is not always so clear, however, in multiparty systems, from which the prime minister emerges as a result of protracted negotiations after the legislative elections.

Third, presidential government is "limited government" as a result of the separation of powers. This stands in stark contrast to the "fusion" of powers in parliamentary systems, where in the case of Great Britain, the executive and legislative authorities almost always are made up of the same party. This puts enormous power into the hands of the prime minister. However, in the American case, the founding fathers ensured that presidential powers are checked and balanced by separate institutions in order to make it as difficult as possible for any one particular institution to dominate the political agenda.

Through examining the disadvantages of presidentialism it becomes clear that in most cases they are simply the obverse of the very advantages just highlighted. For instance, the fixed legislative terms can easily be interpreted as leading to "temporal rigidity," meaning incapacity of the legislature to impose changes on executive authority. Once a president has won an election, there is no mechanism, save for impeachment, to remove him or her from power. This incapacity for changing the commander in chief can prove very detrimental when cataclysmic circumstances such as wars necessitate a quick adjustment of leadership to a changing environment or when a president is involved in questionable affairs. An example is Richard Nixon, who continued to stay in power for over one-and-a-half years after it became public knowledge that he was involved in the Watergate scandal.

Another disadvantage of presidentialism derives directly from the separation of powers argument: Precisely because there is separation of powers, there is gridlock. One could describe the American constitution as "gridlock by design." This was most clearly shown during the Clinton administration when Bill Clinton waved his "veto pen" and blocked budget bills coming from the republican Congress, leading to shut-downs of governmental services on two occasions. This is particularly relevant if there are incoherent majorities between the president and the two houses of parliament, which means that either one or even both houses are of a different party from the president's. It is of course less of an issue if there are coherent majorities.

The third disadvantage is closely connected to the second: If there are incoherent majorities, who is accountable for policymaking? If one or both of the two houses are of a different party than the president's, inevitable finger pointing arises as to whose fault it is if policymaking comes to a screeching halt.

Finally, a fourth disadvantage of presidentialism is that it tends to operate in a environment with low party loyalty. Being a loyal member of a party does not guarantee success at the ballot box. Oftentimes, "running against Washington" is precisely what proved successful for some politicians in America, even when the president was from their own party. In a presidential system, success of a representative depends on what he or she did for the district or state that is going to elect her or not. As a result, the tendency to engage in inefficient pork-barrel policies is much higher in a presidential system than in a parliamentary system.

Advantages and Disadvantages of Parliamentarism

Proponents of parliamentary systems highlight the advantages that come with "fusion" between the executive and legislative powers. As we have noted, after parliamentary elections have taken place, the majority party usually also installs the prime minister, leading to a fusion of executive and legislative power. This means no gridlock, clear accountability, and high efficiency of policymaking. In parliamentary systems, particularly with two parties, it is very clear who is responsible for political outcomes, whether they are good or bad. There is no finger pointing from one branch of government to the next.

Another advantage is that parliamentary systems operate in an environment of strong party loyalties. Intense party loyalty tends to instill political debates that center on national, encompassing issues rather than district-based issues. It is for this reason that pork-barrel policies are much less of a problem in parliamentary systems than in presidential ones.

Alas, just as we have seen in presidential systems, it is possible to see disadvantages in the very advantages of parliamentarism as well. Precisely because parliamentarism is built on the principle of fusion, it could be argued that it gives too much power to the executive. Those who favor more limited government would be very much concerned with the enormous powers of a prime minister.

Finally, because in parliamentary systems executive authority not only emerges from the legislature but is also responsible to it, the legislature can bring down government by a vote of no-confidence. As we have seen in the case of Italy, this device may make for rather unstable governments, although in practice it is really only Italy that indicates high rates of government turnover. While some decry this ability of the legislative to bring down cabinets as "instability," others call it "flexibility."

What becomes obvious is that the choice between presidential and parliamentary systems is driven by negative trade-offs. If effectiveness of policymaking is more important than lengthy debates, a parliamentary system is preferable. If democratic debate, direct election of the president, and separation of powers are more important than effectiveness of policymaking, a presidential system is preferable. Another trade-off refers to stability or flexibility of government: If stability is desired, a presidential system will deliver that, while a parliamentary system will always allow, in the words of Walter Bagehot, a certain "revolutionary reserve"[27] that might come in handy if a change in executive authority becomes necessary.

HEADS OF STATE

The president of France has important executive functions but is also head of state. This is similar to the United States, where the president is both chief executive and head of state. In Europe, however, the normal pattern is that the roles of head of state and chief executive are played by two different individuals. The head of state is either a monarch or an elected president and has mainly representative functions.

Monarchial Head of State

Great Britain probably best illustrates the functions of a monarch in a modern European democracy. The reigning monarch is Queen Elizabeth II. She appoints the prime minister, but this appointment is a pure formality. It makes for a colorful ceremony with a symbolic value when the queen invites the leader of the winning party to come to Buckingham Palace and asks him or her to form Her Majesty's next government. The losing party is called Her Majesty's opposition. An even grander ceremony takes place when the queen opens the first session of Parliament with a speech. The speech is written not by the queen, but by the prime minister, who uses it to announce the new government's program (Photo 4.1).

In former centuries the symbolic trappings of the monarch also had substance. The king or queen was an important political actor who, for example, had a great say in the

Photo 4.1 Queen opens session of Parliament. (*Source*: Tim Graham/Getty Images)

appointment and dismissal of the prime minister. Together with other institutions, such as the House of Commons and the House of Lords, the monarch ruled the country. But, in a slow and long process, the monarchy lost its substantive power. Today, the saying is that the queen *reigns,* and the prime minister *rules*. Only the trappings of the queen's power remain, but these trappings have great symbolic value.

Until recent scandals surrounding the royal family, the monarchy was very popular. In our bureaucratic and anonymous world, the public seems to have a great need for colorful images. This need is not well fulfilled by modern-day politicians who, at best, give the impression of being efficient managers of huge government programs. At worst, they appear power-hungry, inefficient, and sometimes even corrupt. In contrast, the royal family does not have to run for office, and its members cannot be held accountable for what goes wrong in the government. Thus, in an ironic way, for a long time the absence of political power contributed to the popularity of the monarchy. The queen was a symbol holding the British nation together.

So why has the popularity of the royal family decreased in recent years? Box 4.6 gives a vivid explanation. Family quarrels, separations, and divorces are the main reasons. All of a sudden, the royals appear to be an ordinary family with ordinary problems. It has become more difficult to look up to them and to admire them as role models. There were additional problems, such as the fact that the queen agreed only reluctantly to pay taxes. Sensationalism in the media contributed greatly to the problems of the royal family. Prince Charles, next in line for succession, has had particular difficulties. In addition to his divorce problems, he is somewhat unsure about how to define his public role. In addition to the usual ceremonial duties, he sometimes speaks up on controversial issues such as modern architecture and education. It remains to be seen whether he will retain this frankness if, one day,

---

Box 4.6 It Hasn't Been a Good Year for the Monarchy

LONDON—On the 40th anniversary of her accession to the throne, Queen Elizabeth II on Tuesday branded 1992 a "horrible year," and, adopting a rare personal tone, called for a less savage treatment of the embattled royal family by the British media. The queen told a gilt-edged audience of 500 at a lunch, hosted by the Lord Mayor of London at Guildhall, that she could not look on this anniversary year with "undiluted pleasure," understanding the problems by which she has been plagued, including her children's marital problems and the fire last weekend at her Windsor Castle home. In a voice croaking from a cold, the queen conceded that the monarchy was not above criticism. But she also suggested that the running attacks that her family has endured in the tabloid press have lacked "gentleness, good humor and understanding." "There can be no doubt, of course, that criticism is good for people and institutions that are part of public life," she said in her statement, which was unusual in that it seemed to come from the heart from a family more known for its stiff upper lip. But she added: "I dare say that history will take a slightly more moderate view than that of some contemporary commentators."

Source: *Los Angeles Times*, November 25, 1992.

---

he becomes king. This could cause problems, because the monarchy is supposed to stay above politics.

Although Americans may be most familiar with the British monarchy, several other European democracies also have monarchs. These countries include Belgium, Denmark, Luxembourg, the Netherlands, Norway, Spain, and Sweden, as well as the tiny countries of Liechtenstein and Monaco. In some of these countries, the monarchical trappings are not quite as splendid as in Great Britain. An extreme case of a stripped-down monarchy is found in Sweden. According to a 1974 constitutional amendment, the king is not even symbolically allowed to appoint the prime minister or open Parliament. The Swedish king has become more of a citizen like everyone else. He does not even get special parking permits. The main task of the Swedish king is to cut ribbons, open museums, and make state visits.

A bizarre episode in Belgium in 1990 shows how politically weak the position of European monarchs has become. The Belgian king declared that in good conscience as a Roman Catholic, he could not sign a new law permitting abortion. To circumvent the unexpected difficulty, the cabinet temporarily suspended the king and promulgated the law on its own power. Afterward, the parliament was called into a special session to reinstate the king.

Spain illustrates how even in modern times there may be situations where a monarch exercises political power. Spain was a dictatorship until the death of Francisco Franco in 1975. Afterward, the monarchy was reestablished with Juan Carlos I as king. Instead of trying to have dictatorial powers for himself, he helped to lead his country to a democratic form of government. But for some time, the Spanish democracy was still frail because Franco supporters remained influential in the armed forces and the police (see Chapter 11). At one point, these groups attempted a coup to overthrow the democratic government. Some officers holding weapons in their hands entered parliament and began shooting in the air. They hoped to get the support of the king, but Juan Carlos acted forcefully in the defense of democracy and had the coup participants imprisoned. In normal times he prefers to act as the symbolic figurehead of his country, but if new threats to the Spanish democracy should occur, he can be counted on to step in and exercise a political role.

Elected Heads of State

Germany serves as a good illustration for an elected head of state. In the long history of Germany, emperors and kings have played significant roles. After Germany's defeat in World War I, however, the country sent its emperor into exile. When the Federal Republic of Germany was established in 1949, its constitution provided for the office of federal president as head of state. How is the president elected, and what are his functions? Is he as politically powerless as the European monarchs? The German president is elected by a special assembly that consists of all members of the lower house of the federal parliament (the Bundestag) and an equal number of deputies from the state parliaments. Successful candidates must have a reputation that transcends party lines.

The role of president has been interpreted very differently by the persons who have filled the office up to now. The first president, Theodor Heuss, played the role of political philosopher, often speaking out forcefully on fundamental questions of the democratic order. He instructed the German people on the value of democracy in a critical period of their history. Gustav Heinemann tried to be a "citizen president," seeking contact with ordinary men and women, visiting them in their homes. Walter Scheel brought great elegance to the presidency and sponsored many splendid performances by artists at the presidential palace. Richard von Weizsäcker was a rather political president, often speaking out on the great questions confronting the country.

Compared to the European monarchs, the German president exercises more political power and leadership, but also runs the risk of crossing the fine line where he or she might suddenly become too political. Walter Scheel had such an experience at the beginning of his term, when he was rebuked by Chancellor Helmut Schmidt, who told him, in no uncertain terms, that it was not the business of the president to run the foreign policy of the country. This episode shows the delicate nature of the role played by the German president. Unlike a monarch, whose prestige is assured by a royal background, the German president must earn his or her prestige through public statements that must be neither trivial nor too overtly political. At rare occasions the president has to take over important functions. A recent example discussed in Chapter 3 is when in 2005 the president had to decide whether to follow the recommendation of Chancellor Gerhard Schröder to dissolve Parliament and to call for early elections (which he did).

In the other European countries with an elected president as head of state, the situation is basically the same as in Germany, although there is some variation with regard to methods of election and the amount of power exercised by the president. As we have already discussed, the only real exception is France, where the president not only is head of state but also exercises strong executive power.

What implications might we draw from this section for the United States? The fact that the American president is simultaneously head of state and chief executive has led to two sorts of complaints. One is that the president misuses his prestige as head of state to impose his policies as chief executive. The other complaint is that the president is over-burdened with ceremonial tasks as head of state, so that he does not have enough time for his duties as chief executive. It is unlikely that the United States will undertake any great changes in this respect any time soon. But it may still be worthwhile to reflect on two possible changes based on the European experience. One change could be to give the title of prime minister to the chief of staff of the White House. The chief of staff already has great coordinating responsibilities in the daily operations of the American executive. These responsibilities could be made more visible with a stronger title. Such a system would draw heavily on the French experience. Another change, based on the German experience, could be to have a president as ceremonial head of state and a prime minister as chief executive. In the American context, this would not necessarily mean a change to a parliamentary system. The ceremonial president could be elected by a joint session of Congress, while the politically more important prime minister could be elected by the people.

The main message of this chapter is that a parliamentary system is not necessarily unstable. It depends very much on the number and kind of political parties elected to parliament, and this in turn depends to a large extent on the parliamentary election systems discussed in the previous chapter. In order to understand how political parties are constrained by the institutional setting, one has to grasp the complex interactions between rules for parliamentary elections and rules for cabinet formation. To add to this complexity, we introduce in the next chapter the court systems of European democracies.

Discussion Questions

1. The Italian examples raise a most intriguing question: When do governments come to an end in parliamentary systems? When there is a new prime minister? When there is a new election? When there are new parties in government?

2. Who is more powerful: a president or prime minister?

3. Which system, parliamentarism or presidentialism, enjoys more "checks and balances"?

4. How important is "stability" for a political system? Can a system be "too stable"?

5. In parliamentary systems, legislators can depose a government with a vote of no confidence. Is this an expression of "democracy" or does it invite dysfunctional political behavior?

6. In which system, parliamentary or presidential, do parties play a bigger role? Why?

7. In which system, parliamentary or presidential, does money play a bigger role? Why?

---

[1]Craig R. Whitney. A Talk with Helmut Schmidt. *New York Times Magazine*, September 16, 1984, p. 118.
[2]BBC News, Cook Quits over Iraq Crisis. Monday, March 17, 2003.
[3]Philip Cowley. Blair at Mercy of Rebels. *The Guardian*, Friday, May 6, 2005.
[4]Patrick Gordon Walker. *The Cabinet* (London: Jonathan Cape, 1970), 151.
[5]Mark Wickham-Jones. Anticipating Social Democracy, Preempting Anticipations: Economic Policy-Making in the British Labor Party, 1987–1992. *Politics & Society* 23 (December 1995): 486–487.
[6]*The Sunday Times*, April 30, 1995.
[7]David Sanders, Paul Whiteley, Harold Clark, and Marianne Stewart. *British Election 2005*. (American Political Science Association, 2005).

[8]For the classical formulation of why minimal-winning coalitions should form, see William Riker, *The Theory of Political Coalitions* (New Haven, CT: Yale University Press, 1962).

[9]As we have seen in Chapter 2, the Christian Democrats in Bavaria are called Christian Social Union (CSU).

[10]In Germany the prime minister is called *chancellor*.

[11]Times OnLine. Merkel Is New German Chancellor. October 10, 2005.

[12]Three cantons split in the past, resulting in six half-cantons. Each of these half-cantons has only one representative in the Council of States. There are 20 full cantons, hence a total of 46 seats in the Council of States.

[13]*Neue Zürcher Zeitung*, April 10, 1996.

[14]Nicholas Aylott and Torbjörn Bergmann. "Almost in Government, But Not Quite: The Swedish Greens, Bargaining Constraints and the Rise of Contract Parliamentarism." Paper presented at the European Consortium of Political Research, Uppsala, April 2004.

[15]Torbjörn Bergman. Formation Rules and Minority Governments. *European Journal of Political Research* 23 (1993): 55–66.

[16]Carol Mershon. The Costs of Coalition: Coalition Theories and Italian Governments. *American Political Science Review* 90 (September 1996): 534.

[17]*New York Times*, March 31, 1994.

[18]For example, Le Monde, *The Guardian*, Neue Zürcher Zeitung, and Süddeutsche Zeitung.

[19]*New York Times*, March 29, 1994.

[20]*New York Times*, March 24, 1994.

[21] BBC News. David Wiley. "Berlusconi says: 'I am like Jesus.'" Monday, February 13, 2006.

[22] Times OnLine. Bronwen Maddox. "'Sick man has little to gain from victory by Berlusconi.'" April 11, 2005.

[23]Theodore J. Lowi and Martin A. Schain. Conditional Surrender: Charles de Gaulle and American Opinion. *PS. Political Science and Politics* 25 (September 1992): 498–506.

[24]Robert Elgie and Moshe Moar. Accounting for the Survival of Minority Governments: An Examination of the French Case, 1988–1991. *West European Politics* 15 (October 1992): 57–74.

[25]*Neue Zürcher Zeitung*, April 20, 1993.

[26]This debate follows loosely the chapter called "Introduction" in Arend Lijphart (ed.), *Parliamentary vs. Presidential Government* (New York: Oxford University Press, 1992).

[27]Walter Bagehot. [1867] The English Constitution. The Cabinet. In Arend Lijphart (ed.), *Parliamentary vs. Presidential Government* (New York: Oxford University Press, 1992).

CHAPTER 5

Courts

One of the major institutional differences between Europe and the United States is that the Supreme Court in the United States has much more power than the court in any European democracy. Let us take the example of abortion. In the United States it is accepted that the Supreme Court has the ultimate say on matters of abortion (short of a corresponding constitutional amendment, which in this controversial matter is virtually impossible). We will show that in Great Britain the ultimate say on abortion is with the House of Commons, and in Switzerland with the people in a referendum. Although in Great Britain and Switzerland the judicial branch of government has little political influence, in other European countries the judiciary has more political influence; we will use Germany and France as illustrations. The countries of continental Europe are all influenced by the legal tradition of ancient Rome, where code law prevailed. Great Britain deviates from this pattern in having a tradition of common law, where judges continually reinterpret old precedents in the light of new circumstances. Code law, by contrast, is characterized by complex bodies of categories and subcategories that give the courts limited discretion in handling particular cases. The classical code law is the Napoleonic code system, which Napoleon introduced in France after the Great Revolution and which under French revolutionary influence spread to the other countries of the continent. The Napoleonic codes were conceived as positive legal commands that judges were strictly obligated to obey, to avoid a government of judges. As Alec Stone puts it:

> The judge's role was a subservient and bureaucratic one; he was required to verify the existence and applicability of statutory norms to a case at hand, but he could investigate the work of the legislature no further. . . . Judicial review was all but unthinkable.[1]

In the United States, on the other hand, judges have always enjoyed great political influence. They have, in particular, the authority to overturn as unconstitutional decisions of the other branches of government. As Shapiro and Stone explain:

> In the American model of review, any judge of any court, in any case, at the behest of any litigating party, has the power to declare a law unconstitutional. This power is what Americans always think of when they see judicial review.[2]

At first, Europeans took the United States as a negative example of a nation practicing a government of judges. But in the latter half of the 19th century, European legal scholars began increasingly to argue for the merits of constitutional judicial review. Thanks to the influence of one of these scholars, law professor Hans Kelsen, Austria was the first European country to introduce constitutional judicial review after World War I. As constitutional review is practiced in Europe, only separate, specialized courts, so-called constitutional courts, exercise review powers. After 1945, an increasing number of European countries introduced such constitutional courts. When, in the 1970s, authoritarian regimes fell in Greece, Spain, and Portugal, these countries, too, introduced constitutional courts.

In the United States judicial review is of a concrete nature in the sense that a real case or controversy is a precondition for judicial review to take place. Judicial review in this concrete sense is also known in Europe. But, in addition, Europe embraces the concept of abstract judicial review, which means that a legislative text is reviewed by the constitutional court before the text becomes law. Various combinations of the two review forms occur in different countries. Germany, for example, has both a concrete and an abstract form of judicial review; France has only an abstract one. Abstract review is initiated by politicians, who refer legislation directly to the court. As Stone puts it, "abstract review therefore functions to extend what would otherwise be a concluded legislative process." The court undertakes, so to speak, a "final reading" of a bill. In doing so, decision making of the judges is closer to legislative decision making than when they apply the constitution to a concrete litigation.[3]

Some European countries are still without a constitutional court. Two examples are Great Britain and Switzerland, with which we begin. We then turn to Germany as an example of a country with a strong constitutional court.

GREAT BRITAIN

American readers will be surprised to learn that the British have no written constitution in the sense of a single document. British political institutions, practices, and civil liberties have evolved over many centuries. Some of the resulting rules are codified; others exist only as unwritten customs and conventions. Even the most fundamental laws have no special status and can be changed by Parliament, just like any other laws. Great Britain is said, therefore, to have an unwritten constitution.

In their daily work, the courts apply the law to specific cases, but they have no right to say whether a law is constitutional. Questions of constitutionality rest in the hands of Parliament. Does this lack of constitutional judicial review by the courts lead to an arbitrary regime? Is there a danger that the majority in Parliament will abuse its power to rewrite and reinterpret the constitutional rules according to selfish interests? Where are the checks and balances in this system? These are troublesome questions for someone accustomed to the American system.

The British system is based on a very different philosophy of government. In Great Britain, the main task of the voters is to elect Parliament, which alone has the legitimate right to express the will of the people. Because the people give full power to Parliament, it would be illogical—according to British tradition—for a high court to check the actions of Parliament. These checks are made by the people in the next election. If the majority in Parliament interprets the constitution against the wishes of the people, the voters can replace the governing party at the next election with the party in opposition (see Chapter 4).

Does this system run the risk that one day a governing party might restrict democratic freedoms or even cancel future elections? In other words, what prevents a governing party from establishing a dictatorship? The answer is a commonly accepted democratic political culture. The British system is based on the assumption that everyone accepts certain basic rules of the game. One such rule is that free elections take place at regular intervals. There are also many commonly accepted rules concerning the protection of individual freedoms, some of which go back to medieval times. The British assume that no governing party will ever dare touch these fundamental rules. Thus, the stability of the system is ultimately based on an element of fair play.

Within the framework of commonly accepted basic rules, Parliament can take whatever actions it sees fit. Thus, Parliament can nationalize key industries, and no court can intervene with the argument that such a measure violates the constitution. And Parliament can decide abortion matters in whatever manner it sees fit. Parliament is sovereign, and it alone can say what is constitutional. For many American observers, this lack of judicial review is appalling. Which is the better system—the British or the American? One could argue that the voters have greater influence in Great Britain, because they can replace the governing party with the opposition, thereby hoping to reverse earlier decisions of Parliament. Such reversals took place with regard to the nationalization of key industries, which were nationalized by Labour, but voters sent the Conservatives back to power, who denationalized again the key industries. With this system, the will of the people can be quickly translated into political action.

In the United States, voters can influence Supreme Court decisions only in an indirect and tenuous way. They can vote for a particular presidential candidate in the hope that, if elected, he will have the chance to nominate new judges. In the confirmation process, senators often listen to the views expressed by the voters. All this is true, but it must also be considered that often the composition of the Supreme Court does not change very much over many years because there are no term limits for Supreme Court judges—not even a mandatory retirement age. One also has to take account of the fact that judges quite often develop in directions not anticipated by the president nominating them or the senators confirming them. Under all these circumstances, the Court may be unresponsive to the immediate wishes of the people. The decisions of the Court may not correspond to the prevailing public opinion of the time. Although this system appears less democratic than the British system, it has the advantage of giving more continuity to the law of the land. Who should be the watchdog for the constitution: the Parliament, which is directly accountable to the people, or judges, who are more detached from popular pressures? There are good arguments on both sides.

Although Great Britain has no constitutional judicial review, it has so-called statutory judicial review, which means that judges have the right and the obligation to review what in the country is lawful and what is not. This includes reviews of administrative regulations, which may be struck down by the courts. Thus, the role of British courts should not be downplayed too much because, after all, they can interpret the meaning of a law when they apply it to concrete cases. This gives a certain amount of power to the courts.

It should also be mentioned that historically speaking, going back more than 600 years, the House of Lords has certain judicial functions. It serves as the supreme court of appeal, but this function is not exercised by the House of Lords as a whole but by 12 so-called law lords. They are highly qualified judges appointed by the queen on the recommendation of the prime minister. Law lords have a seat in the House of Lords but do not usually take part in controversial political discussions. This quite archaic arrangement reveals the impact of traditions in Great Britain. Recently, however, it was recognized that it is strange if members of a legislative branch have also judicial functions, and in 2005 it was decided that the law lords should be separated from the House of Lords and form a special supreme court of appeal. This special court is expected to begin to operate in 2008.

SWITZERLAND

In contrast to Great Britain, Switzerland does have a single document that serves as its constitution, but, like Britain, Swiss courts do not have the right to determine whether a particular law is constitutional. In the Swiss case, this decision is ultimately made by the people in a referendum. Thus, the Swiss go a step further than the British in giving final authority over constitutional questions—they give it not merely to the representatives of the people but to the people themselves. Most Swiss believe that in a true democracy the most vital decisions must be made not by judges or members of parliament but by the citizens. Are the citizens mature and legally educated enough to decide complex constitutional issues? Switzerland is a good case for examining this question (see also Chapter 6).

How is the Swiss government organized so the voters can decide questions of constitutionality? First, voters have the right to call for a popular referendum on every bill decided by Parliament. The only requirement is that 50,000 signatures be obtained, which is relatively easy in a country of 7.5 million inhabitants. There are many motives for calling a referendum on a particular bill, but one possible reason is that some voters may feel that the bill violates the constitution. It is then up to the voters to decide whether this is so. A bill is enacted into law only if no referendum is called or if the bill is accepted in the popular vote.

The voters also have the final say on constitutional amendments. All constitutional amendments decided by Parliament must be submitted to the voters. A minimum of 100,000 voters can also submit a constitutional amendment of their own, which will first be debated by Parliament but finally decided in a popular referendum. This instrument of the popular constitutional initiative is widely used and can be applied to whatever question the people wish to decide. If the voters wish to amend the constitution in a particular way, neither Parliament nor the courts has the power to intervene. Recently, a constitutional initiative was launched to establish a system of hiking trails throughout the country. Constitutional lawyers might argue that this issue is not important enough to be included in the constitution. But the people decided otherwise, so the Swiss constitution now contains an article about hiking trails.

From the perspective of a clear and systematic distinction between the levels of constitution on the one hand and laws on the other hand, it is bothersome that sometimes the voters approve constitutional amendments that really belong in a law or even an administrative regulation. A far greater problem arises, however, if the voters add an article to the constitution that contradicts other parts of the constitution. Such an extreme case occurred early in the 20th century, when a constitutional initiative was accepted prohibiting the killing of animals according to Jewish kosher rites. On the surface, the proposal was presented as an animal protection measure, but its real intent was clearly anti-Semitic. The referendum allowed anti-Semitic feelings to be expressed in the secrecy of the voting booth. Did such an amendment contradict the religious freedom guaranteed by the constitution? One would assume so. However, if the people themselves decide that the two parts of the constitution are compatible, so be it. The people interpret what is constitutional, and no court can overrule their decision, because the people are the highest authority in the land—the sovereign, as the Swiss like to say.

The example of the kosher rites shows the dangers of giving ultimate power over the most basic constitutional questions to the people. Unlike judges, voters may be less concerned with the logical consistency of their decisions. Because most voters have little, if any, legal training, there is a risk that they follow their emotions and prejudices rather than logic. Thus, the people may act like a whimsical dictator. On the other hand, participation in referenda may help to educate the voters, making them more responsible and consistent in their judgments. Thus, fortunately, the referendum on kosher rites a hundred years ago remains an isolated extreme case.

What about constitutional initiatives that violate international law? In this respect, the Swiss Parliament in 1996 for the first time set limits on constitutional initiatives. The Swiss Democrats, a party of the New Radical Right, had collected enough signatures for a constitutional initiative, whose acceptance would have allowed asylum-seekers to be expelled from Switzerland even if there were still war in their country of origin. Such an amendment to the constitution would have violated an important principle of international law, the principle of *non-refoulement*, according to which refugees have the right not to be sent back to a country at war. Recognizing the obligation of Switzerland to uphold this principle, the Swiss Parliament declared the initiative of the Swiss Democrats as invalid so that it was not submitted to the voters. It is interesting to note that this decision of invalidation was made by Parliament and not by the courts.

GERMANY

Germany is a good illustration of a country with a strong constitutional court. After World War II, it tried to learn from the manner in which Hitler overthrew the Weimar Republic. He based his power, in many respects, on newly written laws. The courts at that time possessed only a very weak tradition of constitutional judicial review and therefore were hesitant to strike down these laws as unconstitutional. As a consequence, Hitler was able to argue that he had acted within legal limits. When the constitution of the Federal Republic of Germany was written, great care was given to avoid the possibility of a dictatorship being established by seemingly legal means. The key responsibility for this endeavor was given to the Federal Constitutional Court, which is located in the city of Karlsruhe (thus, the saying that Karlsruhe has decided).

The structure of the court was heavily influenced by the American occupation authorities, who used the U.S. Supreme Court as a model. The German court, however, consists of two units called senates, which have equal power but exercise mutually exclusive jurisdiction. The First Senate decides issues arising out of ordinary litigation, the Second Senate handles disputes among branches and levels of government. The members of the Constitutional Court are selected by Parliament based on a rule of party apportionment. The court is administratively independent; it has its own budget and the right to hire and fire its employees. In the relatively brief history of the Federal Republic, the court has established its moral and political authority as watchdog of the constitution. Like the Supreme Court in the United States, the Constitutional Court in the Federal Republic has played an important role in the abortion issue. When the government coalition of Social

Democrats and Free Democrats liberalized the abortion law in 1974, Christian Democrats brought the issue to the court, which declared the new law unconstitutional. The judges argued that the right to life guaranteed by the constitution also applied in principle to the unborn child. Following this decision, Parliament enacted a less liberal law. It is noteworthy that the right to life was included in the constitution in order to prevent atrocities such as those committed under Hitler. The hope was that the Constitutional Court would remain strong enough to strike down any act violating the constitutionally guaranteed right to life.

After German unification the court once again had to deal with the abortion issue. East Germany had a much more liberal abortion law than West Germany. The newly elected parliament of the united Germany tried to find a middle ground between the two practices. But the new law, passed in June 1992, was challenged in court. On May 28, 1993, the Second Senate of the Constitutional Court ruled in a very differentiated way, accepting many parts of the law and rejecting others. The basic ruling was that in the first three months abortion was legal only in the case of rape, when the life of the mother was in danger, or when the child had a hereditary defect. In all other cases, abortion would be illegal—but not punishable. At first, this seemed a paradoxical ruling, and there was great confusion in the initial commentaries by politicians and journalists. The ruling ran to 183 pages. When the details emerged, the court was saying that the implications of an illegal abortion were that it could not be done in a state hospital and that state-funded health insurance was not available. Poor mothers, however, could receive welfare payments. This ruling shows to what extent the German Constitutional Court is willing to get immersed in minute legislative details.

Another interesting court decision was made in 1992 concerning public subsidies to the political parties. Such subsidies began in 1959. They were increased significantly by a law in 1989, which was pushed through Parliament by all major parties except the Greens. But the latter took the law to the Constitutional Court, whose decision was that the law was indeed, in large part, unconstitutional. The court did not deny that the political parties had a certain right to be reimbursed by the state for parts of their costs. But it objected to the fact that, according to the new law, parties were financed to about 60 percent by the state.[4] The principle established by the court was that the parties had to draw the major part of their financial resources from private hands. This case is a good illustration of how the German Constitutional Court is able and willing to stand up against the interests of the major political parties.

A last example to illustrate the great importance of the German Constitutional Court stems from the decision in 2005 to have early elections for the Bundestag, the lower house of German parliament. As seen in Chapter 4, the coalition of Social Democrats and Greens under the leadership of chancellor Gerhard Schröder had difficulties to implement its economic reform program because of resistence at the left wing of the coalition. According to the German constitution, Schröder and his coalition did not have the power to call for early elections. Such a decision was up to the president of the country (for this office, see Chapter 4), to whom Schröder recommended that early elections be held. The president followed this recommendation, but some members of the Bundestag brought the matter to the Constitutional Court with the argument that the coalition of Schröder still had a working majority in Parliament, thus calling early elections violated the constitution. Here again, the Constitutional Court had the ultimate say, and as we have seen in Chapter 4, the outcome was that the court allowed early elections.

FRANCE

The constitution of the Fifth Republic in 1958 created a Constitutional Council, which was a very new development for France. The Council has nine regular members who are appointed for a nonrenewable term of nine years by the president of the republic (Chapter 4) and the presidents of the two chambers of Parliament, the National Assembly and the Senate. As a somewhat strange feature for an American reader, former presidents of the republic are de jure life members of the Constitutional Council, adding to the nine regular members.

It is also somewhat strange to an American reader that the French Constitutional Court is not the summit of a hierarchy of courts at lower levels. In this sense the Constitutional Court cannot properly be called a Supreme Court. As Alex Stone puts it, the Constitutional Court "does function as a kind of legislative chamber within parliamentary space, and an umpire in the political game." In what sense is the Constitutional Court an umpire in the political game? It supervises parliamentary work, stepping in at the time point when a law has been voted upon but before it is promulgated. The Constitutional Court has the authority to censure an entire law or part of it. For changes in political institutions of France it is mandatory for the Constitutional Court to step in. For ordinary laws and international agreements the Court only steps in when asked by either the president of the republic, the prime minister, the president of the National Assembly, the president of the Senate, 60 members of the National Assembly, or 60 members of the Senate. Alex Stone concludes that "one simply cannot understand the French legislative process without an understanding of the role, direct or indirect, of the Council." The Constitutional Courts also rules on the lawfulness of presidential and parliamentary elections.

There is another judicial body in France, the Council of State (*Conseil d'Etat*). It has about 300 members who are recruited from the top ranks of the very prestigious school of public administration (ENA, Ecole Nationale d'Administration). The Council of State steps in earlier in the political decision process than the Constitutional Council, namely already before a bill is submitted to the cabinet. The highly professional members of the Council of State examine the judicial soundness of the draft bills. The Council of State is also the highest administrative court in France, ruling on conflicts between different administrative units and complaints against the administration.

This chapter has shown that American lawyers who wish to do business in Europe are confronted with an overwhelming amount of variation among European countries. The complexity is greatly increased when we introduce, in Chapter 14, the European Court of Justice.

Discussion Questions

1. Since Great Britain does not have a written constitution, which body does, in effect, determine whether a law is constitutional or not?

2. What explains the presence of judicial review in the United States, and the absence of it in Great Britain?

3. Who decides in Switzerland whether a law is constitutional or not?

4. The function of "supreme courts" is generally described as "interpreting" the constitution. However, does judicial review not give courts a great influence in shaping, that is making laws? Does this power not interfere with the authority of parliaments whose job it is to make laws?

---

[1] Alec Stone. The Birth and Development of Abstract Review: Constitutional Courts and Policymaking in Western Europe. *Policy Studies Journal* 19 (Fall 1990): 81.

[2] Shapiro and Stone, The New Constitutional Politics in Europe, *Comparative Political Studies* 26 (January 1994): 400.

[3] Stone, The Birth and Development of Abstract Review, 82.

[4] *Neue Zürcher Zeitung*, April 10, 1992.

[5] Stone, The Birth and Development of Abstract Review, 81.

Federalism and Referendum

We have now covered the three classical branches of government—the legislative, the executive and the judicial branches. In this chapter we add two more institutional elements important for the operation of political parties: federalism and the referendum. We give particular emphasis to Switzerland, which has the most federalist structure in Europe and uses the referendum most often. We will then show that more federalism and more use of the referendum is a current topic in many European democracies. We end the chapter with a discussion of the advantages and disadvantages of strong federalism and a strong referendum.

Federalism and referendum are similar in that both institutions bring political decision making closer to the people. In a federalist country, many important political decisions are made not at the national level but at lower levels of governments, such as states and cantons. For federalism to exist, subnational units must have some autonomy, especially in financial matters. Federalism is most secured if subnational units can raise their own taxes. With the referendum, the voters have the final say in substantive political decisions such as taxes, health-care expenditures, and so on. The United States is a federalist country, and it uses the referendum in many states and local communities, although not at the national level. In Europe, Switzerland is the prototypical case of a federalist country with a strong referendum; we use the Swiss case to explain the basic features of federalism and the referendum. Later in the chapter, we will show that there is a trend in Europe toward more federalism and referenda, but also resistance against the expansion of these institutions.

SWITZERLAND: PROTOTYPICAL CASE OF A FEDERALIST COUNTRY WITH A STRONG REFERENDUM

The Latin root word of federalism, *foedus,* means "tie" or "bond." A federalist system of government consists of autonomous units that are tied together within one country. In Switzerland, these units are the 26 cantons. In a federalist government, the individual units are not simply bureaucratic districts of the central government; instead, they have their own independent power, which is constitutionally guaranteed. In other words, under federalism, government activities are divided and sometimes shared between one central and several regional governments. The opposite of a federalist government is a unitary government, in which regional units are merely bureaucratic in nature.

Switzerland has four official languages, which are all explicitly mentioned in the constitution: According to the 2000 census, 63.7 percent of the Swiss population speaks German, 20.4 percent French, 6.5 percent Italian, and 0.5 percent Romansh, which belongs to the family of Romance languages and is spoken only in Switzerland. The remaining 8.9 percent of the population, mainly foreigners, speaks a large variety of languages, with none of them having an official status. With regard to religion, 41.8 percent are Roman

Catholic, 35.3 percent Protestant, 7.5 percent indicate another denomination, while the remaining 15.5 did not give any religious denomination. Switzerland's regional differences range from remote mountain valleys to cosmopolitan cities such as Zurich and Geneva. Despite this diversity, Switzerland enjoys high political stability.

A major reason for this stability is its federalist structure. Its cantons are highly autonomous, and some of them proudly call themselves republics. The official name for the canton of Geneva, for example, is Republic of Geneva. Swiss federalism developed from the bottom up, in the sense that the cantons existed before the Swiss Confederation. The cantons built a *foedus*, to use the Latin expression, or bond, holding them together within a single political system. Thus, federalism in Switzerland can be compared to federalism in the United States, where the original 13 states also existed before the Union.

To understand Swiss federalism, it is important to emphasize that the cantons, not the linguistic communities, are the building blocks. All but four of the cantons are linguistically homogeneous. In the canton of Geneva, for example, public-school students are taught only in French. Leaving educational and cultural matters to the cantons alleviates a thorny problem for a multilingual country; for instance, the Swiss do not have to fight at the national level over which textbooks should be used in the schools. Such issues are handled at the cantonal level.

But other important issues must be dealt with at the national level. And here, there is always the possibility that blocs of cantons may form along linguistic lines, so that the language differential might still have political importance. This happened in 1996, for example, when Swissair, then still the national airline, canceled many intercontinental flights at the Geneva airport to concentrate them in Zurich. The French-speaking cantons reacted with bitter complaints. Divisions among the linguistic groups occur also in foreign policy issues, in particular with regard to the relationship of Switzerland to the European Union, where the French speakers are more willing to join than the German speakers.

Overall, such head-on confrontations between French- and German-speaking cantons are not too frequent. One reason is that the border between French- and German-speaking Switzerland is located in three bilingual cantons, blurring the distinction between linguistically based blocs of cantons. More important, neither the German-speaking nor the French-speaking parts of Switzerland are internally homogeneous. Important differences cut across the linguistic borders, and on certain issues some German speakers may have more in common with French speakers than they do with other German speakers. This is often true from an economic perspective: The tourist and banking industries, for example, are located in all three major linguistic areas. It would be very different if they were concentrated in only one language area. In that case, economic and linguistic interests would reinforce each other.

It is also significant that the Catholic–Protestant division cuts across the border between German and French speakers. Some German-speaking cantons are predominantly Catholic and others are Protestant, and the same internal division can be found among the French-speaking cantons. If the religious and linguistic areas were the same, it would be much more likely that coherent blocs of cantons would confront one another. But with linguistic, economic, and religious lines cutting across one another in a complex way, Swiss politics is characterized by constantly shifting coalitions. A German-speaking mountain farmer of the Catholic faith may have interests in common with other German speakers on one issue, with other Catholics—irrespective of language—on a second issue, and with other mountain farmers—irrespective of language and religion—on still a third issue. Due to these shifting coalitions, no single group is a permanent majority; each group risks being in the minority on at least some issues.

The absence of coherent language blocs also has the consequence that language is not always of prime importance. To be sure, in some issues language affiliation becomes a key consideration. But other identities, such as canton, religion, or occupation, are more important at other times. In addition, German speakers in Switzerland have a great number of distinct dialects, which is yet another base for identification. Given all this complexity, German speakers rarely function as a unified and dominant bloc in Swiss politics, despite their numerical majority.

Switzerland has no dominant capital, another factor that has helped make federalism work. If a country has a strong center, such as Paris in France, it is difficult to decentralize power, not only in form but also in fact. The Swiss parliament and the executive Federal Council are located in the capital, Bern, but the Swiss supreme court is located in French-speaking Lausanne. Bern is only the fourth largest city in Switzerland: Zurich, Basel, and Geneva each have more inhabitants. Bern is also not Switzerland's business or cultural center. In recent years, Zurich's economic importance has begun to be a problem for the complex and subtle balances in Swiss society. Representatives of other cantons complain that more and more of the largest companies are moving their headquarters to Zurich and that Zurich is becoming too much the economic center of Switzerland. On the other hand, Switzerland may need a strong economic center in order to remain internationally competitive.

Swiss federalism gives some powerful instruments for the exercise of power to the economically weaker cantons. As in the United States, Parliament in Switzerland has a second chamber in which each canton holds two seats, regardless of population.[1] Furthermore, when a constitutional amendment is submitted to a referendum, acceptance requires not only a majority of the voters but also a majority of the cantons. Another important aspect of Swiss federalism is that the cantons are regularly consulted about the drafting of federal legislation. Although this involvement seems to give a strong voice to the small cantons, a growing weakness of Swiss federalism becomes apparent in this process of cantonal consultation. As an economically highly developed country, Switzerland is increasingly confronted with very complex issues that require specialized expertise. This development puts the smaller cantons at a disadvantage, because they often lack the necessary professional staff to prepare well-researched answers for the federal authorities. This raises the question of how far decentralization can be taken without endangering the problem-solving capacity of a country.

With regard to the referendum, we have to be aware of the distinction between a representative and a direct form of democracy. If a democracy is of the representative type, the citizens elect their representatives, who then make the substantive decisions. In a direct democracy, substantive matters are decided by the citizens themselves in referenda. The notion of direct citizen involvement in actual decision making has deep roots in Swiss history. In medieval times, the pastures high in the mountains were communal property; thus, decisions about these pastures were made communally—for example when exactly in early summer to bring the cows up to the alpine pastures. When modern Switzerland was established with the constitution of 1848, its founders drew on these ancient traditions. In a mystical way, the Swiss spoke of reviving the old democratic freedoms. They remembered Old Switzerland too nostalgically, however. For example, they forgot that there were many serfs who did not share in the communal property of the pastures. But, however imperfect reference to the historical reality of medieval times was, it was crucially important that the 19th-century founders of modern Switzerland could cite democratic traditions that they were trying to restore. Combined with the revolutionary ideas of the Enlightenment, these old democratic traditions led the Swiss to incorporate the popular referendum in the constitution of 1848. In the beginning, the referendum was limited to constitutional amendments proposed by Parliament. Later in the 19th century, the people themselves received the right to propose constitutional amendments. The voters also got the right to call for a referendum on legislative bills. In Chapter 5 we described the rules with regard to the number of signatures necessary for a referendum to be held.

When the referendum was introduced, it was expected that its effect would be innovative. The founders of modern Switzerland wished to overcome the inaction of the old regime and its dominance by a few ruling families. They anticipated that the voters would be open to change, but in fact, the opposite was true, and the referendum has often had a delaying effect. The best example is the introduction of female suffrage. Parliament was prepared much earlier than ordinary male voters to grant women the right to vote. Several amendments to the constitution that would have established female suffrage were defeated in referenda. The margin of defeat, however, got smaller each time until, finally, in 1971, women were given the right to vote. This example is typical in the sense that it shows how it often takes a long time to convince the Swiss voters to accept a new idea. This is also shown in the slow approach of Switzerland toward the European Union. Switzerland is still not a full member of the EU, but in several referenda Swiss voters agreed to intensify the relationship with the EU with a set of bilateral treaties. An important such step was taken on September 25, 2005, when Swiss voters accepted that the free-labor market with the EU be extended to the new EU members in Central and Eastern Europe (see Chapter 14).

Of course, it is not always undesirable to delay a decision. Delay can prevent precipitous decisions that are regretted in retrospect. There have been quite a few cases in which the Swiss voters were wise not to move as quickly as their leaders desired. For example, some negative referenda prevented Switzerland from expanding its system of higher education as quickly as countries such as the Federal Republic of Germany had done. Today, it is generally agreed that these referenda had the positive result of less crowding in Swiss universities, as compared to overcrowded German Schools.

Although the referendum generally has had a delaying effect, on some occasions new ideas have been brought into public debate as a result of a referendum. Some students had the original idea of making one Sunday every month traffic-free on Swiss roads. This not only would have saved energy but also would have brought some calm to everyday life. Once a month, the highways would have been opened to strollers and bicyclists. The students collected enough signatures to allow the proposal to be submitted to a referendum. All major political parties and interest groups found the idea well-intentioned but impractical. In the popular vote, the students received broad support, but their proposal was still narrowly defeated. Despite this ultimate defeat, this is a good illustration of how the referendum can help to bring unorthodox ideas to public attention.

There are also cases where fresh ideas pass in the referendum. An illustration is the so-called Alp Initiative, where environmental groups collected enough signatures for the demand that within 10 years all heavy trucks passing through Switzerland be put on railroad flatbeds. Although the federal parliament shared the view that more trucks should be put on rails, it rejected the initiative as too extreme. Yet, 52 percent of the voters accepted the initiative.

How responsible are Swiss voters when they participate in a referendum? Is there a danger that they simply vote for their own narrow interests? Is there a threat that the interests of minorities are neglected? There is always the possibility of a tyranny of the majority. And, yes, there are cases in Swiss history when minorities suffered from the results of a referendum. In Chapter 5 we described how an anti-Semitic constitutional amendment prohibiting the slaughter of animals according to kosher rites was approved. Another conflict over minority rights concerns conscientious objectors. For a long time, Parliament was willing to allow them to serve the country outside the army, but attempts to change the constitution in this direction failed in several referenda, until finally the voters, too, accepted the idea that conscientious objectors need protection.

Such examples show the worst side of the referendum. But in other cases the referendum has revealed consideration for minority rights. Illustrative are several referenda on the issue of foreign workers in the 1970s. During the economic boom of the 1960s, Switzerland admitted so many foreign workers that they came to number more than 1 million in a total population that was then 6 million. This foreign presence was felt in many segments of Swiss society: In some school classes foreign children outnumbered Swiss children. Many Swiss no longer felt at home in their own country and began to refer to the "foreignization" of Switzerland. Politically, an antialiens movement developed, demanding a severe reduction in the number of foreigners allowed in Switzerland. This movement launched several constitutional initiatives that would have forced hundreds of thousands of foreigners to leave the country almost immediately. Swiss voters were greatly tempted to accept these constitutional initiatives. Not only was the economic boom over, but also Switzerland gave the impression of being overcrowded, with too much traffic on the highways and a severe housing shortage. To be sure, all major political parties and interest groups recommended rejection of the constitutional amendments as morally wrong. But there was the obvious danger that frustrated voters would vent their antiforeigner prejudices. No rational justification was necessary, only a mark on a secret ballot. The constitutional amendments received broad popular support but were defeated each time, although sometimes quite narrowly. The leading newspapers printed editorials applauding the maturity of Swiss voters.

How does the Swiss voter make his or her decision in a referendum? Is the Swiss citizen a wise sovereign who is well-informed and carefully weighs all arguments for and against a proposal? The referendum has certainly had an educating effect and has raised the level of political knowledge, but the Swiss citizen should not be viewed too idealistically. Propaganda is an important feature in referenda campaigns. Even more than in elections, the views of citizens can be molded in referenda. In elections, most voters have some long-standing party loyalty that is difficult to change. But in a referendum, voters may be very unfamiliar with the issue and consequently much more open to propaganda effects. Money and organization are, therefore, important weapons in referenda. However, a costly campaign can sometimes also backfire by creating sympathy for the financially weaker side.

Voter turnout in referenda is often shamefully low, sometimes only between 30 and 40 percent. At other times, however, the interest of the voters is great; in 1992, an unusually high 78 percent participated in a referendum about membership of Switzerland in the European Economic Area. For the expansion of the free-labor market to Central and

Eastern Europe mentioned earlier, turnout was also rather high—54 percent. Many explanations for the generally low turnout have been offered by scholars and other commentators. Might four times a year (on average) be too often to call on voters to cast their ballot? Have the issues become too complicated? Are the causes deeper? Do they lie, for example, in a selfish retreat into private lives or a general distrust of politics? In fact, the explanation of the generally low voter turnout probably lies in a combination of these and, possibly, other factors.

The greatest weakness of the referendum as practiced in Switzerland is that unconventional minorities are not sufficiently protected. The greatest strength of the referendum is the legitimacy it gives to political decisions. An increasing problem in modern democracies is the lack of legitimacy of many political decisions. Thus, transferring more political responsibility from politicians and bureaucrats to the people means the voters share the blame and cannot complain too much about the democratic legitimacy of the decisions.

EUROPEAN TREND TOWARD FEDERALISM AND REFERENDA

Traditionally, most European countries had a unitary form of government and no referendum, so that Switzerland was, for a long time, a special case. This has changed—a trend toward federalism and referenda is now apparent in many European countries. The most dramatic change from a unitary to a federalist government occurred in Germany after the defeat of the Nazis. Under Hitler, Germany was a unitary state, with all political power concentrated at the center. This government structure was seen as a major factor in Hitler's ability to take total control of his country. After his defeat in 1945, the occupying powers were eager to dismantle Germany's centralized government structure. The French even suggested breaking up Germany into several independent countries, so the military might of the German people would be broken forever. The division of Germany into eastern and western parts after World War II should be seen in this same context. Although the Western powers were not happy that the Soviet Union had established a Communist state in East Germany, they were not too unhappy that Germany was divided into two parts.

The effort to decentralize power in Germany was also apparent in 1949, when a democratic government was established in the three Western zones. The structure of that government—in accordance with the wishes of the three occupying powers, the United States, Great Britain, and France—was federalist in nature. The importance of this was reflected in the new country's name, the Federal Republic of Germany. Like the United States, the Federal Republic was divided into states (*Länder*). There were 11 Länder within the Federal Republic.[2] Some, such as Bavaria, had a long tradition of autonomy, and even independence, in German history. With German unification in 1990, 5 more Länder were added, so that today Germany consists of 16 Länder. Like the American states, the German Länder have areas for which they are solely or mostly responsible, such as education. The federal parliament has a second chamber, the Bundesrat, in addition to the Bundestag. The government of each German state sends representatives to the Bundesrat, where all federal bills that impact on Länder affairs must be passed. Federalism has helped to decentralize power in Germany. Important decisions are made not only at the federal level, but also in the state capitals. The negative side to this system is that government responsibilities are sometimes blurred. Despite this drawback, federalism has become firmly established in the German political culture.

Like Hitler in Germany, Mussolini established a strongly centralized structure of government in Italy. When democracy was restored after World War II, Italy remained a unitary state. To be sure, the 1948 constitution provided for autonomous regions. But this part of the constitution was only implemented for five so-called special regions at the periphery, such as the island of Sardinia. It was only in 1970 that regionalization was extended to the entire country, and Italy is now divided into 20 regions, each of which has a regional parliament and a regional cabinet. Why did this regionalist development occur in Italy? The main reason is not that the central government in Rome had too much power but, on the contrary, that it had too little. For many centuries, Italy had cultural and geographic but not political unity. Only during the second half of the 19th century was the country united politically, and its historically rooted political diversity is still felt today. The people of Naples, for example, have not forgotten that they had their own kingdom for centuries. Given the different historical traditions of the various regions of Italy, it is often difficult for the central government to exercise its authority today. Add to this bureaucratic sloppiness and corruption, and it is easy to see why the central government in Rome is often inefficient. The impetus behind regionalization is the hope that by bringing government closer to the people, its efficiency will increase. This is the same argument made in the United States for transferring more power from Washington to the states.

Can Italy's government now be classified as federalist? Compared with the American states and the German Länder, the Italian regions are weak. The fact that most of their revenues come from taxes collected by the central government and not by the regions is especially detrimental to their autonomy. On the other hand, regional authorities are elected by regional voters, not appointed by the central government. Thus, whether Italy today is classified as a unitary or a federalist government depends on the criteria used. Arend Lijphart is probably correct in his classification of Italy as still unitary because the autonomy of the regions is not yet sufficiently guaranteed by the constitution.[3] Yet, things are in flux, and as we have seen in Chapter 1, Italian regional parties have recently gained momentum, especially the Northern League under its charismatic leader Umberto Bossi.

Spain is another country with a strong regionalist trend. Francisco Franco, like his Fascist friends Hitler and Mussolini, established a strongly centralized government. When democracy was restored after Franco's death in 1975, the central authorities were immediately confronted with demands for regional autonomy. These demands, which were suppressed under Franco, could now be articulated under a democratic form of government. The demand for more autonomy is particularly intense and sometimes even violent in the Basque province, which has a cultural tradition distinct from that of the rest of Spain. The Basque problem is further complicated by the fact that Basques also live across the French border (see Chapter 12). Other Spanish provinces, such as Catalonia and Andalusia, also seek more autonomy.

In Great Britain, too, the central government in London is confronted today with vigorous demands from regional movements. These demands come mainly from the Scots, the Welsh, and the Irish Catholics in Northern Ireland. Although Great Britain's official name is the United Kingdom of Great Britain and Northern Ireland, it remains to be seen how united the country can remain. The Irish Catholics are fighting for independence from Great Britain and unification with the Republic of Ireland (Chapter 12). In Scotland and

Wales, although the main demand is for more autonomy, some people seek independence. The cases of Spain and Great Britain show that a federalist trend can, in fact, become so strong that separation becomes an option. This issue was raised in the United States in the Civil War.

Traditionally, the most unitary state in Europe has been France, the "one and indivisible nation." The basis for its unitary government structure was established in the time of absolutism of the Bourbon kings and was later reinforced by the regimes of Napoleon I and Napoleon III. As a result of these historical developments, Paris dominates the country like no other capital in Europe. Paris is not only the political but also the artistic, intellectual, and economic center of France. Nearly every fourth French person lives in metropolitan Paris. From a Parisian view, the rest of France is often considered, in a condescending way, as provincial. The departments into which France is divided are established as bureaucratic districts of the central government, not as means for local self-expression. Government buildings throughout France display no regional flags, only the national blue-, white-, and red-striped flag. But even in France, regional movements have begun to demand more local power—in Brittany, the Alsace, and on the island of Corsica, for example. Some concessions to these movements have already been made. Thus, it was a gesture of symbolic value when the prestigious École Nationale d'Administration was transferred from Paris to Strasbourg, the main city in the Alsace. As a correspondent of the *New York Times* wrote, "it is one of the more extraordinary sights in France: the future elite of the country, the exquisitely articulate men and women who will rule ministries and state industries, gathered . . . hundreds of miles from the corridors of power in Paris."[4] But it was equally of symbolic value when the highest administrative court of France decided that the elite school had to be moved back to Paris.[5] This episode shows how strong the central tradition in France still is.

Among the smaller European democracies the federalist trend is most apparent in Belgium, which was formerly a strictly unitary country and is now federalist in its institutional structure. The delicate language situation is behind this change in structure. In addition to a small German-speaking group, the two major linguistic groups are French-speaking Walloons and Dutch-speaking Flemish. Relations between Walloons and Flemish are especially tense in the capital, Brussels, and its suburbs, where the language border is often contested. There are endless debates, for example, about the language to be spoken at particular post offices. To the outside world such incidents may seem trivial, but they are indicative of underlying tensions between the linguistic groups. Belgium has now been transformed from a unitary to a federalist government structure. The details of the new structure are complex: Belgium is divided into three regions—French-speaking Wallonia, Dutch-speaking Flanders, and bilingual Brussels. In addition to these three regions, its governmental structure contains three so-called cultural communities: French, Dutch, and German speakers. To make things even more complicated, the Dutch-speaking community has been united with the Dutch-speaking region, so that there are altogether five governmental units. As one newspaper puts it, this looks like a "fragile federalist structure."[6]

A major reason for the federalist trend in Europe is the wish of the citizens to bring political power closer to the grassroots level. This wish also accounts for the trend to have more political decisions made in referenda. Voters increasingly feel that they are qualified enough to speak for themselves. They reject the idea that all decisions should be made by professional politicians, whom they tend to view with decreasing respect. Many recent corruption scandals have eroded public respect for politicians. Today, many European citizens have begun to ask why politicians know what the people need better than the people themselves. A push for referenda also comes from a development described in Chapter 2—namely, that the traditional party labels have lost meaning when it comes to new issues such as drugs and the environment. Voters often have little knowledge of which party to vote for in order to do something about such issues. Would it not be better in such cases to let the voters speak for themselves in a referendum? Even when party labels still do have meaning, many European voters feel that important decisions are made not by the parties but by powerful interest groups and state bureaucracies. A vote for a particular party may not have any great impact in certain cases, and interest groups and bureaucracies are almost immune to election results. Here again, voters may wish to exercise their influence not only in elections but also in referenda.

David Butler and Austin Ranney argued some time ago that referenda "are almost certain to increase in number and importance in the years ahead."[7] This has indeed happened in many European countries. Illustrations are Sweden and Austria, which settled the tricky issue of nuclear power in referenda. In Italy and Ireland, the divorce issue was very controversial for many years and was finally submitted to a referendum. For matters of the European Union (EU) the referendum has gained particular importance (Chapter 14). Thus, Denmark, France, and Ireland let the voters decide the ratification of the Maastricht treaty of the EU. Some of the Central and Eastern European countries decided entry into the EU with a referendum. France and the Netherlands rejected the proposed constitution of the European Union in a referendum.

ARGUMENTS AGAINST FEDERALISM AND REFERENDA

Although there is a trend toward federalism and referenda in Europe, one should not overlook the arguments that are made against this trend. With regard to federalism one hears warnings that public monies may be wasted if each subnational unit tries to solve problems on its own, as unnecessary duplications may occur, for example, with regard to research and development. It is also argued that fairness in the treatment of all citizens can be guaranteed only if national standards, for example for education and health care, are set and implemented. Arguments against referenda are even more vocal because they touch on basic issues of democratic life. Great Britain is the country where one most often hears fundamental objections to the referendum. Whereas supporters of the referendum stress that democracy is, above all else, government *by* the people, the British see the ideal of democracy best-fulfilled in government *of and for* the people. At the core of this notion is the belief that Parliament can better speak for the people than the people themselves. Parliament is *of the people* in the sense that its members are elected by the citizenry; but once elected, Parliament is sovereign and has not only the right but the duty to make decisions for the people. According to British political thinking, Parliament cannot delegate this duty to anyone else—not even to the people.

How do the British justify the idea that decisions are best made in Parliament? There is a certain sacred mystique about the British House of Commons, located in Westminster Palace on the Thames River in the heart of London. Westminster is considered the birthplace of modern parliament, and there, generation after generation, the people have spoken out through their representatives. In the British view, the crucial point is that the voice of the people is not only heard but debated. In this process of debate, the people's true needs are expected to be clarified and to emerge in a "purified" form. Thus, the "sum" of the people's will expressed in the decisions of the House of Commons is more than the mere addition of what all individual citizens desire. Arguments are judged not simply according to the frequency with which they are expressed but also according to their logic and plausibility. Parliamentary debate also takes account of the intensity with which a position is held. The British doctrine is that in a referendum the voice of the people is expressed in raw form, whereas in parliamentary debate these manifold voices are integrated through negotiation into a more coherent overall will. The members of Parliament are able to exercise a strong leadership role with this doctrine. They are not simply messengers for the demands of the voters; their task is, rather, to put those demands into the larger context of the common good. This approach is supposed to lead to the best possible legislation.

As might be expected, the reality of the House of Commons does not correspond to this idealistic doctrine. Debates are often partisan and rancorous, and they sometimes deteriorate into shouting matches. Despite such behavior, the doctrine that parliamentary debate helps to transform the will of individual voters into the general will of the people still helps to justify the belief that a true democracy should be of a representative, not a direct, nature. In their long history, the British have held only a single national referendum: in 1975, over Britain's continued membership in the European Community, now known as the European Union (Chapter 14). Two years earlier, when the Conservatives were in power, Britain had joined the European Community. Labor was badly split on the issue, and they saw no other way to resolve their internal conflict when they came to power than to organize a national referendum. The notion that Parliament is sovereign was not formally overthrown with the referendum, however, because it was explicitly stated that the referendum was to be advisory only. The governing Labour Party followed the advice of the people, who, according to the referendum, wished to remain in the European Community.

The 1975 referendum may have set an important precedent. It can be argued that if a British government ever wishes to withdraw from the European Union, it will first have to obtain the assent of the voters in a referendum. The possibility of a referendum was discussed for the ratification of the Treaty of Maastricht of the European Union. But the Conservative government of John Major prevailed with its argument that the instrument of the referendum was alien to the parliamentary tradition of the country. Major stressed the advantages of parliamentary scrutiny against a decision in a referendum "where many votes may be cast on matters wholly unrelated to the treaty." By contrast, the House of Commons "will scrutinise the bill line by line, clause by clause and vote on it in the same way."[8] John Major presented here in a classical manner the British argument against the usage of the referendum. If Great Britain, however, wants to join one day in use of the euro, the European currency (Chapter 14), the arguments of John Major will probably not hold and a referendum will be organized.

In the United States in the 1970s, there was some movement in Congress to introduce the referendum at the federal level. But this movement never got off the ground, and the issue has disappeared from the political agenda. Based on the European experience with the referendum, should the issue be brought up again in Washington?

In Chapters 3 through 6 we have explained all the major features of the institutional setting within which European political parties compete with each other. Although no democracy can do without political parties, we have to consider in the next two chapters that there are other important actors exercising great influence in European politics: social movements (Chapter 7) and economic interest groups (Chapter 8).

Discussion Questions

1. Does the result of a referendum in general reflect the "will of the people"?

2. Who is most likely to turn out for a referendum?

3. The constitution of the United States is based on "We, the people . . .", and yet, there are no national referendums in the United States. Why is this so?

4. Are referendums in general more applicable to small or large states?

5. Is it correct to say that policies based on referendums are more democratic than policies enacted by legislators in Parliaments?

6. Are referendums equally useful for any political issues? For instance, are referendums equally useful for deciding whether immigrants should have access to public benefits or whether to engage in a mix of fiscal policies and austerity programs in order to create higher economic growth?

---

[1] For the half-cantons, see Chapter 3.
[2] Berlin (West) was also a Länder but had a special status.
[3] Arend Lijphart. *Democracies: Patterns of Majoritarian and Consensus Government in Twenty-one Countries*. (New Haven: Yale University Press, 169–186).
[4] *New York Times*, February 13, 1993.
[5] *Neue Zürcher Zeitung*, June 5–6, 1993.
[6] *Neue Zürcher Zeitung*, April 24–25, 1993.
[7] David Butler and Austin Ranney. *Referendums: A Comparative Study of Practice and Theory*. (Washington, DC: American Enterprise Institute, 1978, 226).
[8] *Financial Times*, September 8, 1992.

Social Movements

This chapter covers the environmental movement, the peace and third-world movement, the women's movement, and the youth movement. Social movements do not compete in elections and they are not represented in cabinets, but as we will see in this chapter, they have many other ways to influence policy outcomes in European democracies.

As political scientist Hanspeter Kriesi correctly states, social movements "are highly elusive phenomena which are inherently difficult to grasp."[1] As noted, this chapter covers the environmental movement, the peace and third-world movement, the women's movement, and the youth movement. What do these movements have in common? Kriesi offers a useful definition of social movements that includes all those just mentioned. He considers a social movement "to be an organized, sustained, self-conscious challenge to existing authorities on behalf of constituencies whose goals are not effectively taken into account by these authorities."[2] The key element of this definition is that social movements attract dissatisfied outsiders who challenge the policies of the authorities. And, in contrast to political parties and economic interest groups, social movements are only loosely organized. As Kriesi puts it, "except for a small group of core movement activists who staff the social movement organization, individual citizens are solicited for active participation in movement campaigns only for limited periods of time."[3] Such campaigns try to catch the public eye using actions such as street demonstrations, hunger strikes, occupations of buildings, petitions, and all sorts of happenings. Kriesi says about action campaigns:

> Each action campaign is spatially and temporally limited. The totality of the action campaigns concerned with a particular challenge makes up the movement. To the extent that there is a degree of coherence and continuity to the challenge, it is secured by the organizational infrastructure of the movement.[4]

Such action campaigns are not specific to Europe; American readers also are aware of the phenomenon from their own country.

ENVIRONMENTAL MOVEMENT

In Europe, as in the United States, there is an increasing concern about the environment. In Europe the concern may be even more immediate, because Europeans live in much more crowded conditions than Americans. Most European countries have a much higher population density than the United States. The Netherlands, the most densely populated European country, has 13 times more people living per square kilometer than the United States. For the European Union at large, population density is four times higher than in the United States.

The environmental concern in Europe began in the 1960s, primarily with regard to water pollution. At that time the problem was basically seen in technical terms. It was thought that sufficient know-how and financial resources could remedy the situation. This expectation was justified with regard to water pollution, and today some European rivers and lakes are cleaner than they were 30 years ago. Swimming is even allowed at a few places where it was prohibited only a short while ago, and salmon can be found today in London's Thames River.

In the 1970s, worries began to develop about the environmental impact of nuclear power, with the discussion taking a more fundamental turn. People questioned whether there should be limits to economic growth in order to eliminate the need for provision of more and more energy. For many environmentalists, disposal of radioactive waste material became a symbol for technological development over which the experts had lost control. Fears were expressed about genetic damage to future generations.

During the 1980s, the environmental question assumed greater urgency when it began to be publicly reported that many of Europe's forests would be dead by the end of the century because of air pollution. This brought home the problem to many who had not been particularly concerned before. Suddenly, warnings about catastrophic consequences to nature were relevant not merely to the indefinite future but also to the present.

The fight against air pollution became a prime political issue. But the task was much more difficult than the fight against water pollution: Dirty air cannot simply be cleaned mechanically like dirty water. The fight for clean air must begin at the sources of pollution, and many environmentalists believe that the fight cannot be won without basic changes in people's lifestyles. (Concerning the question of a simpler lifestyle, see also the discussion on the Green Party in Chapter 2.) Some steps have already been taken to change the lifestyles of Europeans in environmentally sound directions. Strong efforts have been made, for example, to curtail private transportation and to bring about a shift toward using more public transportation. Many European inner cities now ban private cars and allow only public transportation and taxis. (See Box 7.1.)

European business leaders are also increasingly receptive to environmental concerns, accepting the principle that environmental costs of production be added to the selling price of products. Expressed in technical economic terms, this means that external environmental costs are internalized into the selling price. When you buy, for example, a battery for your flashlight, the cost for the recycling of the battery is already included in the price. When you have used up the battery you can bring it back to any store selling batteries. With this system a very high number of batteries are recycled in a professional manner, which is excellent for companies in the recycling business. Thus, the principle that external costs are internalized into the selling price is ultimately good for innovative businesses in this area.

How is the environmental movement in European countries organized? Because of its multilayered historical development, it has anything but a unified structure. Associations for the beautification of nature existed long before the general public became concerned about the environment. Traditionally, these associations promoted such causes as the protection of rare plants and animals and the building of foot trails. Mostly organized in an old-fashioned way, they reacted rather slowly when environmental questions became politically explosive issues. Most of these older associations eventually adapted their organizational structures to the new political situation, and today many of them play an important role in the environmental movement.

A second layer of environmental groups arose more or less spontaneously from specific local issues. These groups became known under the term *citizen initiatives*. When a town or a neighborhood was threatened with some environmental danger, such as toxic

---

Box 7.1 Amsterdam Plans Wide Limit on Cars

AMSTERDAM—Even for a city that relishes the social experiment, this city's plan for a new urban lifestyle may appear unusually radical. Amsterdam wants to be the first major European city that virtually banishes the car from its heart. Wall-to-wall traffic, noise, and fumes in the stovepipe streets and stiff gridlocks on the canal bridges have brought on the decision. The present image of the automobile here is approximately that of a leech on the body of the community. "For years the city was forced to adapt to cars," said Rob Pistor, a city official and one of the plan's chief strategists. "Cars will now have to adapt to the city." In the first stage, beginning this year, the plan aims to curtail traffic and to make life as unpleasant as possible for motorists who insist on nudging their way around the city's inner ring of canals. Cars will be squeezed off by wider sidewalks and new bicycle lanes, and parking spaces will be cut back sharply. In the final stage, all nonvital traffic is to be banned. Though the plan has wide backing from frustrated residents, business groups are warning against the dangers: What may be a victory for the quality of life could bring on the decline if not the collapse of economic life in the inner city. The Amsterdam plan, experts say, will serve as a test case for other cities because, across Western Europe, the competition between man and machine is slowly shifting in favor of the pedestrian. What began as a modest trend in many cities to close off the occasional shopping street is growing into a movement of larger car-free zones.

Source: *New York Times*, January 28, 1993.

---

waste or a nuclear power plant, and no political parties or other organizations were willing to help, ordinary citizens often took the initiative and organized to defend their interests. Because their fights sometimes continued for years, after a while these groups tended to take on a more sustained organization, often directing their attention to other issues and staying together even when the original issue had been settled.

A third layer appeared when environmentalists began to organize their own political party. In Chapter 2 the development of the Greens as an environmental party was described. However, the Green Party does not speak for the entire environmental movement. Many environmentalists prefer to stay outside a party framework, whereas others try to work within the older parties—a fourth layer of the environmental movement. Most of the political parties have recently turned their attention to environmental concerns. This is particularly true of the Socialists but also of the Conservatives. The latter play with the word *conservation* and argue that conservation of nature has always been a key point in Conservative thinking.

When asked in surveys about their most immediate concerns, citizens in Europe rank the environment much lower than 10 or 20 years ago. Other issues, in particular economic issues such as unemployment, top the agenda. The environment is also less of a hot political issue because the environmental movement was so successful that its demands have, in the meantime, almost universally been accepted by all political parties, at least in their programmatic statements. This does not mean that there is no longer work to be done with regard to the environment in Europe. For example, despite excellent public transportation, there are still too many private cars on European roads, contributing to air and noise pollution. Such external costs of private cars are more internalized in the price of gas than in the United States, making gas much more expensive in Europe than in the United States. But the price of gas in Europe would have to be raised still much higher for all external costs of private driving to be internalized.

PEACE AND THIRD-WORLD MOVEMENT

The movement against war goes in cycles in European history. Beginning in the 1920s, after the atrocities of World War I, pacifists sought complete disarmament so no other war would ever occur. But these early pacifists could not prevent the coming to power of Adolf Hitler and the outbreak of World War II, with its even greater atrocities. The 1950s brought mass protests against nuclear armaments, especially in Great Britain and the Federal Republic of Germany. During the late 1960s, students all over Western Europe organized massive demonstrations against the military involvement of the United States in Vietnam. At this time, the European peace movement began to be closely linked with third-world issues. The war in Vietnam was seen as an imperialist enterprise of the foremost power of the Western world against a poor, third-world country.

With the beginning of the Reagan area in the early 1980s, the European peace movement got a new push. The deployment of American nuclear missiles in Europe—decided by NATO in 1979—became the prime target of peace activists, many of whom wished to abolish the entire American military presence in Europe. The professed goal of the peace movement was to distance Europe from the tensions between the Soviets and the Americans. A policy of neutralism or nonalignment was advocated for Europe. Even more than in earlier periods, peace and third-world issues were closely linked. The military help of the United States for the Contras in Nicaragua came under particular criticism by the European peace movement. Another prominent target was the support of Western countries and multinational corporations for the white apartheid regime in South Africa. In both Nicaragua and South Africa, the European peace movement saw the rich West use military force and other forms of oppression against poor, third-world groups.

The end of the cold war brought the European peace movement into a deep crisis. The crisis began in December 1987, when Mikhail Gorbachev, for the Soviet Union, and Ronald Reagan, for the United States, signed the Intermediate Range Nuclear Forces (INF) Treaty, which mandated from both sides the withdrawal of all medium- and short-range missiles in Europe. The first reaction of the peace movement to the INF Treaty was celebration. As political scientist Diarmuid Maguire describes it for Britain:

> On the day the INF Treaty was signed local peace groups lit beacons all over Britain as a mark of celebration. Greater Manchester Campaign for Nuclear Disarmament organized a victory march at which slices of sponge cake were distributed. . . . thousands of women surrounded Greenham Common (a missile site) to celebrate the future departure of Cruise missiles.[5]

Was the signing of the INF Treaty and the ensuing end of the cold war indeed the result of the actions of the peace movement? Did its mass demonstrations in the early and mid-1980s pay off? Although this is what the peace movement claims, another plausible interpretation is that it was the initial deployment of the American missiles in Europe that ultimately helped the cause of peace. Only when the Soviets saw that the Americans were willing to continue to defend Europe did they agree to negotiate about the missiles. According to this interpretation, the peace movement was not a help but, rather, an obstacle to peace. If its mass demonstrations had been successful in preventing the deployment of the American missiles, the danger of adventurous actions by the Soviet Union would have increased greatly. Which interpretation is correct? An objective answer is difficult to give, perhaps even impossible. Both sides will continue for years to insist on their own interpretation.

Despite all their celebrations, the peace activists were also worried. As Maguire has found for Britain:

> Campaign for Nuclear Disarmament organisers were worried that the beginning of change at the top of international politics would lead to the end of the movement from below. . . . the dilemma for Campaign organisers was how to raise movement morale by claiming a success without exacerbating the process of demobilisation.[6]

Unfortunately, the INF Treaty and the end of the cold war did not mean peace in Europe. As we see in Chapter 12, ethnic and national conflicts dramatically increased, in particular in former Yugoslavia. Did this increase in violence lead to new activities of the peace movement? Not at all. To be sure, there were some individual actions in support of peace in Yugoslavia, but no mass movement by any count. In contrast to the time of the cold war, it was much more difficult to identify the villains against whom one could organize mass rallies. Atrocities were committed by all sides—Serbs, Croats, and Muslims. As Alice Holmes Cooper demonstrates, the peace movement was severely split over the war, especially in Germany.[7] When the issue of whether Germany should participate in the peacekeeping action of NATO in Bosnia came up, a part of the German peace movement was supportive, accepting that sometimes weapons have to be used for the sake of peace. But another part of the German peace movement took a fundamental pacifist position, arguing that the use of weapons is always wrong.

A new lift for the European peace movement came with the war in Iraq. There were again large street demonstrations. In Italy, for example, rainbow flags with the peace sign (pace) could be seen at many houses. Generally speaking, the success of the peace movement depends, of course, very much on the international situation, but the general conclusion is that Europe has much more a pacifist tradition than the United States. In Europe there is much more a political left that can be mobilized in the name of peace. The churches are also more willing in Europe than in the United States to become politically active in the name of world peace.

WOMEN'S MOVEMENT

For an American reader, the women's movement in Europe is relatively easy to understand, because it raises, although with some delay, many of the same issues the women's movement in the United States has raised. In this respect, there is indeed a strong American influence in Europe, where American feminist authors have been widely read. In many ways, the women's movement has had a more difficult time in Europe, because individualism is less emphasized than in the United States. (For the lesser role of individualism in Europe, see also Chapter 6 and Chapter 1.) In Europe, the notion that not only individuals but also groups have basic rights is much more common than in the United States. In Europe, the family as a group is treated as a crucial economic unit; the argument is made that the important consideration is that each family has a decent income. From this premise it follows that in the case of a lack of jobs, families with two breadwinners should give up one job to families with no breadwinner at all. This has meant for a long time—and still does to some extent—that a woman has to give up her job in favor of a man. It is precisely against this situation that the growing women's movement protests and argues that women, as individuals, should have their own inalienable rights.

The belief that women are not the equal of men has deep roots in European history. Popular culture has had a profound effect on how women should behave. Under the influence of the women's movement, studies have been done about 18th- and 19th-century books on marriage for young women, which were widely read at the time. The basic message of these books was that wives should be subservient to their husbands. Fulfillment in their lives would come from providing their husbands with a pleasant home where they could find peace and tranquility far from the struggles of the outside world. According to these books, it was a wife's duty to discover the wishes of her husband and to make every attempt to fulfill those wishes. If the husband was in a bad mood and complained loudly, it was recommended that the wife keep calm. There were no such guidebooks to how men should behave toward their wives. Men's task was simply to earn a living. In return, they had the right to be spoiled by their wives.

It was not only in popular but also in high culture that women were put in a subservient role. The women's movement points to many sexist remarks in the long history of European philosophers, poets, and writers. An extreme example is the often-quoted statement by the 19th-century German philosopher Friedrich Nietzsche, in which he said that men should take the whip when they go to a woman. Such writings in both popular and high culture had a strong influence on the behavior of women. Women themselves were eager to follow the set standards because they were socialized to accept them as desirable behavior. As in Marxism (Chapter 10), here, too, we can speak of the existence of a false consciousness. Just as many proletarians did not rebel against their exploited status, many women gladly accepted their inferior position. In this context, it is noteworthy that in Europe many women fought against the introduction of women's suffrage. Politics was considered by them to be something dirty and from which women should be kept, in their own best interests.

In legal terms, the situation for European women has dramatically improved. Women's suffrage has been introduced everywhere. Switzerland was the last country to do so by means of an all-male popular referendum in 1971. Although legal discrimination against women has largely been remedied and women participate more in the labor force, there is still much discrimination. In the universities, for example, presently very few women who have attained the rank of professor. As in the United States, the argument is made that female students need female teachers as role models. Special women's days are organized at many universities to draw attention to these demands. Student newspapers have special issues devoted to women's issues. Research projects are launched to study the discrimination against women. The push for more opportunities for women may be strongest and most visible in the universities, but there are also efforts to increase leadership positions for women in political parties, churches, unions, and other areas.

For the women's movement, this push has not only a quantitative but also a qualitative aspect. The goal is not merely to increase the number of women in leadership positions, but also to redefine the role expectations for women leaders. Women should not simply try to imitate the role patterns of men in leadership positions. What, then, should be the proper behavior of women in leadership positions? This issue is hotly debated among feminists, and many different opinions are articulated. The necessity of a special women's culture is stressed, but it is not altogether clear what the key characteristics of this culture should be. A common theme is that female leaders should think in less compartmentalized terms than male leaders. They would tend to see political issues in more global terms. Thus, female leaders would, for example, be more sensitive to how too-rapid economic growth may negatively influence the quality of life of ordinary people. With such a broader view, women would apply a more general principle of rationality, whereas male leaders would tend to be rational in a narrower sense, concentrating on how a particular decision would influence profit levels but forgetting the impact it would have on the environment. Thus, the argument is not that male leaders would be more rational and female leaders more emotional. Rather, the difference would be that women would include broader elements in their decision making than men would.

That leaders can be both men and women should be expressed more clearly in everyday language is an issue about which the women's movement is very concerned. The specific words we use in both public and private domains determine how we see the world. If language refers to leadership positions only in masculine form, we tend to think of leaders only as men. In languages such as German and French, this problem is even more acute than in English, because in these languages the article has both a masculine and a feminine form. Whereas in English the article *the* can refer either to a man or a woman, in German the article *der* refers to a man and the article *die* to a woman. The same difference exists in French with the articles *le* and *la*. Nouns, too, may have masculine and feminine forms. The English term *director* is, respectively, *Direktor* in German and *directeur* in French in the case of a man, and *Direktorin* and *directrice* in the case of a woman. The women's movement insists that in such cases the feminine form should be used as often as the masculine form so the language properly expresses that directors may be both men and women. Some professions have traditionally been so dominated by men that a feminine form does not even exist. Thus, in French there is only a masculine form for professor, namely *professeur*. Should the feminine form *professeuse* be introduced, or should a female professor be called *madame le professeur*? Some critics consider such issues to be trivial, but many people in the women's movement argue that equal status for women will never be achieved if our languages are not changed properly.

The women's movement also has many specific projects, in particular rape crisis centers, houses for battered women, hotels for women, taxis for women, bookstores for women, discos for women, and self-defense courses for women, music for women, theater for women, and self-actualization groups for women. There is a strong element of group solidarity in the women's movement. In the anonymous world of today, sisterhood gives many women an emotional and natural bond. To be with other women gives them a feeling of satisfaction. There was occasionally an alliance between the women's and the Marxist movements, both of which fight for groups that are exploited in society. But many women found among Marxists the same male chauvinism that appears in society at large and decided to stay among themselves. The hope is that in the women's movement, a feeling of togetherness will develop and that every woman will have the same status and the same say. The women's movement has the ambition to practice internally a lifestyle of fundamental democratization and thus to serve as an example for society at large.

Several studies have shown that Europeans are beginning to develop a more positive attitude toward a stronger role of women in politics and society; thus one may conclude that the women's movement has been quite successful in Europe. European women are also more protected by an extensive welfare state that provides for generous child care, day care, job protection, health care for both mother and child, and many other such programs. As a result, the reason why the women's movement in Europe is not as vocal as the American one is because many women's concerns have already been addressed via the welfare state. Women also have gained more access to important political positions than in the United States. In the Scandinavian countries, for instance, women are quite numerous in important political positions. In Sweden, for example, by 2004, 45.3 percent of members of Parliament were women, compared to 38.4 percent in 1990. During the same time period the number of women in the U.S. House of Representatives increased from 6.6 percent to 14.3 percent. In 2000, France passed the "parity law," which requires that in parliamentary and municipal elections half of the slate of candidates must be women, or fines must be paid. The first test of this law was the 2002 election, which was subject to this rule. With the exception of the National Front, which managed to put up 49 percent female candidates, no other parties even came close to fielding a slate of 50 percent women on their lists.[8] (See Box 7.2.)

Political measures are also taken to expand the role of women in the business sector. An unusually far-reaching measure was put in effect in Norway in 2006, requiring that in the next two years 40 percent of the board members of the nation's large, publicly traded private companies be women. Ms. Bekkemellem, the minister of children and equality, commented on the measure in the following way: "The government's decision is to see that women will have a place where the power is, where leadership takes place in this society. This is a very forceful affirmative action, but it will set an example for other centers of society."[9] That this Norwegian law could go into effect does not mean that all men were supportive. As a male business leader formulated his criticism: "It is contrary to the principles of a free society to tell private businessmen whom they must put on their corporate boards."[10] But she added that businessmen will comply with the law.

YOUTH MOVEMENT

If we compare the younger generation in America and Europe, the most striking difference is a more critical and pessimistic attitude toward the future among young Europeans. To understand the situation of their peers in Europe, young Americans must understand the very different educational system in Europe. Education is organized somewhat differently from one European country to another, but despite such national variations we can speak of a general European pattern, which is quite different from the American pattern. Until about the mid-1960s, the European educational system was geared toward a small elite,

Box 7.2 French Women in Politics: The Long Road to Parity

U.S.–FRANCE ANALYSIS, MAY 2001

The March 2001 municipal elections in France did not produce the expected *vague rose*—or electoral domination of the Left—but French politics are nonetheless taking on a distinctively pinker tint. For the first time since its adoption last year, the law on political parity, ensuring equal access to political representation for both men and women, has been implemented. . .

On June 28, 1999, articles 3 and 4 of the French Constitution were amended. The law promoting equal access for men and women to elected positions was adopted on June 6, 2000. . .

The March [2001] municipal elections have shown that applying the law has not always been easy. In some areas of France, meeting the 50% requirement posed a challenge because of a lack of women volunteers. Aspiring mayors of all political shades have therefore been seeking new women candidates to meet their quotas, and several extreme right lists have had to withdraw for lack of female participation. In a few cases, as in the town of Les Ulis near Paris, too many women proposed to seek office, and some had to step down to ensure that their male counterparts could meet their own share of the quota. . .

The idea of pursuing political parity through strict quotas has not received unanimous support in France. . . In February 1999, 14 prominent women, including philosopher Elisabeth Badinter, lawyer Evelyne Pisier and writer Danielle Sallenave, publicly voiced their opposition to forced parity. They argued that the reform would undermine the concept of universalism in political representation and therefore open the door to demands from other specific groups based on race, religion, or sexual preference. For feminists fighting for gender blindness, the law therefore represented a step backward. Other women have found the idea insulting and unnecessary. They claim that France's political elites will not be able to ignore public opinion favoring a more feminized representation indefinitely. They cite as an example the Scandinavian experience in which high levels of female political representation were achieved without formal quotas. . .

The discussion of gender inequalities in politics and business also masks the more fundamental issue of the unequal division of tasks at home. A government study conducted in 1999 has confirmed that women still bear 80% of domestic tasks. Working women still spent over three hours on domestic tasks every day. This is only four minutes less than in 1986, and still a staggering two hours more than their male counterparts. This heavy burden of work at home remains a practical obstacle for women wishing to take on political and corporate responsibilities. "Responsibilities for day-to-day life still rest on women," said Elisabeth Guigou, now Minister of Labor. "Day-to-day life is particularly difficult for a woman politician since politics is one of the activities that least respects the rhythms of private time. . ." At work as in politics, parity will have to start at home.

Source: Caroline Lambert, Brookings Institution

which alone was eligible for higher education. Since then, Europe has changed to a pattern of mass education, with a larger proportion of young people going to a university. This change caused many problems with which young Europeans have to struggle today.

Under the earlier system, selection for higher education occurred very early, in most places at around the age of 11 or 12. On the basis of strict exams, a small number of students, usually not more than 5 percent of the respective age group, was accepted into university preparatory schools. These schools had different names: in Germany, *Gymnasium*; in France, *lycée*. The curriculum was very demanding, for example, with six hours of Latin per week. At the age of 18 or 19, students were required to take an extensive final exam. If they passed, they were eligible to enter any university and any field. The name of this exam varied from country to country; the term *Matura*—used, for example, in Switzerland—perhaps best expresses the nature of the exam. After a broad education, the student was considered "mature" enough to begin university studies. Unlike in America, no distinction was made between undergraduate and graduate studies in European universities. If students wished to study medicine, they enrolled in the faculty for medicine; if they wished to study law, in the faculty for law; and so forth. Usually only one degree was offered: A doctorate after five or six years of studies.

This system fostered a small, homogeneous, highly educated elite. If one did not belong to this elite, educational options were limited. Mandatory education ended at the age of 15 or 16. Afterward, you could immediately enter the workforce or enter an apprenticeship for three or four years. As an apprentice, you could learn a trade in a practical way, by working in a bakery or a bank, for example. Included in the apprenticeships were also a few hours of trade school per week.

This educational system had the big advantage of being inexpensive. But in the 1960s many Europeans began to wonder whether they needed a more expensive system. The U.S. model seemed particularly attractive, for at this time Americans were economically very successful and much admired in Europe. Europeans were impressed by the broad-based American system of higher education that allowed a large number of young people to continue their education beyond the secondary level. These educational opportunities were perceived as instrumental to American economic success, and most European reformers came to the conclusion that an expansion of higher education would be the key to the development of a stronger economy. From this perspective, the severe shortcomings of the old system were apparent. Early selection of university students was seen as giving an undue advantage to children from a milieu in which education was already important. It was feared that under this system Europe had lost many late-blooming talents.

So it was that, beginning in the mid-1960s, many profound changes were implemented in the European educational system, with some countries, such as the Netherlands and Sweden, moving much faster than others. One crucial change was made in the preparatory schools for university entrance, which set their entering age much later, at 15 or 16. Partly as a result of this change, the number of students in preparatory schools increased dramatically. In many countries preparatory schools begin to resemble American high schools. This expansion naturally led to a strong increase in the number of university students. The United States still has the most students in universities and colleges, but some European countries are now approaching the American situation. The American influence on European universities is most visible in the renaming of the degrees that one obtains.

Based on a decision reached by the European education ministers in the Italian city of Bologna, European universities now follow the so-called Bologna model, according to which there are three degree levels: bachelor, master, and doctorate.

Important changes also took place with regard to apprenticeships, where the emphasis has shifted from practical work to formal schooling. Many apprentices today have two or more days per week of full-time classes. Opportunities also have been opened for continuing education after the apprenticeship. Such further schooling can even lead a student to transfer to a university without first attending preparatory school.

In many respects the reforms have not fulfilled their promise. This is probably due less to the basic idea of the reforms than to their often hasty implementation. Another negative factor was that after the mid-1970s, economic conditions worsened in Europe, so less money was available for reforms. Today there is much confusion, even crisis, in the European educational system. Universities are overenrolled because staff and buildings were not adapted to the large increase in the number of students. Where formerly professors and students interacted in small groups, there are now large lecture classes and a sense of anonymity. Job prospects after graduation are much worse than under the old university system, when jobs were plentiful for the small number of graduates. Most European families still expect that children with a university education will achieve a high-status position in society. Frustration is then all the greater when university graduates land only low-level jobs or no jobs at all. Even medical doctors have difficulty finding work, and countries such as Spain and Italy have thousands of unemployed physicians. Under these unsatisfactory conditions, it is no wonder that pessimism prevails in Europe's universities.

At the apprentice level, the situation is no better. In the past, obtaining a university education was so unrealistic for most young Europeans that they felt proud and privileged to earn an apprenticeship degree. Today, many parents are almost embarrassed to say that their child is "only" an apprentice, because this implies that their child is not smart enough to make it to a university. And, as with university graduates, job prospects for apprentices are bleak, partly because many positions that formerly were reserved for apprenticeship graduates are now taken by university graduates. A further problem is that with hard economic times many employers have cut back on the number of apprenticeship positions, so many youngsters leaving mandatory school are unable to find a job as an apprentice. Generally speaking, youth unemployment is a severe problem, particularly for women. The youth unemployment rate (15–24 year olds) in January 2006 in Germany was 15 percent, in Britain 14 percent and in France it reached a staggering 22 percent as compared to the United States with a youth unemployment rate of 11 percent.[11] (See Box 7.3.)

This overview of the European educational system is important to understanding the youth movement, which is a very heterogeneous phenomenon with fluid boundaries. The current youth movement has very different goals from the student movement of the 1960s. The student leaders of the 1960s developed grand designs for large-scale changes to society. Underlying their protests were hope and optimism for the future. The basic tone of the current youth movement is quite different. The hope of changing society in any fundamental way has been given up; the main goals are to be left alone, to be happy with other young people, and not to be bothered by the adult world. Demands are made for special youth centers where young people can lead their own lives, play music, dance, discuss, paint, and so forth. Where

---

Box 7.3 French Government Backtracks on Youth Labor Law

Paris—President Jacques Chirac caved in to protesters Monday, canceling a law on youth employment that fueled nationwide unrest and raising questions about France's ability to reform labor laws in a globalized world. Unions declared victory, but energized students decided to go ahead with a "day of action" today to try to knock down other measures—designed to reduce the 22 percent unemployment rate among youths—that are viewed as threatening coveted job protections.

In an announcement that amounted to a humiliating admission of defeat, Prime Minister Dominique de Villepin said on nationwide TV that the contested measure would be replaced...The rejected law would have allowed employers to fire workers under the age of 26 at any time during a two year trial period without giving a reason. The government had said that the law was aimed at spurring the hiring of young people. Villepin had sought to add a dose of flexibility to France's rigid labor laws to prime the French economy for the challenges of globalization.

Source: Christine Oliver, *Associated Press*, Tuesday, April 11, 2006

---

political authorities have granted such demands and established youth centers, however, controversies about the legality of the activities inside these centers have arisen, especially in connection with drug use. Young people insist that they have the right to set their own rules. The key word is *autonomy, and much graffiti all over Europe features the letter A,* standing for this demand. The letter *A* also stands for *anarchy and, furthermore, for the Italian amore* (love), expressing the need of young people to live in communities of their own that are more humane than the cold, anonymous world outside. The demand for autonomy and self-rule in youth centers is generally not well received by the general public, which is unwilling to allow ordinary laws to be disregarded in these centers.

The question of legality becomes even more of an issue when young people occupy empty apartment buildings to establish their own youth centers. These buildings are usually scheduled to be torn down and replaced with expensive office complexes. The young people justify this type of occupation by citing a general housing shortage and the immorality of construction speculation. The political authorities are then confronted with the dilemma of either negotiating with the squatters or using the police to clear the buildings. If they do the latter, pictures of police brutality on TV news may raise sympathy for the squatters among other young people, which in turn may lead to demonstrations with the risk of violent incidents. In cities such as Amsterdam, Berlin, and Zurich, the question of how to deal with squatters has become a hot political issue, although recently somewhat less significant than in the 1980s and 1990s.

In addition to demands for autonomous youth centers, the youth movement is also active in the environmental movement. This activity grows out of a fear that the leaders of the older generation may cause the destruction of nature and, ultimately, the human race. Here again, the question of legality comes up when young people try to occupy, for example, train tracks to nuclear waste disposal sites. Such illegal acts are justified by the occupants as elementary self-defense. Members of the clergy often try to play a mediating role.

Rioting and rampaging of young people may erupt for any reason and spontaneously. When we compare the situation of young people in Europe and America, we see that the main lessons seem to go from the new to the old continent. The educational system in the United States, although much criticized at home, is again increasingly being used as a model by European educators. They realize that they learned only half the American lesson when they expanded higher education in Europe. The neglected other half of the lesson is to differentiate educational opportunities as the Americans do. Young Europeans still have only two basic options for further education after mandatory schooling: university studies or an apprenticeship. European universities are not yet ranked in a systematic way according to quality like American universities, because this was not necessary when they served a small elite. Equal ranking of all universities even offered certain advantages, such as easy transfers, and allowed students to study consecutively at several universities. But today, with the large masses of students, the failure to rank universities is a big disadvantage. Brilliant students must take the same classes as average ones, which lowers the overall level of education. In America, access to the top universities is limited to the very best students, who can be pushed to their intellectual limits. But weaker students also have their opportunities at intellectually less-demanding universities and colleges, where they can be educated according to their capabilities. There is currently much discussion in Europe as to how its higher education could achieve this flexibility. For Americans, on the other hand, the moral of the story may well be to maintain the many different levels of their current system of higher education.

This chapter has shown us that in order to understand European politics we have to look beyond political parties and consider also the role of the various social movements. Complexity of European politics is further increased when we add, in the next chapter, economic interest groups and the state to the picture.

Discussion Questions

1. Social movements tend to wax and wane over time. What do you think could explain that variation over time?

2. In what way is it plausible to think of social movements as being inimical to democracy and in what way is it plausible to think of them as being the embodiment of democracy itself?

3. What would you describe as the functions of social movements?

4. How are social movements different from political parties?

---

[1]Hanspeter Kriesi. Support and Mobilization Potential for New Social Movements: Concepts, Operationalizations and Illustrations from the Netherlands. In Mario Diani and Ron Eyerman, eds., *Studying Collective Action.* (London: Sage, 1992, 22). See also Hanspeter Kriesi, Ruud Koopmans, Jan Willem Dyvendak, and Marco G. Giugni. *New Social Movements in Western Europe. A Comparative Analysis.* (Minneapolis: University of Minnesota Press, 1995).
[2]Kriesi, Support and Mobilization Potential for New Social Movements, 22.
[3]Ibid., 23.
[4]Ibid., 22.
[5]Diarmuid Maguire. When the Streets Begin to Empty: The Demobilisation of the British Peace Movement After 1983. *West European Politics* 15 (October 1992): 79.

[6]Ibid., 79–80.

[7]Alice Holmes Cooper. Public-Good Movements and the Dimensions of Political Process. Postwar German Peace Movements. *Comparative Political Studies* 29 (June 1996): 267–289.

[8]BBC News. Le Pen and His Feminine Side. May 28, 2002.

[9]*New York Times*, January 12, 2006.

[10]*New York Times*, January 12, 2006.

[11]*The Economist*, March 18, 2006. France's labour laws. In rare praise of Dominique de Villepin. p. 13.

CHAPTER 8

The State and Economic Interest Groups

In Europe there is often a close cooperation between the state and economic interest groups. Such cooperation goes under the name of *corporatism*, which is quite alien to politics as practiced in the United States. First we have to explain that in Europe the state may often operate as a political actor in its own right. Representatives of the state bureaucracy meet with representatives of the major economic interest groups, and in these meetings attempts are made to find common solutions for the economic problems of the country.

THE STATE AS A POLITICAL ACTOR

The concept of the state has a different meaning in Europe than it does in the United States. For Americans, the term refers primarily to the 50 states of the union. It is also used to refer to important political figures with the term *statesmen*. In Europe, the distinction is made between *state* and *politics*—in German for example, between *Staat* and *Politik,* and in French between *état* and *politique*. One of the difficulties of comparative politics is translating certain key concepts from one language into another. The concept of the state is a good illustration for such difficulties of translation.

In Europe, the concept of the state grew out of a very different historical context than it did in America. No American leader has ever declared, "The state is me" (*L'état, c'est moi*), as did the French King Louis XIV. In France, prior to the revolution of 1789, the term *state* referred to the governmental institutions built by the kings of the Bourbon dynasty over several centuries. This royal family considered it a personal accomplishment to have given France a governmental structure; the French state was, in a way, its private possession. The Bourbon kings used "their" state to rule the territory of France. To give legitimacy to this rule, the kings claimed to act in the name of God. Thus, they were supposed to have a higher mission to fulfill. The instrument of their rule was the state, which took on a sacred character. The doctrine evolved that the state had its own interests. The bureaucrats working for the state were socialized to believe that they were obligated to serve the interests of the state. This was particularly true during the period of French absolutism in the 17th and 18th centuries. Absolutist regimes prevailed during this time in many other European countries, such as Prussia, where the same doctrine of a higher state interest developed.

In contemporary Europe, the notion of a higher state interest is perhaps most pronounced in France. French history of the past 200 years was characterized by many upheavals, and today the French are already living under their Fifth Republic (Chapter 4). But, through all the crises, the state bureaucracy has continued to work and has looked after the interests of the state. Top bureaucrats enjoy very high social status in France. Future state bureaucrats are rigorously trained at special postgraduate schools. Admission to these schools is extremely competitive, and the students who are accepted are immediately treated as the elite of their country. They form a special, distinguished class, with its own norms and values, whose goal is to excel in the service of the French state. A lifelong career with the state is considered to be more attractive and prestigious than a career in the private sector. High political offices are often filled by top bureaucrats.

Knowledge of the high social status of French bureaucrats sheds light on the important role of the state in the French economy. Because they feel they are the elite of the country, state bureaucrats have, for centuries, been empowered to make important economic decisions. To be sure, governments of the Left tend to give more power to the state than governments of the Right. But the political Right, too, has a positive view of the state.

The French bureaucracy exemplifies in a particularly pronounced form the general characteristics of the state bureaucracies in Europe. But the British civil service, for example, is also well known for its high professional standards and independence. And to understand the Italian government, it is important to know that the state bureaucracies continue to function whenever one of Italy's cabinet crises occurs.

Given the important role of state bureaucrats in European countries, we must ask exactly what these bureaucrats mean when they claim to represent the interest of the state. How do they know what is in the interest of the state? As we will see in Chapter 10, Marxist sociologists argue that state bureaucrats simply help to maintain the capitalist system, and when bureaucrats speak of the interests of the state, they really mean the interests of the capitalist class. According to this Marxist analysis, the main function of the state is to preserve order and thus prevent any uprisings of the working class. Another critical view of the role of state bureaucrats is that they mainly defend their own career interests. When they refer to the interests of the state, they primarily mean the interests of the state bureaucracy itself. Thus, they try to get larger and plusher buildings, larger staffs, higher salaries, more travel money, and so on.

For a long time, when American political scientists studied European politics, many of them neglected the phenomenon of the state acting as an independent player in the political game. They looked at Europe through a particular theoretical framework that had grown out of the American context but was not adapted to the European scene.[1] The framework begins with the inputs that the political system gets from its societal environment. These inputs consist of demands aggregated and articulated by political parties, economic interest groups, and various other groups. These demands are then converted by the political system into decisions and actions, or outputs that may or may not satisfy the original demands. If the demands are satisfied, the political system receives an input of support from the affected societal groups. This framework stems from the American tradition that the political system should serve society. Free citizens organize in groups and articulate their demands. The political system is the place where these demands compete and where winners and losers are sorted out. Looking at reality through this framework, the political system appears to have no demands of its own; it is merely the neutral arena where societal groups compete with one another.

Many scholars have criticized the application of the input/output framework to the analysis of European democracies. They argue that it is not sufficient for a thorough analysis of the state as an independent actor. In this context, it is important to note that political appointees are much rarer in Europe than in the United States. With a new American administration, the top echelons of the bureaucracy in Washington, D.C., are replaced with supporters of the new president. In Europe, the normal pattern is that most high-ranking civil servants stay on the job. In this way, there is much more continuity, which contributes to the perception of the state as an independent actor in the political game. Profiting from analyses of European democracies, many political scientists have taken a second look at the usefulness of the input/output framework for the study of the United States itself. Despite more frequent replacements in the top bureaucratic positions, there is much evidence that Washington bureaucrats, too, have become important political actors in their own right. Often, they do not simply implement decisions made by the president and Congress but are themselves decision makers. Thus, the concept of the state is also useful for the analysis of the United States.

Despite its usefulness, the concept of the state still remains rather vaguely defined. It certainly includes the state bureaucrats, but it has clearly a much wider meaning. The concept also refers to rules, norms, values, and historical myths. The state is also visible in everyday life, an aspect emphasized in the following quote from political scientist Timothy Mitchell:

> A construct like the state occurs not merely as a subjective belief, incorporated in the thinking and action of individuals. It is represented and reproduced in visible, everyday forms, such as the language of legal practice, the architecture of public buildings, and the wearing of military uniforms, or the marking out and policing of frontiers. . . . Setting up and policing a frontier involves a variety of fairly modern social practices—continuous barbed-wire fencing, passports, immigration laws, inspections, currency control and so on. These mundane arrangements, most of them unknown two hundred or even one hundred years ago, help manufacture an almost transcendental entity, the nation state. This entity comes to seem something much more than the sum of the everyday activities that constitute it, appearing as a structure containing and giving order to people's lives.[2]

ECONOMIC INTEREST GROUPS

In the United States many economic interest groups are active in the political process. Farmers, teachers, bankers, truckers, miners, and others are politically organized. For Americans, to represent special interests has mostly a negative connotation. The impression evoked is that a special interest group seeks privileges detrimental to the common good of the country. In American political thinking, the influence of such groups should ideally be as limited as possible. Many people believe, for example, that members of Congress should be unencumbered by such special interests and instead should strive to make decisions for the higher common good. In this view, special interest groups should be kept to the lobbies of the Capitol, and it is from this perspective that interest groups are called lobbies in the United States.

The term *lobby* makes less sense in a European context. An official of an economic interest group often may also sit in the national parliament. There he or she usually does not hesitate to speak for his or her interest group. Thus, interest groups are heard not only at hearings and in the lobbies, but also in parliament itself. To understand the situation of economic interest groups in Europe, one must consider the long European tradition of economic interest group participation in political decision making. This tradition goes back to the medieval guild system in which bakers, butchers, and similar occupational groups were tightly organized in European towns. These guilds not only regulated their internal affairs, but also played an important role in the political life of the community. Although the guild system has since been dissolved, the doctrine that occupational groups should have a central place in politics persists. It is a sign of this continuity that guilds still flourish in many European cities, although in a new form—as prestigious private clubs with important social functions. In Zurich, for example, the guilds organize a popular parade through the streets of the city every spring. Most members of these modern-day guilds no longer belong to the respective occupational groups but come from high-status professions such as law, medicine, business, and so forth. Memories of the guilds are also kept alive in the names of streets and fashionable restaurants. With this historical background, it is understandable that in European politics economic interest groups are not relegated to the lobbies of parliament but are allowed entry to parliament itself. This raises the question of the relationship between political parties and economic interest groups.

Many more Europeans join an economic interest group than a political party (for membership in political parties, see Chapter 2). It is seen as a more immediate personal advantage to belong to an economic interest group than to a political party. On average, about 43 percent of the European workforce is organized; in Sweden, Finland, and Denmark it is between 80 to 90 percent.[3] In the United States, by contrast, less than 13 percent of the workforce is organized. It is also important to note that membership fees in economic interest groups are usually higher than in political parties. The combination of larger membership and higher membership fees means that economic interest groups tend to be much more affluent than political parties. The trade unions, for example, are more affluent than the Socialist parties and the business associations more affluent than the Conservative parties. These differences in financial resources are vividly seen in the headquarters, where it is not uncommon to find economic interest groups located in luxurious office buildings with huge staffs, whereas political parties have modest rooms and small staffs. In a few countries, notably Germany, the financial condition of the parties is somewhat better than elsewhere as a result of government contributions.

The overlap between membership in political parties and economic interest groups varies greatly from country to country. Such variation by country occurs clearly for the trade union movement. In Germany, Great Britain, and Sweden, for example, the trade unions have a single national organization, and most trade union leaders also belong to the Socialist Party. In other countries, such as France, Italy, and Switzerland, the trade union movement is split into several separate national organizations, each having a special affiliation with a different party. Switzerland, for example, has three major trade union organizations; the largest is close to the Socialists and the second largest is aligned with the Christian Democrats.

Business associations, as might be expected, have a close affiliation with Conservative and Free Democratic parties. In some countries, farmers have developed their own agrarian parties: In Sweden, the Center Party was originally an agrarian party and still, to some extent, represents farmers' interests. In countries without a special agrarian party, farmers mostly support parties of the political Right, but some small farmers, mainly in Italy and France, are Socialists or even Communists. White-collar employees and their interest groups are usually not close to particular parties but pursue the strategy of having good relations with all the major parties.

Whether leaders of economic interest groups run for a parliamentary seat varies greatly from country to country and from one interest group to another. German trade union officials, for example, are more likely than their French counterparts to run for parliament. From the perspective of democratic theory, is it desirable that leaders of economic interest groups sit in parliament? A negative response might arise from the fear that giving voice to special economic interests in parliament could decrease the chances that decisions will be made for the common good. But one could also argue that it is better to hear the representatives of economic interests in the open forum of parliamentary debates. In this way positions are made clearer to the general public than if interest groups remain in the lobbies. Moreover, the responsibility of a parliamentary seat might lead to more moderation in the positions of interest-group representatives than if they stay outside parliament.

What about the policy programs of the various interest groups? We do not cover them as we did the programs of the political parties. First, the programs of the interest groups are to a large extent self-explanatory and can be deduced from the groups' names. Thus, it is easy to guess that teachers' associations fight for higher wages for their members. At a more specific level, we come immediately to minute details. Do teachers' associations support merit pay, and, if so, how should a teacher's performance be measured? At this specific level, there is wide variation from country to country and even within countries. Entire monographs have been published on the policy programs of teachers' associations in Europe. The same is true for medical associations, bankers' associations, trade unions, trade associations, and so on. More interesting than such detailed program descriptions is the question of how the demands of the various economic interest groups influence the political decision process and its outcome. This question makes the transition to the next section, which looks at the interactions between economic interest groups and the state.

PLURALISM AND CORPORATISM

Pluralism means that there is a plurality of interest groups, all of which try to influence the decisions of the state. The state itself is relatively "weak" vis-à-vis interest groups. The term *weak* refers to the reduced capacity of the state to push its preferences through as compared to the preferences of the various interest groups. In pluralist systems, the autonomy of the state is limited by its inability to keep interest groups at arm's length. The United States is a prime example, where interest groups wield significant influence in the policymaking process. *Corporatism* is a formal cooperation between the state and interest groups with the goal of finding mutually acceptable solutions. Pluralism and corporatism have to be seen as the poles of a continuum with many variations in between. American readers are familiar with interest-group pluralism; corporatism, on the other hand, needs explanation.

The notion of corporatism as a form of government has deep roots in European history, dating from medieval times. In our present era of individualism, it is difficult to imagine how in medieval times the lives of individuals were embedded in and subordinated to the groups to which they belonged. Membership in these groups was not voluntary but compulsory. A baker in a medieval town had no choice as to whether to join the professional bakers' organization; all bakers had to belong to their guild. These guilds were hierarchical. At the bottom were apprentices, who trained to become journeymen and later, perhaps, masters of their craft. The guild established rules specifying how many journeymen and apprentices a master could employ. Standards were also set as to how much could be produced—for example, how many breads a baker could bake. In addition to guilds, there were other "corporations," such as universities, whose internal differentiation was primarily between professors and students. In Latin, *university* comes from *universitas magistrorum studentiumque*, meaning "corporation of professors and students."

Corporations played a crucial role in the government of a medieval town. Together with town officials, they managed public affairs. Decision making was characterized by mutual accommodation and bargaining; the ideological basis was a harmonious model of society. Each corporation was seen as a part of a living body, and the parts had to cooperate for the entire body to stay healthy. The main function of the individual in this organic view of society was his or her contribution to the whole. In fact, the word *corporatism* finds its roots in the Latin term *corpore*, which means "body." When all the different parts of society work together, the "whole is more than the sum of its parts," as so powerfully stated by one of the most important corporatists, Emile Durkheim.

It was only during the Enlightenment that philosophers began to place the individual at center stage. They proclaimed that individuals had natural rights independent of the groups to which they belonged, a notion alien to medieval thinkers. The French philosopher René Descartes (1596–1650) made the influential statement, *"Cogito, ergo sum"* (I think, therefore I am), indicating that the potential to think is the crucial element in human existence. The capacity of thought makes the individual free and gives him or her inalienable rights—among others, the right of free association. Individuals should be able to choose freely the groups to which they belong. Based on this right, political parties were founded, bringing together people of similar ideological orientations. This was the beginning of modern democracy, first put in practice in the United States and, shortly thereafter, in France. The old harmonious model was replaced with the notion of competition. The emerging political parties competed for members and votes. Decisions increasingly were made with the device of the majority principle. The building blocks of society were no longer organic groups but individuals free to choose for themselves.

But notions of democracy based on individualism and competition in 19th-century Europe led to much turmoil, unrest, and bloody revolutions. As a result, there was a backlash, accompanied by nostalgic longing for the old order of cooperation and harmony and a view of modern democracy as divisive and contrary to the laws of nature. Motivated by such views, in 1922 Benito Mussolini overthrew the frail Italian democracy and established fascism based on a corporate form of government (see also Chapter 11). Although similar forms of government were established in other countries, Mussolini was most explicit in the implementation of corporatist ideas: The will of the people should be represented not by political parties but by the natural economic forces of society. A national assembly should bring together the interests of farmers, businesses, workers, and so forth. Because everyone belongs to an economic sector of society, everyone would be represented. Interests would not be antagonistic but would complement each other for the good of the entire country. It would only be necessary for the *Duce* (leader)—Mussolini himself—to give clear directions as to which way the country should go. The result would be the reestablishment of order and strength for the Italian state. As a symbol for this strength, Mussolini used the Roman term *fasces,* which led to the concept of fascism (Chapter 2).

Because of its association with fascism and its atrocities, the concept of corporatism was discredited for many years after World War II. It has only been since the 1970s that some political scientists have once again begun to use the term *corporatism*. To distinguish their idea of corporatism from Mussolini's, these political scientists speak often of *neocorporatism, liberal corporatism, societal corporatism,* or *democratic corporatism*. Whatever term they use, they claim that some European democracies have a corporatist form of government. The example cited most often is Austria, where laws have established chambers of business, labor, and agriculture. Membership in these chambers is compulsory. Representatives of the chambers meet regularly under the chairmanship of the federal chancellor to hammer out crucial economic decisions. Other countries frequently characterized as corporatist are Norway, Sweden, and the Netherlands. By contrast, the United States, Canada, New Zealand, and Australia are considered to be classical cases of interest-group pluralism.

At its core, corporatism in a modern democracy deals with the interactions among organized business, organized labor, and the state bureaucracy. These three actors cooperate at the national level in the pursuit of what they see as the public good. It is important for this definition that negotiations are not merely bilateral between business and labor, but trilateral—that is, inclusive of the state bureaucracy as well. The participation of the state bureaucracy as an independent actor in its own right is a crucial element of corporatism. The state bureaucracy's representatives meet around the same table with the representatives of the major business and labor organizations. These economic interest groups are not merely consulted but are themselves active decision makers. The style of decision making is characterized by bargaining. The interests of the three actors in corporatist decision making are usually quite divergent in the initial phases, but the three share a common belief in the existence of an optimal solution for the public good.

The representatives from all three sides are usually professional economists who are proficient in the same economic language; consequently, problems are usually addressed in a highly technical and professional way. To determine an optimal wage settlement, for example, a huge amount of data is brought into play concerning inflation, unemployment, balance of payments, money supplies, budgets, and so on. The negotiators generally expect that a careful analysis of all the data will allow them to determine the optimal wage level for the long-term interests of the country. In these negotiations, state bureaucrats are not only mediators between business and labor but also defenders of the interests of the state as a special entity. If corporatist decision making is successful, the final outcome is acceptable to all three sides, although it will most likely not correspond precisely to the initial demands of any one of the partners.

Besides wage settlements, other economic issues may be dealt with in a corporatist way, such as public works programs or measures to help exporters. The range of issues may be even broader, including questions of old-age pensions, taxes, and budgets. Through such an extension of corporatist decision making, political parties and parliament may lose many of their essential functions. To be sure, decisions reached in a corporatist way must still pass the parliamentary procedure, but this can amount to pure formality if the proposals submitted to parliament have already been accepted by the corporatist actors. As a qualifier to the argument that corporatism weakens political parties, one must add that party leaders may play an important role in labor and business organizations.

Though classical corporatism is trilateral—that is, between business, labor, and the state bureaucracy—other actors, such as farmers, bankers, and consumers, can be added.

The concept of corporatism becomes increasingly fuzzy as one moves away from its core definition. Is it still useful to use the term *corporatism* when the state bureaucracy calls in, for example, medical professionals and social workers for a decision about the implementation of a disability program? As we see later in this chapter, such conceptual fuzziness plagues empirical research about corporatism.

As said at the beginning of this section, corporatism can be seen as the polar opposite of pluralism. In a pluralist system of government, economic interest groups stand outside the institutional framework of government. Their representatives are not appointed to official governmental commissions; they therefore do not act as decision makers, as they do in corporatism. Their role is, rather, to influence government actions from the outside, mainly through lobbying elected officials and state bureaucrats. In these lobbying efforts, business, labor, and other economic interest groups are in competition with one another, and each group exercises as much pressure as possible. Therefore, pluralism may also be called *pressure-group politics*. Whether economic interest groups exercise more influence in a corporatist or a pluralist system cannot be answered a priori but is an open question for empirical investigation.

THE THEORY OF CORPORATISM

If countries differ in the degree to which their decision making is corporatist or pluralistic, these differences must be explained in their causes and consequences. The literature offers several explanatory factors. The vulnerability of a country to international market forces is said to be of prime importance for the emergence of corporatist decision making. This factor would explain why corporatism is particularly prominent in smaller countries that depend heavily on imports and exports. The name of the game in such countries is not so much internal competition between business and labor as it is survival of the country in the world market. Political scientist Klaus Armingeon compares the situation of such countries in the world market to a nutshell on the high seas. Just as such a nutshell has no control over the waves of the sea, a small country has no control over the waves of the world market.[4] Under these circumstances, labor is very much aware that the country's products must remain competitive in international markets to prevent high domestic unemployment. Business, on the other hand, knows that it needs a satisfied and productive labor force in order to stay internationally competitive. Because both labor and business realize how much they depend on each other, they are more willing to engage in corporatist decision making. In a small country, this would be all the more likely to happen because there tend to be many close personal contacts among the national elites and because a small country may more easily develop a sense of community among the entire population.

A second factor identified by theorists of corporatism as contributing to corporatist decision making is a strong labor movement. For a labor movement to be strong, membership must be high, and a single, centralized organization must exist. Under these conditions, business is confronted with an adversary that it cannot easily ignore, and one that has the advantage of being able to negotiate settlements that will be upheld by the entire labor force. In contrast, if the unions have few members and are split and decentralized, business has little assurance that a settlement negotiated with union leaders will also be accepted by the rank and file. Thus, it is hypothesized that strong unions facilitate corporatist decision making.

Some corporatist authors argue, however, that this hypothesis is valid only if still another factor comes into play: a Socialist government.[5] Under this additional condition, the unions are interested in helping their "friends" in government to stabilize the economy. The Socialists, in turn, use their governmental power to guarantee that the settlements reached in corporatist decision making are actually implemented. Consequently, the unions will not fear being left in the cold by a hostile government. If, on the other hand, strong unions face a Conservative government, chances for corporatist decision making decrease. The unions may be reluctant to help the government and, thus, to increase its electoral chances. The unions may also be afraid of being ultimately betrayed by a Conservative government.

Is corporatism more likely when the economy booms or when it is in crisis? In the former case, it is labor that is more likely to withdraw from corporatist arrangements, and in the latter case, business. When the economy booms, the workforce is in short supply, which gives labor a strong position with regard to wage demands. It may hope to get these demands better fulfilled by strikes or threats of strikes than by corporatist negotiations. When the economy is in crisis, on the other hand, business may no longer be interested in corporatist negotiations but prefer to obtain lower wages through threats of layoffs or actual layoffs. These arguments show that corporatism has as a precondition that both labor and business take a long-term perspective, at least over an entire business cycle and possibly over several cycles. The state bureaucrats, as the third actors in corporatism, are likely to encourage such a long-term perspective because the interests of the state are, by nature, long range.

At a more general and speculative level, some theorists argue that corporatism is a result of advanced capitalism, which is characterized by increased organizational concentration. Major interest groups and some individual companies become so large and powerful that they have a virtual veto power in many economic areas. State authorities therefore have no choice but to assemble these interests around a common table if anything at all is to be accomplished.

What are the consequences of corporatist decision making? Here, too, the literature presents interesting hypotheses. The effects of corporatism on the economy of a country are seen by some theorists as positive. They hypothesize that corporatist decision making allows for a more flexible response to changes in the international market because internal domestic compensation is possible. If a sector of the economy is threatened by changing international factors, corporatist decision making allows the system to come to its aid. On the other hand, free market purists argue that in the long run a country will be haunted by such rescue operations because they are undertaken against the verdict of market forces. Economist Manfred E. Streit speaks in this context of the danger of "institutional sclerosis." He warns that the participants in corporatist decision making are less able to solve the problem of reliable knowledge to steer the economy than the free market does.[6] But supporters of corporatism reply that human and material costs are sometimes too high if market forces alone are allowed to dominate, so joint steering by the state and the major economic interest groups may be needed in certain cases.

In another respect, corporatism is seen in a still more negative light. It is argued that successful corporatist negotiations presuppose a subservient trade union membership, so labor leaders have sufficient leeway for making deals. If rank-and-file members criticize such deals, their criticism must be repressed in order for corporatist decision making to continue. In other words, corporatism is not compatible with true internal democracy in the trade unions. As a consequence of the lack of internal democracy, labor leaders may begin to look out more for their own personal interests than for the interests of their members. They may also be tempted to accommodate business leaders and even to adopt their lifestyle. Manfred E. Streit speaks in this context of "the feudal barons of our time,"[7] and argues that, eventually, ordinary members of the unions will realize that their needs have been forgotten, and they will revolt against the decisions reached in a corporatist way. This argument leads to the conclusion that corporatist decision making is ultimately unstable because of its elitism, which eventually causes dissatisfaction and disruption at the rank-and-file level of the working class.

The discussion about the consequences of corporatist decision making shows that there is basic disagreement in the literature over whether corporatism helps with the "governability" of highly industrialized countries. This disagreement can also be seen in the public debate in the United States, where corporatism is better known as "industrial policy." The bailout of the Chrysler Corporation was a typical case of industrial policy, in which the federal government, labor, and the corporation owners mutually worked out a deal. Whether the government and labor should be involved in such business decisions is still hotly debated. Generally, the attitude toward corporatism, or industrial policy, is more critical in the United States than in Europe.

A first necessary step for an empirical test of the corporatist theory is a classification of a sufficiently large number of countries on a continuum from corporatist to pluralist. To arrive at such a classification with the necessary reliability and validity is a formidable task. Although for most countries there is general agreement among scholars on the approximate location on the corporatist–pluralist continuum, there is much disagreement on the specific locations. There are even some countries for which wide disagreements exist on the approximate classification.

The classification of the degree of corporatism in a country is usually based, in a first approximation, on the presence or absence of particular institutions. One particular indicator of corporatism is the existence of a permanent institution such as an economic and social council, where the representatives of the state bureaucracy and the major economic interest groups meet on a regular basis. However, such institutions are sometimes merely shells without much substance. In such cases, the original classification must then be modified. France, for example, has the Economic and Social Council, whose existence seems to indicate a high degree of corporatism. But in fact, this council has little political importance.

For Switzerland, the problem is, in a way, reversed. Switzerland has no economic and social council and has no similar permanent institution, so corporatism seems weak; yet some authors classify Switzerland as strongly corporatist. For the Netherlands, some classifications have shifted over time. On the one hand, the Dutch have the Social and Economic Council, but, on the other hand, this council seems to have lost much of its importance since its heyday in the 1950s.

Great Britain offers still another example of why it is not sufficient to look at institutions in order to classify a country on the corporatist–pluralist continuum. In 1962, the National Economic Development Council was created, which brought together representatives of government, business, and labor. When Margaret Thatcher became prime minister in 1979, this institution lost all practical importance but continued to exist on paper until it was formally dissolved in 1992.

Despite all the difficulties with the corporatist–pluralist continuum, we, working together with Arend Lijphart, arrived at a classification of a large number of countries on this continuum.[8] The idea was to establish a composite measure of corporatism based on the judgments of 12 corporatist experts published in the literature. Included were those countries for which at least six scholarly judgments were available, which resulted in a total of 18 countries, ranked in the following way, from the most corporatist to the least corporatist:

> Austria, Norway, Sweden, Netherlands, Denmark, Switzerland, Germany, Finland, Belgium, Japan, Ireland, France, Italy, Great Britain, Australia, New Zealand, Canada, and the United States

For the interpretation of this ranking, it is important to note that there was relatively little disagreement among the experts on the classification of the countries at the extremes of the continuum. Austria, Norway, and Sweden were classified by all experts as strongly corporatist; the United States and Canada were classified as strongly pluralist. The greatest disagreements emerged for the classifications of Japan and Switzerland, for which the judgments of the experts varied widely.

With the six most-corporatist countries being small in size, the ranking confirms the hypothesis that small size increases the likelihood of corporatism. A closer look at the ranking also confirms that the more-corporatist countries tend to have strong trade unions and, frequently, Socialist governments.

Many empirical studies have demonstrated that corporatism matters. Corporatist countries tend to have lower strike rates, lower inflation, lower unemployment and higher economic growth.[9] Corporatist countries also tend to have lower income inequality than pluralist countries, tend to spend more on the welfare of their people, have fewer citizens in poverty and lower crime rates, and have even lower environmental pollution levels than pluralist countries.[10]

The Future of Corporatism

Despite these impressive results, many observers have noticed three developments that may ring the death-knell of corporatism: postmaterialism, postindustrialism, and globalization.

Postmaterialism (see Chapter 2) refers to the rise of new political issues such as environmental, women's rights, pacifism, and a general orientation toward more grassroots democracy. Postmaterialism is incompatible with corporatism on two grounds: a substantive and a procedural one. The substantive one is self-explanatory: Corporatism centers around materialist issues, such as economic growth, unemployment, inflation, working conditions and others. "Post"-materialism is exactly about opposite issues, such as the environment. Increasingly, these "productive interests" (i.e., corporatist interests) clash with the so called "protective" interests, such as environmental concerns. Why do they clash? Because the "secret of corporatism" has always been to establish social harmony on the basis of economic growth. Unfortunately, economic growth is often incompatible with environmental concerns, leading to new alliances between left and right against environmental interests. For example, in the winter of 1984 the Austrian government decided to build a hydroelectric dam on the Danube River. When the bulldozers came to clear the land, they found students had chained themselves to trees to protect what was the habitat of a rare frog. Political protests erupted in the streets of Vienna, where unions marched together with representatives of the employer's organization against environmentalists and representatives of the Green Party. The political Left and Right found themselves on the same side against a new challenger: the Greens.

Postmaterialism also clashes with corporatism on procedural grounds. For corporatism to work, as mentioned, it has to be organized in centralized, hierarchical structures. Postmaterialism is the opposite—it believes in decentralization and grassroots democracy. Many of the central organizational features of corporatism, particularly in the Austrian case—such as organization of interests in peak association, compulsory membership, and the principle of unanimity—are incompatible with notions of grassroots democracy and decentralization of power.

The second reason why corporatism may decline in importance is the rise of postindustrial society. We have already highlighted the fact that the power of labor organizations is directly connected to their unionization rates—the more workers are organized, the more power they have vis-à-vis the employer's organizations. Corporatism is built on the traditional 19th-century industrial class conflict between mass labor unions who organize against the captains of industry. However, at the beginning of the third millennium, these images do not apply anymore. The secondary sector (the industrial sector) of most all of the modern European economies contributes less than 25 percent to the GDP, with the service sector contributing typically between 65 and 70 percent to the nation's GDP and with agriculture contributing the rest, around 5 percent. People who work in the service sector (lawyers, bankers, professors, insurance agents, real estate agents, teachers, etc.), so-called "white-collar" workers, are much more difficult to organize than blue-collar workers in the industrial sector. The reason is that many of these white-collar workers are very much removed from the strongly hierarchical nature of the 19th-century factory production process. The relationship between a "boss" and a "worker" in a modern law office or bank is much more collegial than the strictly class-based, hierarchical relationship in the old days of unfettered capitalism. In addition, part of the qualification of white-collar workers is to think for themselves, to be creative, innovative, and think "out of the box." All of this conspires to a reduced willingness of many white-collar workers to be led by an organization that emphasizes hierarchy. As a result, not only are unionization rates dropping in industrial unions, but particularly in service sector unions, again unsettling the balance of power between capital and labor.

The third contender for the "end of corporatism" thesis is globalization (Chapter 15). Corporatism is a "national" concept, that is, it is a nation-specific approach to deal with economic and political challenges. As mentioned, the central actors of corporatism are the state, the labor unions, and the employer's organizations. Over the last decade, however, some observers have raised the issue of globalization, meaning that as a result of advances in information, transportation, and communication technologies, capital can move to whichever location best maximizes profits. This allows capital an "exit" option: If labor unions do not agree to the demands of capital, the latter can pack up and move their production facilities outside of the country to a location with lower wages and fewer or no regulations. Capital can move; domestic labor in industrialized democracies usually cannot. In order to avoid such "capital flight," labor has to give inducements to capital to stay at home, such as tax reductions, wage reduction, and fewer regulations such as in the area of the environment (see Box 8.1). Sometimes, capital might even play off one country's offers to attract investment against another country's, leading to what is sometimes called "race to the bottom"—that is, the company has an incentive to move to the location with the lowest wages, the lowest worker's protection, the lowest environmental regulation, and so on. Capital's exit option shifts significant bargaining power to its side, with labor having little to counter the exit threat, unsettling the "balance of power" between capital and labor.

Box 8.1 Globalization: Chirac Urges Social Welfare Rethink

Jacques Chirac, France's President, has announced plans for tax reforms in an attempt to discourage companies from dismissing French workers or moving production overseas. In his televised New Year's Even address, Mr. Chirac called on his government to meet the challenges of globalization by changing the way it raises funds for social welfare—including unemployment benefits, family assistance, pension and health care. This rethink represents a significant new idea in Mr. Chirac's address, as he adopted a more friendly tone towards global capitalism than in previous speeches calling on French people to "make globalization an asset for our growth and our jobs." Instead of taxing companies based on the number of employees, which experts say encourages them to dismiss workers and discourages them from hiring staff, the government is expected to examine alternative ways to raise funds for social welfare. "Today the more jobs a company cuts, the more production it moves overseas, the less social charges it pays. Our system of corporate charges must favour companies that employ people in France," said Mr. Chirac. The tax reform plan is seen as a response by the president to concerns sparked by an announcement last year by Hewlett-Packard, the IT company, that it was cutting 1,240 jobs in France as part of a global restructuring.

Source: *Financial Times*, January 3, 2006.

As a result, many scholars have noticed a decline in corporatism even in the most traditional corporatist countries such as Austria and Sweden. One of us (Crepaz) comes to the conclusion that "Austrian corporatism is on the wane and is slowly but surely being replaced by a more competitive, innovative, authentic but maybe less stable or even effective pattern of interest representation."[11]

Globalization challenges corporatism on an even more fundamental level as it question the very viability of the state. Labor and capital are both tied to the state; however, globalization offers many more opportunities for business to be mobile than it does for labor. The close connection between business and the state, as exemplified in the American statement "What is good for General Motors is good for America," does not apply anymore in the new global context where hitherto "national" companies are increasingly owned by foreign private equity investors with very little sympathy for the fates of the nation's workers. Such international investors, such as TPG (Texas Pacific Group) or CSFB (Credit Suisse First Boston) often wield significant influence even though they only hold minor shares in national companies raising the specter of who actually controls the company. As the part-owners of companies are becoming "foreigners" their attachment to the nation state, its people and workers, is proportionately reduced (see Box 8.2).

Sweden, another country with a long corporatist tradition, fares no better when evaluated by Leif Lewin, who writes that, "During the 1980s we have, however, witnessed a gradual decline of this neocorporatist model of interest representation. Europe is approaching the American pluralist model instead. Sweden, once the prototype of the Social Democratic Corporatist State, is the best example of this change."[12] Jonas Pontusson and Peter Swenson agree with Lewin that corporatism has declined in Western Europe and that

Box 8.2 Anti-Capitalism Debate

MARX OR MARKETS: GERMAN POLITICIANS DEBATE THE DANGERS OF CAPITALISM

... Two weeks ago, the head of Germany's ruling Social Democratic Party (SPD) compared private equity firms to a "swarm of locusts" that "graze" on under-priced businesses, lay off employees and then proceed to resell the firm for a sweet profit. Executives of these companies, he said, are "extremists with no sense of responsibility." And this weekend, Muentefering upped the ante by circulating a so-called "locust list" within his party, linking company names and faces to the crop-destroying insects, which are used to symbolize destruction in the Bible.

Critics say that Muentefering's words are aimed at disenchanted voters in North-Rhine Westphalia, which is due to have elections in just a few weeks. ..

Muentefering is however trying to prove to skeptics that his words are more than simply pre-electoral posturing: He has called for a raft of laws that would bet-ter protect the German market from wage dumping by introducing tighter con-trols on foreign companies, particularly those from Eastern Europe. He also wants business taxes to be standardized across the European Union in order to elimi-nate the competitive advantage enjoyed by countries with low corporate tax rates.

Source: Spiegel Online, May 5, 2005.

this decline has not spared Sweden.[13] For Sweden, they demonstrate how export-oriented engineering employers wanted more wage flexibility to compete in the world markets and how they dismantled the corporatist system: "The wage rigidities inherent in centralized bargaining as it had evolved in Sweden thus became increasingly unacceptable to engi-neering employers."[14] Wage bargaining in Sweden now mostly occurs at a decentralized level, which allows for more flexibility in setting wages.

In this chapter the level of difficulty of the textbook has clearly been raised. Whereas in the previous chapters the focus was more on description, the focus in the current chap-ter has shifted to theory building. At a more sophisticated level, political scientists not only try to describe political phenomena, but also to establish causal relations among important political phenomena. This is called *theory building*. In this theoretical spirit, we have not only described the level of corporatism in the various European democracies, but we also address the question of the preconditions and consequences of a high level of corporatism. In this process of theory building, logically sound hypotheses need to be formulated and then tested with empirical data. As we have seen, it is often not easy to establish in a con-vincing way whether the data support a particular hypothesis or not. Different scholars may come to different conclusions, and this contributes to vigorous and stimulating scholarly discussions.

Discussion Questions

1. Corporatism is often described as "elitist." The United States does not have levels of corporatism comparable to Europe. Does that mean that crucial decisions about politi-cal and economics are made by "the people" or are there other kinds of elites in the United States? If yes, who are they?

2. Why is a European type of corporatism unthinkable in the United States?

3. Corporatism is closely connected to the "state." Why is this so?

4. Many observers have argued that corporatism is no longer sustainable in an age of globalization. Why?

5. The ideology of postmaterialist, or "green" parties is often described as being incompatible with corporatism. Why is this so?

6. What is the difference between pluralism and corporatism?

7. Corporatism sometimes goes under the label "expertocracy," meaning that it is government by experts. Should corporatism wane, as many observers have argued, who would take their place?

---

[1]David Easton. *A Systems Analysis of Political Life*. (New York: Wiley, 1965, 32).

[2]Timothy Mitchell. The Limits of the State: Beyond Statist Approaches and Their Critics. *American Political Science Review* 85 (March 1991): 81, 94.

[3]Klaus Armingeon. Korporatismus im Wandel: Ein internationaler Vergleich. In Emmerich Tálos (Hg), *Sozialpartnerschaft: Kontinuität und Wandel eines Modells*. (Vienna: Verlag für Gesellschaftskritik, 1993, 291). Klaus Armingeon. *Staat und Arbeitsbeziehungen. Ein Internationaler Vergleich*. (Opladen: Westdeutscher Verlag, 1994).

[4]Armingeon, Korporatismus im Wandel, 299.

[5]R. Michael Alvarez, Geoffrey Garrett, and Peter Lange. Government Partisanship, Labor Organizations, and Marcoeconomic Performance. *American Political Science Review* 85 (June 1991): 539–556. Nathaniel Beck, Jonathan N. Katz, R. Michael Alvarez, Geoffrey Garrett, and Peter Lange. Government Partisanship, Labor Organization, and Macroeconomic Performance: A Corrigendum. *American Political Science Review* 87 (December 1993): 945–948.

[6]Manfred E. Streit. Market Order and Welfare Politics: The Mirage of Neo-Corporatism. Research Unit for Societal Developments, University of Mannheim, Working Papers, No. 3, 1987.

[7]Ibid.

[8]Arend Lijphart and Markus M. L. Crepaz. Corporatism and Consensus Democracy in Eighteen Countries: Conceptual and Empirical Linkages. *British Journal of Political Science* 21 (1990): 235–256.

[9]Markus M. L. Crepaz. Corporatism in Decline? An Empirical Analysis of the Impact of Corporatism on Macroeconomic Performance and Industrial Disputes in 18 Industrialized Democracies. *Comparative Political Studies* 25 (July 1992): 139–168.

[10]Markus M. L. Crepaz. Explaining National Variations of Air Pollution Levels: Political Institutions and Their Impact on Environmental Policy-Making. *Environmental Politics*, Vol. 4 (1995): 391–414.

[11]Markus M. L. Crepaz. From Semisovereignty to Sovereignty. The Decline of Corporatism and Rise of Parliament in Austria. *Comparative Politics*, Vol. 27 (1995): 45–65.

[12]Leif Lewin. The Rise and Decline of Corporatism: The Case of Sweden. *European Journal of Political Research* 26 (1994): 59.

[13]Jonas Pontusson and Peter Swenson. Labor Markets, Production Strategies, and Wage Bargaining Institutions. The Swedish Employer Offensive in Comparative Perspective. *Comparative Political Studies* 29 (April 1996): 223–250.

[14]Ibid., 225.

[15]Jelle Visser and Anton Hemerijck. A *Dutch Miracle. Job Growth, Welfare Reform and Corporatism in the Netherlands*. (Amsterdam: Amsterdam University Press, 1997).

CHAPTER 9

Policy Outcomes

In this chapter, we try to bring students into our discussion of European politics in a more active way by challenging them to explain variation in policy outcomes among European democracies and also in comparison with the United States. We will define what is meant in political science by a policy outcome, and then we will give comparative data on a wide range of policy outcomes in Europe and the United States. The task then is to explain, for example, why taxes are higher in Sweden than in Switzerland, or why poverty is higher in the United States than in the Netherlands. There is a wealth of explanations on such questions in the political science literature, and there is a lively and vigorous debate about the merits of the various explanations. As we wrote at the end of Chapter 8, such debates are both expected and healthy when it comes to establishing causal connections among political variables. On purpose, we do not try to summarize the wide literature on explanations of policy outcomes; in this chapter, we leave that task to our readers. Perhaps this chapter could be summarized as a term paper assignment. For possible explanatory variables, students should look at all previous chapters. Do features of the parliamentary election systems, for example, have causal impact on the level of governmental health expenditures? Do political systems that allow for referenda have lower or higher tax levels?

Even with the casual view of a tourist, it is easy to discover differences in policy outcomes from one European country to another. Trains, for example, are more punctual in Switzerland than in Italy. And, because trains are mostly government-run, their punctuality can be considered a governmental policy outcome. One might ask why the Italian government is less able than the Swiss government to make its trains run on time. If tourists become ill on a European vacation, they can compare the quality of health care in the various European countries. Parents moving from one country to another can see where their children get the best education. There are literally thousands of criteria according to which one can evaluate the policy outcomes of a country. A specialist in education may wish to know on a cross-national basis how well students learn to read, whether there is sex discrimination in the educational system, what the social status of teachers is, and so on. An expert in criminology will have a similar multitude of questions regarding crime.

How can we systematically explain differences in policy outcomes? In the first eight chapters we encountered many factors that may help us with such explanations. Does the economic performance of a country, for example, depend on the strength of the various political parties, on the pattern of cabinet formation, or on the level of government centralization? Does it have something to do with the influence of interest groups on the policy making process? Or, can the differences in policy outcomes even be linked to the different processes of modernization in Europe and the United States?

Whatever the answer, the very assumption is that politics makes a difference. The operative term of most every political campaign is "change," meaning that if enough voters vote for a particular party, some kind of change will occur. This means that the candidates and the voters must believe that politicians actually have the *capacity* to affect change.

After all, if things couldn't be changed, why bother to vote in the first place? Unfortunately, it is not that easy. As we have already learned in Chapter 8, and will revisit in the last chapter of this book (Chapter 15), the degree to which politics can affect particular outcomes has been seriously challenged by globalization, calling into question the sovereignty of states to achieve particular outcomes. Still, the basic proposition of democratic politics is that people have choices and depending on what they choose, they will get different outcomes.

In this chapter we will compare various European Democracies together with the United States across a range of outcomes. In analyzing differences it is important to realize that "change" can occur along two dimensions: across time and across space. It is important to keep in mind that changes over time *within* one country are qualitatively different as compared to differences *between* countries. Making comparisons across countries requires an understanding of "systemic effects." For instance, it is difficult for an American voter to imagine that political parties in Sweden run, and win, on the basis of tax *increases*. Carl Bildt, conservative challenger to the Social Democrats, campaigned for tax cuts in the 1998 general election campaign. He lost to the Social Democrats who were running on the basis of tax *increases*. Referring to the 1998 general election campaign, "talking about tax cuts in this campaign is like swearing in church" said Toivo Sjoren, the research director of the Sifo opinion surveying firm.[1] A similar scenario was present during the 2002 campaign. The Swedish Prime Minister Göran Persson, leading up to the 2002 election, declared that "Welfare is not free. You have to pay for it, and that is why we say no to the tax cuts."[2] Such a scenario is almost unthinkable for an American voter. What is different in Sweden that makes it possible for politicians running on tax *increases* to actually win an election?

Comparing outcomes across systems, it is important to know something about the "systemic" differences between countries. By *systemic* we mean things such as different political institutions, different forms of interest representation, different "cultures," and many of the elements we have highlighted in this book so far in Chapters 1 through 8. What follows are country rankings across many different policy fields. The task for students in this chapter is draw upon the insights gained from the previous chapters and attempt to analyze and understand why countries occupy particular positions compared to other countries. The location of countries compared to others is not accidental—policy outcomes represent the combined interactions of modernization, political parties, interest groups, the electoral system, social movements, and all the other elements we covered in the earlier chapters. Most graphs include three ex-Communist Eastern European countries, the Czech Republic, Poland, and Hungary. In interpreting their location it is useful to keep their history in mind.

At this point it is useful to briefly discuss the difference between policy *output* and policy *outcome*. Policy output might mean, for example, a political program, or taxes, or particular regulation to achieve a particular outcome. In other words, policy output is not the "result" itself, it is a way to achieve, via political programs, taxes, regulation, and so on, a particular result. Say, for example, a country wants to reduce air pollution and in doing so produces legislation that forces factories to install so-called "scrubbers" in their chimneys to clean the air. If after a particular period of time, all factories have such scrubbers installed, that is an example of policy output. It does not represent the actual result yet. The actual outcome of that policy, it is hoped, would be reduced air pollution.

There are many instances where a particular policy output fails to achieve the expected policy outcome. One example is immigration policy in Germany. After the first oil shock in 1973/74, Germany stopped labor immigration. Yet, the number of immigrants continued to increase in Germany as a result of family unification and later as a result of asylum seekers. This incapacity to control the borders led to horrific attacks on immigrants in Germany and is at least partly responsible for the electoral success of radical right-wing parties in eastern parts of Germany. Another example is health policy in the United States. America has by far the most expensive health-care system in the world, yet its health outcomes, measured in terms of life expectancy and infant mortality, are below par given that its health-care system encompasses one-sixth of the American economy. Other countries achieve much better results with much lower costs.

This chapter is an exercise in "applied political science." In other words, it is an attempt to demonstrate that history, institutions, political structures, and so on, matter. They have actual, systematic, and sometimes even predictable outcomes. However, connecting outcomes and outputs is sometimes quite difficult because, surprisingly, relatively little research has investigated the determinants of policy outcomes. Not all outcomes are only driven by these factors we have highlighted in the previous eight chapters. Some outcomes can be explained by individual behavior, others by the natural resource endowment of countries, and others simply by the geographic location of countries. However, even in the arena of seemingly individual choices, such as whether to smoke or not, buying guns or not, or what foods can be purchased and eaten, the impact of politics is ubiquitous. Thus, public policy affects what appear to be individual choices as well as the provision of public goods, such as the environment. Think of the government's antismoking campaigns, for example, or the obligation to wear seat belts in cars, or the fashion in which governments manage public lands and attempt to protect natural resources. Politics enters into all the policy outcomes and outputs presented in the next section even though it sometimes seems that the outcomes are a matter of individual behavior. Some outcomes, such as obesity, which is fast becoming a major public health crisis in many developed democracies, at first appears to be simply a matter of individual choice. But is it really? Or is it a matter of "class"? Are obese people generally well to-do or are they generally poor? If it is the latter, political explanations are highly relevant in explaining variation of obesity across countries. In the next section, let us pretend to be policy analysts and let us go on this creative, and perhaps somewhat speculative, journey to find out whether there is a systematic way of understanding the bewildering variety of policy outcomes. This section is particularly useful as a starting point for more extensive research to delve deeper into the determinants of policy outcomes and outputs and lends itself ideally to term paper assignments.

EXPLAINING POLICY OUTCOMES

What are some of these policy outcomes most people are concerned about? Certainly it appears that macroeconomic outcomes such as unemployment, inflation, and economic growth are crucial results that directly affect most, if not all, citizens of a country either directly or indirectly. The state of the economy is traditionally one of the hottest topics during an election campaign. We heard in the chapter on cabinet formation (Chapter 4) how the German cabinet under chancellor Gerhard Schröder lost a crucial Land election as a result of his attempt to get unemployment under control, which in the spring of 2005 exceeded 10 percent. In some regions of Eastern Germany, unemployment reaches 20 percent, giving rise to regional radical right-wing parties. Similarly, inflation—which measures the changes in the consumer price index—is a crucial measure of government performance. Inflation appears in the form of rising prices, which can directly affect people's disposable income if their wages do not rise concomitantly with prices. Finally, economic growth, which is generally measured as the annual increase in the value of all goods and services produced (GDP—gross domestic product) is the most important measure of the economic well-being of a society. Figure 9.1 shows these three measures across a range of European Democracies and also for the United States.

What could explain the variation of these three measures across the set of industrial societies? Are there particular reasons to believe that some political parties may favor more or less unemployment and/or inflation? Would leftist parties favor policies that produce lower unemployment than inflation or vice versa? Would rightist parties favor economic policies that would create lower inflation than unemployment or vice versa? What about economic growth? Are there reasons to believe that some parties on the political spectrum would not favor economic growth? Or would all political parties favor economic growth? What are the potential "costs" of economic growth, and which political parties' fortunes might be positively affected by highlighting the "costs" of economic growth?

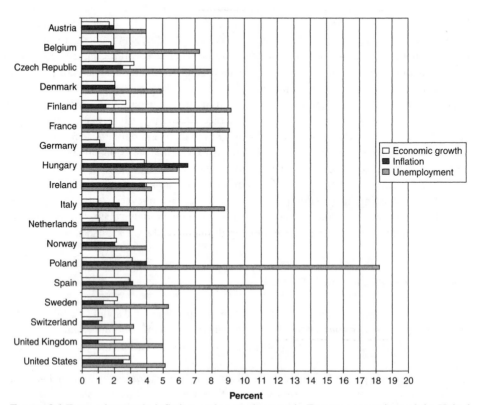

FIGURE 9.1 Economic growth, inflation, and unemployment in European countries and the United States. (*Source: OECD Economic Outlook* 77, June 2005.)

Other important economic measures are how much the state spends on social expenditures. Figure 1.1 in Chapter 1 shows the amount of social expenditures across many modern societies, with Denmark, Sweden, and France spending over 25 percent of their GDP on social welfare such as old-age benefits, health benefits, family benefits, and others, while the United States is last in that list, spending only a little over 14 percent. How can that be explained?

Similarly, Figure 1.2 in Chapter 1 shows what we termed the "redistributive capacity of the state," meaning the effect of taxes and transfer payments to reduce poverty (i.e., the percentage of household living below 50 percent of median income). For example, Belgium indicates a percentage of about 83. This means that taxes and transfer payments were able to reduce the percentage of people living below 50 percent of the median income by 83 percent. Sweden, Norway, Finland, and the Netherlands also show a high capacity to reduce poverty via taxes and transfer payments. These states can reduce poverty via taxes and transfer payments by over 75 percent. Why do you think these states have such a high capacity of poverty reduction compared to, say, the United States, where only 34 percent of households are lifted out of poverty via taxes and transfer payments?

The degree of poverty is a highly relevant policy outcome in its own right. Poor people tend to be less educated, encourage education less among their children, live in unhealthy conditions, tend to vote less, and, in general, have fewer "life chances" than the middle class. Figure 9.2 shows two policy outcomes: the percentage of households living in poverty (defined as the living below 50 percent of the median income) and total taxes as a percent of GDP. This is an example of the difference between policy output and policy outcomes. Taxes represent an example of policy output, whereas poverty is an example of policy outcome. Taxes are a "steering instrument" to achieve a particular outcome. The taxes dimension indicates the degree of "state interventionism" and highlights to what extent people are willing to tolerate the state extracting funds from them for redistribution toward specific outomes such as equalizing life chances or increasing military security.

Figure 9.2 is ordered from highest to lowest poverty, indicating the United States is at the top of the poverty scale while the Scandinavian countries, and the Czech Republic, an Eastern European country, indicate the lowest poverty. Although the United States shows the highest poverty, it also shows the lowest tax rates as compared to the Scandinavian countries, which tend to have higher total taxes. What might account for the varying rates in poverty and total taxes across these modern democracies?

One of the often heard definitions of politics is Harold Lasswell's: Who gets, what, when, and how? Who gets which pieces of the economic pie? A central principle of democracy is equality—where each voter's vote counts the same. But what about the economic system: Is there equality? How egalitarian are modern societies? Is economic inequality between groups consistent with the idea of democracy? The Greek philosopher Plutarch was very much aware of the corrosive forces of inquality. He declared that, "The most fatal ailment of all republics [is] the imbalance between rich and poor."

The *Gini coefficient* is the most useful of all measures of income inequality, as it captures inequality across the whole range of incomes. The Gini coefficient was developed by the Italian statistician Corrado Gini in 1912. The range of the coefficient is between 0 and 1. Zero means perfect equality with everybody having the same income, and 1 means perfect inequality; in other words, one person has all the income and nobody else has anything.

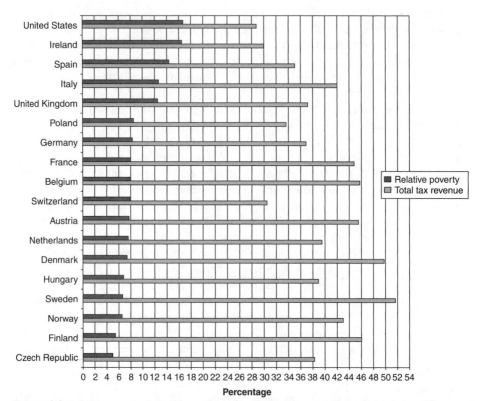

Percentage

Figure 9.2 Relative poverty for total population in 2000* (percent of households below 50 percent of the median income) ordered from highest to lowest poverty, and total tax revenue 2005 (as percentage of GDP). (*Source*: For relative poverty: Luxembourg Income Study. LIS Key Figures: For total taxes: OECD, Organization for Economic Cooperation and Development, *Factbook 2005: Public Policies, Total Tax revenue.*)
*Percentages are mostly for the year 2000 except for the Czech Republic (1996), Denmark (1992), France (1994), Hungary (1999), Netherlands (1999), Poland (1999), and the UK (1999).

In Figure 9.3 countries are ordered from highest to lowest income inequality, with the United States and the United Kingdom leading that list and with Finland and Denmark indicating the lowest income inequality. How can this be explained? Is equality of incomes important?

Perhaps a more rounded measure is necessary in order to capture the concept of "life chances." The Human Development Report (HDR) published by the United Nations Development Program (UNDP) argues that "Human development is about freedom. It is about building human capabilities .... Individual rights matter a great deal, but people are restricted in what they can do with their freedom if they are poor, ill, illiterate, discriminated against, threatened by violent conflict, or denied a political voice."[3] To that end, the HDR has developed various statistical measures capturing health, education, and access to resources. One such measure, specifically designed for high-income countries, is the human poverty index, as shown in Figure 9.4.

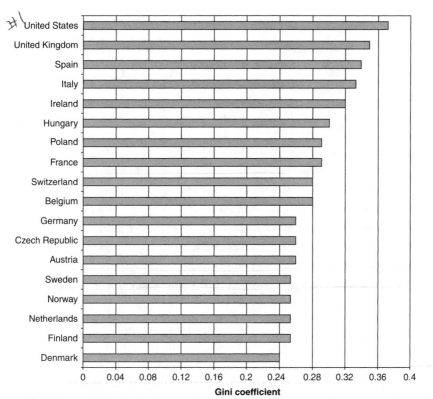

FIGURE 9.3 Gini coefficient for 18 democracies in 2000. (*Source*: Luxembourg Income Study, Key Figures.)
*Coefficients are mostly for the year 2000 except for the Czech Republic (1996), Denmark (1992), France (1994), Hungary (1999), Netherlands (1999), Poland (1999), and the UK (1999).

The index consists of four elements: the probability at birth of not surviving to age 60 (average 2000–2005), the percentage of population lacking functional literacy skills (average 1994–2003), long-term unemployment (2003), and the percent of population below 50 percent of the median income (1999–2000).

Using this composite measure, the Scandinavian countries rank the lowest in terms of human and income poverty, with the United States and particularly Italy indicating high human and income poverty. The plot thickens. How would you explain this outcome?

It may be possible that some of the outcomes we are trying to explain are a result of political participation of voters. Ultimately voting is the essence of democracy. How do the various countries stack up in political participation vis-à-vis each other? One measure of political participation is voter turnout. People vote for very different reasons: because they feel very strongly about a particular issue, or they are socialized into a particular political milieu that emphasizes voting as a duty of citizens, or they may vote simply out of habit. Figure 9.5 shows that there is quite some variation across modern democracies in terms of voter turnout. What might explain this variation?

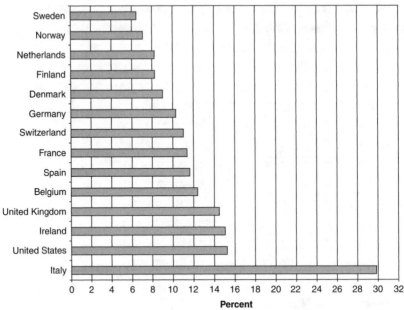

FIGURE 9.4 Human and income poverty ordered from lowest to highest. (*Source: Human Development Report*, 2005. UNDP (United Nations Development Program), New York).

Another measure that some observers argue is important is participation of women in parliaments. Even though both of these measures are included in the same graph, this does not suggest that there is necessarily a connection, although there might be. Women, it is argued, have different political interests than men, and if women were more equally represented in parliaments, policy production would reflect more of women's interests, such as parental leave, day care, social welfare issues, and others. Four Scandinavian countries are at the top, having the highest percentage of women in parliaments (lower house), and the United States, France, and Italy bring up the rear. What can explain the distribution of women in parliaments across these modern democracies?

Staying with the theme of gender, the World Economic Forum has recently established an index called the "global gender gap." It consists of five elements: economic participation (the presence of women in the workforce), economic opportunity (the *quality* of women's economic involvement), political empowerment (equitable representation of women in decision-making structures), educational attainment (literacy rates, school enrolment rates, and average years of schooling), and health and well-being (access to sufficient nutrition, health-care and reproductive facilities, and issues of fundamental safety and integrity) of women. The index ranges from 0 to 7, with 7 showing the lowest gender gap and 0 showing the highest gender gap.

In addition, Figure 9.6 shows the "growth competitiveness index," also created by the World Economic Forum. Again, for economy of presentation, both indices are shown together in the same graph. The growth competitiveness index is composed of three elements that are critical to economic growth: the quality of the macro-economic environment, the

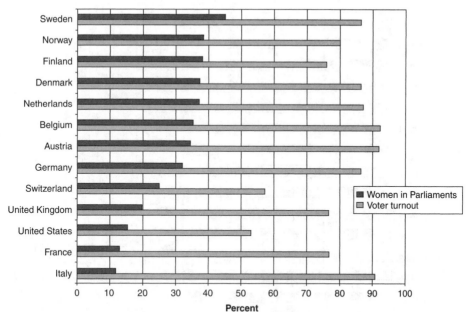

FIGURE 9.5 Women in parliaments (percent of women in the lower house) in 2005 and voter turnout (average from 1945–1999) ordered from highest percentage of women in parliaments to lowest percentage. (*Source: Women in Parliament: Interparliamentary Union 2005,* http://www.ipu.org. For voter turnout: Mark N. Franklin, "The Voter Turnout Puzzles." Paper presented at the Fulbright Brainstorm Conference on Voter Turnout, Portugal, February 2002, p. 7.)

state of the country's public institutions, and the country's technological readiness. The index also ranges from 0, meaning low growth competitiveness, to 7, meaning maximum growth competitiveness. Figure 9.6 is ordered along the growth competitiveness index.

The countries with the biggest gender gap are Italy, Switzerland, and Spain, whereas Sweden, Denmark, and Finland are the countries most friendly to women's interests. In terms of growth competitiveness, Finland, the United States, and Sweden are in the lead and the Czech Republic, Italy, and Poland are at the bottom. Looking at all the previous chapters in this book, do they contain any explanations that might shed light on these rankings?

One of the most important policy outcomes is health. For a society to be productive, it has to be healthy. Countries lose billions of dollars per year as a result of workers who are absent from work due to illness. In addition, treating sick people from preventable diseases such as AIDS, lung cancer caused by smoking, or obesity absorbs huge resources that could be employed in other areas. For example, the United States Food and Drug Administration estimates that obesity alone created economic costs to the tune of over 117 billion dollars in 2004.[4] In the United Kingdom, obesity has tripled during the last 20 years. Obesity in the UK is responsible for an estimated 18 million sick days a year, a reduction in life-span by nine years on average, and its economic costs are an estimated 2 billion pounds a year.[5]

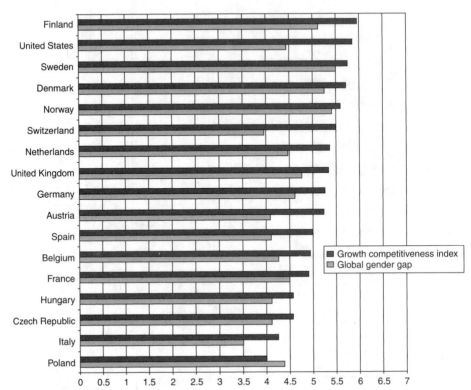

FIGURE 9.6 Global gender gap (2005) and growth competitiveness index, 2004. (*Source*: World Economic Forum, *Measuring the Global Gender Gap and Global Competitiveness Report*, 2005–06. http://www.weforum.org.)

Figure 9.7 shows three measures: health spending as a percentage of GDP (an output measure), and two outcome measures—Infant mortality (deaths per 1,000 live births) and obesity (percent of population aged 15 and above with a body mass index of more than 30). The graph is ordered from highest to lowest health spending. Figure 9.7 shows that the United States has the highest health expenditures with by far the highest level of obesity and high infant mortality. In fact, only two ex-Communist Central and Eastern European countries, Hungary and Poland, have higher infant mortality rates. Finland, Norway, and Sweden show the lowest levels of infant mortality achieved with lower, particularly in the case of Finland, health expenditures while at the same time achieving lower levels of obesity. What might explain the varying levels of health expenditures, obesity, and infant mortality?

The "gold standard" for the health of nations is life expectancy. As Figure 9.8 demonstrates, there are significant differences in life expectancies across different nations. The nations with the lowest life expectancies are the former Communist nations of Eastern Europe, Hungary, Poland, and the Czech Republic, whereas people in Italy, Sweden, and Switzerland live the longest. What could explain these differences in life expectancies?

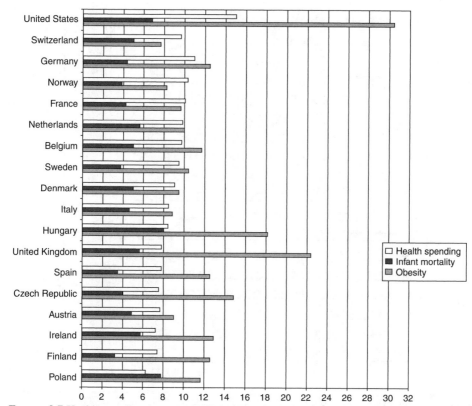

FIGURE 9.7 Health spending (percent of GDP, 2003), obesity (percent of population aged 15 and above with a body mass index of more than 30, 2005), and infant mortality (deaths per 1,000 live births, 2001). (*Source*: OECD (Organization for Economic Cooperation and Development), Paris, Health Data 2005.)

There is hardly a government that does not realize how crucial an educated citizenry is. At a very basic level, democracy itself is not possible without an educated citizenry. But even at more mundane levels, education is crucial in a globalized world where skills are absolutely essential to succeed, not only for individual companies but also for countries as a whole. In the international competition for foreign direct investments (i.e., private companies that are investing significant resources in a country other than where they are headquartered), a highly educated workforce combined with an excellent infrastructure and political stability are about the most important reasons why such companies invest their resources. Today, it is understood that "human capital" (i.e., knowledge and education), is as important as investment capital (i.e., land and machinery).

Figure 9.9 shows two "output" measures and one "outcome" measure. The outcome measure is the so-called PISA measure, which stands for OECD's "Program for International Student Assessment," whose purpose it is to "assess how effective school systems are in providing young people with a solid foundation of knowledge and skills that will

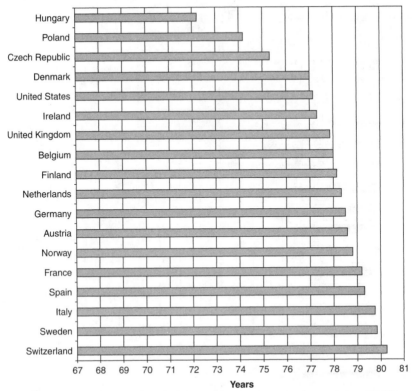

Figure 9.8 Life expectancy at birth (2001). (*Source*: OECD, Paris, Health Data 2005).

equip them for life and learning beyond school."[6] The survey covers mathematics, reading, science, and problem solving. The two output measures are total (public and private) education expenditures and expenditures in research and development, both measured as percentage of GDP. The graph is ordered from the highest to the lowest PISA scores, showing Finland and the United Kingdom at the top and Norway and Denmark at the bottom of that scale. In terms of combined public and private education expenditures, the United States and Finland spend the most on education, and the Czech Republic and Ireland are at the bottom of that list. When it comes to expenditures on research and development, the two ex-Communist countries Hungary and Poland are at the bottom and Sweden and Finland are at the top. What could explain their ranking?

The state of the environment has become a critical political issue over the last two decades. Figure 9.10 shows three outcome measures: the first is carbon dioxide emissions per capita in metric tons. Carbon dioxide is one of the main contributors to global warming and stems mostly from the burning of fossil fuels, such as gasoline and oil, but also from gas flaring and the production of cement. One of the biggest contributors to the production of carbon dioxide is driving: burning one gallon of gasoline produces 22 pounds of carbon dioxide.[7] Environmental issues have become so pressing that in many European countries during the 1980s, Green parties gained representation in their parliaments.

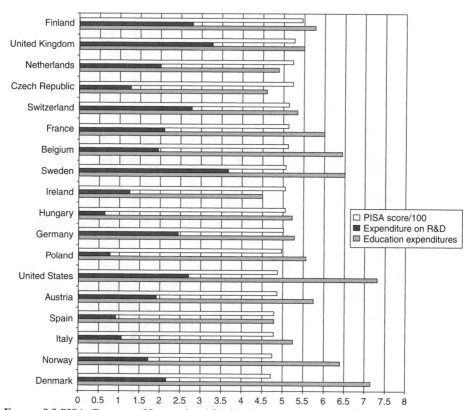

FIGURE 9.9 PISA (Program of International Student Assessment) scores/100, science scale (2003), expenditures on research and development (percent of GDP, 1999), and combined public and private education expenditures (percent of GDP, 2001). (*Source*: OECD, Paris, Factbook 2005.)

Note: PISA scores have been divided by 100 to make them comparable to the scale for the other two measures. For Poland and Switzerland only the public education expenditures are available. The PISA score for the UK refers to the year 2000, and score for R&D in Switzerland refers to 1996.

The United States indicates the highest per capita carbon dioxide emissions, 20 metric tons per person, which is significantly higher than the next largest country, Norway, which produces a little over 12 metric tons per person. Sweden, Switzerland, and Hungary are the bottom of that list, producing not quite 6 metric tons of carbon dioxide per person. In terms of municipal waste generation, the United States and Switzerland are most wasteful, producing 730 kg and 660 kg of waste per person, respectively. Finally, in terms of electricity consumption, Norway, Finland, and Sweden use by far the most electricity per capita while Poland, Hungary, and the Czech Republic use the least amount of electricity. These are intriguing results. How would you explain them?

Some of these outcomes are a result of the size of the country, their geographic location, and their specific resource endowment, although they are all mediated by politics. A more useful measure would capture the capacity for "environmental sustainability," that

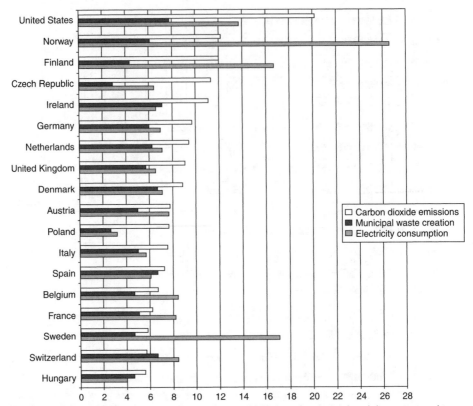

FIGURE 9.10 Carbon dioxide emissions per capita 2002 (metric tons), electricity consumption per capita, 2002 (megawatt hours), and municipal waste creation (in 100-kilogram units per capita), 2002. (*Source*: For carbon dioxide emissions per capita and electricity consumption per capita: Human Development Report, UNDP, 2005. For municipal waste creation: OECD, Paris, Factbook 2005.)

is, the capacity of a country to produce goods and services without unduly damaging the environment. Fortunately, such a index has recently been constructed by the Yale Center for Environmental Law and Policy together with the Center for International Earth Science Information Network at Columbia University in cooperation with the World Economic Forum and the Joint Research Center of the European Commission. They call their measure "Environmental Sustainability Index" and it is designed to "benchmark the ability of nations to protect the environment over the next several decades."[8] The index consists of five components: the degree to which environmental systems are maintained at healthy levels, the degree to which human-induced environmental stresses are low or being reduced, the degree to which human vulnerability to environmental stresses is reduced, the degree to which countries have a social and institutional capacity to respond to environmental challenges, and the degree to which a country is willing to cooperate with others to manage common environmental problems. See Figure 9.11.

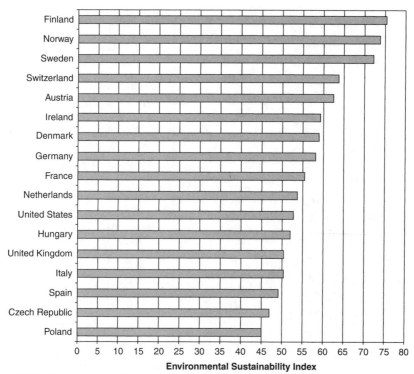

FIGURE 9.11 Environmental Sustainability Index. (*Source*: Daniel C. Esty, Marc Levy, Tanja Srebotnjak, and Alexander de Sherbinin, *2005 Environmental Sustainability Index. Benchmarking National Environmental Stewardship* (New Haven: Yale Center for Environmental Law and Policy, 2005).)

According to this index, which ranges from 0 to 100, the countries that rank the highest are Finland, Norway, and Sweden and those that rank the lowest are Spain, the Czech Republic, and Poland. These are intriguing rankings—what might explain them?

Finally, to what extent are developed nations willing to support development in other countries? One measure of that commitment is called "official development assistance." The United Nations has a long-standing goal that developed nations should commit .7 percent of their gross national income to official development assistance. Official development assistance is defined as "government aid to developing countries designed to promote the economic development and welfare of recipient countries. Loans and credits for military purposes are excluded."[9] Aid includes grants, "soft loans" (where the grant element is at least 25 percent), and the provision of technical assistance. A significant proportion of development assistance is aimed at promoting sustainable development in poorer countries, environmental protection, and population programs.

Official development assistance is often taken as a measure of "compassion" of the rich countries toward the plight of the poor countries. No developed country wants to be appear "stingy," yet the statistics speak louder than politician's talk. This was highlighted when a UN official, in the wake of the horrific tsunami in Southeast Asia on Boxing Day

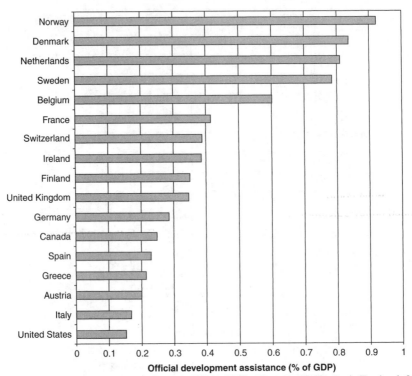

FIGURE 9.12 Official development assistance (ODA) 2003. (*Source*: OECD, Paris Factbook 2005.)

in 2004, complained about the fact that "the foreign assistance of many countries now is 0.1 or 0.2 percent of the gross national income. I think that is stingy, really."[10] It was mostly the United States that felt offended by this statement, although, as measured in terms of a percentage of GDP, the United States is not alone among rich countries in missing the UN goal of 0.7 percent. However, as Figure 9.12. makes clear, compared to its wealth, the United States is indeed the stingiest of developed countries, contributing only .15 of its GDP. It is important to realize, though, that in terms of actual money, .15 percent of American GDP (about 15.8 billion dollars) is significantly higher than .92 of Norway's GDP (a little over 2 billion dollars) in 2003.[11] Yet, it is true also that most of American Development Assistance goes to Israel and Egypt, two major allies of the United States in the Middle East. The most generous donors, as shown in Figure 9.12, are Norway, Denmark, and the Netherlands and the least-generous donors are Austria, Italy, and the United States. What might explain this ranking?

There are many more policy outcomes that could be analyzed, for instance, the percentage of people imprisoned, gun ownership, government deficits, subsidies, production of crucial strategic goods such as coal and steel, migration levels, hours worked, labor productivity, trade, savings rates, and foreign direct investment, to name but a few. The important lesson of this chapter is that most, if not all, of these policy outcomes and outputs are a direct result of many of the factors we highlighted in the first eight chapters of this book. The questions posed in this chapter should make for some exciting term papers as they highlight the connection between political parties, electoral systems, social movements, different histories in terms of modernization, and actual political outcomes that affect us all. The perhaps even more important lesson of this chapter is that politics matters. This is worth remembering when the next election comes around and citizens are asked to vote. After all, is it not true that in democratic systems people get the policy outcomes they deserve?

Discussion Questions

1. Above we cautioned students to distinguish between "policy outcomes" and "policy outputs." What is the difference between them?

2. What could turn the most well intentioned policy output into failure (i.e. an unintended policy outcome)?

3. In Chapter 8 we learned that globalization affects the political economics of all nations. How? Would globalization make it easier or harder for governments to achieve the intended policy outcomes? Why?

---

[1]Hoge, W. Swedish Party Pledging Expanded Welfare Gains Slim Victory. *New York Times* (1998).
[2]BBC News. Saturday, September 14, 2002.
[3]*Human Development Report 2005*. United Nations Development Program, New York, p. 18.
[4]U.S. Food and Drug Administration. *HHS Tackles Obesity*. (May 2004).
[5]British House of Commons. Ninth Report. *Tackling Obesity in England*. London.
[6]OECD, Paris, Factbook 2005. International Student Assessment. Definition.
[7]The National Energy Foundation. CO2 Calculator. See:
http://www.nef.org.uk/energyadvice/co2calculator.htm.
[8]Daniel C. Esty, Marc Levy, Tanja Srebotnjak, and Alexander de Sherbinin. *2005 Environmental Sustainability Index. Benchmarking National Environmental Stewardship*. (New Haven: Yale Center for Environmental Law and Policy, 2005). The report is available on the Internet: at http://www.yale.edu/esi.
[9]OECD, Paris, Factbook 2005.
[10]Relief Efforts Stingy, says UN official. *The Tribune*, Online Edition. (December 29, 2004).
[11]Anup Shah. The US and Foreign Aid Assistance. Global Issues. Sustainable Development. (2005). See http://www.globalissues.org/TradeRelated/Debt/USAid.asp.

The End of the Cold War

We add now one more layer to the explanation of current European politics: the cold war after 1945 and its end 1989. In order to understand current European politics, we must come to terms with the fact that the continent was divided for almost half a century by an Iron Curtain dividing the Communist East and the Democratic West. In order to make the argument that the cold war still matters, we can refer to the term of *path dependency*. This is an important concept in political science meaning that the historical path of a country always has some influence on the present. The past constrains to some extent the viable options for the present. Renowned political scientist Stein Rokkan has demonstrated in his seminal research that current party systems are dependent on the path that a country took centuries back, for example in the Reformation and the French Revolution.[1]

If such long-ago events still have a contemporary influence, this is all the more so for such a recent event as the cold war, especially because the cold war was such a crucial episode in European history. People in Central and Eastern Europe were trapped in a large prison and could not escape, and if they tried, they risked being shot. When visiting Berlin, one is still reminded of the Wall dividing the city during the cold war and the people who were killed attempting to cross over it. In the Communist countries in Central and Eastern Europe people who dared to speak up against the regime were severely punished; they lost their jobs, were sent to prison and labor camps, and even may have lost their life in mysterious car accidents with probable involvement of the secret state police. We recently visited Warsaw and Budapest and have seen many monuments, plaques, and exhibits reminding us that in these countries the memories of the cold war are still fresh and painful.

The continuing impact of the cold war can also be demonstrated with the statistical data presented in Chapter 9. To the extent that data were available we included three former Communist countries, the Czech Republic, Hungary, and Poland. Figure 9.8 reveals that these three countries are at the very bottom of life expectancy. This low ranking occurs also for the growth competitive index in Figure 9.6, although here Italy is lower than the Czech Republic and Hungary. For unemployment Poland has a terrible record, with almost 20 percent unemployed; for the Czech Republic and Hungary the employment situation is better but not great (Figure 9.1). According to Figure 9.11, the Environmental Sustainability Index, Poland is last, the Czech Republic second last, and Hungary somewhat better, sixth last. These data make clear that the cold war still has an influence on how well European countries are currently doing, Western countries generally faring better than Central and Eastern countries.

That Central and Eastern Europe came under communism is to a large extent due to the imperialistic power of the Soviet Union. But communism also held some intellectual attraction, so that it had some support in Western Europe as well, in particular in Italy and France. The intellectual base of communism was Marxism, which was developed in the 19th century. In a first section, we go back to these Marxist roots of communism to see what the attraction was.

176

CLASSICAL MARXISM

Who was Karl Marx, the man who had such a great influence on the Communist movement? A German philosopher, Marx was born in 1818 in Trier, in southwestern Germany, and died in 1883 in exile in London. Among his famous publications are *Das Kapital* and, together with Friedrich Engels, *The Communist Manifesto*. What are the assumptions on which the philosophy of Marx is based? The most basic axiom is that human thinking and behavior are determined by economic factors. Marx speaks of an economic infrastructure and a noneconomic superstructure. Therefore, all meaningful explanations must begin with the economy of a society: its infrastructure. Causality begins with the material aspects of human life. All other aspects, such as politics, religion, education, and the arts, belong to the superstructure. These superstructural aspects can be understood only on the basis of their economic infrastructure. Thus, in the Marxist view, religious beliefs can be understood only on the basis of the society's economic infrastructure.

The economy is a broad concept, so which characteristics of economic life are of particular importance according to Marx? Here we come to a second basic assumption: The ownership of the means of production is the crucial factor. Marx distinguishes three means of production: land, capital, and labor. The basic distinction in society is whether someone owns land and capital or can offer only his or her labor. In industrial societies, the former are capitalists and the latter proletarians. During the early period of industrialization, when Marx wrote, many people could not clearly be classified as belonging to one of these two social classes. A baker, for example, who worked with his family and perhaps an apprentice, was neither a capitalist nor a proletarian. Marx predicted that such intermediate cases would become less and less frequent and that society would increasingly be divided into only the two classes, capitalists and proletarians. This prediction corresponded to what was to him a historical law, one he thought he had discovered in studying the industrialization of his time. With the increased costs of new technologies, companies needed to become bigger and bigger to survive. If the baker wanted to remain competitive, he had to transform his family bakery into a big factory. If he was not successful, he would become a laborer in such a factory. Land and capital would accumulate in the hands of fewer and fewer capitalists, and these capitalists would become richer and richer. But competition among capitalists would remain fierce, and to finance their expansion they would need a lot of money. The place where they can easily get this money is the proletariat. In this context, Marx coins the concept of *surplus value of labor*. This is the value of work done by the proletarians that is not returned to them in the form of wages, but is kept by the capitalists in the form of profits. According to Marx, this surplus value of labor would steadily increase so that less and less would remain for the proletarians, who would sink more and more into poverty. This is what Marx meant when he called the capitalists *exploiters* and the proletarians *exploitees*.

Marx argued that the frustrations of the proletariat would eventually lead to a revolution that would overthrow the capitalists and bring the proletariat to power (see Box 10.1). Following the historical laws that Marx thought he had discovered, this revolution would occur by necessity. The only question was where and when it would happen. According to Marx, it was also certain that the revolution ultimately would be successful. After the revolution, the proletariat would establish a dictatorship. Marx called this the Socialist phase. This dictatorship was necessary to prevent a counterrevolution of the capitalists, who were

Box 10.1 Excerpts from the Communist Manifesto

The proletariat will use its political supremacy to wrest, by degrees, all capital from the bourgeoisie, to centralize all instruments of production in the hands of the State, i.e., of the proletariat organized as a ruling class; and to increase the total productive forces as rapidly as possible. . . . The Communists disdain to conceal their views and aims. They openly declare that their ends can be attained only by the forcible overthrow of all existing social conditions. Let the ruling class tremble at a Communistic revolution. The proletarians have nothing to lose but their chains. They have a world to win. Working men of all countries, unite!

Source: *The World's Great Thinkers. Man and the State: The Political Philosophers* (New York: Random House, 1947, pp. 509, 523). (Originally published in 1847 by Karl Marx and Friedrich Engels.)

also likely to operate from foreign countries. Consequently, it was necessary to bring the proletarian revolution to the entire world. The capitalists, with their selfish profit orientation, must be defeated everywhere, and until this was achieved, the proletariat would have to maintain its dictatorship.

The transition from the Socialist to the Communist phase could occur only when the capitalist mentality had been eliminated from the world. At this point, the dictatorship of the proletariat would no longer be necessary. All people would have been educated to think in an altruistic, unselfish way instead of the earlier egotistical way. With this new orientation, all people would take from society only what they needed, and they would contribute everything that was within their capabilities. As a consequence, there would be no more scarcities, only a happy situation of plenty. Under these circumstances, the state would fade away. It would have become unnecessary. Because everyone would be morally pure, no police, no military, and no courts would be needed. And taxes wouldn't even have to be collected because all members of society would contribute on a voluntary basis—all having become altruists.

How would people actually live in this final Communist phase? Marx, writing together with Friedrich Engels, claimed that Communist society would make it "possible for me to do one thing today and another tomorrow, to hunt in the morning, fish in the afternoon, rear cattle in the evening, criticize after dinner."[2] As political scientist William James Booth correctly argues: "Marx does not raise the issue of whether, for example, hunting is to be preferred to philosophy or, in general, of what the good life is. It is sufficient, for Marx, that . . . the individual be free of constraint."[3]

Given this vision of no constraints and ultimate salvation, Marxism may be interpreted as a religion or, at least, as a substitute for a religion. This is the way the French writer Albert Camus interprets Marx.[4] In communism, as in a religion, the promise of one day reaching a utopian land of no evil encourages people to sacrifice in the present. The uncertainties of the present can be overcome by the certainties of the future. The sociologist Daniel Bell, too, interprets Marxism as a religion:

What were the attractions of revolutionary Marxism that drew so many passionate intellectuals to its flag? What was the faith that, like that of the first-century Christian martyrs, summoned many to die for a cause? In one respect, the answer is simple: What once had appealed in the name of God crossed over to the banner of History. The belief remained in an eschatology that would end a divided consciousness, which placed men in a state of alienation. Marxism was a secular religion.[5]

Are Camus and Bell on the right track to interpret Marxism as a religion? Or is it blasphemy to see Marxism in these terms? After all, Marx declared religion as the opiate for the masses.

Neo-Marxism

By the 1950s, Marxism had become intellectually out of favor. It seemed that its socio-logical class analysis was all wrong. Instead of having an increasingly two-class system in highly industrialized societies, a broad middle class seemed to emerge. Thus, the potential for a proletarian revolution outside the Soviet bloc appeared increasingly remote. The arguments raised at the time against Marxist class analysis were as follows:

1. Workers in capitalist societies have not sunk into an impoverished proletarian situation. Compared with the 19th century, when Marx wrote, they have been able to improve their standard of living, and today many of them enjoy a considerable wealth of consumer goods, although there are still large pockets of poverty.

2. Stocks are not concentrated in the hands of fewer and fewer individuals. On the contrary, more and more people participate in the stock market, in particular through new means such as mutual funds.

3. Business decisions are influenced not only by those who own stocks but also by a wide range of managers with special skills in law, engineering, economics, and so on.

4. Class structure is flexible, and there are many people who, thanks to their energy and intelligence, move from the bottom to the top in their own lifetime. On the other hand, there is also downward mobility.

5. There is a growing public sector of teachers, police, civil servants, and so on for whom the distinction between capitalists and proletarians does not apply.

6. There is a growing service sector in the private economy of health-care workers, hotel and restaurant workers, and so on, and people working in this sector are hard to organize in trade unions because they do not perceive themselves as workers in the classical sense.

7. Since the time Marx wrote, democratic forms of government have become more prevalent in highly developed capitalistic countries. In democratic elections everyone has one vote without regard for ownership of land and capital, although more affluent people have a higher chance to influence the election campaign.

8. Besides the difference between social classes, there are other important social distinctions, for example, those based on religion, race, language, and region. Important substantive issues such as abortion also cut across social classes.

PHOTO 10.1 Marx and Lenin speculations as to why communism may have failed. (*Source:* Roy Peterson, *Vancouver Sun*)

All of these arguments against the class analysis of Marx add up to a pluralistic view of society. This view does not deny the fact that some people are very rich and others are very poor. Most people, however, are somewhere in the middle—some a little higher, others a little lower.

By the 1960s and 1970s, however, a new brand of Marxist scholars—neo-Marxists—gave new vigor to class analysis. Their analyses often differed in details, but their overall conclusion was always the same: Highly developed capitalist countries basically have a two-class structure of capitalists and proletarians. Their position was roughly as follows:

1. To give the workers access to consumer goods has a double advantage for the capitalists. First, it helps to pacify the workers. If they have cars for traveling and television sets for watching sports, they lose their revolutionary zeal. But to possess consumer goods does not mean the workers have gained any control over the important economic decisions in society; it only means they forget that they have no real economic influence at all. The workers have moved into a state of false class consciousness. Blinded by the richness of consumer goods, they think subjectively that they are no longer exploited, whereas objectively they still are. Second, giving consumer goods to the workers keeps the capitalist system going. Capitalists are aware of the danger of an impoverished proletariat that is not able to buy the increasing number of goods produced by the capitalist system. To prevent this danger, the capitalists are willing to increase the workers' wages. Although these wage increases marginally diminish the profits of the capitalists in the short run, their profits will soar in the long run as a result of higher production levels. Overall, giving consumer goods to the workers in no way threatens the powerful position of those who own land and capital.

2. What about the argument that today many workers are themselves owners of stocks? Can't these workers exercise power in shareholders' annual meetings? Not really, say neo-Marxists. To have true power in a company, one must own a large block of its stocks, not just a token few. With five or ten shares, workers get some dividends, and perhaps a nice meal at the shareholders' meeting, but have no real economic influence. The major effect is a reinforcement of their false class consciousness. With the possession of a few shares of stock, or participation in mutual funds, workers think of themselves as members of the middle class. Hoping to share in the profits, they now support the capitalist system. Thus, the dominant position of the capitalists is strengthened if they disperse stocks broadly among the population, as long as they keep the majority of the stocks in their own hands.

3. How do neo-Marxists handle the argument that many important business decisions are influenced not by shareholders but by managers, most of whom count themselves among the middle classes? A neo-Marxist would respond that one must distinguish between top managers on the one hand and middle- and lower-level managers on the other hand. The latter are merely useful tools in the hands of the capitalists. They help to control the workers, which does not mean they have any broad-based economic power. Although they are not aware of it, these middle- and lower-level managers are just as exploited as the workers, in many ways even more so, because they have fewer opportunities to escape the pressures of work. The top managers, on the other hand, belong to the capitalist class, with which they share the same social background and values. Quite often, these top managers also own a high number of stocks.

4. Aren't there many top managers who have advanced their careers through hard work and intelligence? Neo-Marxists do not deny the existence of such upward mobility, but they insist that such cases are rare and do not threaten the capitalist system. Before someone is allowed to reach the top level of a company, that person is carefully scrutinized to make sure he or she accepts the basic values of capitalism. Therefore, such upwardly mobile people constitute no threat to the existing class structure. Their success stories even help to reinforce this structure by giving it the appearance of flexibility. Here neo-Marxists allude to the tendencies of the mass media to publicize the life stories of people who move from the bottom to the top. But these stories are always of a few rare cases, and the fact that the overwhelming majority of proletarians never have a chance to enter the capitalist class does not change. Yet, seeing others move up, proletarians begin to attribute their own failure to personal shortcomings instead of the objective characteristics of the existing class structure. Such a perception further diminishes the class consciousness of the proletariat.

5. How does the increasing number of public employees fit into the neo-Marxist distinction between capitalists and proletarians? Just as in the private sector, a distinction is made between top public employees and those in middle and lower levels. The top bureaucrats belong to the capitalist class, with which they share the same social background and values. Whenever a basic conflict between the social classes arises, the top bureaucrats virtually always take the pro-capitalist position. Specifically, this means the top bureaucrats defend the concept of private property. If in rare cases they do not do so, they may lose their jobs or at least their promotion chances. In this sense, business has a privileged position to influence basic decisions of top civil servants. Top bureaucrats only remain neutral in conflicts between two property rights, such as between two automobile

companies. Middle- and lower-level public employees are merely useful tools in the hands of the top bureaucrats. Teachers in the public schools help to socialize the children to the values of the capitalist system. To support this argument, neo-Marxists refer to textbooks that teach children in subtle ways how the profit motive contributes to the betterment of society. The police help the capitalists to control the proletariat, and tax collectors extract money from the lower class. Although teachers, police, tax collectors, and other public employees in similar positions are probably not aware of it, objectively they are in an exploited proletarian situation.

6. Employees in the service sector of the private economy are just as powerless and exploited as workers in the manufacturing sector. A hairdresser working for a wage is not in a different situation than a mechanic getting wages from an automobile company. The kind of clothing one wears for work does not make a difference, although workers in the service sector often think so.

7. Doesn't the principle of one person, one vote, in democratic elections contribute to some extent to equality among all citizens? Again, neo-Marxists disagree with this contention. First, decisions made by politicians are relatively unimportant compared with the decisions made in the boardrooms of the big multinational corporations. The main function of the political game is to entertain the public while diverting its attention from the more important business decisions. Second, to the extent that elections have any importance, they are manipulated by capitalist money that buys influence over nearly all parties and candidates. To understand the outcome of elections, it is important to know that newspapers, television, and radio are all directly or indirectly controlled by capital. Third, even if parties of the Left win elections, these parties merely do useful repair work for the capitalistic system without changing it in any fundamental way. Capitalists may sometimes even be glad when the Left wins, because a prime minister or a president of the Left may further help to cover up the real power structure in society, in the sense that leftist voters may get the wrong impression that they exercise real political power.

8. It may be true that there is an important social distinction between the superrich and everyone else. But aren't other social differences also important? Not according to neo-Marxists. These other distinctions either reinforce the class difference or are merely superficial. The former situation is said to exist in the conflict between whites and blacks in the United States, where the capitalist class is almost exclusively white and most blacks have proletarian status. This does not mean, of course, that there are not masses of white proletarians, only that nearly all capitalists are white. In the view of neo-Marxists, the race element helps to hide the real class structure. Capitalists are defended by white proletarians who are not aware of their real class interest, which, objectively, would be with the proletarians, regardless of race. Differences other than those based on social class can also be purely superficial, such as the language divisions in Switzerland, where capitalists come from all three major linguistic areas. Large banks are located in German-speaking Zurich, French-speaking Geneva, and Italian-speaking Lugano. Objectively, the proletariat from all three linguistic groups has the same class interest. To play one linguistic group against another is merely a surface conflict that helps to divert attention from the real class conflict. The same would be true, according to the neo-Marxist argument, for conflicts over issues such as abortion, which are only a means to divert attention from the class conflict.

In the 1960s and 1970s, neo-Marxist analysis had great intellectual appeal in Western Europe's academic circles, and also among intellectuals in other parts of the world such as Latin America, but much less so in the United States. Why is it that the United States was much less receptive to Neo-Marxist analysis? *Perhaps because of the strong role of religion in American society? Or the pragmatic-individualistic nature of American culture? Or because of its status of superpower, the United States has seen Marxism as a deadly enemy in the cold war, more so than other countries?*

COMMUNISM IN WESTERN EUROPE

Communists in Western Europe during the cold war were certainly supported in many different ways by the Soviets. But they were not simply Soviet agents; they had their own reasons to be Communists. For Americans, who tend to identify communism with the Soviet Union, it is not easy to understand why during the cold war a fairly large number of Western Europeans chose to vote for Communist parties. Communism in Western Europe was referred to as *Eurocommunism*.

It is important to note that Eurocommunists had strong internal disagreements, which indicates that they did not simply execute orders from Moscow. Heated debates ensued about exactly what Marx meant by the concept of revolution and how he would interpret this concept under Western European conditions. The terrorist Left argued that violence needed to be used to overthrow the existing class system, whereas the official Communist parties took the position that revolutionary change could be caused through participation in the electoral process.

The terrorist Left was particularly active in the 1970s and the early 1980s. Estimates are difficult to make, but probably no more than a few thousand people in all of Western Europe were ever active in the terrorist Left. It consisted of no single organization, but was split into a large number of groups that often were in fierce competition with one another. Well known were the Red Brigades in Italy, the Red Army Faction in West Germany, and Direct Action in France.

Through kidnapping, assassinations, and other spectacular terrorist acts, the terrorist Left attracted worldwide attention to their cause. Just exactly what was this cause? What were they fighting for? The terrorist Left in Western Europe believed capitalism could only be overcome through violence. But because most proletarians had lost their class consciousness, the violent overthrow of capitalism had become difficult. Before a successful revolution can take place, the proletariat must be stripped of its false consciousness so that it can recognize the extent of its exploitation by the capitalists. How can this be demonstrated with sufficient clarity and vividness? The answer of the terrorist Left was to provoke the capitalists so they would be forced to show their "real face." If you shoot them in the knees and kill a few, they will bring out their military and police forces, and the brutality of their regime will become visible. The eyes of the proletarians will be opened to their true class situation. It turned out that the terrorist Left strategy failed. Instead of turning against the authorities, most workers turned against the terrorists.

Who were the terrorists? Were they the poorest of the poor in society, acting out of desperation? Not at all. Most terrorists came from affluent families and attended good schools. Women were heavily involved in the terrorist Left. Originally, many of these people had high ideals—a vision of a utopian, classless society with happiness for all. But, once engaged in terrorist activity, they were so busy hiding, robbing, and acquiring weapons that they no longer had the time and leisure to reflect on what this classless society might look like.

The Communist parties in Western Europe tried to organize politically and to participate in elections. The greatest success the Communists had was in Italy. In the first parliamentary election after World War II in 1946, the Communists received 19 percent of the votes. Their share then steadily increased from election to election, to a high point of 34 percent in 1976. Afterward, a slow decline resulted in 27 percent in 1987, the last election before the end of the cold war. The other country where for a long time the Communists had substantial electoral support was France. After World War II and until the mid-1950s, the French Communist Party received about 25 percent of the votes at each election. Their voter share then decreased to around 20 percent, and stayed at this level until the end of the 1970s. A further decline occurred in the 1980s, to about 10 percent of the votes. There were no other Western European countries where the Communists had as much electoral success as in Italy and France. But in four countries—Finland, Greece, Portugal, and Spain—the Communists received, at least for some elections, two-digit support.

During the cold war, Americans could easily understand how communism had a grip on the satellite countries of the Soviet Union in Central and Eastern Europe, and how the terrorist Left tried to destabilize the democracies in Western Europe. But most Americans had difficulty understanding what the Communist parties in Western Europe were up to. Were they not steered by the Soviet Union, and would they not ultimately band together with the terrorist Left? Was participation in elections not just another means to destabilize the West? The Communist parties in Western Europe always declared that they were not involved in any terrorist activities and that they respected basic democratic principles. Increasingly they began to criticize the Soviet Union, for example, over the invasion of Czechoslovakia and Afghanistan and the existence of concentration camps in Siberia. The Italian Communist Party was particularly vocal in its criticism of the Soviet Union, the French Communists much less so. In their election campaigns, the Eurocommunists promised to bring more justice to the societies of Western Europe. They advocated stiffer taxes on the rich and more generous social programs for the poor.

How do we evaluate the rhetoric of the Western European Communist parties during the cold war? Was it all a well-orchestrated campaign of disinformation, or did some Communists in Western Europe really believe in democratic principles? Box 10.2 shows how

Box 10.2 Jean-Pierre Quilgars, French Factory Worker

"Being a Communist has brought me many things. It has brought me friends, a way to reflect on both political and personal life. It has permitted me to have confidence in myself and believe in myself. I couldn't think of not being a Communist. It's my life. I don't make an effort to be a Communist. I live it. . . . I am proud to be a Communist and have always been proud to be a Communist. There were difficult times on the international front, Afghanistan, for example, but I was never embarrassed to call myself a Communist."

Source: *New York Times*, January 23, 1989.

at the very end of the cold war, a French factory worker still expressed his faith in the Communist ideals. It is hard to distrust completely the sincerity of such statements.

In Italy and France, many local communities had Communist parties in power for a long time. How was this power exercised? Were basic civil liberties curtailed? The answer is clearly no. A well-known example is the old Italian city of Bologna, which has been ruled for many years by the Communists and has enjoyed a good local administration. Do such examples prove that the Communists had accepted democratic principles? Not necessarily. Local communities are subordinated to the national governmental authorities, who are obliged to intervene if local communities violate basic democratic principles.

During a brief period following World War II, France had some Communist cabinet ministers. More important, from 1981 to 1984 the French cabinet was formed by Socialists and Communists. Did the Communist Party misuse this power to limit democratic freedoms? Again the answer is no. But, again, this is not proof that the Communists had accepted democracy as a form of government, because they were merely the junior coalition partner and thus had only limited power. At one time or another, Communists also exercised national executive power in Finland, Portugal, and Greece but, as in France, only as junior partners; so the question remains open as to how the Communist Party would have acted if it had gained full governmental control in a Western European country.

Whether a party is internally democratic should be an indication of whether it accepts democracy as a general principle for society at large. This is a severe test, because most non-Communist parties also violate to some extent the principles of internal democracy. It is widely documented that some internal debate took place, in particular, in the Italian Communist Party. Skeptics may object that such debates were merely organized to project the image of internal democracy. Other Communist parties, such as in France, tolerated much less internal debate than the Italian party.

From these indicators no definite conclusion can be drawn about how Communists would have behaved if, during the cold war, they had gotten full political control in a Western European democracy. So we will never know for sure what would have happened if, for example, the Italian Communists had won a majority in a parliamentary election.

What happened to the Western European Communist parties after the end of the cold war? The Italian Communist Party made a vigorous effort to adapt to the new situation. It changed its name to the "Democratic Party of the Left" and cast itself in the Western European Socialist tradition. Nearly a third of the delegates, however, opposed the changes and walked out of the convention hall to form a group of their own, the Reform Communists. In France, the Communists have kept their name and were quite slow to change. In Belgium, the Communists were even more reluctant to move away from orthodox Marxist thinking. In the Netherlands, on the other hand, the Communists shed their Marxist heritage and became the Dutch Green Left. Generally speaking, Martin J. Bull concludes that:

> The West European communist movement as we have known it is dead. This is not to suggest that communist parties will no longer exist in the West, but those which remain cannot be the same as before. However firm their refusal to countenance change, they have to face the fact that the collapse of international communism embodies a change in their own nature.[6]

COMMUNISM IN EASTERN EUROPE

After World War II, the Soviet Union established a brutal rule on the countries of Central and Eastern Europe. As Winston Churchill expressed it eloquently, the Iron Curtain went down, and behind this curtain, the Soviets enforced State Communism. This meant that the economies of the Central and Eastern European countries were to a large extent nationalized, and state bureaucrats planned economic activities in a centralized way. There were no free elections and no freedoms of speech and religion. Political dissidents were sent to prison and concentration camps. This was clearly a dictatorial regime. From a Marxist view, one could argue that this was a historical necessity, because after the revolution the proletariat had to establish a dictatorship in order to erase all traces of capitalist thinking (see the first section of this chapter). There were many Marxists in the West who, for a long time, accepted this interpretation. But there were many other Western Marxists who began to recognize that what happened in the Soviet Union and its satellite countries had nothing to do with Marxism but was a continuation of Russian absolutism and imperialism from the time of the czars. The proletarian revolution, after all, would first have to occur in the most industrialized countries, such as England and Germany, but certainly not in mostly rural Russia. How much can Karl Marx be held accountable for what happened in his name under Soviet rule?

The year 1989 was a memorable one—for this was when State Communism crumbled in Central and Eastern Europe. This was an important turning point, not only for the countries involved, but also for world politics. The cold war, which had raged for more than 40 years, came to an end. The dramatic events of 1989 came as a surprise to nearly everyone. There was always much speculation about the future of the Communist countries in Central and Eastern Europe, but none of the predictions turned out to be correct. As Ronald A. Francisco puts it in retrospect:

> The ossified regimes of Eastern Europe toppled like so many dominoes in the autumn of 1989. . . . Taken as a whole, this was arguably the most significant event since 1945. Yet no one foresaw it. . . . There was widespread recognition of serious problems, but no one predicted the sequential collapse of successive regimes in revolutions largely devoid of violence.[7]

Prior to 1989 there were two prominent predictions about what would happen in the future in Eastern Europe. One prediction was that in Communist totalitarian regimes no real internal changes would ever occur. The other prominent prediction about the future of Communism was that increased contacts with the West would cause slow, gradual changes in Central and Eastern European countries.

What exactly happened in Eastern Europe in the historic year of 1989? To understand the events of that year, one must be aware that these countries were satellites of the Soviet Union and not masters of their own destiny. It is impossible to say what would have happened if the Central and Eastern European countries could have chosen their own Communist path. In this context, it is interesting to mention the Spring Movement of 1968 in Czechoslovakia, when the Communist Party of that country, under the leadership of Alexander Dubcek, launched reforms that were meant to lead to Communism "with a human face." That spring was a time of great hope and excitement. The reform-minded Communist leaders in Czechoslovakia saw the possibility that the ideas of Marx could finally be implemented in a true sense and not perverted as in the Soviet Union. Social justice and democracy seemed possible in a Communist-run country. For a few months, Czechoslovakia was in a fever. Freedom of speech existed, the arts blossomed, and there was lively discussion about the exact direction of the reforms. But the experiment was stopped in August of the same year, when Soviet tanks rolled into Prague. The people in the streets tried to hold discussions with the Soviet soldiers, putting flowers into their guns, but in vain. The reformers were ousted, stripped of their influence; some of them were arrested, some sent to labor camps. Thus, it is impossible to say where the reforms would have led. It remains speculation whether Communist Czechoslovakia without the Soviet interference could have turned democratic with all basic liberties.

What we have, then, is a test of Soviet-style communism. And this type of communism failed dismally with regard to the economy, the environment, and most important, basic freedoms. The secret state police had a devastating influence on the life of ordinary people, who lived in constant fear. Even the Communist Party members became more and more disillusioned with the failed system. But State Communism in Central and Eastern Europe would not have dissolved itself so easily without the momentous events in the Soviet Union itself. The real trigger for what happened in 1989 was the decision of the Soviet leader Mikhail Gorbachev to let the Central and Eastern European countries go their own way. At first, there were merely vague hints that a basic policy change might take place. Thus, early in 1989, the Soviet foreign ministry spokesman began to speak in a light-hearted way of the new "Sinatra doctrine," referring to a song by Frank Sinatra with the lyric "do it my way." The implication seemed to be that the countries in Central and Eastern Europe should do it their ways, too. On July 7, 1989, the Warsaw Pact repealed the doctrine, according to which it had the right to intervene in "brother" countries in order to protect communism. It was this doctrine that justified the Soviet tanks rolling into Czechoslovakia in 1968. But by the summer of 1989, the real intentions of the Soviet Union still remained ambivalent. It was only in mid-October 1989, during the crisis in East Germany, that it became fully clear that the Soviet Union had withdrawn its threat of military intervention.

What happened in Central and Eastern Europe, once the threat of Soviet military intervention vanished? Each country took a somewhat different path. To be sure, 1989 can be seen as a year of one big revolution, but there were interesting national differences in the manner in which the revolution took place. As illustration we compare Hungary, Poland, and East Germany.

Hungary

In Hungary, the Communist Party itself launched the reforms. The reform process had already begun in the early 1970s, although in a very slow and gradual way. Step by step, some free-market elements were introduced into the planned economy. Politically, reforms were much slower to come. It was only in 1988, when Gorbachev was already in office, that some political liberalization began to occur. The great surprise was how quickly this liberalization swept the country in 1989. During a visit to Hungary in July 1989, we[8] witnessed this liberalization firsthand. As we sat in sidewalk cafés in Budapest, most of our Hungarian hosts spoke freely to us about the situation in the country, not sparing their critiques of the Communist Party. When we asked whether such frankness in a public place was not dangerous, the reply was "no more." Traveling through the countryside, we found the same frankness among much of the rural population. A railroad worker told us that recently he had spoken openly with his superior, a Communist Party member, and that only a year ago such frankness would have put him in prison. By the summer of 1989, the fear of the Communists had gone, although there was still some apprehension.

The Communists in Hungary were not forced by street demonstrations to grant basic reforms. It was rather the reform wing within the party itself that pushed for the reforms. The leading reformer was Imre Pozsgay who, like Alexander Dubcek in 1968 in Czechoslovakia, claimed to fight for communism "with a human face." The Hungarian Communists conceded publicly that in the past they had made grave mistakes, in particular by participating in the bloody repression by the Soviets of the democratic Hungarian revolution in October 1956. This mistake was prominently acknowledged in June 1989 when Imre Nagy, the leader of the 1956 revolution, was allowed a hero's reburial in Budapest. The entire Communist leadership was present, together with a huge crowd. During my visit, the bookstores were full of critical and touching accounts of how the Communists had crushed the 1956 revolution.

In the spring of 1989 the Communist rulers tore down the barbed wire at the western border of the country, and Hungarians were free to travel to the West. Indeed, a farm family, whom I had met during my trip, did visit us in Switzerland a few weeks later, receiving the travel visa without any difficulties. Further signs of a fundamental change occurred when the Communists were willing to take their symbol, the Red Star, from public buildings, and when freedom of religion was adopted. The most important element of political liberalization was free elections. As early as the summer of 1989 there were two by-elections for parliament that were free; in both cases the Communist candidate lost. General elections for parliament took place in March 1990.

Poland

In 1981 developments in Poland seemed to support the claim that Communist regimes never truly change. When Solidarity, the trade union led by the charismatic Lech Walesa, became too active and too popular among the Polish people, the Communist Party cracked down hard. Solidarity was banned, many of its leaders were arrested, and a state of emergency was declared. Once again—as in 1968 in Czechoslovakia, 1956 in Hungary and Poland, and 1953 in East Germany—Communism had shown its iron fist. Despair and frustration spread among the Polish people. The stiff and grim-looking General Wojciech Jaruzelski, who headed the government, became the symbol for the apparent unchangeability of communism. In the Soviet Union, Brezhnev was still in power and Soviet troops were at hand, threatening intervention if the Polish Communists were not tough enough.

When Gorbachev came to power in Moscow in 1985, the situation began slowly to change for the better in Poland. In 1986 all political prisoners were released. In 1988 the Communist government made some timid steps to liberalize the economy, and travel to the West was made easier. In 1989, Solidarity, which had continued to be active underground, was legalized again, and the Communists began roundtable discussions with Lech Walesa and his Solidarity colleagues. Why the softening of the Communist rulers? Of crucial importance was the deteriorating economic situation, in particular the staggering foreign debt. Interest on this debt could no longer be paid, and Poland seemed at the brink of collapse. The Communist leaders could not think of any other way out than to begin a dialogue with the banned opposition. Thus, the course of events in Poland was quite different from that in Hungary. Whereas the Hungarian Communists launched the reforms on their own, the Polish Communists were forced to change because of the desperate state of the country and the continued underground activities of Solidarity.

The talks between the Communists and Solidarity led to a complicated deal about a formula for elections to the Sejm, the Polish parliament. Solidarity was allowed to run candidates, but only one-third of the parliamentary seats were open for competition. The Communist Party, still insisting on keeping its leading role in the state, claimed the other two-thirds for itself. Therefore, it was guaranteed from the beginning that the Communists would keep their parliamentary majority. The elections took place on June 4, 1989. They brought a triumph for Solidarity, which swept all seats that were contested. But formal power was still in the hands of the Communists. They recognized, however, that they had to share power with Solidarity. Complicated negotiations began again. The result was a complex scheme of power sharing. Parliament elected Jaruzelski president and, in this capacity, head of state. In return, the Communists were willing to select someone from Solidarity as prime minister. Lech Walesa declined the offer for himself, and one of his close associates, Tadeusz Mazowiecki, became prime minister on August 24, 1989.

A further twist in the arrangement was that, within the cabinet, the military and the state security apparatus remained in the hands of the Communists. Overall, the arrangement did not reflect at all the fact that Solidarity had won all parliamentary seats that were open for competition. The Polish people clearly supported Solidarity, but the Communists were dragging their feet. Despite the verdict of the people, they were unwilling to yield the crucial power of the military and the security forces. Poland shows how difficult it was, even in 1989, to unsettle the Communists. But the momentum against the Communists became so strong that they were unable to cling to their remaining power. There was so much push for free elections that in the May 1990 local elections and the October 1991 national elections, all seats had to be opened for competition.

East Germany

Under Communist rule, East Germany called itself the German Democratic Republic (GDR). In West Germany, many people hoped that the "Democratic" in the name of the East German state would gradually become more meaningful as contacts between the two German states became more frequent. This was, in particular, the position of the West German Social Democrats, but their hopes were greatly disappointed. The East German Communists were unwilling to liberalize. In the summer of 1989, when the Chinese Communists crushed the student movement in a very brutal and bloody way, East German high officials supported the Chinese action, the only high-ranking Communist officials in Central and Eastern Europe to do so.

Yet 1989 brought dramatic changes to East Germany, too. The crucial element was the demonstration effect of events in Hungary and Poland. East Germans had easy access to West German television and were thus well informed about the reforms in the two countries. Watching how others moved forward made their own situation all the more unbearable. It was particularly important for the East Germans to see that the Soviets did tolerate the developments in Hungary and Poland, making no threats to intervene militarily. Thus, it became increasingly credible that the Soviets were indeed willing to let the Central and Eastern European countries go their own ways.

In September 1989, Hungary influenced the changes in East Germany not only indirectly, but also in a very direct way by allowing East Germans staying in Hungary to emigrate to the West. Travel within the Communist countries was always relatively free, and many East Germans spent their summer vacations in Hungary, which was known for its tourist attractions. When, in the spring of 1989, the Hungarians began to tear down the barbed wire at the western border to Austria, many vacationing East Germans exploited the situation to escape to the West. Austria put up tent cities at its borders to accommodate all the refugees who were mostly teachers, doctors, engineers, and other skilled professionals. The conditions soon became so chaotic, with hundreds of East Germans attempting the flight every night, that the Hungarian government finally and officially allowed the East Germans to travel to the West. This action was a breach of a treaty with East Germany, which greatly infuriated the East German government. It was unheard of in the Eastern bloc for one country to let the citizens of another country travel freely to the West.

When the East German government made it increasingly difficult for its citizens to go to Hungary, many went to neighboring Czechoslovakia, at the time still a hard-line Communist country. These East Germans sought refuge at the West German embassy in Prague. In front of the embassy, dramatic scenes occurred, with the Czech police trying to prevent East Germans from climbing over the embassy fence. These scenes were shown on TV all over the world and could also be seen in East Germany on West German TV. Symbols are always important in politics, and here was a very powerful symbol of how eager and desperate thousands of East Germans were to leave their country. What made these scenes so damaging for the East German regime was that most refugees were young people who apparently saw no future in their country.

The West German embassy in Prague became so overcrowded that the situation became untenable with regard to hygiene. Finally, the East German government gave in and allowed the refugees to travel by special trains to West Germany, although insisting that the route be through East German territory. This turned out to be a serious mistake, because other East Germans tried to board the train when it stopped in the East German city of Dresden. Again, pictures of great symbolic power flashed over the TV screens of the world, showing the refugees with tears of joy in their eyes arriving at West German railway stations. These pictures could also be seen in East Germany, and there were emotional moments when young refugees waved, with the help of the TV cameras, to their aging parents left at home.

More and more East Germans went to the streets to demonstrate for reforms. Of particular importance were the marches every Monday evening in Leipzig. How did the Communist leaders react? With many of them having publicly supported the Chinese crackdown earlier in the year, would they apply the same method in their own country? Erich Honecker, the 77-year-old party boss, seemed unyielding. Although he denied it later, he is said to have given the order to the police to shoot at the demonstrators, but he was ousted and replaced by a younger man, Egon Krenz. The opening of the Berlin Wall November 9, 1989, was not a carefully calculated decision but rather the result of much confusion and bumbling in the East German leadership. However the decision was made, it was immediately greeted with great ecstasy, well captured in Box 10.3 and Photo 10.2. The celebrations of East and West Berliners standing on the Wall were the most powerful

Box 10.3 The Opening of the Berlin Wall

East Germany on Thursday declared the end of restrictions on emigration or travel to the West, and within hours thousands of East Germans swarmed across the Berlin wall in a mass celebration of their newly won freedom.... The East German leadership announced permission to travel or emigrate would be granted quickly and without conditions. The leadership said East Germans would be allowed to move through any crossing into West Germany or West Berlin, including through the wall. . . . "We know this need of citizens to travel or leave the country," said Günter Schabowski, a member of the Politburo who made the announcement at a news conference on Thursday evening. "Today the decision was made that makes it possible for all citizens to leave the country through East German crossing points." A tentative trickle of East Germans testing the new regulations quickly turned into a swarm of ecstatic people, who were met in the middle of the crossings by crowds of flag-waving, cheering West Germans. Some West Berliners came in cars and offered to take those from the East on a tour, and others clambered on top of the wall, unbothered by border guards. By 1 A.M. today, celebrating Berliners, East and West, had filled the celebrated Kurfürstendamm, blowing on trumpets, dancing, laughing and absorbing a glittering scene they had only glimpsed before on television.

Source: *New York Times*, November 10, 1989.

Photo 10.2 Berlin Wall, November 9, 1989. (*Source:* TimeLife Pictures/Getty Images)

of the pictures that symbolized the end of the cold war. Many American presidents and other Western leaders had called for the Wall, the symbol of the division of the world, to be torn down, and now it was open!

After the opening of the Wall, it was discovered that the leaders in East Germany had lived in great luxury. They had maintained hunting lodges stuffed with Western goods. In Wandlitz, north of Berlin, they had an exclusive housing enclave protected day and night by the state's secret police. These revelations brought an outcry from the population, in particular from Communist rank-and-file members, who felt betrayed by their leaders. Some of the top leaders, including Honecker himself, were expelled from the party. Later, Honecker and several other former high officials were arrested on charges of high treason. The indignation at Honecker and his regime increased still more when it was discovered that leftist terrorists of West Germany had been offered refuge in Communist East Germany for many years. Honecker was brought to court, but for health reasons he was never tried, and finally he was allowed to move with his wife to join their daughter in Chile, where he died. A few other East German leaders were actually tried and convicted.

It is important to stress that Honecker did not give up power voluntarily. It was an unusual set of circumstances that forced him out. It was also good luck that his orders to shoot were not obeyed, so that a bloodbath was prevented. He remained a cruel dictator, exploiting his people, spying on them through the state secret police, giving orders to kill those who tried to escape to the West, all the while living in luxury and splendor. In early 1990, 2,000 to 3,000 East Germans left every day for West Germany. There was increasing demand for unification of the two German states. At demonstrations the main slogan changed from "we are the people" to "we are one people." In March 1990, free elections took place in East Germany. In the aftermath of these elections, Germany was united October 3, 1990.

Are there still any prospects for Communism in Europe at all? One conclusion is firm: Communism in its Stalinist version is dead. There is no longer any support at all for the belief that the Communist party has a right to a monopoly on power. The notion of a dictatorship of the proletariat is no longer tenable. How about the prospects of the terrorist Left? As a political force, it is as discredited as Stalinism. The romanticism of violence has for the most part vanished among young Europeans of the Left, although there are still some sporadic leftist terrorist actions, in particular in Italy where the Red Brigades are lingering on.

The political death of Stalinism and to a large extent also of the terrorist Left does not mean that Karl Marx is dead as an intellectual force. After all, he was a philosopher of the 19th century, and it is not altogether clear how he would have reacted to the developments in the Soviet Union or the actions of such terrorist groups as the Red Brigades. One could very well argue that he would not have approved at all. As we saw earlier in this chapter, Marx used the concept of revolution in a rather abstract form and left ambivalent the matter of whether violence should be part of the revolution. The lasting contribution of Marx is his economic interpretation of society, and in this sense Marx will continue to have an intellectual influence on the European Left. At the same time, it must also be said that the influence of Marx has greatly diminished since the heydays of the 1960s and 1970s; for new issues of the Left, such as ecology and feminism, Marxism is no longer seen as relevant. Although Marx will continue to have an influence, the European Left should not be identified with Marxism alone. In the past 200 years, there was a great diversity of ideas on the Left, and this diversity has again become more apparent. Thus, there was always a tradition of the Left warning against the dangers of too much centralization and demanding more autonomy for small groups, in particular workers at their workplace and local communities.

Having described in this chapter how Soviet-style communism was overthrown in Central and Eastern Europe, the next chapter will explain what exactly happened afterward, how the transition to democratic regimes took place in Central and Eastern Europe, and what the problems were in this transition.

Discussion Questions

1. With the fall of the Berlin Wall and the collapse of the Soviet Union, does that mean that Marxism as a political philosophy is also finished?

2. Why was communism such an attractive ideology right after the WWII in Europe, particularly in Italy?

3. What was the ultimate goal of Marxism?

4. What do you think were the main reasons why communism failed?

5. Some observes have termed the fall of communism worldwide, the "end of history," meaning that the bitter battle between two rival ideologies has ended with liberal capitalism as the victor. Are there no major similar contenders "out there" that could challenge the purported predominance of liberal capitalism?

6. The Soviet Union collapsed on December 31, 1991. How do you think that event affects you personally?

7. Why is it that the United States was much less receptive to Marxist analysis?

---

[1]Stein Rokkan. *Citizens, Elections, Parties: Approaches to the Comparative Study of the Process of Development*, (Oslo: Universitetsforlaget, 1970).

[2]Karl Marx and Frederick Engels. *The German Ideology, Collected Works* (Vol. 5). (New York: International Publishers, 1976, 47).

[3]William James Booth. The New Household Economy. *American Political Science Review* 85 (March 1991): 71.

[4]Evelyne Pisier and Pierre Bouretz. Camus et le Marxism. *Revue française de science politique* 35 (December 1985): 1056.

[5]Daniel Bell. The Fight for the 20th Century: Raymond Aron Versus Jean-Paul Sartre. *New York Times Book Review* (February 18, 1990): 3.

[6]Martin J. Bull. The West European Communist Movement in the Late Twentieth Century. *West European Politics* 18 (January 1995): 90.

[7]Ronald A. Francisco. Theories of Protest and the Revolutions of 1989. *American Journal of Political Science* 37 (August 1993): 663.

[8]Author Steiner and his wife.

Transitions to Democracy

In the last chapter we discussed how the Communist dictatorships toppled in Central and Eastern Europe. Not every fall of a dictatorship necessarily leads to a democratic regime—a dictatorship may very well be replaced with another dictatorship. Thus it is interesting to explore how a transition from dictatorship to democracy may actually work. Of critical importance is the holding of the first free and fair elections, so-called *founding elections*. Such founding elections determine to a large extent the form a democratic system will take. Besides successful founding elections, a country also needs a culture favorable to democracy. In Chapter 12 we will turn to the cultural aspect, discussing nationalism and ethnicity.

In the current world, the study of transitions from dictatorship to democracy is of great practical importance; let us think, for example, of Afghanistan and Iraq. Is China on a successful path to democracy? How are transitions to democracy shaping up in Africa? Europe offers several recent examples of successful transitions to democracy. We describe first how the Federal Republic of Germany and Italy, after the overthrow of the dictatorships of Hitler and Mussolini in World War II, established their democratic systems. Our third case will be Spain after the death of its dictator Franco in 1975. How did the Spaniards make the transition from a dictatorship to democratic elections? The Central and Eastern European countries after the overthrow of communism in 1989 also provide further examples of the transition to democratic elections; as illustrations we will take Hungary and Poland. Finally we will look at the very recent case of the Ukraine in 2004.

THE FEDERAL REPUBLIC OF GERMANY AFTER 1945

World War II ended in May 1945, and the first democratic elections in the Federal Republic of Germany took place in August 1949. Thus, the transition from the Nazi dictatorship of Hitler to democratic elections took more than four years, quite a long time. Part of the reason for the delay was the division of Germany that took place in the meantime. After the defeat of the Nazi regime, the country was divided into four military occupation zones, with the Soviets having their zone in the East and the Americans, the British, and the French in the West. The Soviets established a Communist regime in their zone, the so-called German Democratic Republic, whereas the Western Allies established the Federal Republic of Germany in their zones.

When the first democratic elections in the Federal Republic of Germany took place in August 1949, the country was still militarily occupied by the three Western Allies. And it was indeed the case that the occupation powers had a great influence on how the elections were organized. It must first be noted that the leaders of the Nazi regime had no influence on the drafting of the election law. As we will see later in this chapter, there are countries where the leaders of the old regime are allowed to play some role in the transition to democratic elections. This was definitely not true in the Federal Republic of Germany. If they

194

did not commit suicide like Hitler himself, the Nazi leaders were tried at the Nürnberg War Crime Tribunal; some of them were hung, others sentenced to long prison terms. It is true, however, that quite a few Nazi members who did not belong to the top leadership continued to play a political role in the Federal Republic, often hiding their Nazi past.

The Western occupation powers chose the strategy to begin the process of democratization from the bottom, beginning with the local level and then continuing with the state level. Eleven states were established, called Länder. On July 1, 1948, the three Western Allied military governors convened a meeting in Frankfurt with the chief executives of the 11 states. The purpose of the meeting was to establish a constituent assembly that was to draft a constitution for the three Western zones. By this time, political parties had already begun to organize on the territory of the Western zones. The most successful organizers were the Social Democratic Party (SPD) and the Christian Democratic Union with its sister organization in Bavaria, the Christian Social Union (CDU/CSU). Before the Frankfurt meeting, the prime ministers of the states met with the leadership of these two major parties. Thus, the base of participation of German political leaders was somewhat broadened. But the key actors continued to be the Western Allied occupation powers.

Out of the July Frankfurt meeting came the decision to convene a constituent assembly by September 1948. The states were charged to send delegates to this assembly—thus ordinary citizens had no direct say. However, great political indifference existed among most West German citizens, who were busy putting their shattered lives back together. How elections should be organized was far from their top priorities. It took the constituent assembly only nine months, from September 1948 until May 1949, to come up with a draft of a constitution, called Basic Law. Initially, the Western occupation powers had planned that this draft would be submitted to a referendum in all three Western zones, but ultimately ratification by the state parliaments was considered sufficient. The rule was set that two-thirds of the states had to accept the draft for the Basic Law. Ten states did so. Only the state of Bavaria rejected the draft, objecting to too much centralization. Despite this objection, Bavaria recognized the Basic Law as being legally binding.

The key principles for democratic elections were set in the Basic Law. According to article 38, "the deputies to the German Bundestag shall be elected in general, direct, free, equal, and secret elections. They shall be representatives of the whole people, not bound by orders and instructions, and shall be subject only to their conscience." Details of the election rules were regulated in a special law. These specific rules were explained in Chapter 3, where we learned that the election system is basically by proportionality, but with two important modifications: First, half of the members of the Bundestag are elected not on party lists, but in single districts, making the election rules more personalized. Second, political parties must reach a threshold of either 5 percent of the national vote or three direct seats in order to receive any representation in the Bundestag. As also already explained in Chapter 3, the Western occupation powers, in particular the United States and Great Britain, urged the adoption of a winner-take-all system as practiced in their own countries, fearing that a system of proportionality would lead to severe party fragmentation. The fact that the chosen system was basically by proportionality, although with two important modifications, as noted, shows that the Western occupation powers did not simply ram through their ideas but were open to arguments from the German side.

It turned out that the fears of the Western occupation powers were unfounded, as SPD and CDU/CSU emerged as the two major parties with not too many other competitors.

In the first election of 1949 the CDU/CSU received 142 seats, the SPD 136 seats. A third party, the Free Democrats, got 53 seats, all other parties together 80 seats. Four years later, these minor parties were already down to 45 seats, and eight years later to 18 seats. Thus, in the first few elections the Federal Republic of Germany did not suffer from severe party fragmentation. Having a threshold against parliamentary representation of tiny parties certainly helped to keep party fragmentation to a moderate level.

In summary, two aspects stand out with regard to the transition to democratic elections in the Federal Republic of Germany. First, the Western Allied occupation powers had a strong influence, particularly in the process leading up to the establishment of the election system. For the substance of the specific election rules, the Western Allied occupation forces were more open to the arguments of the German side. Second, ordinary citizens were hardly involved at all. Which election rules should be used was very much decided at the elite level, for the most part behind closed doors. Both aspects speak for the undemocratic nature of the establishment of Germany's election system. Nonetheless, the system was quickly recognized as legitimate by large parts of the population; the first election took place in a calm atmosphere and turnout was high—78.5 percent.

ITALY AFTER 1945

In 1943, still during World War II, King Victor Emmanuel III, even though a mere figurehead, had the Fascist dictator Mussolini arrested and put into a mountain hideout. The Italians realized that further resistance against the Allies was not fruitful. They surrendered, changed sides, and fought the Germans on the side of the Allies. Then the Germans came back into Italy to defend it against the invading Americans. Mussolini was rescued in a daring operation, and the Germans installed him in a puppet regime in Salo, on the shores of Lake Garda. In April 1945, shortly before the end of the war, Mussolini and his mistress were captured in a hideout in Northern Italy, summarily tried, executed, and hung upside down in Milan. Many other summary executions took place, on the one hand of leftist partisans by Fascists and on the other hand of Fascists by leftist partisans.

In contrast to Germany, Italy was not militarily occupied after the war. This was mainly due to the fact that Italians helped a great deal to topple their dictatorship. In addition, Mussolini was considered to be a somewhat less brutal and ruthless dictator than Hitler. The absence of occupation forces allowed Italy to organize its own transition to democratic elections. The first sticking point was the issue of the monarchy. In the view of many Italians, the king had not taken a clear enough position against the dictatorship of Mussolini. What sealed the fate of the monarchy was that the king fled to the Southern Italian town of Brindisi after the German's return to Italy, instead of standing up to face them. The question of the monarchy was submitted to a popular referendum in June 1946. With 89 percent, turnout was very high. 54 percent of the Italian voters chose to have a republic; the king abdicated and had to leave the country. The same day, a constituent assembly was elected by the voters. A year and a half later, by December 1947, this assembly had approved a new constitution. The ensuing parliamentary election in 1948 was bitterly fought, pitting the Popular Front of Communists and Socialists against the Christian Democrats, and there was quite a high level of violence marring the elections. The Christian Democrats received 307 seats in the Chamber of Deputies, the Popular Front 215 seats, and the remaining 52 seats went to minor parties.

In summary, Italians were able to take the transition to democratic elections mostly in their own hands, although both the Soviet Union and the United States tried to influence the election outcome with financial support—the United States for the Christian Democrats, and the Soviets for the Popular Front. In fact, American military forces were ready to be deployed in the case of a Communist victory. Political interest among Italian citizens was high, and they had the opportunity to take a direct influence in settling the issue of the monarchy and the composition of the constituent assembly. Interestingly enough, this setup of the transition to democratic elections brought not more but less political stability than in Germany. Does this mean that transitions to democratic elections are easier when citizens are less involved? Or was Italian society much more divided than German society, so that the Italian transition to democratic elections would have been messier even if the question of the monarchy and the election of the constituent assembly would not have been submitted to a popular referendum? This is an interesting question to ponder, and good arguments can be made on both sides. The extent of citizen involvement in the transition to democratic elections is always a tricky question. High citizen involvement may increase the legitimacy of the election outcome, but it may also increase political tensions.

SPAIN AFTER 1975

In 1975 the Spanish dictator Francisco Franco died, and two years later democratic elections took place. In 1936 Franco had launched a military coup against a democratically elected leftist government. But it was only after a bloody civil war that Franco could establish his dictatorship in 1939. In this civil war, Franco was helped by Hitler and Mussolini. But he was shrewd enough not to get directly involved with Hitler and Mussolini in World War II, which allowed him to stay in power until his death in 1975. Long before his death Franco thought about the best way for his regime to continue. He came to the conclusion that the best bet was to be succeeded by a king. In 1931 Spain had become a republic, and the king went into exile in Rome. There his son Juan Carlos was born in 1939. In the hope that he might one day become king of Spain, his father had him educated in Spain, where he studied law and economics. Juan Carlos also became a pilot in the Spanish air force. In 1962 he married Princess Sophia of Greece, thus solidifying his claim on the Spanish throne.

In 1969 Franco made an arrangement with Juan Carlos that after the death of Franco, Juan Carlos should be his successor. This is indeed what happened in 1975. Juan Carlos was sworn in as head of state. But he was not interested in continuing the dictatorial Franco regime—he wanted to become a constitutional monarch in a true democracy as, for example, the monarchs in Belgium and Sweden (see Chapter 4). Having a sworn-in king immediately after the death of Franco gave Spain some initial stability at the beginning of the transition period. This stability was used to hold democratic parliamentary elections in 1977. The newly elected Parliament as its first order of business worked out a draft of a constitution, which was accepted in a popular referendum in 1978.

Overall, this was a smooth transition to democratic elections. The transition was helped by the fact that the last years of the Franco regime had seen some political liberalization, with much less police brutality against dissenters than in former times. Economically, Spain was even more launched on a path of liberalization. The economy improved, greatly helped by the influx of large numbers of foreign tourists to the Spanish beaches.

Thanks to these political and economic liberalizations in the last years of the Franco regime, no need was felt to punish the old officeholders, a great contrast with Germany and Italy after 1945. Many of the officeholders under Franco even openly continued their political careers under the new democratic regime. The smooth transition to democratic elections was also helped by the fact that in the mid-1970s Spain was not in the chaotic aftermath of a lost war, another great contrast with Germany and Italy after 1945.

A challenge came to Spanish democracy in 1981, when some officers in the armed forces longing for the old days of the Franco regime attempted a coup. They entered Parliament holding weapons in their hands and began shooting in the air. They hoped to get the support of the king, but Juan Carlos acted forcefully in the defense of democracy and had the coup participants imprisoned. This incident shows how sometimes the fate of a country depends on a single individual. Juan Carlos rendered his country a great service in accepting the role of a constitutional monarch and having the courage to stand up for this role.

HUNGARY AFTER 1989

In Chapter 10 we described how the Communist regime was toppled in Hungary. We now turn to the events of the first free election in 1990. Each voter had two votes: one for a candidate in a single district and one for a party list. Overall there were 386 parliamentary seats to be filled. From this total number, 176 seats were filled in single districts according to the winner-take-all system. In addition to the 176 single districts, Hungary was also divided into 20 larger districts, which corresponded to its 20 counties. At the county level, the remaining 210 seats were filled according to party list proportionality.[1] Thus, each voter could vote for a candidate in a small district and for a party list in a large district. Why exactly 176 seats by winner-take-all and 210 seats by proportional representation? Nothing magic about it, this was simply the outcome of the bargaining about the electoral law.

For the first free elections, debate ensured not only about the election rules, but also about the time of the elections. Parliament, which was still controlled by the Communists, decided that elections of the president should come first, before the parliamentary elections. The date set for the presidential elections was January 7, 1990; the date for parliamentary elections was set for later in the year. Four opposition parties—the Free Democrats, the Young Democrats, the Independent Smallholders' Party, and the Social Democrats—objected to this plan. They argued that parliamentary elections should be held first. The four opposition parties feared that early presidential elections would give an undue advantage to the Communist candidate. They considered it to be undemocratic to choose so important an official while the Communists still controlled all essential offices and such vital political advantages as access to state-run television and most of the press.

The four parties collected signatures in order to challenge the decision of Parliament about the date of presidential elections. For a decision of Parliament to be submitted to a referendum, 100,000 signatures were required. The four opposition parties had no difficulties in attaining this limit, and they even reached more than double the needed number of signatures. The referendum was set for November 26, 1989. In the referendum campaign, the fronts took a rather complicated shape, because another opposition party, the Democratic Forum, supported the Communists' desire for early presidential elections. The proposed Communist candidate, Imre Pozsgay, was a moderate, and the Democratic Forum expected that it could work with him.

Thus, it was not easy for the Hungarian voters to decide which way to vote. The choice was not simply to support or oppose the ruling Communist Party. It was feared that voter turnout would be low, which would have been a bad start for the process of democratization. Fortunately, nearly 60 percent of the voters turned up at the ballot boxes, despite a severe snowstorm that set in during the evening. A turnout of 50 percent was required for the referendum to be valid. If it had fallen below this threshold, the referendum would have failed, whatever the outcome. The four opposition parties could celebrate a double victory: Not only was the referendum valid, it was also decided, although by a narrow margin, to delay presidential elections until after parliamentary elections.

The Communists accepted the outcome, and Pozsgay wisely said: "While in Eastern and Central Europe hundreds of thousands of people are marching in the streets to express their opinions, Hungarians are going to the ballot box to express their political will."[2] The Associated Press quoted a voter as saying, "We wanted to take into our own hands the possibility to decide on the people's future."[3] Following the referendum, parliamentary elections indeed came first, on March 25, 1990. The campaign did not have the professional smoothness of those in established democracies. Many things went wrong: Microphones did not work, computers broke down, and so on. But these were mere technical flaws. What really mattered was that the campaign and the election itself occurred with very few irregularities. There were no incidents of violence and no intimidation of voters. According to the general consensus of foreign observers, the election took place in an atmosphere of freedom.

The headlines in the Western media after the elections were about the big defeat of the Communists.[4] This result may seem surprising, because, as we saw in Chapter 10, Hungary was the only Central and Eastern European country where reforms were pushed by the Communists themselves. But they received little credit from the voters on election day. Only 10.9 percent voted for the party list of the Hungarian Socialist Party, the new name chosen by the Communists. Most Hungarians were tired of the Communists, however reform-oriented they were. To the credit of the Communists, it should be noted that they gave up power graciously. Their party chairman declared: "We will be an opposition party. This, to use a religious term, will be penance for the party." Along the same gracious line, the outgoing Communist prime minister stated: "I will hand over the reins head high and with a clear conscience. I don't have bitterness in my heart but satisfaction."[5] Who would have thought that one day Communists would yield power in this way?

When in 1989 the Communists embarked on a course of reform, the more Marxist-oriented wing split from the party and founded their own Hungarian Socialist Workers' Party. But it fared even worse than the Reform Communists, getting 3.7 percent for its party list, which was below the 4 percent threshold required to be seated in Parliament. This minimum threshold was also not reached by the Social Democratic Party, which had the support of its sister parties in Western Europe. Thus, altogether the parties of the Left did poorly in Hungary.

Who were the winners? We look first at the results for the party lists and turn later to the winner-take-all part of the elections. The two top vote-getters for the party lists were the Hungarian Democratic Forum with 24.7 percent and the Alliance of Free Democrats with 21.4 percent. The Democratic Forum roughly corresponds to the Conservatives in

Dem. Forum vs. Free Dems.

Western Europe, as described in Chapter 2. It displays a Christian image, and its overall message has rather strong nationalist overtones. Economically, the Democratic Forum stood for the free market, although advocating a cautious transition. The Free Democrats more or less correspond to their sister parties in Western Europe. More than the Democratic Forum they stressed a quick transition to a free-market economy. The Free Democrats are also strongly individualistic, not putting as much emphasis on church and nation as the Democratic Forum. With 11.7 percent of the party lists, the Independent Smallholders' party came in third. Before the Communist regime, it was the largest party in Hungary. Its major campaign plank was that all land should go back to those who owned it in 1947, before Communists took over.

We turn now to the election results in the 176 single districts. The electoral rules specified that to be elected in the first round, a candidate had to receive more than 50 percent of the votes. If no candidate reached this threshold, a second round of elections was organized two weeks later. The top three finishers, plus all candidates who acquired at least 15 percent of the first-round vote, were eligible to compete in the second round. Candidates were so numerous that only five districts were able to declare a candidate elected in the first round. Thus, 171 seats were left to be contested in the second round. For both rounds together, the Democratic Forum was the big winner, taking a total of 114 of the districts; the Free Democrats were far behind, winning in only 35 districts. The Smallholders' Party won in 1 district and the Socialist Party in 1 district. The remaining 15 districts went to several small parties and some independent candidates. Thus, as expected, the winner-take-all part of the election favored the largest party. As the British say of the winner-take-all system, what counts is who is first past the post (see Chapter 3). Having come out as the frontrunner in the first round, the Democratic Forum had the necessary momentum to capture many districts in the second round. In the winner-take-all system, nothing is as successful as anticipated success, because supporters of smaller parties do not like to waste their votes and therefore cast them for a candidate with a real winning chance.

The election was able to weed out the minor parties and limit the political game to relatively few viable parties. Thus, as a "founding election"—to borrow a term from Guillermo O'Donnell and Philippe Schmitter[6]—it fulfilled its purpose in establishing a manageable party system. The Hungarian election system shares with the German system the characteristic that some members of Parliament are elected by winner-take-all in single districts and others by party list proportionality in larger, regional districts. We should also note, however, an important difference between the two systems. As we remember from Chapter 3, in Germany only the votes for the party lists determine the total number of seats a party gets in Parliament. In Hungary, by contrast, the two parts of the elections are independent of each other, so that the Hungarian system is more truly a mixed system.

POLAND AFTER 1989

Whereas the "founding" elections in Hungary resulted in a manageable party system, this was not at all the case in Poland. Together with Hungary, Poland was at the forefront of the process of democratization. As we saw in Chapter 10, Poland was the first Communist country to have elections with a real choice for the voters. But the elections of June 1989 were not entirely free. The Communist Party reserved two-thirds of the parliamentary seats for itself and allowed free competition only for the remaining third. This free part of the election brought triumph to the opposition Solidarity movement, which swept all contested seats.

The first completely free Polish election, with all seats open for competition, took place on May 27, 1990, at the local level. The results were a big victory for Solidarity and a total defeat for the Communists. The latter had tried to save themselves by confessing to all their mistakes in the past. Box 11.1 shows the self-criticism of Mieczystaw Rakowski, the first secretary of the Communist Party, at the party congress in January 1990. He acknowledged "the abandonment of political democracy" as the main failing. The party went so far as to dissolve itself and create a new party with the label Social Democratic. The Communists avidly tried to distance themselves from their past. But all these efforts were in vain, and even as a new party with a new name, the Communists received only 0.2 percent of the votes in the local elections of May 27, 1990, indeed a catastrophic result!

In the councils of the big cities, Solidarity won the overwhelming number of seats: in Warsaw 301 of 345, in Gdansk 56 of 60, and in Cracow 72 of 75. For the entire country, Solidarity received 41 percent of the votes. Where did all the other votes go? They went to independent candidates, and to a great variety of tiny parties. The most striking result was that none of the newly created parties could really catch on. With these local elections, Poland had not yet crossed the threshold to a true multiparty system. Instead of dominance by the Communists, Solidarity dominated. This does not mean that basic changes in the direction of democracy had not taken place. The local elections were indeed completely free, and Poland now enjoyed all the basic civil liberties, such as freedom of speech and freedom of religion. But a country needs more than one strong party for a functioning democracy.

National parliamentary elections were held in October 1991. They still did not lead to a clear party system. The largest party received only 12.3 percent of the votes in the Sejm, the lower house of Parliament. Altogether, 29 parties were represented in the Sejm. As soon as Parliament gathered, the situation became even more confusing, because some of the parties split or united and individual deputies changed parties or became independents.

Was the fragmentation in the Polish parliament mainly a consequence of the electoral system? At first it may appear so, but a second look reveals that other factors must have played a more important role. A system of party list PR was used for the election of the

---

Box 11.1 Self-Criticism of Rakowski, First Secretary of Polish Communist Party

Mr. Rakowski's hourlong speech opening up the congress was a rare concession by a party leader about the mistakes made during Communist rule. He said Marxist socialism had "caused the slowdown of economic development, the disappearance of incentives for innovation and effective work, and the formation of a strong bureaucracy."

He added that "the main weakness of the Communist movement and the source of all its failings was the abandonment of political democracy."

Source: *New York Times*, January 28, 1990.

Sejm, and no minimal threshold had to be reached for a party to enter Parliament. The only advantage for the larger parties was that they received a bonus in the sense that 15 percent of the seats were set aside for parties that received at least 5 percent of the total vote. This put the small parties at a small disadvantage, but still allowed them to enter Parliament. Thus, it appears that it was indeed the election system that allowed so many small parties to receive parliamentary representation. This was the interpretation of a *Newsweek* correspondent who wrote of "proportional representation gone wild."[7]

There are, however, two arguments against such an interpretation of the election results. First, there was no single national electoral district, which would have favored small parties as in the Netherlands (Chapter 3). Rather, Poland had relatively small districts, with an average of only 10.6 deputies per district. Therefore, 10 percent of the votes were needed to get representation in the average district. But the outcome was that from district to district different parties got representation, so that the overall number of parties in the Sejm reached the high number of 29.

Second, and more important, the elections to the Senate, the upper house, were held by the winner-take-all system, which, as in Great Britain, should work against small parties. But in the Senate, the number of parties gaining representation was even higher than in the Sejm. In the Senate races only winning counted, but candidates from very different parties won from district to district. The conclusion is that, to some extent, the electoral system may have contributed to the fragmentation of the Polish legislature, but there were other factors involved. The main factor being that, with its heroic history, the Solidarity movement was such a strong umbrella that its various factions found it difficult to emerge as well-structured independent parties. In contrast to Hungary, the "founding" Polish parliamentary elections led to a diffuse party system.

The Democratic Union grew directly out of Solidarity. It corresponds roughly to the Free Democrats in Hungary. Another party that grew directly out of Solidarity was the Center Citizens' Alliance. It was somewhat more for state economic interventions, somewhat more authoritarian than the Democratic Union and, somewhere more at the center of the party system—as its name implies. The former Communists ran under the label Democratic Left Alliance and did quite well, much better than in the local elections of the previous year. Several parties ran with a Catholic platform; others claimed to represent peasants or particular regions. There were also several nationalistic parties, for example, the Confederation for an Independent Poland. Two parties used the label Solidarity, although most Solidarity members had organized in other parties. There were also some frivolous aspects in the emerging party system, in particular with regard to the Beer Lovers' party. In a democracy citizens may certainly organize however they wish, and beer drinkers may have common interests that they want to represent in Parliament.

To understand Poland's transition to democratic elections, it is necessary to cover also the second national elections that took place in September 1993. For these elections an important modification in the electoral law was in force. With the goal of reducing the number of parties in Parliament, the Polish parliament had introduced a 5 percent threshold for a party to enter Parliament. The example of the 5 percent threshold in Germany had a great influence on this decision (Chapter 3). The former Communists, now called Democratic Left Alliance, reinforced their comeback.[8] After receiving merely 0.2 percent of the votes in the May 1991 local elections, and having increased their support to 12.0 percent in the October 1991 national elections, they were now up to 20.4 percent. The Polish Peasant

Party increased its voters' share also, from 8.7 to 15.4 percent. The Democratic Union declined slightly, from 12.3 to 10.6 percent. Three other smaller parties reached the 5 percent threshold: the Union of Labor, the Confederation for an Independent Poland, and the Non-Party Bloc to Support Reform.

The 5 percent clause had fulfilled its purpose: The number of parties represented in the Sejm was dramatically reduced from 29 to 6. An important unplanned consequence also occured: The Democratic Left Alliance with 20.4 percent of the votes received 37.2 percent of the seats (171), and the Peasant Party with 15.4 percent of the votes arrived at 28.7 percent of the seats (132). Thus, the two leading parties, although together they had merely 35.8 percent of the votes, got 65.9 percent of the seats. And yet the electoral system was meant to be proportional, with the exception of excluding tiny parties with less than 5 percent. Why the discrepancy between votes and seats? What had happened? Apparently something very different from the pattern in Germany, where the proportion of voter support tends to correspond closely to the proportion of parliamentary seats.

The big difference between these first Polish elections with a 5 percent threshold and the German situation was that many more Poles "wasted" their votes as compared to Germans. Indeed, about 35 percent of the Polish voters supported parties that stayed below the 5 percent threshold. Why the difference? The German voters had adapted their behavior to the 5 percent threshold and were careful not to vote for a party with no chance of making the threshold. As the Poles learned how the system works and gathered more information about the chances of success of the various parties, they, too, became more careful not to waste their votes.

After the Polish elections of 1993, the *New York Times* wrote of a "victory of the former Communists."[9] Was it actually a victory? Yes and no. The former Communists were certainly winning in the sense that they received the most votes of all the parties. It was also a victory for them that the other successful party, the Peasant Party, had been a close ally during the Communist regime. The Peasant Party had been one of the so-called bloc parties, which were allowed to run their own candidates but factually belonged to the Communist bloc. The Peasant Party could be considered the rural branch of the Communists. Now, in the 1993 elections, which were absolutely free, these two former Communist parties together received two-thirds of the parliamentary seats! As the reporter of the *New York Times* writes, this was indeed a victory. But it must also be stressed that the two parties received only about one-third of the votes, and that it was only thanks to the change in the electoral system that they got two-thirds of the seats in Parliament.

Having made this argument, it must also be recognized that the 1993 elections brought a spectacular comeback for the former Communists. Why? A first reason was that the change to a market economy brought, for many voters, hardship and insecurity:

> Forty years of Communism had ingrained expectations of social security that the new parties failed to provide. The architects of Poland's "shock therapy" knew that there would be victims in their game plan—pensioners, unskilled young people, middle-aged workers made redundant by privatization—but gambled that those losers would not stall the march to a full market economy.[10]

A second reason for the good showing of the former Communists was that many educated young people, especially women, resented the newly gained strong political influence of the Catholic Church. Of particular concern to these voters was the strict antiabortion legislation rammed through Parliament by the parties close to the Catholic Church. The parties supported by the Catholic Church suffered a severe defeat. The Church had overestimated its political influence. Although very religious, Poles did not wish the Catholic Church to dominate the political life of the country. Under communism the church could play an important political role as protector of the democratic opposition. But now with democracy established, Poles wanted the Church to concentrate on its religious duties.

A third reason for the good election result of the former Communists was that they had changed greatly. The leader of the Democratic Left Alliance, Aleksander Kwasniewski, had played only a minor role in the old regime. At the time of the 1993 election, he was only 39 years old. As a student of economics at Gdansk University, he had been chairman of the Communist student organization of Poland. He then became editor of two youth newspapers, and in 1985, junior minister in the Communist government. In the election campaign, Kwasniewski tried to make a clear break with the old-line Communist past, declaring:

> There shouldn't be a shadow of a doubt to the party's position on Stalinism and other Communist crimes. Does it make me sad that a lot of these people who were Communists, committed these crimes? Yes, it does. . . . We are ready to take part in a pragmatic coalition which looks toward the future, not the past. We are about resolving problems in domestic and foreign policies. We need competent people in office. . . . Our program has not a single thing that would remind you of Communism. If someone in our party proposed a return to a central command economy, he would have to be expelled, not for being a Communist but for being an idiot.[11]

The Democratic Left Alliance is comparable to the Social Democrats in Western Europe (Chapter 2). It supports democracy and, to a large extent, the free market also. So it was somewhat misleading when the Western media wrote of an election victory of the former Communists. To be sure, most leaders of the Democratic Left Alliance belonged to the old Communist Party, but they were in its reformist wing. By 1993 the old hard-line Communists had completely vanished from the political scene of Poland.

The description of the Polish transition to democratic elections should have shown us once again in a forceful way how election results may be shaped by the election rules. These rules are never neutral but always favor some parties over others. We have already made this argument in Chapter 3, and the Polish situations described here should help to reinforce the argument.

Ukraine in 2004

In the Ukraine, it took a long time for the old Communists to yield power to an opposition party. The change came only in December 2004, and in a highly dramatic form. The Ukraine had been part of the Soviet Union, and when the latter broke apart in 1991, the Ukraine declared its independence in a popular referendum with the approval of over 90 percent of the voters. The same day as the referendum, the voters elected Leonid D.

Kuchma president. He had been an important figure in the Soviet Union, among other things manager of the largest missile factory. Kuchma was reelected president 1994 and 1999. These elections were, however, quite strongly rigged in his favor. There was much corruption, and Kuchman was even implicated in the murder of a journalist, although never put to trial.

When Kuchmas third term was up in 2004, he wanted his prime minister, Victor F. Yanukovich, to succeed him. This time, the opposition put up a popular candidate, Victor A. Yushchenko. Again, the party of Kuchma tried to rig the election in its favor, and, as soon as the election results were in, it quickly declared Yanukovich the winner. But popular resistance was strong, and large numbers of citizens came out to protest the rigging of the elections. After many days and nights of protest, the Supreme Courts declared the elections invalid and ordered new elections. Testimonies before the Supreme Courts revealed widespread fraud and ballot stuffing. Adding to the overall crisis situation was that the candidate of the opposition was poisoned with dioxin, which led to severe health problems including a disfiguration of the face. There were only speculations of who could have done the poisoning, and no one was charged. In the new elections, Yushchenko won (Box 11.2). He had to concede, however, that his power was somewhat weakened in favor of Parliament, where the old regime still enjoyed quite a lot of power.

The main lesson of the Ukrainian transition to truly free elections is that ordinary citizens have power if they dare to go to the streets to protest a corrupt regime. The mass demonstrations in the capital Kiev and elsewhere in the country led to a real revolution, called the Orange Revolution, named after the campaign color of Yushchenko. Hundreds of thousands of his supporters protested in bitter cold and did not give up until new elections with fairer rules were called. Because Yanukovich also had supporters, especially in the countryside, there were fears of civil war and a breakup of the country. But fortunately this did not happen. Mass demonstrations do not necessarily have to turn violent. Among the protesters, an uplifting feeling persisted that they had the power to direct the country in a democratic direction; and the old regime was wise enough not to use police force to

---

Box 11.2 *Yushchenko, a Survivor of Fraud and Poisoning, Takes the Lead*

Victor A. Yushchenko, the opposition leader, appeared headed for a resounding victory early Monday morning in a riveting presidential race marked by intrigue, charges of poisoning, fervent street demonstrations and wide-spread abuses of state power. There were no independent reports of the egregious violations that had discredited the previous round of voting. Mr. Yushchenko, addressing supporters at his headquarters, predicted an end at last to an extended and bitter election season. "It has happened," said Mr. Yushchenko, his face still disfigured from dioxin poisoning this fall for which he has blamed his adversaries in the government. "Today we are turning a page of lies, censorship, and violence." Ahead, he said, lay a "new epoch of a new great democracy."

Source: *New York Times*, December 27, 2004.

dismantle the demonstrations. Unfortunately, corruption also is rampant in the new regime, which shows that erasing a pattern of corruption in a country is not an easy task. The Orange Revolution also did not bring the desired political stability to the country, as much in-fighting broke out among the new rulers. The case of the Ukraine reveals that it is one thing to overthrow an authoritarian regime but quite another thing to establish afterwards a stable political order.

A second lesson of the Orange Revolution is that the international community can exercise a positive influence. The president of Poland and high-ranking representatives of the European Union and the Organization for Security and Cooperation in Europe arrived quickly on the scene to push for new elections. At the same time, they acted as mediators helping to increase the power of Parliament and thus leave substantial amounts of power to the old regime. This mediation, however, was not easy to accomplish because the Russian president Vladimir Putin supported the candidate of the old regime, whom he recognized quickly after the fraudulent elections as the winner. Putin felt ideologically close to the old regime and considered the Ukraine as being in the Russian sphere of influence; but ultimately Putin accepted that Yushchenko became president. The Ukrainian example shows that the international community may not always speak with one voice when it comes to the transition of a country to democratic elections. Thus, a power game may go on not only internally in the respective country but also internationally.

EXPLANATIONS

We have now covered six cases of transitions to democratic elections: the Federal Republic of Germany, Italy, Spain, Hungary, Poland, and the Ukraine. It is striking how much variation there is among the seven cases. Each case is different from the others. This raises the question of whether any generalizations are possible. The challenge in comparative politics is to recognize that each country is idiosyncratic, with very specific characteristics, but one must still attempt to generalize to some extent. Such generalizations are made easier if more cases are added. For the transition to democratic elections, one could add Greece and Portugal, which made the transition, like Spain, in the 1970s. One could also add other Central and Eastern European countries. In some of them transition to democracy was not very smooth, for example, in Albania, Romania, and Bulgaria. Still staying within Europe, one could go to history and study, for example, the French Revolution in 1789, or the unsuccessful German revolution in 1848. Latin America in recent times offers many examples of successful and unsuccessful transitions to democratic elections. Afghanistan, Iraq, and many other cases around the world could also be studied. For American students it would be of particular interest to investigate how the very first democratic elections in their country took place and then make comparisons with other countries.

Much scholarly literature also exists on transitions to democratic elections. Why are some transitions smooth, others rough, and still others not taking place at all? Students may choose for their term papers a few countries and try to come up with some explanations for the variation among these countries. What are possible explanatory factors?

The next section suggests a list and raises further questions.

Discussion Questions

1. *Culture:* The culture of a country is characterized by specific values and social norms. Which values and norms make a transition to democratic elections easier? For example, does an emphasis on individualistic values and norms facilitate a smooth transition to democratic elections? Or is it better to have more of an emphasis on collective values and norms?

2. *Religion:* Much has been written about the influence of religion on politics. With regard to the transition to democratic elections, one may ask whether it is smoother in more religious or more secular countries. Does it depend on the kind of religion? Or on the number of religious groups in a country?

3. *Education:* Does a highly educated populace make the transition to democratic elections easier? Does it depend on the kind of education, for example, such as an emphasis on liberal arts?

4. *Economy:* Is the affluence of a country an influence? Or, more specifically, is a transition to democratic elections easier during an upturn or a downturn of the economy?

5. *Old elites:* Should the old elites be put to trial? Is the death penalty an appropriate punishment in these circumstances? In South Africa after the overthrow of the Apartheid regime, there were no criminal trials, but a truth commission; does such a commission make the transition to democratic elections easier? Another possibility is simply to let the old elites participate in the transition to democratic elections, as in Spain and Hungary. Are there general rules regarding how the old elites should be treated, or does it very much depend on the specific cases, in particular on how brutal the old regime was?

6. *Institutions:* The founding democratic elections may be organized in very different ways. Do the elections rules have an influence on how smooth the election process will be? Is the winner-take-all system to be preferred? Or is it better to go with rules of proportionality, and does it matter which specific rules of proportionality are chosen? Other institutional features may have an impact, too, for example, whether a country has a monarch, or whether it has a centralized or a federalist structure.

7. *International pressure:* In each of the cases we discussed the international community played a very different role. Here again many questions can be asked. Does a military occupation help or hurt the transition to democratic elections? Does it depend on who the occupiers are? Are international election observers useful? Who should these observers be?

---

[1]Seats are distributed according to the Droop Largest Remainder formula. Unlike the pure Droop formula, however, remainder seats are allocated only to parties with vote remainders greater than two-thirds of the vote quotas. Unawarded seats and unused votes are transferred to the national level for distribution.

[2]*New York Times,* November 28, 1989.

[3]*New York Times,* November 27, 1989.

[4]For the electoral fate of the former Communist parties in the various Central and Eastern European countries, see John T. Ishiyama. Communist Parties in Transition: Structures, Leaders, and Processes of Democratization in Eastern Europe. *Comparative Politics* 27, January 1995: 147–166.

[5]*The News and Observer,* Raleigh, NC, March 26, 1990.

[6]D. O'Donnell and P. Schmitter. *Transitions from Authoritarian Rule: Tentative Conclusions About Uncertain Democracies.* (Baltimore, MD: Johns Hopkins University Press, 1986).

[7]*Newsweek,* October 28, 1991.

[8]Ishiyama, Communist Parties in Transition, 159–160.

[9]*New York Times,* September 21, 1993.

[10]*New York Times,* September 21, 1993.

[11]*New York Times,* September 15 and 19, 1993.

Nationalism and Ethnicity

In this chapter we address an important aspect of the culture of a country: nationalism and ethnicity. Culture has much to do with identity. Who are we? How do we define ourselves? Identity can be defined at an individual level. Readers of this book may ask themselves whether they see themselves primarily as boys or men, girls or women—a question of identity definition often not easily solved by American students in their transition from high school to adult life. Identity can also be defined at a collective level. With what group is my strongest identification? Here, the nation and ethnic groups as sources of identity come into play. We will show that some European nations are multiethnic whereas other nations are more ethnically homogeneous. We will also show that some ethnic groups aspire to become nations whereas other ethnic groups have no such aspirations. Furthermore, we will learn that some ethnic groups cross national borders.

Relating this chapter to the previous chapter on transitions to democracy, it is interesting to ponder whether strong nationalism helps or hurts successful transitions to democracy and whether successful transitions to democracy are easier or more difficult in ethnically homogeneous or ethnically heterogeneous countries. We will come back to these issues in Chapter 13 on power sharing.

It is not easy to separate the concepts of nationalism and ethnicity. The phenomenon of ethnicity implies that a large number of individuals feel and act as one "people." What is meant in this context by "people"? The term has many different connotations. The connotation important for the definition of ethnicity is that a "people" has a common culture and a common history. The members of a "people" feel emotional ties to each other, even if they don't know each other on a personal basis. There is a shared feeling of belonging together, a feeling of being "we," of being different from all others.

Thus defined, a "people" is an ethnic group. Such groups often share common ascriptive attributes, such as skin color, language, or religion. But sometimes, an ethnic group is merely held together by a common history, or more precisely, by the *perception* of a common history. To what extent such a common history actually exists is less important. It may consist mainly of sagas and myths.

Ethnic groups often strive to have their own independent states. If they reach this goal, they are no longer called ethnic groups but nations. A good illustration are the Slovenes, who were an ethnic group in former Yugoslavia. When they reached independence, they were no longer called an ethnic group, but a nation. Ethnic feelings became national feelings. Sometimes, an ethnic group is satisfied to receive more autonomy within an existing nation, for example the Bretons within France. Some ethnic groups cross national borders, for example the Basques, who live on both sides of the French–Spanish border. Nations may be based on a single ethnicity, or they may be multiethnic. In the latter case, nationalism has to make a bridge between the various ethnic groups. Belgian nationalism, for example, has to take account of both the Flemish and the Walloon ethnicities. To make the terminology even more complicated, certain ethnic groups within a nation state may call themselves nations. The Catalans in Spain are a prominent example in this respect; they consider themselves a nation within Spain. Thus, the distinction between nations and ethnic groups is rather blurred in the European context.

Strong national and ethnic identities may not be harmful and may even be considered a good thing, giving a feeling of belongingness to people. However, negative consequences of such identities may lead to political instability and even violence. Unfortunately, Europe is not yet free of such negative consequences. The worst example is the former Yugoslavia, which in the 1990s broke apart among tremendous atrocities. Europeans had hoped that after World War II such atrocities would no longer occur on its soil. We begin the chapter with this war in former Yugoslavia.

WAR IN FORMER YUGOSLAVIA

Yugoslavia became Communist after World War II, but could keep its distance from the Soviet Union. After the fall of the Berlin Wall in 1989 and the disintegration of communism in Central and Eastern Europe, the international community held no immediate worries about Yugoslavia. Attention was directed to other places such as Romania, East Germany, and the former Soviet republics. Thus, it was all the more unpleasant and surprising when violence broke out in Yugoslavia in 1991. Communist leaders such as the Serb Slobodan Milosevic and the Croat Franjo Tudjman turned into fierce nationalists. Ordinary citizens who did not seem to care too much about their ethnic and national identities began to shoot at each other. In the city of Sarajevo, where the various ethnic groups seemingly had lived peacefully together and where in 1984 well-organized Winter Olympics had taken place, fierce fighting broke out. What happened to cause nationalism and ethnicity to suddenly reveal its ugly face?

To understand the situation one needs to go way back into history. The term *Yugoslavs* means "South Slavs," which refers to the time of the great European migration around A.D. 600. At that time, these Slavs moved from northeastern Europe southward to the Balkans and were therefore called South Slavs. Thus, initially all South Slavs belonged, broadly speaking, to the same ethnic group. This common origin explains why it is very difficult to distinguish members of the current ethnic groups by their physical appearance. Why did the various groups differentiate themselves from their common origin? The Croats and Slovenes lived mostly to the west and thus closest to Rome, the center of the Roman Catholic Church, which explains why these two groups became Roman Catholic. The Serbs and the Macedonians were mostly in the east, and under the influence of the Russian Christian Orthodox Church they became Christian Orthodox.

The Muslims were originally Christians too, living in the central region of Bosnia-Herzegovina. They practiced a controversial kind of Christianity that was considered heresy by the other Christian churches. They were inspired by the teachings of Mani, a prophet born in Babylon in A.D. 216, who stressed the human aspects of Jesus. Being without the backing of a powerful outside religious center, these so-called Manichaeans sought the protection of the Ottoman Empire when it expanded its influence on the Balkans and converted to Islam.

There is also the special case of the Albanians, who are ethnically not South Slavs. They are the dominant group in Kosovo. The minority are Serbs, and, as we will see shortly, the fact that Albanians and Serbs are of very different ethnic groups has greatly contributed to the problems in Kosovo.

According to the 1990 census, before war broke out, 36 percent of the people in the whole of Yugoslavia identified themselves as Serbs and 20 percent as Croats. The next largest group were the Muslims with 9 percent, living mostly in Bosnia-Herzegovina. As described earlier, these Muslims were also South Slavs, and in order to differentiate themselves from the other South Slavs, they identified themselves by their religious affiliation. Another 8 percent were also Muslims, those living in Kosovo, but since they are of a very different ethnic group they like to be seen as Albanians. If this sounds complicated, it is. The ethnic and religious composition of the former Yugoslavia was indeed of a perplexing complexity. Let us add that there were also 8 percent Slovenes, 6 percent Macedonians, while the remaining 13 percent were members of even smaller minorities such as Montenegrins, Turks, and Hungarians.

Looking back at history, over the centuries there was much fighting among the various groups. Nobel Prize–winner Ivo Andrić, in his *The Bridge on the Drina*, gives a vivid literary description of how, over many generations, Muslims and Serbs lived together in a small town in eastern Bosnia at the Drina River.[1] He describes much cruelty between the two groups, but also warm friendships across ethnic lines. His novel was meant to give hope that despite all the differences, ethnic groups would learn to live peacefully together. Unfortunately, his hopes were not fulfilled. When the iron fist of communism was lifted from Bosnia-Herzegovina, the old hatreds emerged again.

Over the centuries, the Balkans were very much under foreign domination, by the Ottoman Empire from the south and the Austro-Hungarian Empire from the north. In the 19th century the Ottoman Empire began to decay, which allowed the Serbs to form their own kingdom of Serbia and the Montenegrins their kingdom of Montenegro. In World War I the Ottoman Empire fell completely apart, as did the Austro-Hungarian Empire. What should happen with the Balkans? Without asking the people themselves, the Versailles Peace Conference created a very artificial entity first called Kingdom of Serbs, Croats, and Slovenes. The king was a Serb; he established a very authoritarian regime. In 1929 he renamed the kingdom *Yugoslavia*. The other ethnic groups resented the dominance of the Serbs, and in 1934 a Croat assassinated the king.

In World War II, the power relations changed dramatically between Croats and Serbs. Croatia became a puppet regime of Hitler, and committed many atrocities against Serbs including concentration camps for Serbs. After World War II, Marshal Tito, who had fought the Nazis in the war, established a Communist regime. As noted, Tito was able to liberate himself from Soviet dominance, and there were no Soviet soldiers on Yugoslav soil. For Tito ethnicity was not compatible with Communist ideas, and he organized the country in such a way that political lines did not follow ethnic lines. Figure 12.1 shows the division of Communist Yugoslavia into republics that were ethnically quite heterogeneous. The republic of Croatia, for example, had a Serb minority of 11 percent.

Completing the ethnic picture of Yugoslavia in 1990, we should add that language did contribute to the ethnic divisions. Slovenes and Croats used the Roman alphabet; the other ethnic groups used the Cyrillic script. Thus, how people wrote gave a clear indication early on as to what ethnic groups they belonged to. There were also huge economic inequalities among the ethnic groups. Slovenia, on the Austrian border, had a per capita income that

FIGURE 12.1 Yugoslavia in 1990.

was about seven times higher than that in Kosovo and about three times higher than that in Macedonia and Montenegro.

After 1990 events in Yugoslavia took a dramatic turn. Slovenia and Croatia attempted to become independent countries. Should the international community accept such a move? Two fundamental international principles came into conflict with each other: territorial integrity and self-determination. Territorial integrity means that international borders can be changed only by peaceful means and by common agreement. Self-determination means that all people who so desire have the right to a sovereign and independent state.

Initially, the international community gave preference to the principle of territorial integrity. Thus, U.S. Secretary of State James Baker, during a visit to Yugoslavia in June 1991:

... told the presidents of the republics of Slovenia and Croatia, who are planning to announce some form of independence in the next few days that the U.S. and its

European allies would not recognize them if they wanted to unilaterally break away from Yugoslavia and that they should not expect any economic assistance.[2]

The Slovenian parliament had decided on September 27, 1990, that the Yugoslav federal law would no longer apply within the borders of Slovenia. On December 23, 1990, 89 percent of Slovenian voters approved independence in a popular referendum. Croatian voters followed Slovenia's lead on May 19, 1991, when 93 percent approved independence for Croatia. The Yugoslav prime minister warned Slovenia and Croatia on June 24, 1991, that "the Federal Government will use all means to stop the republics' unilateral steps towards independence."[3] Despite this grave warning, Slovenia and Croatia formally declared independence the following day. On June 27, 1991, armed hostilities broke out between the Yugoslav Federal Army and the Slovenian Militia (Box 12.1). By early August, the hostilities spread to Croatia.

Shortly after the beginning of hostilities, Germany began to push for international recognition of Slovenian and Croatian independence. As political scientist Beverly Crawford shows, there was strong domestic pressure in Germany for giving Slovenia and Croatia the right of self-determination. A link was made with the recent German unification, and, as the general secretary of the ruling Christian Democrats expressed it, Germany could not apply another yardstick to Yugoslavia "when we achieved the unity and freedom of our country through the right of self-determination." The two opposition parties, the Social Democrats and the Greens, also supported the principle of self-determination for the crisis in Yugoslavia.[4] German Foreign Minister Hans-Dietrich Genscher presented the German view as follows: "To refuse recognition to those republics which desire their independence must lead to a further escalation of the use of force by the national [Yugoslav] Army."[5] For the Germans, the principle of territorial integrity of Yugoslavia was superseded by the principle of self-determination for Slovenia and Croatia. France,

---

Box 12.1

"Slovenia Is at War," Defense Chief Says as Fighting Spreads

The Slovene defense minister, Janez Jansa, speaking after Yugoslav Army tanks pushed into his republic, said Thursday that Slovenia was at war. Mr. Jansa said in a television interview that fighting was going on in at least 20 places in the republic and he estimated there were more than 100 dead and wounded on both sides. "To put it briefly, Slovenia is at war," he said. Slovenia military units earlier shot down a Yugoslav Army helicopter, killing the pilot and a crewman, Slovene police sources said. They said that two missiles hit the helicopter over a residential area on the outskirts of the republic's capital, Ljubljana. Two burned bodies were visible in the twisted metal of the helicopter. The shooting occurred after the Yugoslav Army sent tanks driving through Slovenia to the international borders. The shooting that broke out Thursday was the first between army troops and rebel militiamen since the republics of Slovenia and Croatia declared independence Tuesday.

Source: *New York Times*, June 28, 1991.

Great Britain, and the United States were at first reluctant to follow Germany's lead. But the newly united Germany used its strength to impose its will. Genscher flew to Slovenia and Croatia and received an enthusiastic welcome. The entire episode stirred troubling historical associations, because Nazi Germany dominated the two Yugoslav regions during World War II. On January 15, 1992, the European Union recognized Slovenia and Croatia as sovereign, independent states. The United Nations followed suit May 22, 1992.

In Slovenia, the hostilities were never severe and came to a quick end. Slovenia had the advantage of being the most homogeneous of the Yugoslav republics, with 90 percent of the population being Slovenes. In addition, it was the most Westernized and economically the most developed. Of all the parts of former Yugoslavia, Slovenia was the only one to reach some degree of political and economic stability relatively quickly. In 2004 it even joined the European Union as the first region of the former Yugoslavia.

Croatia had many more difficulties to overcome than Slovenia on the road to peace. As we have seen, Croatia had a substantial minority of Serbs, who were concentrated in a region called Krajina, located in the south-center of Croatia. In the old Yugoslavia, these Krajina Serbs had lived together with the Serbs of the Serbian Republic within the same national borders. Now, all of a sudden, they found themselves within the national borders of Croatia, and Serbia had become for them a foreign country. This situation was not accepted by the Krajina Serbs. They were supported in their resistance by the Serbian leaders in Belgrade who still controlled the Yugoslav Federal Army. Heavy fighting erupted and planes of the Yugoslav Federal Army even attacked the Croatian presidential palace in Zagreb.

In the international media, the Serbs appeared as the aggressors. Under the leadership of Milosevic in the late 1980s and early 1990s, they indeed displayed fierce nationalism and expansionism. Actions such as the attack on the Croatian presidential palace made the Serbs look like the guilty party. In fact, the situation was more complicated. We will present both sides of the arguments in this Croatian–Serbian war. It is then up to the reader to make a judgment. Let us begin the discussion with two American analogies, the War of Independence and the War of Secession. If we take the perspective of the American War of Independence, the Croats have all the rights on their side. Just as the American colonies liberated themselves from British domination, the Croats liberated themselves from Serb domination. But if we take the perspective of the American War of Secession, things look different. When the American South tried to secede from the Union, President Lincoln used all the federal forces to prevent this secession. In an analogous way, the Yugoslav federal authorities in Belgrade tried to prevent the secession of Croatia. Lincoln was successful; the Yugoslav federal authorities were not. Could it be that this is the reason that Lincoln is seen as hero, the Yugoslav federal authorities as villains?

With regard to the specifics of Croatia, there is no question that with its unilateral declaration of independence it violated the territorial integrity of Yugoslavia. It was clearly an illegal act of the Croats to blockade the Yugoslav federal troops stationed in their garrisons in Croatia. But how else could the Croats have secured their right to self-determination? Was there any way to do so in a peaceful way and by mutual agreement?

How about the rights of the Krajina Serbs? Did they also have a right to self-determination? They thought so, and wished either to be independent or to join Serbia. Although the Krajina region had no common border with Serbia, it could have joined Serbia as a Croat enclave. This is not an uncommon solution in international law. Croatia severely restricted the rights of the Krajina Serbs, forcing them, for example, to replace Serbian road signs in their villages with Croatian signs. The European Union was aware of the problem of the Krajina Serbs. It stated the following condition for diplomatic recognition of Croatian independence: "Guarantees for the rights of ethnic and national groups and minorities in accordance with the commitments subscribed to in the framework of the Conference on Security and Cooperation in Europe."[6] Personal assurances by the Croatian President Tudjman that the Krajina Serbs would be given a "special status" were sufficient for the European Union to consider the required condition as fulfilled. Was this sufficient assurance, or should the European Union have undertaken investigations on location to determine whether the rights of the Krajina Serbs were truly guaranteed? What were these rights anyhow? The European Union distinguished conceptually between "minorities" and "territorially defined administrative units." The Krajina Serbs were considered only a minority, with the right of autonomy but not independence. Croatia, on the other hand, was considered a territorially defined administrative unit and was therefore entitled to independence. Did this conceptual distinction make sense? Could not the Krajina Serbs also claim that they were territorially defined, since they lived in a relatively well-defined area? Should they not also have the right to self-determination? They made an effort to claim such a right and created the Serbian Republic of Krajina, but neither Croatia nor the international community recognized this entity. The Krajina region became more and more isolated and economically devastated. As a newspaper report put it, "the Krajina Serbs feel [they are] being pushed to the end of the world. The Croatian capital Zagreb is hostile territory, and the Serbian capital only to be reached over insecure roads."[7] In June 1993, the Krajina Serbs organized a referendum in which they decided overwhelmingly to join Serbia and the Serbs in Bosnia-Herzegovina in a Greater Serbia. But, again, the international community didn't recognize this referendum, which was called by a leading newspaper a "phantom referendum."[8]

Finally, there is the question of whether the international community played a proper role in the Croatian–Serbian conflict. The Secretary General of the United Nations had initially stated that recognition of Croatia and any other Yugoslav entity "can only be envisioned in the framework of an overall settlement,"[9] meaning that issues such as the fate of the Krajina Serbs should be settled before diplomatic recognition of any new states could be considered. As we have seen, this position was at first supported by the United States, Great Britain, and France. Should this policy have been pursued even when Germany went ahead to recognize Croatia and Slovenia? The Secretary General of the United Nations feared that premature recognition would lead to even greater violence. As we have seen, German Foreign Minister Genscher took the opposite view. In retrospect, who was right? With regard to the German policy, the question must be raised whether the Germans were sensitive enough to the historical aspect of Croatia having been a Nazi puppet regime in World War II. Could the hero's welcome of Genscher in Croatia not be interpreted by the Serbs as the beginning of a new German conquest? Was talk of a "Fourth German Reich" extending to Slovenia and Croatia only Serbian propaganda, or was such talk based on real fears? These are all difficult questions to ponder. In retrospect, political scientist Dusan Sidjanski argues that the early international recognition of Croatia "did not appease but, on the contrary, may have rekindled the nationalistic ambitions and the conflict between Croatia and Serbia."[10] Is he right? Because it is not possible to know what would have happened without early diplomatic recognition of Croatia, there is no definite answer to this question, which will be debated among historians for generations to come. In the current world, the proper behavior of the international community has great importance. As the war between Serbia and Croatia shows, it is not so easy for the international community to simply stay uninvolved. It was confronted with the question of whether or not to recognize Croatia as an independent country. Not to do anything and not to give recognition would have been an action too. Thus, the international community was forced to act one way or the other. To stay out of the conflict was not an option.

If the situation in Croatia was complicated, it was even more complicated in Bosnia-Herzegovina, which had three major groups: 39 percent Muslims, 32 percent Serbs, and 18 percent Croats. For the Muslims this was the only part of former Yugoslavia where they were the largest group. On March 1, 1992, 63 percent of the electorate voted for an independent Bosnia-Herzegovina. Compared with the referenda in Slovenia and Croatia, this support was not very high, indicating opposition by many Serbs and Croats living in Bosnia-Herzegovina. Quite a few Serbs and Croats did not even vote, boycotting the referendum altogether. Thus, from the very beginning, the Muslim-dominated government of Bosnia-Herzegovina was on shaky ground. The European Union was aware of the dangers ahead and warned the government of Bosnia-Herzegovina "to grant to the members of the minorities and ethnic groups the totality of human rights and fundamental freedoms recognized by international law."[11] Based on the promise to do so, Bosnia-Herzegovina was recognized by the European Union, and, on May 22, 1992, by the United Nations.

But quickly a horrendous war broke out in Bosnia-Herzegovina. Box 12.2 and Photo 12.1 testify to the atrocities committed in this war. It seemed unbelievable that such

PHOTO 12.1 Young woman seeking cover during shelling in the town of Mostar in Bosnia-Herzegovina. (Copyright Associated Press.)

Box 12.2

UN's GRIM DOCUMENTATION AT A MASSACRE SITE IN BOSNIA

STUPNI DO—Until about 3 P.M. on Saturday, this village in the mountains of central Bosnia was a haven from the war that has engulfed much of this former Yugoslav republic, a cluster of houses high in a valley where the immediate concern of the Muslim inhabitants was gathering in beets, potatoes, and squashes before the snow began. Then the brutality came up the winding dirt road from the town on the valley floor, in cars and trucks that arrived so suddenly that some of the 250 villagers had time only to pull on one sleeve of their winter jackets before rushing for the safety of the woodlands above the village. As they fled, they dropped a trail of shoes, gloves, and half-emptied cigarette packs along the muddy paths. But the speed they gained from their fear was not enough to save dozens of them from the wrath of the Croation nationalist soldiers who came to rape, to cut throats, to smash children's skulls, to machine-gun whole families. At noon today, the funeral pyres set by the Croats in the moonlight of Saturday night were still burning, and the stench of burnt bodies wafted down the hillsides, mingling with the fall scents of leaves and freshly turned sod. The only life left in the village after the massacre, a few dogs and some chickens and sheep, picked at bodies that had escaped the pyres. "Crazy, it's all crazy," said Maj. Daniel Ekberg, a 30-year-old Swedish officer whose persistence in trying to reach the village through three days of armed menace by Croatian troops finally paid off on Tuesday afternoon. His persistence meant that for the first time in the 18-month Bosnian war, the United Nations military command here arrived at a massacre scene soon enough, and well enough prepared, to determine exactly what had happened and who was responsible.

Source: *New York Times*, October 28, 1993.

brutalities could still occur in Europe. One had hoped that after the Nazi war crimes life had become more civilized in Europe. But, shamefully, the worst possible crimes happened: the rape of women, the killing of children, mass executions, concentration camps, the expulsion of civilians from their homes. Serbs killed Muslims and Croats, Croats killed Muslims and Serbs, Muslims killed Serbs and Croats. The worst offenders were the Serbs, particularly with the 1995 massacre in Srebrenica where Serbs separated men from women and children and executed about 8,000 men. Estimates are that more than 100,000 people lost their lives in the Bosnian war.[12] As a consequence of these atrocities, the Security Council of the United Nations decided that an international war tribunal should investigate these crimes and bring the guilty to court. This was the first time since the Nazi crimes that the international community established a war tribunal.

Macedonia was the fourth Yugoslav republic to be granted independence by the United Nations. This happened with much delay only in April 1993. The problem for Macedonia was that Greece was opposed to its independence, because immediately to the south of Macedonia was a Greek province with the same name. Greece feared that an independent

Macedonia could put claims on the Greek province, trying to expand into a Greater Macedonia. During the Greek civil war in the late 1940s, the Yugoslav leader Tito had tried to piece together such a Greater Macedonia stretching to the Aegean Sea. Thus, the Greek fears were not unfounded. As the Greek Prime Minister said in an interview: "The generation that went through this war still remembers these things, and it's natural that the Greek people should be very sensitive concerning this issue."[13] Salonika, the capital of the Greek province Macedonia, is the birthplace of Alexander the Great. As one shopkeeper in Salonika said: "We are the true Macedonians. We've been here 3,000 years."[14] Given such emotions, it was not easy to find a solution. Finally, in the compromise that was worked out, the former Yugoslav republic received independence, but under the awkward name Former Yugoslav Republic of Macedonia. It was only in 2004 that the United States recognized that the name be abbreviated to Republic of Macedonia, and even then only under protests from Greece.

Then there is Kosovo, which did not get independence. It was not a proper republic in former Yugoslavia, but merely a province within Serbia. The rule adopted by the international community was that only republics of the former regime should get independence and not subunits of republics. This somewhat arbitrary rule played against the Krajina and also against Kosovo. For an understanding of the situation in Kosovo it is important to know that on its territory the Serbs fought their most important historical battle, the battle of Kosovo in 1389. They lost this battle against the Turks, but turned the defeat into a legend. "There is no holier place in the Serbian mind, and there are few Serbs who have not memorized parts of epic poems about the battle."[15] Kosovo's population is about 90 percent Albanian, most of whom are Muslim. As we have shown, the Kosovo Albanians are not South Slavs but a very different ethnic group. They claim to have always lived in this region and wish an independent Kosovo. The Serbs, on the other hand, want to keep this most holy place of their history in their own hands. In all of former Yugoslavia, Kosovo turned out to be the most difficult issue to resolve, and it is still not resolved.

In attempting to solve the problems in Bosnia-Herzegovina, Macedonia, and Kosovo, the international community tried to impose institutions of power sharing. Because Chapter 13 is entirely devoted to power sharing, we will discuss there to what extent these power-sharing efforts were successful in the regions of former Yugoslavia.

NORTHERN IRELAND

Northern Ireland is another trouble spot where nationalism and ethnicity led to violence and more than 3,000 deaths since the 1960s (for a tragic illustration, see Photo 12.2). The conflict is easier to explain than the one in former Yugoslavia because in Northern Ireland there are basically only two groups confronting each other: British Protestants and Irish Catholics. The problem appears on the surface to be a religious one, and the mass media usually speak of civil strife between Protestants and Catholics. But, below the surface, the battle is really between two ethnic groups: the British Unionists and the Irish Nationalists. The former happen to be Protestants and the latter, Catholics, but the conflict is not primarily about religious matters, although the religious dimension has some importance, too. But essentially it is much more a struggle between two cultures unwilling to share the same territory. The Protestants want to remain part of the United Kingdom, therefore the term

PHOTO 12.2 Scene after a bomb killed seven construction workers riding the bus in the background. The IRA claimed responsibility for the blast. (Copyright Associated Press.)

Unionists, and the Catholics want to be part of the Irish nation. This is also the view of political scientist Arend Lijphart:

> Ethnic cleavages may superficially look like religious, ideological, or some other kind of divisions. The clearest case in point is Northern Ireland, where the groups in conflict are commonly referred to as Protestants and Catholics; the labels are religious, but the two communities are true ethnic groups. This does not mean that their religious differences are unimportant but, rather, that religion is only part of the distinctive set of characteristics that define the groups.[16]

John McGarry and Brendan O'Leary stress, too, that the conflict in Northern Ireland "is primarily ethno-national."[17] In medieval times only Irish lived on the island; ethnically they were Celtic. In the 16th and 17th centuries, Scottish settlers arrived in the northern part. They were the British Protestants just mentioned.

Politically, the entire island eventually came under British domination, which was harsh and never accepted by the Irish. The British rulers treated the Irish as inferior beings, and Irish literature is filled with angry descriptions of how the British prevented the Irish from being Irish on their own territory. Even during the time when Great Britain had an impressive colonial empire, the Irish issue occupied British leaders. The Irish wanted independence, which they called Home Rule. Finally, at the end of World War I, following a bloody uprising in Dublin in 1916, Ireland got its independence from Great Britain in 1921. Dublin became the capital of the Republic of Ireland, but Great Britain kept the island's Northern provinces. There the majority of the population was British by ethnic background and Protestant by religion. But a substantial minority of Irish Catholics also lived in Northern Ireland.

What we have seen in Northern Ireland are the difficulties British and Irish people have in trying to live together peacefully. The Irish want to make Northern Ireland part of the Republic of Ireland and consider the British foreign invaders. The British, on the other hand, argue that Northern Ireland is their home, where they have lived for centuries. As the majority in Northern Ireland, they want to remain a part of Great Britain and object to the notion that a minority could impose its preference on a majority. The important point is that the Catholics do not have a primarily religious grievance. Their complaint is, rather, that they are forced as Irish people to remain part of Great Britain. In this context students may wish to discuss the question of when people can claim a right to live on a piece of land. After about 400 years, did the Protestant settlers have the right to stay in Northern Ireland?

When the Republic of Ireland obtained its independence in 1921 and Northern Ireland remained British, a parliament (Stormont) with extensive powers was established in Belfast, the capital of Northern Ireland. Protestants held a two-to-one majority in the country, and they practiced democracy in the traditional British way—by applying the majority principle both for parliamentary elections and cabinet formation. Given their numerical dominance, they easily won one parliamentary election after another and exercised all the governmental power. The local prime minister and all his cabinet members always belonged to the Protestant subculture, while the Catholics remained politically impotent. Over the years, this led to increasing dissatisfaction and frustration among the Irish Catholic population. In 1968 violence broke out, referred to by the British in a rather benign way as the "troubles" in Northern Ireland. But these were more than mere troubles. The Irish Republican Army (IRA), which was active in the liberation struggle of Ireland in the 19th century and the beginning of the 20th century, was reactivated and began to use terrorist methods. Ultimately, British troops intervened, and in 1972 the Belfast parliament was dissolved and direct rule by London was imposed.

The British tried to restore calm in Northern Ireland through a form of power sharing. A cabinet of moderate Protestants and Catholics was established in Northern Ireland, but within a few months a general strike of Protestant workers brought this experiment to a halt. The large majority of Protestants was not willing to change from a majoritarian to a power-sharing pattern of decision making. The Catholics, for their part, reacted with further civil strife. In Chapter 13 we will discuss, in the general context of the power-sharing literature, the specific obstacles to power sharing in Northern Ireland and how, finally, with the Good Friday Accord some important steps were made in the direction of power sharing.

BASQUE COUNTRY

The Basque country is yet another place in Europe where nationalism and ethnicity has caused widespread violence, with about 1,000 deaths since the 1960s. The Basque country, economically quite affluent, is located at the Northeastern corner of Spain and reaches also into France. The Basques are an ethnic group with a very long tradition. They are united by a unique language whose historical origin is still unclear. It seems to be the oldest language in Europe, different from all the Indo-Germanic languages. For a long time, both Spain and France tried to suppress Basque language and culture on their respective territories. This suppression was particularly harsh under the dictatorship of Francisco Franco in Spain (for the Franco regime, see Chapter 11). It was during this dictatorial regime that in 1959 an organization was founded to fight for Basque independence. The name of this organization was *Basque Fatherland and Liberty Group*, in Basque language *Euskadi Ta Askatasuna* (ETA).

This ETA organization was willing to use terrorist methods to reach its goal. Its targets were mainly security forces, government officials, and politicians, but also tourist places to hurt the Spanish economy. Its most spectacular action occurred in 1973 with the assassination of Admiral Luis Carrero, the presumed successor of Franco. When after the death of Franco in 1975 Spain made a successful transition to a democratic regime, the Basque country received considerable autonomy with its own local parliament. Although many Basque people were quite satisfied with this progress, the ETA insisted on Basque independence and continued its terrorist activities. The ETA operated with small, self-sufficient cells so that it was very difficult to penetrate the organization and break it up.

The ETA has a political wing, the Herri Batasuma, which participates in elections. The Spanish authorities have great difficulties in handling this political wing of the ETA. On the one hand, attempts were made to separate the political leaders of Herri Batasuma from the ETA. But on the other hand, it also happened that the entire leadership of Herri Batasuma was arrested and sentenced to prison terms for collaborating with an armed group. The ambivalent position of the Spanish authorities was also revealed when they entered secret but unsuccessful talks with ETA representatives. The authorities also did not know how to act when the ETA declared a ceasefire. Was this genuine or was it just a stalling tactic to allow the ETA to reorganize and rearm? The Spanish population remains very upset with the terrorist activities of the ETA, and several times large numbers took to the streets to protest the activities of the ETA.

An interesting twist in the Basque issue occurred in December 2004 when the Basque parliament approved, by a vote of 39 to 35, a proposal that says the Basque region has the right to secede from Spain. The Spanish Prime Minister reacted immediately, rejecting the Basque Declaration and arguing that it violated the Spanish constitution, the proposal having "no legal foundation."[18] The Basque parliament did not necessarily express a demand for independence; its point was rather that it was up to the Basques to determine their relationship with Spain. As was stated in the decision of the Basque parliament: "We express our will to form a new political pact that grows from a new model for relations with the Spanish state based on freedom of association." The President of the Basque region and main author of the plan did elaborate on the meaning of the decision of the Basque parliament: "We are not proposing a project for breaking away from Spain, but we are formalizing a project for friendly coexistence between the Basque region and Spain. . . . The Basque country is not a subordinate part of the Spanish state. The only way there will be a shared relationship with the state is if we decide there will be one."[19] This episode raises most interesting questions of democratic theory: Is it up to each region of a country to determine for itself what association it wishes to have with the other parts of the country? How important is it for the collective identity of a region to have this right of self-determination? Both questions were answered in the affirmative by the Basque parliament. According to its decision the Basques are happy to remain part of Spain, but only if they can decide freely to do so.

How important is the question of independence in current Europe anyhow? Both France and Spain belong to the European Union and use the euro as common currency, and people can travel freely back and forth. As we will see in Chapter 14 on the European Union, regions play an increasingly important role, with some of them crossing national borders. Is the Basque country not an ideal region within the European Union? There are indeed many signs of the emergence of a cross-national Basque region. Basque is again taught in school, on both sides of the French–Spanish border. If it is geographically more convenient, schoolchildren are allowed to attend school on the other side of the border. In the town of Ainhoa, for example, located on the French side, about one-fifth of the children come from the Spanish side. Many people in the Basque region speak three languages: Basque, French, and Spanish. The traditional Basque ball game, pelota, which is comparable to squash, is played in the entire Basque region, regardless of the border between France and Spain. Farmers are allowed to graze their sheep on both sides of the border. Firefighting and recycling are organized across the border. In the daily life of the Basque country, the national border between France and Spain has lost much of its importance. Here, as a journalist notes, "Europe of the regions has become reality."[20] Given this situation, the notion of national independence has lost much of its importance, so that it seems antiquated that the ETA still continues to some extent its terrorist activities. The Basque country is well and alive as a vibrant European region with one part of the Basques also belonging to Spain, the other part also to France. The ETA thus fights an old battle that no longer fits the emerging political order of the European Union.

IMMIGRATION

Within the countries of the European Union it has become very easy and unproblematic to move from one country to another (see Chapter 14). This, however, is not at all the case if someone comes from outside the European Union, especially from former Yugoslavia,[21] Turkey, or Africa. Many people from these regions try to find work in Europe. Many refugees also try to come to Europe. Often the line between immigrant workers and refugees is blurred, which puts the European authorities in severe dilemmas concerning whom to accept and whom to reject. If someone attempts to escape the economic misery, even starvation, in an African country, is this sufficient ground to be considered a refugee? These are the hard cases to be decided by European authorities.

In former times, refugees were no problem when they came in small numbers from Communist countries. There were two main waves of refugees fleeing from communism. In 1956, many Hungarians were able to escape before the Soviet tanks crushed the uprising in Budapest. In 1968, many were able to flee from Czechoslovakia before the Soviet tanks stopped the reform movement there. These refugees were most welcome in Western Europe. Most of them were highly educated, and during the economic boom of the time they were easily integrated in their host countries.

The welcome for such migrants soon wore out in Europe. In contrast to the refugees from Communist countries during the cold war, the new asylum-seekers integrated less easily into the European societies. First, their status was uncertain, and most knew that their request for asylum would ultimately be rejected. Second, they were too different to be able to integrate successfully. For both reasons, they most often preferred to stay among themselves and to give one another comfort. Some poor neighborhoods in the big European cities were thus transferred into ethnic enclaves of immigrants of all kinds, a mixture of refugees and immigrant workers.

In the German city of Mannheim, one of us (Steiner) has visited a neighborhood nearly exclusively inhabited by Turks. Turkish was spoken in the streets; the stores had Turkish signs and sold Turkish items, in particular Turkish food; women, according to Turkish tradition, wore black clothes and had their hair covered with white shawls. New Turkish immigrants naturally went to such a neighborhood, where they felt more at home. There they joined other Turks who had already lived in Germany for a long time. All over Europe, immigrants from less-developed countries have established their own subcultures in the big cities. This new multiethnicity makes many Europeans ill at ease and hostile (see Box 12.3).

After September 11, 2001, and the war in Iraq, tensions with Muslims in Europe have further increased. Many Muslims feel vulnerable and even less welcome than before. On the other side, there are increasing complaints that many Muslims become fundamentalist and are unwilling to integrate into European societies. This conflict came most visibly to public attention when in 2004 the Dutch filmmaker Theo Van Gogh was assassinated by a Muslim extremist of dual Dutch-Moroccan nationality. Van Gogh, a descendant of the 19th-century painter, was an outspoken proponent of free expression. His short film *Submission*, shown on Dutch television, criticized the Muslim treatment of women. The film told the fictional story of a Muslim woman who was forced into a violent marriage, raped by a relative, and brutally punished for adultery. It featured actresses portraying abused Muslim women, naked under transparent Islamic-style shawls, their bodies marked with texts from the Koran that supposedly justify the repression of women.

The film provoked an angry outcry in the Muslim community. The killer of Van Gogh was most brutal, shooting the filmmaker on an open street of Amsterdam, slitting his throat, and stabbing his chest. Two knives were left in the torso, one pinning a five-page note threatening Western governments. In the aftermath of this assassination, mosques were put on fire, not only in the Netherlands, but, for example, also in Germany. All over Europe, this tragedy led to an intense soul-searching. Did Van Gogh legitimately use his right for free expression? Are there limits to what one can do in a film? To what extent is it allowable for non-Muslims to criticize the teachings of Islam? Should Muslim immigrants make an effort to integrate into European societies? Should non-Muslims be encouraged to learn more about Islam and its history? How can Muslims and non-Muslims live peacefully together in Europe? These are all troubling questions showing that the immigration issue is a most difficult one for Europeans—more difficult than for Americans, who live in an immigration country, whereas Europe has much less of an immigration tradition.

In Europe there is the risk that because of immigration, cleavages between natives and immigrants will become increasingly deeper, with the latter more and more stressing their ethnic and even national identities.

SPORT EVENTS

It is often claimed that sport events bring people of different countries closer together. This is certainly sometimes true, and the United Nations even has a program to use sport events

Box 12.3

"Knallhart"

For years, discussing Germany's failing cultural integration policy (to the extent that one actually existed) was taboo.... Now the country has been forced to face a rather unpleasant reality, first in fictional form. The movie "Knallhart," or "Brutally Tough," depicts the brutalization of a German teenager by a Turkish youth gang at a school in Neukölln, a district in Berlin with a high proportion of foreigners. Not so long ago, a plotline casting immigrants as the villains tormenting a (blond) German would have been unimaginable.... And that was even before Germans learned how authentic the movie really was. Last week it was reported that teachers at a school in Neukölln sent a letter to the city council asking for nothing less than their school to be shut down because of intolerable violence there. More than 83% of the students come from immigrant families, with 61% either from Arab or Turkish families.... The media is now awash with stories of beatings, stabbings, drug dealing, sexual assaults and other violent crimes at German schools— to a disproportionate degree perpetrated by students with a migrant, mostly Turkish, background, according to official statistics.... Those tempted to use this unusually frank discussion about immigration and crime to lash out against foreigners should be reminded that the immigrant and non-immigrant criminals have certain things in common. They are often unemployed young men with limited education springing from low-income households in big cities. There is, though, a cultural element to the violence. Girls are often attacked as "prostitutes" for not adhering to Muslim dress codes. "Pork-eater" has apparently become a common slur for non-Muslim kids. Western and German values are often rejected. While Germans may have added to a certain alienation among the migrant community by making it too difficult to become German, these problems also derive from making it too easy to get away with misbehavior. Cultural relativism and misunderstood political correctness among Germans have limited the demands made on foreigners. Their unwillingness to integrate is met with tolerance.

Source: *Wall Street Journal*, April 5, 2006.

to further international peace. But, unfortunately, on many occasions sport events enflame nationalism, provoking ugly and violent incidents. Soccer, the most popular sport in the world is particularly prone to have fans of different national teams provoking one another. The top soccer games in Europe are very much organized according to national criteria. There is a European tournament of national teams. At the level of club teams, there is first a competition within each country, but then the national champions compete with each other to become the European champion.

In a game between England and Germany, the popular English media presented the game as a replay of World War II. The *Daily Star*, for example, printed the headline "Watch out Krauts. England are gonna bomb you to bits." The *Sun's* headline was titled "Let's Blitz Fritz," with *Blitz* being a clear reference to World War II.[22] A game between the English and Irish national teams had to be stopped after a band of English fans making Nazi salutes ripped up seats and pelted other fans and players with pieces of wood, plastic, and metal.[23] As seen in the following report of the *New York Times,* soccer violence takes on increasingly nationalistic political overtones:

> Soccer violence in Europe used to be largely a matter of drunken youths, inflamed team loyalties and spontaneous brawls, and it usually seemed to involve the English. But soccer associations, the police and researchers have been tracking a steady growth in disturbances at and around games across Europe. And although many incidents are still ignited by beer, boredom and being on the wrong end of the score, experts said there was a growing tendency for hooliganism to be premeditated and organized for political purposes by right-wing extremists.[24]

MORE BENIGN ASPECTS

Up to now we have focused on negative aspects of nationalism and ethnicity, and indeed many disturbing negative aspects are evident. But benign aspects also exist. Let us take the Scots as a positive example. Scotland has a long and rich history, during which it developed many traditions. Since the 17th century, Scotland has been part of Great Britain, and in recent years the Scots have once again become more conscious of their separate historical roots. There has been a rebirth in the popularity of old Scottish songs and poems. Increased attention to Scottish history and culture and an influx of tourists have made many Scots truly aware for the first time that they are different from the English. This heightened awareness is reinforced when Scots move to London, where their Scottish identity often increases rather than decreases. The rebirth of Scottish identity is not limited to the older generation but also occurs among young, highly educated people. Politically, the new Scottish nationalism has gained importance, and Scotland has gotten its own local parliament.

This increased importance of Scottish identity is benign because it has not led to any particular animosities against the English, and certainly not to any violent incidents. For the Scots themselves an increased identity is probably mostly a good thing. The modern world has become more anonymous, with family and neighborhood ties breaking apart. In this situation, ethnic groups offer ties firmly rooted in the past. Nobody can take away the Scots' membership in the Scottish community; even if they move away from the region, they will always remain Scots. As long as one lives, one is united with the brothers and sisters of his or her ethnic affiliation. This belonging also links individuals with preceding generations and generations to follow, creating a historical perspective. What we have noted for Scotland is true for many other ethnic groups in Europe, for example the Catalonia in Spain, Brittany in France, Frisia in the Netherlands, and Bavaria in Germany.

The crucial point is that a strong ethnic identity does not necessarily lead to hostile feelings and even violent actions against other ethnic groups. But it is important that an identity is not exclusive but also allows the existence of other identities. In the modern world multiple identities have positive consequences for political stability and cooperation. In its history, the great danger for Europe was fierce nationalism leading to many bloody wars. Fortunately, there are signs of a multilevel order emerging in Europe, with citizens still having a national identity but in addition also European and regional identities.

A historical perspective shows that the concept of the nation-state is not older than 400 years (see also Chapter 1). It was created in Western Europe, with France as the prototypical example. In medieval times, there existed no French nation-state, nor any other nation-state, in Europe. Under the system of feudalism, no clear borders divided the sovereignty of one ruler from another. Rather, the various rulers—kings, dukes, barons, bishops, cities, monasteries, and so on—had overlapping rights. Within a particular village, both a duke and a monastery may have had the right to levy taxes. An individual peasant may have had obligations to both a bishop and a city.

It was only in the 16th century, with the beginning of absolutism, that the concept of national sovereignty became relevant. Within specific territorial borders a single ruler took over all the political power. To consolidate this power, the ruler tried to establish a common national identity among his or her subjects. Of particular importance was the imposition of a common language. This process of building the European nations took a long time. In France of the 19th century, for example, many people still did not speak French as a native language. Thus, it is historically quite a new phenomenon that Europeans feel part of nation-states.

European history of the 19th and 20th centuries has shown how the concept of the nation-state, based on an exclusively defined national identity, can lead to catastrophic wars. The temptation is great for a nation-state to try to expand its borders and thus its national sovereignty. National interests risk clashing with one another at any time.

The idea for a more stable and cooperative European order is to redefine the concept of sovereignty in less national terms. Sovereignty would no longer belong exclusively to the nation-state but be divided among the European, the national, and the regional levels. The nation-states would certainly continue to exist and exercise important power, but some of their power would be transferred upward to the European level and some downward to the regional level. As we will see in Chapter 14, the European Union makes efforts precisely in this direction. It is important to stress here that the European Union is characterized both by a process of regionalization and a process of supranational integration.

For a new political order in Europe it is also important that regional political units are allowed to cut across national borders. As we have seen earlier in this chapter, the Basque region is a good example to illustrate this aspect. It stretches across the French–Spanish border at the North Atlantic Ocean. The Tyrol is another example of a region that was cut across by a national border but now flourishes again as an entity. The Tyrol belonged to the Austro-Hungarian Empire, within which it had developed its own cultural identity. After the demise of the Austro-Hungarian Empire in World War I, the southern part of the Tyrol was transferred to Italy, while the northern part remained with Austria. Italy tried to assimilate South Tyrol into the Italian nation, in particular with regard to language. But there was fierce resistance among the South Tyrol people, who wanted to stay with their native German language and culture. Occasionally, resistance even took the form of armed attacks against the Italian authorities. Today, with both Austria and Italy being members of the European Union, tensions have vanished in the South Tyrol. People there are once again allowed to be taught German in school. Contacts with the Austrian part of the Tyrol have been greatly facilitated. Although the Tyrol still belongs to two different nation-states, it again enjoys a life of its own with many common cultural and economic affairs. There is a strong

Tyrol identity, but in the South it is coupled with an Italian identity and in the North with an Austrian identity, and both the South and the North have some European identity.

Cross-national regions may also grow out of functional economic circumstances. An example is the Regio Basiliensis in Greater Basel. The city of Basel is located in the northwestern corner of Switzerland, where Germany, France, and Switzerland come together at the Rhine River. Many German and French commuters work in nearby Basel. Many consumers from Basel shop for bargains in German and French stores. The airport of Basel is located on French territory, and a German railway station is based on Swiss soil. These and many other examples indicate how much the agglomeration of Basel forms an economic unity across national borders of three countries. At an organizational level, Regio Basiliensis has the task of coordinating economic activities in the entire region, regardless of national borders.

Cross-national economic regions emerge also in Central and Eastern Europe. An example is the Euroregion Pomerania, at the border between Germany and Poland; another example is the Euroregion Karpatian in the border area of Poland, Slovakia, Hungary, and the Ukraine.[25] All these examples show how important regional thinking has become in Europe, even if the regions cut across national borders.

If Europe moves in the direction of a multilayered order with cross-cutting borders, one may ask whether such an order is not too complex. It does not seem too complex if we think of the problems confronting Europe. These problems are of a high complexity, and to solve complex problems, one needs a complex organization. The traditional organization based on nation-states is just too rigid. To be sure, there are still many problems for which the nation-state is the appropriate unit. But other problems need to be handled at the European level. And still other problems belong to the regional level, with some regions cutting across national borders.

The real issue is not whether Europe needs a complex political order. It is rather whether Europeans are able to adjust their thinking styles and their identities to such a complex order. Political thinking is, of course, easier if the national interest is the sole guiding post. Deciding whether something is good or bad for your nation is a simple question. In Europe of the future, thinking has to be more complex. Political issues need to be addressed at different levels. A particular solution may not seem in the immediate interest of your nation, but it may be beneficial for your region or for Europe at large. Because all levels ultimately depend on each other, in the long run the solution may be good for your nation, too. With such a thinking style, politics is transformed into a positive-sum game, which means that overall gains are higher than overall losses; in a positive-sum game, a gain for one side does not necessarily mean a loss for another side.

Symbolically, the new European order may best be expressed in the variety of flags that one would see in Europe. The national flags would still wave on the rooftops. But equally often one would see regional flags and the European flag. Because we are all also citizens of the world, the flag of the United Nations may also have its place in European towns and villages.

Discussion Questions

1. Does history side with winners?

2. To what extent does the American analogy of the Revolutionary and Civil War laid out above, apply to the Yugoslav situation?

3. Why was Tito able to keep the peace for such a long time in Yugoslavia?

4. Was the war in former Yugoslavia a civil war? If yes, on what grounds would you justify the interference of the United States and Nato?

5. How would you describe the nature of the war in former Yugoslavia? Was it primarily fought over religious differences (Muslims against Christians), or ethnic differences (Croats against Serbs)?

6. Europe is fraught with pockets of local resistance to the centralized state, such as the Catalans in Spain, the Basques, or "Padania" (northern Italy). What explains such resistance?

7. Immigration, particularly Muslim immigration into Europe has caused serious confrontations with the native population. Why is it particularly Muslim immigration that seems to create particularly serious tensions? Does the United States face a similar problem with its Muslim immigrants?

[1]Ivo Andriç. *The Bridge on the Drina* (London: Allen & Unwin, 1959).

[2]*New York Times*, June 22, 1991.

[3]*Financial Times of London,* June 25, 1991.

[4]Beverly Crawford. Explaining Defection from International Cooperation: Germany's Unilateral Recognition of Croatia. *World Politics* 48, July 1996: 505.

[5]Marc Weller. The International Response to the Dissolution of the Socialist Federal Republic of Yugoslavia. *The American Journal of International Law* 86, 1992: 587.

[6]European Press Consortium (EPC) press release. Doc. 128, 1991.

[7]*Neue Zürcher Zeitung*, June 11, 1993 (translation Jürg Steiner).

[8]*Neue Zürcher Zeitung*, June 21, 1993.

[9]Report of the Secretary General Pursuant to Security Resolution 721. Doc. S/23280, 1991.

[10]Dusan Sidjanski. The Consequences of the Crisis of Ex-Yugoslavia on the European Union. *Newsletter of the IPSA Research Committee on European Unification* 6, Spring 1993: 2.

[11]Conference for Peace in Yugoslavia, Arbitration Commission, *Avis* No. 2, Para. 4.

[12]*Neue Zürcher Zeitung*, May 27, 2005.

[13]*New York Times*, February 4, 1993.

[14]Ibid.

[15]*New York Times*, November 15, 1992.

[16]Arend Lijphart. The Power-Sharing Approach. In Joseph V. Montville (ed.) *Conflict and Peacemaking in Multiethnic Societies* (Lexington, KY: D. C. Heath, 1989).

[17]John McGarry and Brendan O'Leary. Five Fallacies: Northern Ireland and the Liabilities of Liberalism. *Ethnic and Racial Studies* 18, October 1995: 859.

[18]*New York Times*, January 4, 2005.

[19]*New York Times*, December 31, 2004.

[20]*Neue Zürcher Zeitung*, July 31/August 1, 1993.

[21]With the exception of Slovenia, which is now a member of the European Union.

[22]*Neue Zürcher Zeitung*, June 26, 1996.

[23]*New York Times*, February 19, 1995.

[24]*New York Times*, February 19, 1995.

[25]Personal communication, Professor Kazimierz Sowa of the University of Rzeszów, Poland.

CHAPTER 13

Power Sharing in Deeply Divided Societies

In Chapter 12 we explored how ethnicity can lead to deep divisions in a society. Deep societal divisions can also be caused by other factors, in particular language, religion, race, and social class. A society is deeply divided if its subgroups have strong identities and hostile feelings among the subgroups. Iraq is certainly a deeply divided society. In the European context, Northern Ireland, Bosnia-Herzegovina, and Kosovo are clear examples of deeply divided societies. How deeply is the United States divided, in particular along racial lines?

How can political stability be attained in such deeply divided societies? Political science theorists see the answer in the sharing of power among the deeply divided groups. This theory of power sharing is also called *consociational theory*.[1] The term *consociational* is rarely used in everyday language, but it has become prominent as a technical term in political science. Consociational democracies stand in contrast to competitive majoritarian democracies, the latter being characterized by a voting mechanism whereby a majority can impose its will on a minority.

DEVELOPMENT OF THE THEORY OF POWER SHARING

The distinction between consociational and competitive democracies was first made by Arend Lijphart and Gerhard Lehmbruch at the 1967 World Congress of the International Political Science Association in Brussels.[2] Their contributions opened an interesting discussion that continues up to the present. Lijphart and Lehmbruch coined the term *consociational democracy* to draw attention to some smaller European democracies that were neglected in prior theorizing. In the 1950s and early 1960s, the thinking of political scientists about democratic regimes was influenced primarily by the experiences of the United States, Great Britain, France, Germany, and Italy. The first two countries seemed to have long traditions of democratic stability, whereas the latter three were plagued by periods of instability. This comparison raised the question of which factors might account for the level of democratic stability. A very influential hypothesis was formulated in 1956 by Gabriel A. Almond, who identified the political culture of a country as a crucial factor.[3] He postulated that a homogeneous political culture, like that of the two Anglo-American countries, is conducive to democratic stability, whereas a fragmented political culture, as in the large continental European countries, tends to lead to democratic instability.

However, Austria, Belgium, the Netherlands, and Switzerland seemed to contradict Almond's hypothesis because they appeared culturally fragmented yet democratically stable. Lijphart and Lehmbruch explained this deviation by observing that these countries practiced a consociational, rather than a competitive, mode of decision making. From this line of theoretical reasoning, a more optimistic view emerged than that contained in Almond's hypothesis: Culturally fragmented countries could hope to attain democratic stability if they used consociational, rather than competitive, decision making. In the meantime, attempts have been made to apply this consociational theory to divided countries such as Afghanistan, Iraq, Lebanon, South Africa, Northern Ireland, and Bosnia-Herzegovina. We will discuss such applications for some European countries later in the chapter.

Before we do so, however, we must clarify three crucial concepts of the theory. First, we must define what is meant by a culturally fragmented society and how it is different from a culturally homogeneous society. Second, consociational decision making must be clearly distinguished from competitive decision making. Third, we must establish what is meant by democratic stability and instability. Only with these clarifications will it become apparent what Lijphart and Lehmbruch had in mind with their theory.

For a country to be culturally fragmented or divided, the various groups must differ in such attributes as race, language, religion, and historical roots. Such attributes are known as *ascriptive* attributes, having been present from birth; they are virtually permanent. Ascriptive attributes may be contrasted with *achieved* attributes, such as occupation and education, which are the result of individual achievement and can be changed relatively easily during a lifetime. Differences in ascriptive attributes are a necessary, but not sufficient, condition for cultural fragmentation. For a country to be culturally fragmented, the people sharing the same ascriptive attribute must also develop a common identity and express it in a politically relevant way. If this additional condition is fulfilled, specific subcultures can be distinguished—for example, a Catholic and a Protestant subculture. People feel an identity as either Protestants or Catholics and are politically active in Protestant and Catholic organizations.

What exactly do Lijphart and Lehmbruch mean when they say that the decision process among subcultures is consociational rather than competitive? A first characteristic is that executive cabinets contain representatives from all of the subcultures. If a country is divided between a Catholic and a Protestant subculture, for example, consociational cabinet formation means that both subcultures share power in the cabinet. Such encompassing coalitions are called *grand coalitions*. Besides the cabinet, grand coalitions may also form in other bodies, such as advisory commissions. A second feature of consociational decision making is a veto power for each subculture on matters involving its essential interests. If Catholics are a minority, parliamentary rules would require that changes in abortion laws, which are so important to Catholics, could not be enacted without the consent of the Catholic minority. A third characteristic is that parliamentary elections, the appointment of public officials, and the distribution of public funds among the subcultures are guided by the principle of proportionality. If Catholics make up 40 percent of the population, they should receive 40 percent of the top positions in the armed forces, for example. In other words, each subculture should receive its quota. Finally, consociational decision making means that the individual subcultures have a great deal of autonomy in regulating their own affairs—having control over educational and cultural matters, in particular.

These consociational principles are very distinct from the principles of majoritarian decision making. If the majority principle is applied in resolving conflicts among subcultures in a fragmented society, minorities will always lose. If Protestants, for example, comprise two-thirds of the population and Catholics one-third, the former will always win. As we will see later in the chapter, this was exactly the situation in Northern Ireland, with Protestants as the larger group winning one election after another and controlling the executive branch of government. No wonder that Catholics were not satisfied with this form of government.

The crucial point in Lijphart and Lehmbruch's argument is that consociational decision making increases the probability of democratic stability in culturally fragmented societies. By democratic stability, they mean essentially that a country has a low level of civil violence and disorder, both actually and potentially. The application of consociational devices is necessary particularly when the cleavage structure of society is reinforcing, rather than cross-cutting. By cleavage structure we mean societal divisions such as religion, language, socioeconomic differences, race, region, and other divisions over which conflicts have erupted since time immemorial. A reinforcing cleavage structure is one in which a society is not only divided along one dimension, say language, but that division is overlaid by additional cleavages such as religion, and/or region and/or race. When cleavages are aligned in a reinforcing pattern, conflict is more likely because any member of society sees the "other" as not only being different in terms of language, but also in terms of region and race, and perhaps even additional differences. Thus, we say that such cleavages "reinforce" each other, leading to a very high potential for conflict. It is precisely in such societies that consociational devices are even more necessary than when cleavages are "cross-cutting." (Figure 13.1)

Cross-cutting cleavages are less problematic for social harmony because they slice up society into a microcosm of differences and no single group is large enough to impose itself on others. In such a situation, power sharing is less necessary because cleavages cross-cut each other to such an extent that any group in power represents a microcosm of society and, as a result, will produce policies that will not systematically exclude other groups.

Why does one fragmented country make use of consociationalism and another does not? Much depends on the wisdom and foresight of the subcultures' leaders. If they are sufficiently aware of the centrifugal tendencies in their society, they may choose to attempt to counterbalance these tendencies via consociationalism. According to the term used by Lijphart, leaders need a spirit of accommodation.[4] This is not to say that leaders with such a spirit of accommodation are always free to adopt a consociational approach to decision making. Certain conditions may prevent consociational decision making, even if the

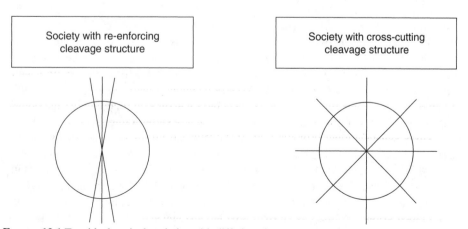

FIGURE 13.1 Two ideal-typical societies with differing cleavage structures.

leaders wish to use it. Consociational decision making is facilitated if at least some of the following conditions are present. Students may wish to discuss in their classes why these conditions are favorable for consociational decision making.

None of the subcultures has a numerical majority.

The subcultures have clear boundaries and can therefore easily be identified.

There is relative economic equality among the subcultures.

Each subculture has preeminent leaders who are internally respected and can speak for the interests of their subculture.

There is some overarching loyalty across all subcultures to the country as a whole, whose very existence is not questioned.

The population of the country is relatively small.

The country is under international pressure that is seen by all subcultures in the same light.

The country has some tradition of accommodation and compromise.

The overall load of unresolved problems on the country (unemployment, inflation, etc.) is not very great.

In Austria, Belgium, the Netherlands, and Switzerland, these conditions were mostly favorable, which allowed their leaders to practice consociational decision making. This practice was so successful that all four countries can now again afford to introduce more competitive elements into their decision making. This move away from consociational decision making is also part of the theory. If, as a result of consociational decision making, relations among subcultures remain peaceful for some time, cultural fragmentation begins to lose some of its importance, so that consociationalism is no longer necessary to preserve harmonious relations. You could say that successful consociationalism makes itself superfluous.

The Austrian case can be used to illustrate the dynamic workings of the consociational theory. After its defeat in World War I and the demise of the Hapsburg Empire, Austria made an initial attempt at a democratic form of government in the 1920s and 1930s. At that time, Austria was a very fragmented society with two subcultures, the so-called red and black camps (Lager). That the military term *camp* was used to designate the two subcultures indicates just how deeply divided Austrian society was. The blacks were the middle-class bourgeois Conservative Catholics; the reds were the working-class anticlerical Socialists. The two camps were very segregated from each other, and Austrians spent most of their daily lives with members of their own camp. Politics was played according to the majority principle. The result was instability, civil strife, and even a brief civil war in the early 1930s. Austria then became easy prey for annexation by Hitler in 1938. After the atrocities of World War II and the concentration camps, surviving leaders of the two groups decided in 1945 to form a grand coalition of the two large parties. For about 20 years, blacks and reds ruled the country together according to the four consociational devices. Relations between the two subcultures became much more harmonious, and the subcultures themselves lost much of their importance. Marriage across subcultural lines, for example, was no longer uncommon.

The Netherlands was deeply divided between Catholics, Calvinists, and a secular group; the latter was further divided along class lines between Socialists and Liberals. As suggested by consociational theory, the politics of accommodation initiated in 1917 brought increasing stability, which in turn, particularly after the 1960s, decreased the importance of the subcultural rifts.

In Switzerland, consociationalism was used both for linguistic and religious cleavages (see also Chapter 6). Religiously, the cleavage was between Catholics and Protestants, and over the centuries there were five civil religious wars. Increasingly, consociationalism was practiced between the two religious groups, and today religious divisions have greatly decreased. Linguistically, Switzerland has four official languages—German, French, Italian, and Romansh—and here too consociationalism was practiced quite successfully, although the language issue is still quite sensitive.

In Belgium, the significance of consociationalism was strong for the language question and also for the relations between clerical and anticlerical Catholics. As in Switzerland, consociationalism has lost much of its importance for the religious issue, but not for the language issue.

CRITIQUE OF THE THEORY OF POWER SHARING

How good is the consociational theory? Has its "medicine" been tested sufficiently to ensure that it has the desired effect? Less metaphorically: Does consociationalism or power sharing really increase the probability of democratic stability? Do Austria, Belgium, the Netherlands, and Switzerland convincingly support the causality postulated by the consociational theory? Here we encounter a difficult methodological problem common to all research in comparative politics: the small number of cases and their great complexity. Four countries obviously constitute a very narrow empirical basis. Even 10 or 20 countries would be too small a number of cases to allow for the use of sophisticated statistical analyses. Contributing further to the methodological difficulty is the great complexity of the individual cases, which often prevents unambiguous identification of the causal effect of an individual factor. If a country changed from competitive to consociational decision making and all other variables remained constant, the independent effect of the change in decision mode could be determined. In reality, however, such experimental situations do not exist.

We first use again the Austrian example to illustrate the difficulty of determining the direction of causality. As described earlier, the decision-making style in Austria's First Republic was majoritarian before civil war broke out in the early 1930s and an autocratic regime was established. By contrast, the Second Republic in the years after World War II practiced consociationalism, and democratic stability prevailed. If nothing save the decision mode had changed, we could safely conclude that this change caused an increase in democratic stability. But, because the Austrian situation changed in many other aspects as well, other plausible explanations for the increased democratic stability are available. One could argue, for example, that economic conditions after 1945 were much better than in the 1920s and early 1930s and that this improvement in the economic situation allowed democratic stability to blossom. Advocates of consociationalism might reply that the economic boom after World War II was itself the result of power sharing. But, in other European countries, such as the Federal Republic of Germany and France, economic recovery occurred under a majoritarian form of government. Thus, the Austrian economy might also have boomed without the grand coalition of the two major parties.

Increased democratic stability in Austria could also be explained by changes in the religious life of the country. In the years after 1945, religious devotion declined rapidly, so that the old rift between clericalists and anticlericalists lost much of its importance. With the decreased prominence of religion, the division between blacks and reds became less divisive, thereby allowing a more stable democracy.

In addition, the social stratification of Austrian society changed noticeably during this period. The simple dichotomy between the bourgeois middle class and the working class, corresponding to an earlier phase of industrial development, was increasingly replaced with a more diversified social structure. Both the middle class and the working class became more heterogeneous, blurring class distinctions. Less class distinction meant less fragmentation between blacks and reds, providing yet another possible explanation for the higher level of democratic stability.

We can thus identify at least five variables that had different values in the First Republic and the beginning years of the Second Republic: decision mode, democratic stability, economic affluence, religious practice, and social stratification. How can we sort out possible causalities among these and perhaps still more variables? Truly convincing conclusions could only be reached if we could manipulate the variables in an experimental way. Because that is not possible, conclusions can only be more or less plausible.

The data for Belgium, the Netherlands, and Switzerland also allow for interpretations that conflict with the assumptions of consociational theory. Do these ambiguities mean that the theory should not be applied to countries like Northern Ireland, Bosnia-Herzegovina, the Ukraine, Afghanistan, Iraq, Lebanon, and South Africa? Certainly not. It is in the nature of comparative politics that the causal effect of a variable can never be laboratory tested. To require such tests would mean postponing practical applications forever and would make comparative politics irrelevant in crisis situations. Yet crisis situations exist in many parts of the world, and they cry out for solutions. Political scientists have the moral obligation to offer help. They must only be sure that their advice is given with the proper care and caution.

A precondition for testing a theory is the ability to measure its variables in a reliable and valid way. Here we encounter additional difficulties with consociational theory, as we would with any other theory. If consociational theory says that power sharing increases the probability of democratic stability in culturally fragmented societies, all three of the variables contained in this hypothesis should be measurable. What indicators can we use to tell us how fragmented a society is, how much its political leaders use the consociational method of decision making, and how democratically stable its political system is? The Swiss case illustrates the problems inherent in answering these questions.

With regard to fragmentation, it is often stated that consociational theory is applicable to Switzerland because of its linguistic fragmentation into German, French, Italian, and Romansh. Other researchers argue, however, that despite the existence of four languages, Swiss society is quite homogeneous, so that consociational theory is not applicable to the Swiss case. We must distinguish carefully between linguistic diversity and linguistic fragmentation. The former means that two or more languages are spoken in a country. Such linguistic diversity is a necessary, but not sufficient, condition for linguistic fragmentation. People speaking the same language may or may not develop a common and politically relevant identity. How is linguistic identity measured in Switzerland? One may use survey methods, asking people how strongly they identify with their language group. In such a survey in 2004, 14 percent answered that they identified most strongly with their language group, compared with 33 percent who identified primarily with their local community, 24 percent with Switzerland at large, 19 percent with their canton, 6 percent with the world, and 4 percent with Europe. One should also consider that 14 percent gave language as their second most important identity. Thus, 28 percent said that language was among their top two identities.[5]

How do we interpret these survey results? The task is not easy because the picture is mixed. Linguistic identity is of great importance for some Swiss but not for others. To make the interpretation of these data more complex, one also needs to consider that the relative importance of a person's identities may change from one life situation to another. In this context, the experiences of two students from the University of Geneva, who studied for a year at the University of North Carolina, are relevant. During their stay in the United States, they felt primarily Swiss. On arriving back at the airport in German-speaking Zurich, they felt that their primary identity was French. When they returned by train to the French-speaking region, still another change in identity took place; each now identified primarily with a canton—Geneva for one student and Jura for the other. This story illustrates the dynamic perspective of identities. A person's primary identity may change from one situation to another. It is difficult to capture such a fast-changing picture with survey techniques. Be aware, also, that surveys are conducted at the attitudinal level, and it is a well-known phenomenon that attitudes do not always translate easily into behavior.

Hence, we must also look at behavioral data. How does the behavior of the Swiss indicate their linguistic group identity? An often-used indicator is marriage across language lines. Do Swiss marry primarily within their language group? Take the example of French speakers: 77 percent marry other French speakers.[6] Again, the data are difficult to interpret. Because French speakers are concentrated in one region of the country, it is not surprising that most of them choose partners who live close by—other French speakers. Under these conditions, is it significant that 23 out of 100 marry someone with a different primary language? Some researchers think so and conclude that this figure indicates a low level of identity among French speakers.[7] But does a French speaker marrying outside his or her linguistic group necessarily have a low identity with other French speakers? Perhaps marriage to a spouse who speaks another language actually increases a person's linguistic identity, even if that person uses the spouse's language in daily life. Take the example of a man from Geneva who is married to a German-speaking wife and both are living in Zurich. Even if he speaks German with his wife, he may develop a stronger French-speaking identity than when he lived back home in Geneva. He may become more aware that as a French speaker, he has different values from German speakers. Of course, it is also possible that, in many cases, marriages between linguistic groups do, indeed, indicate a low level of linguistic identities. This discussion again shows the difficulty of interpreting data to measure cultural fragmentation.

Although surveys and intermarriage data may speak to the strength of subcultural identity, additional data are necessary to determine how a subcultural identity is expressed in a politically relevant way. To be politically relevant, a subcultural identity must find some form of organizational expression. Do French speakers in Switzerland have their own political party? This is not the case, and all attempts to establish such a party have failed. Does this mean that French speakers do not operate as an organized force in Swiss politics? Not quite. Looking at the Swiss party system in more detail, we see that French speakers often form a coherent subgroup in the large political parties. Thus, linguistic identities are expressed not among but within parties. Also, there are always some issues in the national parliament on which French speakers vote more or less as a bloc.

We should also determine to what extent the three other linguistic groups in Switzerland have identities that they express in a politically relevant way. Based on the data from all four groups, we could then make a judgment about how linguistically fragmented Switzerland is. Such a judgment is obviously much more difficult than measuring the annual snowfall in a country. Meteorologists have commonly accepted yardsticks, but no such measure exists for linguistic fragmentation; rather, constant debate continues in the literature about how best to measure the level of fragmentation. Because agreement has not been reached, it is not surprising that some authors classify Switzerland as linguistically quite homogeneous, whereas others see it as relatively fragmented. As a consequence, there is no agreement on exactly what the Swiss case tells us. For some researchers, Switzerland is a good test case for the consociational theory because it is linguistically fragmented. For others, however, Switzerland is irrelevant for the theory because it has no potentially destabilizing fragmentation.

Such difficulties of classification also emerge for other countries. To be sure, it is generally agreed that Northern Ireland is highly fragmented and that Denmark is homogeneous. But what about the linguistic cleavage in Canada, or the racial cleavage in the United States? Are these rifts so deep that the two countries qualify as test cases for consociational theory? Is the racial cleavage in the United States deeper than the linguistic cleavage in Switzerland? How are cleavages compared if they are based on different attributes, such as language and race? Does a marriage across linguistic lines have the same meaning as one across racial lines? Such questions indicate once again the difficulty in measuring fragmentation.

Similar difficulties appear in trying to determine the prevailing political decision mode within a country. Again, the language situation in Switzerland serves as a good illustration. If we begin with the composition of the executive cabinet, the Federal Council, as an indicator, decision making among the language groups seems to be consociational. Although German speakers comprise 70 percent of the population with Swiss nationality, they never have more than five seats, and most often only four, in the seven-member Federal Council. Two or three seats always go to the linguistic minorities. This rule is not based on a constitutional article or a law but on custom and tradition, which guide the members of Parliament when they elect members to the Federal Council. The principle that linguistic minorities get a proportionate share is applied to virtually all government positions. In the Swiss army, for example, there are seven three-star generals; usually these positions are held by four German speakers, two French speakers, and one Italian speaker, which even gives some overrepresentation to the minorities. Federalism, another consociational device, is also strongly developed in Switzerland (Chapter 6).

Are these indicators sufficient for classifying decision making among Swiss language groups as consociational? Many researchers think so, but perhaps we should look more closely at how decisions are actually made. The linguistic minorities may have two or three representatives in the Federal Council, but they can still lose if the Council makes its decisions in a majoritarian way. Decision making in the Federal Council is, in principle, treated as confidential, but occasionally there are leaks about how a particular decision was made. In the past, it seems that decisions were made rarely by majority vote. But rumors have it that it is now more common that a majority outvotes a minority in the Federal Council. This development shows that the pattern of decision making may change over time, so that one has to be careful to clarify the time period when making a definitive statement.

The picture is clearer for Parliament, where deliberations are open to the public. In many cases, the Swiss parliament makes unanimous or near-unanimous decisions. Such cases have often been studied by consociational authors, who use them as illustrations to support their theory. But, in many other cases, Swiss parliament takes close votes, and such votes sometimes pit a German-speaking majority against the linguistic minorities. In Chapter 6, on federalism, we mention a few such cases. How frequent are they? Do they involve essential or only marginal issues for the linguistic minorities? If such votes occur, are some concessions nevertheless made to the minorities, or are they simply outvoted? These questions show that it is not a simple matter to measure the degree of consociational and majoritarian decision making.

The problem is further complicated because decision making takes place in other arenas of Swiss politics in addition to Parliament; the so-called expert committees, where most legislation is prepared, are a good example. Interviews with committee members have revealed that, in this preparliamentary phase, consensual and majoritarian decision making are used with about equal frequency.[8] But, here again, how many of the majority votes are taken along linguistic lines? How important were the issues, and were concessions made to the minorities despite the application of the majority principle? These questions have not yet been studied in detail. Even if they had been, scholars would probably disagree on the exact interpretation of the data. There would most likely be disagreement over how to determine the importance of an issue for a language group or over how to measure the number of concessions a winning majority makes to the minorities, given that each side's original position was perhaps exaggerated for tactical reasons.

The study of expert committees has revealed further that consensual and majoritarian decision making are not the only alternatives. We identified a third decision-making mode, which we call *decision by interpretation*.[9] This mode is a mixture of the two other modes. In the Swiss expert committees, decisions by interpretation are used with about the same frequency as the other two modes. In a decision by interpretation, no explicit consensus is reached, but neither is the voting mechanism used to separate a majority from a minority. Rather, the chair sums up the sense of the meeting, and the other members tacitly go along with the summary. It remains unclear how much consensus has actually been reached. Some members may still dissent, but they prefer not to challenge the summary of the president. Sometimes such summary interpretations are made in the minutes of the meeting.

Decisions by interpretation seem to be common, for example, in the British cabinet, as we have seen in Chapter 4. The existence of decisions by interpretation, in addition to consensual and majoritarian decisions, reinforces the argument of how difficult it is to determine the prevailing decision-making pattern in a country. As in the case of cultural fragmentation, we do not wish to argue that measurement is impossible; we only wish to draw attention to the difficulties present in such measurement. As a consequence, we should not expect to be able to rank countries on a precise scale from consociational to competitive. Decision making among Swiss linguistic groups is certainly more consociational than is decision making among ethnic groups in Northern Ireland. But, if we compare the level of consociationalism in Switzerland and Austria, the judgment is much more difficult. And what about the United States? How consociational are relations between whites and blacks? Is it significant that a tradition seems to have developed to have one African American on the Supreme Court? Can this be seen as a consociational device?

Of all the variables contained in consociational theory, the degree of democratic stability is the most problematic to measure. Switzerland, for example, seems democratically very stable. Very little civil violence and disorder arises from the language question.[10] This seems to indicate that all language groups accept the democratic legitimacy of the political order. In the consociational literature, it is commonly accepted without much further inquiry that Switzerland is a stable democracy. But other literature, inspired by a Marxist view, ranks the democratic quality of Switzerland much lower. Its basic argument is that consociational arrangements are merely a ruse to cover up the real power structure. The most extreme formulation of this argument stems from sociologist and left-wing Socialist Jean Ziegler, who claims that essential power in Switzerland rests with the bankers in Zurich.[11] Ziegler speaks of structural violence against the working class and the linguistic minorities, by which he means that these groups are repressed in such a subtle way that they are not even aware of it. In this view, consociational devices help to make legitimate the existing repressive order in the eyes of the large masses of the people.

Without going as far as Ziegler, other critics complain that economic power is increasingly concentrated in German-speaking Zurich. Consequently, representation of the linguistic minorities in governmental bodies becomes somewhat symbolic if they lose their say in the corporate headquarters. Federalism could become an empty shell if most of the important economic decisions are made in Zurich. Do such critiques indicate an increasing dissatisfaction among the linguistic minorities, perhaps even a potential for future unrest? Is Swiss democracy not as stable, after all, as it appears to the consociational authors? Again, no agreement can be found in the literature.

Is the fact that they cannot agree on how to measure the key variables of their theory a bad sign for the consociational scholars? Physicists had little difficulty in agreeing on the definition of a meter or a kilogram. But, in physics, the observer and the object of observation are separated, although measurements by the observer may have some influence on the phenomena being studied. This is all the more so in the social sciences, where both observer and observed are human beings. When social scientists publish their results, these results may be read by the objects of the study. Social scientists in this way become actors in the world they observe. To take the example of consociational theory, when Ziegler teaches and writes that Switzerland is characterized by subtle repression, his students and readers may begin to perceive Swiss reality in this light. Similarly, perceptions may be influenced by descriptions of Switzerland as a stable democracy.

How to define and measure a political variable is influenced by the political values of the researcher. For all researchers to have the same values is not a desirable goal. With a pluralism of values, researchers will naturally arrive at different results. The application of the consociational theory to Switzerland is a good example in this respect. For some researchers, Switzerland is linguistically fragmented and only remains a stable democracy thanks to the practice of power sharing. For others, Switzerland is relatively homogeneous, and consociational arrangements serve only to legitimize the power of a small elite cartel. Such different interpretations are not due merely to errors of measurement but also to fundamental differences in the value premises on which the research is based. It is healthy that such fundamental differences are aired in scholarly debate, and it speaks well for the consociational theory that it has led to heated but interesting and enlightening discussion.

Among all theories recently developed in political science, consociational theory is perhaps the one most widely applied to trouble spots all over the world. Arend Lijphart has served on several occasions as an influential consultant to politicians in deeply divided countries. In the media, the term *power sharing* is often used to express the idea of consociational decision making. What are the chances of power sharing in such troubled countries as Northern Ireland, Bosnia-Herzegovina, the Ukraine, Afghanistan, Iraq, and Lebanon?

None of the consociational theorists, of course, is naive enough to think that it would be a simple matter for such countries to adopt the consociational solution and that everything would then be fine. The theory explicitly recognizes that some countries are so deeply fragmented that there is no hope for power sharing to work. In such cases, the result is often civil war among the subcultures or the establishment of an authoritarian regime by one of the subcultures. If fragmentation is not extreme but still very high, power sharing may provide a glimmer of hope, and, as the consociational authors argue, probably the only hope. Considering this reasoning, the outlook for countries like Afghanistan and Iraq is not very optimistic. But any hope must be based on the notion of power sharing. These countries are so deeply divided that a majoritarian form of democracy is not a realistic option. The hatred between the subcultures is so great that none would accept an electoral defeat based on majority voting, fearing that the victor would unduly exploit its victory so that the opposition would never have a chance to win a future election. Power sharing, on the other hand, would allow each subculture to maintain some control over the country's decision making. As Lijphart formulates it, the realistic choice for many fragmented societies "is not between the British normative model of democracy and the consociational model, but between consociational democracy and no democracy at all." Therefore, Lijphart advocates power sharing for multiethnic societies:

> Because it is the optimal—indeed, usually the only—solution, regardless of whether the background conditions are favorable or unfavorable. To aspiring power-sharers who find themselves in an unfavorable situation, it does not say: "Give up." Instead, it counsels: "Be aware of the obstacles you face, and try extra hard."[12]

Lijphart becomes impatient with people who are overly pessimistic about power sharing, and he warns them that if nobody tries power sharing, it will certainly not be adopted:

> If everyone is convinced that power sharing cannot be applied, nobody will even try to introduce it, and consequently it will certainly not be adopted. Or if it is introduced in a particular multiethnic society, the conviction that it is bound to fail will kill any effort to make it succeed—and that will surely cause it to fail. It is vastly preferable to think of success and failure in terms of probabilities rather than absolutes.[13]

In the next section, we will look more closely at the chances of power sharing in deeply divided Northern Ireland. Then we will turn to former Czechoslovakia and former Yugoslavia.

NORTHERN IRELAND

As we have seen in Chapter 12, Northern Ireland is deeply divided into British Protestant Unionists and Irish Catholic Nationalists. A first application of consociational theory can be made for the time after 1921, when the Republic of Ireland obtained its independence and Northern Ireland remained British. As we remember, Northern Ireland got autonomy within the United Kingdom and a Parliament (Stormont) with extensive powers was established in Belfast, the capital of Northern Ireland. We also remember that Protestants held a two-to-one majority and practiced democracy in the traditional British way—by applying the majority principle both for parliamentary elections and cabinet formation. Given their numerical dominance, they easily won one parliamentary election after another and exercised all the governmental power. The local prime minister and all his cabinet members always belonged to the Protestant subculture, while the Catholics remained politically impotent. Although Protestants had enough numerical strength to win parliamentary elections, they rigged the system even more to their advantage.

Consociational theory expects that in deeply divided countries the majoritarian model of democracy endangers political stability, and this is precisely what happened when civil strife began in 1968. Northern Ireland is a good illustration to show that the majoritarian model will not work in deeply divided societies. This is a negative lesson telling us what should not be done. Sometimes it serves as good advice to learn what should *not* be done.

If the majoritarian model does not work in a deeply divided society, this does not necessarily mean, of course, that the power sharing model will work. But consociational theory expects that the power-sharing model has at least a better chance to be successful. And Northern Ireland has indeed had some success with the power-sharing model, although problems still linger on to some extent.

Inspired by the successful Swiss experience with power sharing, in the 1970s the British government tried to restore calm in Northern Ireland through a form of consociational power sharing. A cabinet of moderate Protestants and Catholics was established in Northern Ireland, but within a few months a general strike of Protestant workers brought this initial experiment to a halt. The large majority of Protestants was not willing to change from a majoritarian to a consociational pattern of decision making. The Catholics, for their part, reacted with further civil strife.

Why was it such a slow process with many setbacks to introduce power sharing in Northern Ireland? Let us apply the list of facilitating conditions for power sharing that we established in the first section of this chapter to the Northern Irish situation in the 1970s. We note first that there was no overarching loyalty of Catholics and Protestants to Northern Ireland as a political unit. The Protestants wished to remain British, whereas the Catholics wanted to join the Republic of Ireland. There was no loyalty to a common land. In this respect, the situation was different from that in Switzerland, where Catholics and Protestants, German, French, Italian, and Romansh speakers have always felt like members of one political community despite all their differences.

Power sharing might still have worked if other factors would have been favorable, but they were not. It would have been easier if Protestants and Catholics each had a comparable numerical strength, as the blacks and reds in Austria did when they formed their grand coalition in 1945. An even more favorable condition would have been if there would have been three or four subcultures and none in a majority; this was the situation in the Netherlands when power sharing was introduced successfully. Northern Ireland had the most unfavorable condition with only two subcultures and one in a clearly dominant numerical position.

The fact that no clear territorial boundaries existed in Northern Ireland between Protestants and Catholics was a further unfavorable condition for power sharing. The two groups lived interspersed in the same cities, towns, and villages: One street was Protestant, another street Catholic. The lack of spatial separation made it impossible to apply the consociational device of subcultural autonomy, in which the subcultures themselves could have regulated much of their own internal affairs. In this context a comparison can be made to Belgium, where relations between Flemish and Walloons are most problematic in Brussels, the city in which the two communities have no clear boundaries. The old saying that "good fences make good neighbors" seems to have some validity.

A further negative factor in Northern Ireland in the 1970s was the internal rivalries and quarrels within both the Catholic and Protestant leadership. Neither group had uncontested leaders who could speak authoritatively for it. Therefore, neither subculture had representatives who could make deals that were also binding on their own members. An attempt by a political leader to negotiate a compromise with the other side was likely to be that leader's kiss of political death within his or her own group, because competing leaders would exploit such a step as weakness. The result was a tendency for the leaders of each side to outbid each other for the most extreme position.

Still another obstacle to power sharing in Northern Ireland was the region's many unresolved problems, especially a desperate economic situation characterized by a high rate of unemployment.

A seemingly easy way out would have been a territorial separation, with Protestants remaining in the United Kingdom and Catholics joining the Republic of Ireland. Unfortunately, this solution was not feasible because the communities of Catholics and Protestants were so highly interspersed. Massive resettlements, impossible from a practical perspective and morally repugnant, would have been required. In 1989, political scientist Richard Rose expressed the view that a solution may be impossible:

> Northern Ireland is a challenge to the comforting belief that describing a situation as a problem guarantees the existence of a solution. In this strife-torn land where the United Kingdom meets the Republic of Ireland, there is no solution—if a solution is defined as a form of government that is consensual, legitimate, and stable.[14]

Since 1989 when Richard Rose expressed this pessimistic view, some positive development happened in Northern Ireland. One glimmer of hope was the rally for peace in Dublin in 1993 after a terrorist attack of the Irish Republican Army (IRA) had killed two children in England. But a month after this peace rally, the IRA launched another attack in the very heart of London (Box 13.1). Increasingly, violence has also been used by the

---

Box 13.1 London's City Digs Out After Bombing

The Irish Republican Army said Sunday that it was responsible for a huge bomb that devastated the heart of London's financial district. One person was killed and 44 were wounded. Officials said Sunday that despite extensive damage, the financial district should be operating nearly normally on Monday, the *New York Times* reported from London. The stock exchange and all other financial markets, as well as the Lloyds of London insurance market, will be open for business as usual, the official said. Thousands of workers, however, will be unable to enter offices in the buildings that took the worst of the blast, including the National Westminster Bank tower and the headquarters of the Hongkong & Shanghai Banking Corporation. Most companies said that they were arranging for alternative office space and that they did not expect any major disruption to any essential parts of their business.

Source: *International Herald Tribune*, April 26, 1993.

Protestant side in Northern Ireland, in particular by the Ulster Freedom Fighters and the Ulster Defense Association. Both organizations have been outlawed by the British government, but they continue their terrorist activities.

A positive sign was the increasingly close collaboration between Great Britain and the Republic of Ireland with regard to Northern Ireland. On December 15, 1993, the two prime ministers, John Major and Albert Reynolds, signed a Joint Declaration on Northern Ireland. In this declaration, Great Britain concedes that it has no strategic or economic interests in Northern Ireland, which may join the Republic of Ireland if it wishes. The Republic of Ireland, on the other hand, concedes that any change in the status quo needs the support of a majority in Northern Ireland, thus giving to the Northern Irish Protestants a veto power. These were important principles articulated in a spirit of cooperation between London and Dublin. The opening passage of the Joint Declaration reads as follows:

> The Joint Declaration is a charter for peace and reconciliation in Ireland. Peace is a very simple, but also a very powerful idea, whose time has come. The Joint Declaration provides from everyone's point of view a noble means of establishing the first step towards lasting peace with justice in Ireland. The central idea behind the Peace Declaration is that the problems of Northern Ireland, however deep and intractable, however difficult to reconcile, have to be resolved exclusively by political and democratic means.[15]

The pledge of the British government to let the people of Northern Ireland decide their own fate was formulated as follows:

> The Prime Minister, on behalf of the British Government, reaffirms that they will uphold the democratic wish of a greater number of the people of Northern Ireland on the issue of whether they prefer to support the Union or a sovereign united Ireland. On this basis, he reiterates, on behalf of the British Government, that they have no selfish strategic or economic interest in Northern Ireland. Their primary interest is to see peace, stability and reconciliation established by agreement among all the people who inhabit the island.[16]

The Irish government, for its part, formulated its pledge to respect the majority will of the people of Northern Ireland as follows:

> The Taoiseach [formal title of Irish prime minister], on behalf of the Irish Government, considers that . . . it would be wrong to attempt to impose a united Ireland in the absence of the freely given consent of a majority of the people of Northern Ireland. He accepts, on behalf of the Irish Government, that the democratic right of self-determination by the people of Ireland as a whole must be achieved and exercised with and subject to the agreement and consent of a majority of the people of Northern Ireland.[17]

Another positive sign in the Northern Irish conflict was the declaration of a cease-fire by the IRA on August 31, 1994. In its announcement the IRA wrote:

> Recognizing the potential of the current situation and in order to enhance the democratic peace process and underline our definitive commitment to its success, the leadership of the I.R.A. have decided that as of midnight Wednesday, August 31, there will be a complete cessation of military operations. All our units have been instructed accordingly. At this historic crossroads, the leadership of the I.R.A.

salutes and commends our volunteers, other activists, our supporters and the political prisoners who have sustained this struggle, against all odds, for the past 25
years. Your courage, determination and sacrifices have demonstrated that the
spirit of freedom and the desire for peace based on a just and lasting settlement
cannot be crushed. We remember all those who have died for Irish freedom and
we reiterate our commitment to our republican objectives.[18]

The paramilitary organizations of the Protestants, the Ulster Freedom Fighters, and the
Ulster Defense Association joined the cease-fire shortly afterward. On October 4, 1994,
Gerry Adams, president of Sinn Féin, the political arm of the IRA, wrote on the op-ed page
of the *New York Times*:

It happened in the Middle East and South Africa, and now it is happening in
Ireland. The momentous events of the past five weeks, starting with the Irish
Republican Army's cease-fire on August 31, make it clear that people in power
finally understand that the ability to live together—and to work out a political
framework that accommodates different perspectives—is the greatest gift they
can pass on to future generations. . . . The Unionists have as much right to the land
of Ireland as we have. I appeal to my Protestant brothers and sisters to join us in
the search for a settlement acceptable to all Irish people—for a constitution that,
like America's, includes checks and balances and a bill of rights with full protection for Ireland's minorities.[19]

Despite the conciliatory tone, neither the cease-fire announcement of the IRA nor Gerry
Adams's article renounced the goal of a united Ireland. What the Protestants were offered
was a constitution and a bill of rights protecting them as a minority in a united Ireland. But
most Protestants still wanted to stay within Great Britain. Thus, in the fall of 1994, nothing was settled. But at least the killing had stopped. On March 17, 1995, Protestants and
Catholics in Northern Ireland paraded together for St. Patrick's Day and hope began to
spread (Box 13.2).

In the meantime, the British and the Irish governments continued their collaboration,
and in February 1995, they published a Joint Framework Documents that outlined ideas
for the negotiations to come. A key passage of the documents reads:

Both Governments consider that new institutions should be created to cater adequately for the present and future political, social and economic interconnections
on the island of Ireland, enabling representatives of the main traditions, North and
South, to enter agreed dynamic new, cooperative and constructive relationships.[20]

After several setbacks in the peace process, a great breakthrough came with the Good
Friday Accord in the spring of 1998. Preceding this accord, intense international pressures
acted on the warring parties. These pressures came from the governments of London and
Dublin that increasingly worked closer together to bring about a solution to the troubles in
Northern Ireland. Even more important, strong pressures came from the United States.
President Bill Clinton invited the leaders of both sides several times to Washington, D.C.,
where he did some heavy arm-twisting. Issue for discussion: Was this intervention of President Clinton in the Northern Ireland conflict a good example of how the United States
should exercise its influence in the world?

For the actual negotiations, former U.S. senator George Mitchell was of crucial importance. At first, the leaders of the Catholic and Protestant groups were not even willing

Box 13.2 Catholics and Protestants Parade Together in Ulster for St. Patrick

Patrick Gordon rubbed the stubble of his 65-year-old face, peered up the crowed cobblestone street where the sound of the drums and the brass was getting louder, and said, yes, all things considered, "the peace will hold." "The longer its lasts, you see, the harder it will be for anyone on either side to pick up a gun," he said. "We're all getting used to living like this, without the bombs and the killings. Even the normalcy is beginning to seem normal." A few minutes later, when the first dozens of bands on the St. Patrick's Day parade marched by with twirling batons, tinkling glockenspiels and noses and knees tipped with red by the rain and the cold, Mr. Gordon's face was wreathed in smiles. The innovation he had come to see had just happened. For the first time since "the troubles" began 25 years ago, dividing this town and all of Northern Ireland into two hostile camps based on a religious divide that strikes the outside world as anachronistic, the young scouts holding the colors for the parade were mixed and marched side by side—blue uniforms for the Catholics, green for the Protestants.

Source: *New York Times*, March 18, 1995.

to talk with each other. Thus, Mitchell met separately with the two sides to find some common ground. An important step was when Catholic and Protestant leaders were willing to shake hands. Gerry Adams on the Catholic side and David Trimble on the Protestant side emerged as the key leaders who dared to make some steps toward each other. This was indeed a daring enterprise because both of these leaders had to fear for their life—now being considered as traitors by extremists within their groups. The Good Friday Accord resulting from these negotiations contained the following stipulations.

Elections to the local parliament in Northern Ireland, the Stormont, shall be held according to principles of proportionality.

For the executive cabinet all major political parties shall form a grand coalition.

The Republic of Ireland eliminates from its constitution the claim that Northern Ireland is part of the Republic of Ireland.

Although having a large amount of local autonomy, Northern Ireland remains a part of the United Kingdom. If one day, however, the people in Northern Ireland express their wish to join the Republic of Ireland, the United Kingdom shall honor this wish and let Northern Ireland go.

A Joint Irish-Northern Irish Council shall be established, which will have the power to deal with practical matters of importance to both sides of the border such as tourism, the environment, traffic, agriculture.

The Good Friday Accord was written in a spirit of accommodation and contained key power-sharing elements, in particular the principles of proportionality and grand coalitions. There was a "give and take" in the sense that the Republic of Ireland gave up its constitutional claim on Northern Ireland, and in return the United Kingdom accepted that Northern Ireland could one day join the Republic of Ireland if the people of

Northern Ireland decided to do so. The Good Friday Accord was put to a popular referendum for the citizens of Northern Ireland and was overwhelmingly accepted, with clear majorities among both Catholics and Protestants.

An important further step was made on November 17, 1999, when the two major political parties in Northern Ireland, the Ulster Unionists on the Protestant side and Sinn Féin on the Catholic side, made conciliatory public statements.[21] A key passage of the statement of the Ulster Unionists reads as follows:

> It is our belief that the establishment of the new political institutions and the disarmament of all paramilitary organisations will herald a new beginning for all sections of our people—a new, peaceful and democratic society, free from the use or threat of force. . . . Both of our traditions have suffered as a result of our conflict and division. This is a matter of deep regret and makes it all the more important that we now put the past behind us.

In similar accommodative terms, Sinn Féin states:

> Sinn Féin is totally committed to the implementation of the Good Friday agreement in all its aspects. We believe that the wholehearted implementation of the agreement has the capacity to transform the existing situation through constructive and dynamic political development. It is an unprecedented opportunity to start afresh. An opportunity to put behind us the failures, the tragedy, and the suffering of the past. There is no doubt that we are entering into the final stages of the resolution of the conflict.

Shortly after the publication of these two statements, in February 2000, the power-sharing cabinet began to operate with the Protestant David Trimble as first minister. But in Northern Ireland nothing is ever as simple as it sounds. There was still one sticking point not addressed in the Good Friday Accord—namely, the disarmament of all paramilitary forces, called *decommissioning* in Northern Ireland. Decommissioning was so sensitive that no solution could be envisaged in the Good Friday Accord.

Decommissioning was an issue for both Protestant and Catholic paramilitary forces. But it had particular urgency for the Catholic IRA because Protestants were unwilling to cooperate as long as the IRA was not disarmed, and because Protestants were the majority in the country they had more leverage than the Catholics on the issue of decommissioning. The IRA was in principle willing to decommission, but it should not be seen as a humiliating military defeat. Many Protestants, on the other hand, were precisely interested in humiliating the IRA. An attempt was made to proceed with the disarmament of the IRA under the supervision of international mediators under the chairmanship of a Canadian general, John De Chastelain. These mediators certified on September 27, 2005, that the IRA had destroyed its weapons. As De Chastelain put it, "we are satisfied that the arms decommissioned represent the totality of the IRA arsenal."[22] But this was not enough for Protestant extremists, who insisted that this turning in of weapons should occur in public, which the IRA rejected as an attempt to humiliate its members. The leader of these extremists, the Rev. Ian Paisley, exclaimed: "Instead of openness, there was the cunning tactics of cover-up and a complete failure by General De Chastelain to deal with the vital numerics of decommissioning."[23] By this Paisley meant that it was not in the public eye how many weapons the IRA had and how many of them were actually destroyed.

The issue of disarmament was further complicated by the suspicion that the IRA was increasingly involved in ordinary criminal activities, such as a spectacular bank robbery in December 2004. The suspicion was fed by the great sophistication of some of the criminal activities committed in Northern Ireland. As the Independent Monitoring Commission, in charge of tracking paramilitary activities, put it:[24]

> Seldom in the developed world has this high proportion of the most serious criminals been associated with groups originating in terrorism, with an organizational structure and discipline, and the experience of planning, learning, and conducting sophisticated clandestine operations, and with traditions of extreme violence.

Having lost its political functions, suspicions arose that the IRA now used its skills to engage in ordinary criminal activities. Even the Prime Minister of Ireland, usually a supporter of Sinn Féin, said in a radio interview after the daring bank robbery of December 2004 that he was suspicious that the IRA was involved and this would be "a serious setback" for the peace process.[25] Gerry Adams, the president of Sinn Féin, vehemently denied any involvement of the IRA in the bank robbery and asked sarcastically: "What happens if and when it emerges that the IRA weren't involved? Do you all apologize to me?"[26] The atmosphere was clearly poisoned, delaying further a full implementation of the Good Friday Accord. As Box 13.3 shows, the cycle of violence has not yet come to an end. Box 13.3 describes an incident in which Protestants rioted because a parade by the Protestant Orange Order was banned from passing through Catholic neighborhoods. Such incidents reveal how deep-seated feelings of hostility still thrive in Northern Ireland. To have the right kind of power-sharing institutions is not enough. What is also needed is an improvement in the culture of mutual mistrust and hostile feelings. And such improvements take a long time, certainly in Northern Ireland.

Box 13.3 Protestants Riot for 2nd Night in Belfast

Protestants mobs rioted on Sunday for a second consecutive night in Belfast and in towns on the city's outskirts, seriously injuring at least 30 police officers.... Sir Hugh Orde, Northern Ireland's chief constable, said the clashes posed "one of the most dangerous riot situations in the history of policing in the United Kingdom especially because Protestant paramilitary groups attacked the police with automatic weapons." ... The disturbances began Saturday after the government banned a parade by the Orange Order, a Protestant men's organization, from passing through a Roman Catholic neighborhood in Belfast.... Sectarian tensions have repeatedly flared since July, despite hopes that such violence would subside after the Irish Republican Army's announcement of an end to its armed campaign against Britain.... The I.R.A. has yet to fulfill its pledge to disarm, and many Protestants feel that Catholics have benefited disproportionately from the province's 10-year-old peace efforts.

Source: *New York Times*, September 12, 2005.

FORMER CZECHOSLOVAKIA

A theory in political science can be used in a postdictive and a predictive way. *Postdiction* means that after an event has occurred, a theory is used to make sense of this event and to explain it in a post hoc way. With prediction, the theory is used to forecast an event. Political scientists oriented toward the natural science model of explanation claim that only successful predictions can say something about the validity of a theory. Political scientists oriented more toward the model of explanation used by historians work more with postdictions. Issue for discussion: Which model is more appropriate for political science?

In our own view, both postdictions and predictions have a place in political science. Discussing the case of Northern Ireland, we used consociational theory in a postdictive way. The former Czechoslovakia situation allows us to apply consociational theory in a predictive way. When consociational theory was formulated and developed in the 1960s and 1970s, Czechoslovakia was not considered because it was under Communist rule, so that power sharing was not an option. When communism was toppled in Central and Eastern Europe in 1989 (Chapter 10), power sharing indeed became an option in Czechoslovakia because the country had two ethnic groups, Czechs and Slovaks. In an undergraduate honors seminar at the University of North Carolina at Chapel Hill, we used the list of favorable conditions for power sharing presented in the first section of the current chapter to make a prediction for Czechoslovakia. This prediction was published in the second edition of this textbook (1991, pages 247–253) and stated that power sharing would be successful in Czechoslovakia.

At the time, we identified the numerical relationship between the Czechs and Slovaks as the only negative factor. Of the total population of the country, two-thirds were Czechs, one-third Slovaks. According to consociational theory, this is the worst possible situation, because the minority is at the mercy of the majority. Other factors, however, seemed more facilitating for power sharing in Czechoslovakia—For example, the nature of the boundaries between the two ethnic groups. The consociational theory is based on the old saying that "good fences make good neighbors." In 1990 Czechoslovakia had clear boundaries between Czechs and Slovaks; in the Czech Republic, there were only 3.8 percent Slovaks; in the Slovak Republic, only 1.1 percent were Czechs.[27] As a consequence—this is the argument of the theory—there should have been little potential for conflict in everyday life, which in turn should have facilitated power sharing at the elite level.

Another factor favorable for power sharing was the religious composition of Czechoslovakia. Of the people indicating a religious affiliation, 85 percent declared themselves Roman Catholic, 15 percent Protestant. This relative religious homogeneity should have helped to hold the country together across ethnic lines. It also should have helped that the Protestant minority was not concentrated in one ethnic group but was about equally represented in both groups.

The relative economic equality between Czechs and Slovaks seemed still another factor favorable for power sharing. To be sure, as Jiri Musil points out, "the overall process of modernisation in Slovakia started later than in the Czech Lands."[28] But in recent times, the gap had narrowed; "from the macrostructural point of view, both societies became more and more alike."[29] By the year 1990, the income per capita in the Slovak Republic was 86 percent of the figure in the Czech Republic. For power sharing, it would certainly have been better if there were no economic gap at all. But Czechoslovakia was clearly better off than many other multiethnic countries, for example South Africa, where the economic gap between whites and blacks is much wider.

Another favorable condition for power sharing was an overarching loyalty of all ethnic groups to the country at large. As we will see in the next section, Yugoslavia had very unfavorable preconditions in this respect. In Czechoslovakia, the situation was not ideal either, but it was much better than in Yugoslavia. Before 1918, both Czechs and Slovaks belonged to the Austro-Hungarian Empire, and thus already had a certain common history. After World War I and the demise of the Austro-Hungarian Empire, Czechoslovakia was created as an independent political unit, and in the interwar period practiced a quite successful democratic regime. During World War II the Nazis made Slovakia formally an independent country, but, in fact, they dominated both parts of Czechoslovakia. Under communism great efforts were made to downplay the ethnic differences between Czechs and Slovaks. In making our predictions in 1990, we assumed that Czechs and Slovaks had developed a certain overarching loyalty to the country as a whole. This loyalty was helped by successful national sports teams, especially in ice hockey.

The consociational theory links the position of a country in the international system with the pattern of its domestic decision making. The specific hypothesis is that a common threat from abroad increases the likelihood of power sharing. An often-mentioned example is the presence of Soviet occupation troops in Austria from 1945 to 1955, which is said to have contributed to the Austrian power-sharing arrangement. In Czechoslovakia, even more common suffering stemmed from Soviet domination. Both Czechs and Slovaks were active in the dissident movement and often suffered together in the labor camps. This common fate is vividly described by Václav Havel in the letters to his wife Olga, written from the labor camp.[30] We assumed that this factor facilitated power sharing after the demise of communism.

With 16 million people, Czechoslovakia was a relatively small country, which was yet another favorable factor for power sharing. Finally, the living standards in Czechoslovakia were relatively high as compared with the other former Communist countries. This, too, should have helped with power sharing. Our overall conclusion was that Czechs and Slovaks had quite good conditions to practice power sharing.

Initially, this prediction turned out to be true. For the first free elections that took place in June 1990, the principle of proportionality was used, which was in accordance with consociational theory. Additionally, the Slovaks as the minority group got further protection. They had their own electoral district; and in the second chamber, the Chamber of Nationalities, they received the same number of seats as the Czechs. Cabinet formation also very much followed principles of power sharing, in the sense that each deputy minister had to be from the other ethnic group than the minister. If the minister of justice, for example, was a Slovak, the deputy minister of justice had to be a Czech, and vice-versa. It was also of great symbolic value that when Havel as a Czech was made president of the country, great care was taken to ensure that the important position of president of Parliament was filled by the Slovak Dubcek. Havel also made many efforts to show that he was president of both Czechs and Slovaks—for example, opening a presidential office in the Slovak capital Bratislava. With regard to the name of the country, sensitivities of the Slovaks were considered. As one Slovak deputy said in the deliberations on this issue: "When you are abroad, you always hear Czech, Czech, Czech. Slovakia is always left out."[31] To take care of such complaints, the cumbersome name Czech and Slovak Federative Republic was chosen, which expressed that the country had two distinct cultures.

In June 1992, the second free elections took place, and in the aftermath of these elections the country split into the Czech Republic and Slovakia. The key aspect of these elections was that the results were very different in the Czech and the Slovak parts of the country.

Václav Klaus emerged as leader in the Czech Republic, Vladimir Meciar[32] in the Slovak Republic. Each could put together a winning party coalition in his part of the country, but these coalitions were of a very different nature.

Political scientist Herbert Kitschelt has located the two leaders in a two-dimensional space.[33] An economic dimension ranges from "spontaneous market allocation" to "political redistribution"; a cultural dimension from "libertarian-cosmopolitan" to "authoritarian-particularistic." *Libertarian* means to stress the importance of individual liberties; *cosmopolitan* means being open to the world. *Authoritarian* means obedience to authority rather than exercise of individual judgment; *particularistic* means to look after the interests of one's own group. Using Kitschelt's two dimensions, Klaus and Meciar were exactly at opposite ends. Kitschelt characterizes Klaus as market-oriented and libertarian-cosmopolitan, Meciar as economically redistributive and authoritarian-particularistic.

Separation was the outcome of the power struggle between these two leaders, neither of whom was willing to yield. Each recognized that the other could block him at the national level, but not within his own republic. Thus, separation was ultimately in the political self-interest of both of them. There were suggestions that the voters should decide the matter in a referendum. Opinion surveys indicated that the voters were for more autonomy of both republics, but not for separation. Finally, the decisions were made by the politicians in very complex and sometimes obscure parliamentary maneuvers. Each side blamed the other for lack of flexibility. Separation was made against the will of the people. To be sure, Czechs and Slovaks had expressed opposite political orientations in the June 1992 parliamentary elections, but they did not know at the time that these results would lead to separation.

What does this separation say about the validity of consociational theory? The theory always had a strong voluntaristic element in the importance it gives to the free will of leaders. The usual assumption is that the leaders of the various subcultures are more farsighted than the masses and that they use their free will to practice power sharing. In Czechoslovakia, the opposite happened. The leaders, against the wishes of the people, refused to share power, and they separated the country. Would the result have been different with leaders other than Meciar and Klaus? Perhaps. There was perhaps a failure on the part of Havel, who, as president, was personally committed to the unity of the country. He, indeed, tried to organize a popular referendum on the issue of separation. If the polls were correct, such a referendum would have gone against separation. But Havel lacked the necessary political skills to implement the idea of a referendum.

The factors identified in consociational theory allowed us to predict that at the mass level there would be a willingness to share power. To be sure, Czechs and Slovaks voted in the elections in opposite political directions. The appropriate consociational reaction to these election results should have been to give more autonomy to each side. Federalism is, after all, a key element of consociationalism. But driven by Klaus and Meciar, the development went all the way to separation. For a while it seemed that an economic and currency union would still be possible. But at the leadership level, the momentum for separation was simply too strong. It is important to note, however, that separation took place without any bloodshed and in an orderly, legal way. Political stability in the region was never really threatened. In this sense, the favorable conditions identified by consociational theory indeed had some positive effect. They could not prevent the "divorce," but at least they made it civilized. This is a good illustration of how sometimes it is difficult to judge whether a particular country fits or does not fit consociational theory.

FORMER YUGOSLAVIA

In Chapter 12 on nationalism and ethnicity, we described the intricacies of the situation in former Yugoslavia, how civil war broke out in 1991 and how the country fell apart. For Yugoslavia, too, we made predictions about the chances of power sharing—in the fall of 1989, before the civil war started in Yugoslavia. In contrast to Czechoslovakia, for Yugoslavia we identified only one favorable factor for power sharing: the number and numerical strength of the ethnic groups. With five to six major ethnic groups and none of them in a majority position, Yugoslavia seemed at first sight well fitted to practice power sharing. One could expect a fluid multiple balance of power with changing coalitions. No group would be permanently left out and none would always win. According to consociational theory, this seemed an ideal situation for power sharing.

All other factors, however, were unfavorable for power sharing. A first negative factor was that Yugoslavia lacked clear boundaries between the ethnic groups. As the map in Figure 12.1 in Chapter 12 shows, there were six republics: Serbia, Croatia, Slovenia, Macedonia, Montenegro, and Bosnia-Herzegovina. The borders between these republics did not correspond to the ethnic boundaries. The most ethnically homogeneous republic was Slovenia, but even here only 90 percent were Slovenes. In Croatia, 75 percent were Croats; in Montenegro, 69 percent Montenegrins; in Macedonia, 67 percent Macedonians. The most heterogeneous republic was Bosnia-Herzegovina, with 39 percent Muslims, 32 percent Serbs, 18 percent Croats, and the remaining 11 percent dispersed among other ethnic groups. Within Serbia, there were two autonomous provinces, Kosovo and Vojvodina. Kosovo was overwhelmingly Albanian; in Vojvodina there were many Hungarians. In Serbia proper, 85 percent were Serbs. Overall, Yugoslavia had very fluid boundaries among its ethnic groups, which, according to consociational theory, made power sharing difficult.

Another factor unfavorable for power sharing was the religious diversity of the country. As we have seen in Chapter 12, the three main groups were Christian Orthodox, Roman Catholic, and Muslims. What made the religious situation in Yugoslavia particularly difficult for power sharing was that Roman Catholics were concentrated in Slovenia and Croatia; Christian Orthodox in Serbia, Macedonia, and Montenegro; and Muslims in Bosnia-Herzegovina and Kosovo. Thus, religious cleavages were superimposed on ethnic cleavages, which is a much more explosive situation than if the two cleavage lines cut across each other. In Yugoslavia, religious conflicts could easily spill over into ethnic conflicts, and vice versa. To make matters worse, there was also a language cleavage superimposed on the two other cleavages: Slovenes and Croats used the Roman alphabet; the other ethnic groups used the Cyrillic script. Thus, how people wrote already gave a clear indication early on as to what religious and ethnic groups they belonged to.

In addition to the boundaries between the ethnic groups and the nature of the groups, there was a third factor unfavorable for power sharing in Yugoslavia—namely, the huge economic inequality among the groups. Slovenia, on the Austrian border, had a per capita income that was about seven times higher than that in the autonomous province of Kosovo and about three times higher than that in Macedonia and Montenegro.

Yugoslavia also lacked an overarching loyalty among its people. As described in Chapter 12, after World War I it was put together out of very disparate parts without any say of the local people. Slovenia, Croatia, and Bosnia-Herzegovina were remnants of the Austro-Hungarian Empire. The new country also included the kingdom of Serbia and the kingdom of Montenegro. This was a state with very little common history. It was therefore difficult to develop overarching loyalties to the country as a whole.

With regard to the international situation of Yugoslavia, the key element was that under the leadership of Marshal Tito, the country liberated itself in 1948 from Soviet domination. Yugoslavia remained Communist, but it had no Soviet soldiers on its soil. Therefore, after World War II, there was no common suffering from foreign occupation, which could have brought the various ethnic groups closer together.

Another negative factor for power sharing was the poverty of the country. Measured by per capita income, Yugoslavia was twice as poor as Czechoslovakia. After 1985, a particularly severe financial and economic crisis hit Yugoslavia. The poor economic situation of the country was also expressed in such indicators as high infant mortality (25 deaths per 1,000 living births in Yugoslavia, compared with 13 in Czechoslovakia).

A last factor, size of the population, could be considered as neutral in its influence on power sharing. With a population of 24 million, Yugoslavia was a middle-sized country in the European context.

Overall, in our undergraduate honors seminar at the University of North Carolina at Chapel Hill in the fall of 1989, we came to the prediction that Yugoslavia had little chance for power sharing. Even more darkly, we predicted that "(t)he country is now confronted with the danger of disintegration."[34] Although we did not expect the horrendous atrocities that occurred in the civil war (see Chapter 12), our analysis led us correctly to the prediction that the country would disintegrate. Issue for discussion: Could such a prediction have been made without the analytical help of consociational theory? Would other political science theories have been equally or even more accurate? It should be noted that the disintegration of Yugoslavia came as a great surprise to the international community, whose attention at the time was elsewhere, in particular on East Germany, the disintegration of the Soviet Union, and the Maastricht Treaty of the European Union (for discussion of the latter, see Chapter 14).

Although power sharing was not even attempted for Yugoslavia at large, it may still work for some of the new nations emerging from the breakdown of Yugoslavia. Great hopes in this respect are for Bosnia-Herzegovina. After its extremely bloody civil war, attempts were made to establish a regime of power-sharing. The international community still works hard in this direction. What are the chances for success? As we remember from Chapter 12, there are three major groups in Bosnia-Herzegovina—39 percent Muslims (who identify themselves by their religion), 32 percent Serbs (who are Christian Orthodox), and 18 percent Croats (who are Roman Catholic).

The United Nations was the first international organization to try to bring the civil war in Bosnia-Herzegovina to an end. The U.S. government was at first hesitant to take an active part in the Bosnian conflict. This began to change in February 1994, when the United States supported an ultimatum of the United Nations to the Serbs to withdraw their heavy weapons within 12 miles of Sarajevo or to hand them over to the United Nations. The same ultimatum required the Muslims to put their heavy weapons under U.N. control. The ultimatum was set for February 21, at 1 A.M. local time, and NATO forces under U.S. command were charged to execute air strikes against targets not in compliance. Despite adverse weather conditions with heavy snow, the ultimatum worked. Some credit also went to the Russians, who put pressure on their fellow Christian Orthodox Serbs. Russian U.N. troops were moved into the Sarajevo area, which gave the Serbs additional assurance. Two days after the ultimatum, the *New York Times* published a front-page picture showing residents strolling the streets of Sarajevo and the caption "A Respite from Fear for Sarajevans."[35]

With this success, the United Nations became more assertive. On February 28, 1994, it took a decisive step to enforce the no-flight zone over Bosnia-Herzegovina. Such a no-flight zone was supposed to have been in effect since the previous April, but there were numerous violations from all warring factions. As with the ultimatum for Sarajevo, NATO under the leadership of the United States was charged with the enforcement. In the morning hours of February 28, 1994, American F-16 fighters discovered six Serbian light-attack aircraft in the process of bombing a munitions plant controlled by the Muslims. After ignoring two warnings, four of the Serbian aircraft were shot down, while two escaped. This was the first time in its 44-year history that NATO forces were involved in a military clash.

After these two incidents in which the international community had threatened and actually used military force, things began to move also at the diplomatic front. The United States brought about an agreement between Muslim and Croatian representatives who had come to Washington. The agreement was that Muslims and Croats in Bosnia-Herzegovina should join in a federation and that this federation should enter into a confederation with Croatia. The federation of Muslims and Croats would be made up of cantons in which the majority of the population would either be Muslim or Croatian. These cantons would have authority over police, education, culture, housing, public services, tourism, and radio and television. The federation would be responsible for foreign affairs and national defense. The confederation with Croatia would be of an economic nature. At the signing ceremony in Washington on March 18, 1994, President Clinton said, "The agreements signed today offer one of the first clear signals that parties of this conflict are willing to end the violence and begin a process of reconstruction."[36] However, this accord did not address the situation of the Serbs in Bosnia-Herzegovina. For President Clinton this was the next step, and he warned that "Serbia and the Serbs in Bosnia cannot sidestep their own responsibility to achieve an enduring peace."[37]

During March 1994, there were more hopeful signs on the ground. The siege of Sarajevo was lifted to some extent and a few residents could leave the city, although only with special permits. In the city itself, the bridge linking the Muslim and the Serbian neighborhoods was opened again. There was even a soccer game between a local team and a team of the United Nations. But in other parts of Bosnia-Herzegovina, there continued to be disturbing signs of violence, and war broke again out on a large scale; it took another year and a half, to the fall of 1995, until an accord could be reached in Dayton, Ohio, to end the war. Massive military interventions by NATO forces were necessary to achieve this result. These interventions came in reaction to a horrendous shelling of the Sarajevo marketplace on August 28, 1995 (Box 13.4). The reaction of the NATO forces was quick and, this time, very powerful (Box 13.5).

On October 5, 1995, Bosnia's warring parties set a cease-fire brought about by the United States, and then the leaders of Bosnia, Croatia, and Serbia were invited for peace talks in Dayton, Ohio. After fierce negotiations, an accord was initialed on November 1, 1995, by Secretaries of State Warren Christopher for the United States, Alija Izetbegovic for Bosnia-Herzegovina, Slobodan Milosevic for Serbia, and Franjo Tudjman for Croatia (Box 13.6). The peace accord was formally signed on December 14, 1995, in a ceremony in Paris in the presence of President Clinton and other world leaders (Box 13.7).

Box 13.4 Shelling Kills Dozens in Sarajevo; U.S. Urges NATO to Strike Serbs

Two shells slammed into the central Sarajevo market area today, killing at least 37 people and wounding 80 in the most devastating single attack on the Bosnian capital since a similar one 18 months ago led NATO to vow that the city would be protected. Limbs and flesh were splattered on storefronts, and bodies fell to pieces as they were lifted into cars. After 40 months of Serbian siege and bombardment, the scene was familiar, but the horrified frenzy among an exhausted population was still intense. The United States blamed the Bosnian Serbs for the attack, and the United Nations officials in Sarajevo suggested that the 120-millimeter mortar that had caused most of the damage had been fired from Serbian positions south of the capital. In Washington, a senior Administration official said the United States had urged the United Nations and NATO to respond militarily.

Source: *New York Times*, August 29, 1995.

Box 13.5 Artillery and Air Attacks Hit Serb Positions

ZAGREB, CROATIA—After 40 months of awkward hesitation, NATO today stepped squarely into the midst of the Bosnian war, pounding Bosnian Serb targets with air strikes across the country and declaring that the bombardment would not stop until Sarajevo was secure. The onslaught unfurled in at least five waves, beginning in the early-morning darkness and proceeding throughout the day. Large fires burned in Vogosca, a Serbian-held suburb northwest of Sarajevo, and Lukavica, the Serb's main barracks, as NATO bombs struck ammunition and fuel dumps. The fires followed a night illuminated by flashes as NATO fighters hit Bosnian Serb positions all around Sarajevo. Residents of the city, who in three years under siege have grown deeply cynical about the intentions of the West, watched in stunned amazement. More than 200 sorties were flown by NATO planes, including at least 48 American aircraft, in what amounted to the largest military action undertaken by the Western alliance since it was established in 1949, said Franco Veltri, a spokesman at NATO's southern command in Naples.

Source: *New York Times*, August 31, 1995.

The highlights of the Dayton accord were:

The warring parties must withdraw their forces behind the agreed cease-fire lines.

Sixty thousand peacekeepers under NATO command, headed by an American general, monitor the cease-fire and control the airspace. About a third of the peacekeepers will be Americans.

Persons indicted by the international tribunal as war criminals cannot hold office.

Refugees have the legal right to reclaim their homes or to receive compensation.

Box 13.6 All Sides Make Concessions to End Four Years of Conflict

DAYTON, OHIO—The presidents of three rival Balkan states agreed today to make peace in Bosnia, ending nearly four years of terror and ethnic bloodletting that have left a quarter of a million people dead in the worst war in Europe since World War II. The leaders—Alija Izetbegovic of Bosnia, Franjo Tudjman of Croatia and Slobodan Milosevic of Serbia—initialed the peace agreement and 11 annexes in a hastily arranged ceremony in the same conference room on the Wright-Patterson Air Force Base where they opened their talks 21 days ago.

Source: *New York Times*, November 22, 1995.

Box 13.7 Bosnia's Warriors Sign Pact to End Four Years of Cruelty

PARIS—The leaders of Bosnia-Herzegovina, Serbia, and Croatia signed a peace agreement in silence Thursday, even as scattered violence in Bosnia made clear that real peace was not yet at hand. President Bill Clinton and the other international sponsors of the agreement urged the former belligerents to make the agreement work, and vowed to contribute 60,000 NATO peacekeeping troops and hundreds of millions of dollars to rebuild the country and make peace a reality after nearly four cruel years of war.

Source: *New York Times*, December 15, 1995.

Bosnia-Herzegovina maintains its current borders, and a constitution creates a central government according to power sharing principles.

Bosnia-Herzegovina is divided into two subentities, the Federation of Muslims and Croats with 51 percent of the territory and the Serb Republic with 49 percent of the territory. Each subentity has its own governmental institutions.

Officials at all levels are to be chosen in internationally supervised elections.

Box 13.8 describes how American soldiers quite smoothly disarmed Serb soldiers on a snowy day in late January 1996. Elections in Bosnia-Herzegovina were held September 14, 1996. They went relatively smoothly, certainly better than many feared. The elections were supervised by the Conference on Security and Cooperation in Europe. Despite some irregularities, this organization declared the election results valid, which opened the door for the elected officials to assume their duties. The presidency consisted of three members, with one seat reserved for each ethnic group. The Muslims elected Alija Izetbegovic, the Croats Kresimir Zubak, the Serbs Momcilo Krajisnik. These three men all represented not moderate but nationalistic parties within their ethnic groups. Having received the most votes, Izetbegovic chaired the presidency, but this did not give him more power because each member of the presidency had veto power. In the Bosnian national parliament, it was

---

Box 13.8 G.I.'s Moment of Truth: Face-to-Face with Serbs

HADZICI, BOSNIA AND HERZEGOVINA—This was the moment the soldiers of Company C had waited for with some anxiety: standing before them in the snowfall here today were three Bosnian Serb soldiers, two with loaded AK-47s. At midnight, the deadline had passed for all combatants to move out of the zone that separates Muslims from Serbs. The three Serbs would, in theory, have to hand over their guns. The Serbs squinted at a copy of the deadlines in the peace agreement that Sgt. Lee Bruneau, 25, gave them. Finally, looking over five American soldiers with their own guns ready, one Serb with graying hair lifted his palms and, in English, said, "Yes, Yes."

Source: *New York Times*, January 21, 1996.

---

also a victory of the nationalist parties of the three ethnic groups, and here, too, each group had veto power. Another element of power sharing was that a Muslim and a Serb rotate on a weekly basis in the prime ministership and that a Croat was made speaker of Parliament. If we add the federalist structure of the country, all formal elements of power sharing were assembled. Does this mean that the international community was able to impose a regime of power sharing on the warring factions? On paper, this was true, but it was altogether another question whether power sharing would work in praxis.

As we remember from the first section of this chapter, successful power sharing is not only a matter of the right institutions but also of the right spirit of accommodation. And in this respect, much was left to be desired. Having gone through a bloody civil war, it was difficult for Serbs, Croats, and Muslims to find trust in each other, an important precondition for successful power sharing. But there are at least two factors that should facilitate power sharing in the long run. Having three major ethnic groups with none of them controlling a majority of the population is considered a good precondition for power sharing. The small size of the country, about 4 million people, also speaks for successful power sharing. For the time being, however, the international presence is still necessary to keep the three groups from beginning fighting again. In 2004, the responsibility for the international troops was transferred from NATO to the European Union, and the number of American troops was greatly reduced. Issue for discussion: Do you consider the military involvement of the United States in Bosnia-Herzegovina as a positive example of American foreign policy, or should the handling of the crisis have been left to Europeans?

In Kosovo the prospects for power sharing are even less favorable than in Bosnia-Herzegovina. As we remember from Chapter 12, Kosovo did not have the status of a republic in the old Yugoslavia, but was rather merely an autonomous province within the Republic of Serbia. When communism was toppled, Milosevic, the Communist leader in Serbia, began to play the nationalistic card and abolished the autonomy of Kosovo. As we have seen in Chapter 12, the most important military battle of Serb history was fought on Kosovo land, and this land is considered as sacred by Serb nationalists. Therefore it was a shrewd move of Milosevic to demonstrate his nationalism in bringing Kosovo under direct Serbian control. This control was exercised in a brutal and ruthless way with massacres, rapes, and expulsions against the Albanians, who are about 90 percent of the Kosovo population, against only about 10 percent Serbs. In 1999, NATO, under American command, intervened—not with ground troops, but only with air power. It worked, and the Serb armed forces were driven back to Serbia proper. Shortly afterwards Milosevic was toppled and brought to the international war tribunal in The Hague. After the Serbian troops had left, the Albanians in Kosovo committed, in their turn, brutal atrocities against the Serb minority. With this background it is understandable that power sharing is most difficult between Albanians and Serbs in Kosovo. The situation is greatly complicated because the future status of Kosovo is still completely unresolved. The Albanians demand independence, whereas the Serbs want to keep Kosovo as part of Serbia. There is heavy international presence to keep the two groups apart, but this is not always successful with new atrocities being committed from both sides. Issue for discussion: Is a compromise solution possible between the two extreme claims? Could Kosovo get independence with Serb enclaves in their holy places and some kind of linkage between the Serbs in Kosovo and Serbia? A model could be the multilevel order emerging in other parts of Europe, as described in Chapter 12.

In Macedonia the situation is reversed, with the Albanians in a minority and the Macedonians (who are ethnically close to the Serbs) in a majority. Although some violence flared between the two groups, it was much less than in Kosovo. Therefore the chances for successful power sharing are better. A member of the Macedonian parliament brought the criterion for successful power sharing to the point when he exclaimed: "We have improved the constitution to reduce ethnic conflicts, now we must improve the mentality that has caused these ethnic conflicts."[38] This is indeed the crucial point: Power-sharing institutions are necessary in a deeply divided society but they are not enough; these institutions also need to be filled with an accommodative mentality, what is called a "spirit of accommodation" in consociational theory.

In newer research we attempt to conceptualize the somewhat vague concept of spirit of accommodation in a clearer way. The concept is replaced with the concept of deliberation, which is solidly grounded in the philosophical tradition represented in particular by Jürgen Habermas.[39] Such philosophical grounding allows to get a better handle on the cultural aspect of consociational theory. After all, the strength of the theory has always been that it looks both at institutional and cultural aspects. As the theory developed, too much emphasis was given to the institutional aspects. With the replacement of the concept of spirit of accommodation with the theoretically more solidly grounded concept of deliberation, the cultural aspects should come again more to the forefront.

NORMATIVE EVALUATION OF POWER SHARING

The concept of power sharing has become very much part of the everyday political discourse in many countries around the world. Consociational scholars are involved in consulting activities in many places. Thus we must deal with a field of political science that is very much linked to political praxis. This closeness makes it urgent that we reflect carefully on the normative implications of the power-sharing model.[40] One critique of the model is that ordinary citizens have too little say if the elites work so closely together. It is criticized that power sharing really amounts to an elite cartel. Are the relations among the elites not too cozy and too secretive so that they are tempted to look primarily for their self-interest to the detriment of the interests of ordinary citizens? How can citizens hold the ruling elites accountable if they cannot replace them with a set of elites in opposition?

We agree with the critics that there is a danger in consociational countries that the elites are in too cozy a relationship with each other, mutually protecting their respective fiefdoms. In the German language, the term *Filz* ("felt") captures well this aspect of a close-knit elite cartel. Power sharing, however, does not necessarily mean a closed elite cartel. It is certainly true that in its initial formulation consociationalism meant the making of deals among the elites behind closed doors. But in a modern form, consociationalism can very well be made compatible with a spirited public discourse about the political differences in a grand coalition. If the participants in a grand coalition are willing to respect each other's opinions, a widely open public discourse may very well occur. Thus, the citizens may learn where the various partners in a grand coalition stand on specific issues. If, furthermore, a strong referendum is combined with a grand coalition, the danger of undue elitism can be reduced. With a strongly developed referendum, a competitive element is added to consociationalism. The role of opposition is taken up not by an opposition party like in the Westminster model but directly by the citizens. Citizens can inform themselves about the various policy alternatives discussed in the grand coalition and then make a final decision on key issues of the political agenda.

We agree with the critics that the concept of democratic stability, so central to consociational theory, is problematic or at least misleading. If democratic stability simply means that democracy is maintained, the concept is not problematic. But such a definition is only begging the question of what exactly is meant by *democracy*. If the essence of democracy is defined as stability in the sense of the absence of political protests and political unrest, the concept becomes highly problematic. Political protests and political unrest such as street demonstrations, sit-ins, and strikes may be signs of a vibrant democracy. This is not to say that deaths and serious injuries resulting from such events are a positive sign for any democracy. All this shows that it is not easy to determine how political protests and unrest fit within a good definition of democracy. Consociational scholars were perhaps not always careful enough in how they defined democratic stability. Sometimes they used the concept too much in terms of an absence of political protests and unrest. More reflection is needed in this area. Too much tranquility and calm may be harmful for a good democracy. In our view, for the sake of conceptual clarity, the ambiguous concept of democratic stability should best be replaced with the concept of democratic quality. The real question is how good a democracy is. If we put the question in this way, we can arrive at a broad definition of democracy, which should at least include the following elements: civil liberties, citizen participation, competitive elections, absence of severe violence, civility in the political discourse, respect for minorities, equal opportunities. Refocusing the investigation on democratic quality would allow to put consociational theory in a broader philosophical context of democratic theory.

A third normatively grounded critique is that consociational scholars have become political advocates of the consociational pattern of decision making and thus to have unduly entered the political arena as actors of their own.[41] Have consociational scholars with their consulting activities indeed become undue advocates of the pattern of consociational decision making? After the end of the cold war, the biggest challenge of the world may very well be to keep relations among different cultural groups relatively peacefully. From Rwanda to Bosnia, we know too well to what atrocities intercultural conflicts may lead. Should political scientists only observe such dreadful events and not try to have a positive influence? In our understanding, political scientists always have some influence even if they are not conscious of it. Just in teaching and writing, they influence how their listeners and readers think about the world.

The point is that we as political scientists are never purely objective outside observers, but always have some influence on the world. A first step is to reflect on this influence. For consociational scholars this means that they should make explicit to themselves and to the outside world from what normative perspective they make their policy recommendations when they engage in consulting activities. What is, for example, the relative importance they attach to the values of nonviolence and social justice if the two are in conflict? What is also needed on the part of consociational scholars engaged in consulting activities is that they spell out both the potential but also the limits of their research. If these conditions are fulfilled, there is nothing wrong if political scientists go to Bosnia and Rwanda to offer advice. To the contrary, through such activities they contribute to a high level of public discourse about the problems of this world. Issue for discussion: How do you view the potential and the limits of consociational scholars giving practical advice based on their research on power sharing?

Discussion Questions

1. Is there an alternative to consociational democracy in highly divided societies?

2. Why is consociational democracy often considered to be "elitist"?

3. Cooperation between the top representatives of the various societal segments often comes at the cost of increasing tensions between the followers of any specific groups and their leaders. Why is this so?

4. In which societal structure is civil war more likely: one that is characterized by re-enforcing cleavages, or one that is characterized by cross-cutting cleavages?

5. "Success" for consociational democracy basically means establishing peace and harmony in deeply divided societies. Is such success purely a function of its institutional configuration, or are other supporting elements also necessary? What might such elements be?

6. Does the case of Czechoslovakia strengthen or weaken consociational theory?

7. Is it always better of avoid violence and settle on a political compromise?

---

[1]The term *consociational* is derived from Johannes Althusius's concept of *consociatio* in his *Politica Methodice Digesta* (1603), reprinted, with an introduction by Carl Joachim Friedrich (Cambridge, MA: Harvard University Press, 1932).

[2]Arend Lijphart. Consociational Democracy. *World Politics* 21, January 1969: 207–225; Gerhard Lehmbruch. A Noncompetitive Pattern of Conflict Management in Liberal Democracies: The Case of Switzerland, Austria, and Lebanon. In Kenneth MacRae (ed.), *Consociational Democracy: Political Accommodation in Segmented Societies* (Toronto: McClelland and Stewart, Carleton Library, No. 79, 1974).

[3]Gabriel A. Almond. Comparative Political Systems. *Journal of Politics* 18, August 1956: 391–409.

[4]Arend Lijphart. *The Politics of Accommodation. Pluralism and Democracy in the Netherlands.* (Berkeley: University of California Press, 1968, 104.)

[5]gfs. bern, Sorgenbarometer, October 2004.

[6]Based on national census of 2000.

[7]For example, David Earle Bohn. Consociational Democracy and the Case of Switzerland. *Journal of Politics* 42, February 1980: 179.

[8]Raimund E. Germann and Jürg Steiner. Comparing Decision Modes at the Country Level: Some Methodological Considerations Using Swiss Data. *British Journal of Political Science* 16, January 1985: 123–126.

[9]Jürg Steiner and Robert H. Dorff. *A Theory of Political Decision Modes. Intraparty Decision Making in Switzerland.* (Chapel Hill: University of North Carolina Press, 1980).

[10]The only violence that occurred with regard to the language question was in the Jura. The issue was whether the French speakers in the predominantly German-speaking Bern canton should have their own canton and where the borders of this canton should be.

[11]Jean Ziegler. *Une Suisse au-dessus de tout soupçon.* (Paris: Editions du Seuil, 1976).

[12]Arend Lijphart. *Democracy in Plural Societies.* (New Haven, CT: Yale University Press, 1977, 238).

[13]Ibid., 497.

[14]Richard Rose. Northern Ireland: The Irreducible Conflict. In Joseph V. Montville (ed.), *Conflict and Peacemaking in Multiethnic Societies.* (Lexington, KY: D. C. Heath, 1989, 13).

[15]Joint Declaration by An Taoiseach, Mr. Albert Reynolds, T.D., and the British Prime Minister, the Rt. Hon. John Major, M.P., December 15, 1993, printed by Cahill Printers Ltd., Dublin.

[16]Ibid., 4.

[17]Ibid., 5.

[18]*New York Times*, September 1, 1994.

[19]*New York Times*, October 4, 1994.

[20]*New York Times*, February 23, 1995.

[21]*The Times*, November 17, 1999.

[22]*New York Times*, September 27, 2005.

[23]Ibid.

[24]*New York Times*, January 19, 2005.

[25]Ibid.

[26]Ibid.

[27]For the data, we consulted the statistical yearbook of Czechoslovakia and various other publications. For helping with the translation, we express thanks to Joseph Anderle, a colleague at the University of North Carolina at Chapel Hill.

[28]Jiri Musil. Czech and Slovak Society. *Government and Opposition* 28, Autumn 1993: 480.

[29]Ibid., 493.

[30]Václav Havel. *Letters to Olga.* (New York: Knopf, 1988).

[31]*New York Times*, March 28, 1990.

[32]For the phenomenon of Vladimir Meciar in Slovak politics, see Samuel Abraham. Early Elections in Slovakia: A State of Deadlock. *Government and Opposition* 30, Winter 1995: 86–100.

[33]Herbert Kitschelt. The Formation of Party Systems in East Central Europe. *Politics & Society* 20, March 1992: 7–50.

[34]This prediction can be found on page 248 of the second edition of this textbook, published in January 1991.

[35]*New York Times*, February 23, 1994.

[36]*New York Times*, March 19, 1994.

[37]Ibid.

[38]*Neue Zürcher Zeitung*, November 16, 2001.

[39]Jürg Steiner, André Bächtiger, Markus Spörndli, and Marco R. Steenbergen. *Deliberative Politics in Action. Analyzing Parliamentary Debates.* (Cambridge University Press, 2004, in particular Chapter 1).

[40]More on the normative aspect of power sharing in Jürg Steiner and Thomas Ertman (eds.). *Consociationalism and Corporatism in Western Europe. Still the Politics of Accommodation?* (Amsterdam: Boom, 2002; also published as a special issue of *Acta Politica,* vol. 37, Spring/Summer 2002).

[41]Ian S. Lustick. Lijphart, Lakatos, and Consociationalism. *World Politics,* vol. 50: 88–117.

The European Union

More than 200 years ago, the 13 American states joined together in a single political system—the United States of America. Today, there is a movement toward European integration. Will there ever be a United States of Europe similar in form to the United States of America? Probably not. The historical circumstances are so different that Europe will not simply copy the American model. The main difference is that the European countries have far older historical traditions than the American states had when the United States of America was founded.

Nonetheless, European integration is already a reality to a certain extent. European voters participate regularly in elections for the European Parliament. Other governmental bodies include the European Council of Ministers, the European Council, the European Commission, and the European Court of Justice. What are the functions of these institutions, and how much power do they have? What is the relationship between these European institutions and the political institutions in the member countries of the European Union (EU)? These questions are very important for American students who in their later professional lives may be involved in European affairs. With regard to business dealings in Europe, the main responsibilities in many areas are no longer in the national capitals but in Brussels, the capital not only of Belgium but also of the EU. To export oranges from Florida to Great Britain, the paperwork must be handled by European bureaucrats in Brussels. If an American company wants to sell kitchen tools in France, it must be aware of the safety standards that are set by European authorities. The influence of the EU even extends across the Atlantic. In 2001, Mario Monti, the European competitition commissioner, blocked a merger between General Electric and Honeywell, two American companies that had secured approval from the U.S. Justice Department for their merger.[1] In this chapter we give an overview of the history of European integration and describe the institutions of the European Union.

HISTORY OF EUROPEAN INTEGRATION

European countries warred for many centuries. A serious effort to stop the seemingly endless European wars once and for all was made after World War I. In 1914, European leaders had sent their countries' youths to war fired with enthusiasm. Each side expected a quick and heroic victory. The eventual Allied victory, however, came only after four years of trench warfare and tremendous losses on both sides. After the war, many well-meaning people became active in the so-called Pan-European movement, which demanded the unification of Europe so war could never again break out. Members of this movement urged Europeans to recognize their common cultural heritage. But the time for this movement was not yet ripe. Mussolini's Fascist Party took over Italy in 1922. In 1929, the Great Depression began. In 1933, Hitler became dictator of Germany, and in 1939, another world war began.

World War II was, if such comparisons are possible, even more dreadful than World War I. Aerial bombardment increasingly spread the suffering directly to the civilian population. After the war, the idea of European unification was quickly brought up again. In a famous speech in Zurich in 1946, Winston Churchill called for the construction of a "kind of United States of Europe."

A first step was the foundation of the *Council of Europe* in Strasbourg, France, in 1949. Its members were drawn from the national parliaments of the Western European democracies. The Council of Europe had only a consultative character. It required no surrender of national sovereignty, and its decisions were based on unanimous votes, giving each country a veto power. The Council of Europe still exists today and does important work; its Commission on Human Rights investigates human rights abuses. The Council of Europe also has a Court of Human Rights. Although it has no means to enforce its rulings, they are widely followed by the member states, as there is great moral pressure to do so. In order to increase this pressure, the Council of Europe decided in April 1996 that countries violating human rights may be suspended temporarily from some activities of the Council.[2]

Resistance to rulings of the European Court of Human Rights sometimes appears, in particular in Great Britain, against which the court has ruled on several occasions. In March 1996, for example, the court upheld the appeal of the journalist Bill Goodwin against the British courts' refusal to acknowledge that he should be entitled to protect professional sources from disclosure.[3] Reacting to such cases, the British government criticized the court in the following terms:

> Account should be taken of the fact that democratic institutions and tribunals in member states are best placed to determine moral and social issues in accordance with regional and national perceptions. [The aim is] to promote fairness and to ensure that the Strasbourg institutions take all factors into account.[4]

The Council of Europe has also established the European Social Charta, expanding its activities to the area of social rights. The Charta guarantees, for example, the right to work, the right to health care, and the right to welfare. Such rights, however, are even more controversial than human rights, so that in the social rights area the Council of Europe has even less influence.[5]

After the breakdown of communism in Central and Eastern Europe in 1989, it was the Council of Europe that offered these countries their first access to a European institution. Compared with the European Union, the Council of Europe is much less important. Though the Council of Europe meets in Strasbourg in the same building where the parliament of the European Union meets, it is important to differentiate between the two institutions.

The current EU had its institutional beginning in the *European Coal and Steel Community (ECSC)*, which was founded by the Treaty of Paris on April 18, 1951. At the time coal and steel were the crucial elements in any war effort. It was felt that pooling these important raw materials on a European level should prevent future wars in Europe. With this goal in mind, the key aspect was to include both France and the Federal Republic of Germany, which had gone to war with each other three times in the preceding hundred years: 1870–1871, 1914–1918, and 1939–1945. Also participating in the ECSC were Italy, Belgium, the Netherlands, and Luxembourg. The initiative was made successful through such leaders as Jean Monnet and Robert Schuman of France, Alcide de Gasperi of Italy, and Paul-Henri Spaak of Belgium, who are today counted as the founding fathers of the European Union.

In 1954, European integration suffered a painful setback. The six member countries of the ECSC had planned to extend their collaboration to the establishment of a European Defense Community. Five countries had already ratified the corresponding treaty when the French National Assembly voted against it, not wishing to have French troops under a common European command.

After this setback in defense affairs, the economic route to European integration was pursued further. A common market for coal and steel having been established, its six member countries extended their economic collaboration to other areas. In 1957 they signed the crucial Treaty of Rome, establishing the *European Economic Community (EEC)*. For the peaceful use of nuclear energy, they created a special organization, the *European Atomic Energy Community (Euratom)*. The three communities, ECSC, EEC, and Euratom, were never merged into a single entity. However, there were good reasons to regard them as constituting one unit insofar as their political and legal structure was concerned. In the media and in everyday life, the three communities were commonly called the *European Community (EC)*. On February 16, 1978, the European Parliament acknowledged this usage and accepted a resolution that the three communities "be designated the European Community."

Despite Churchill's Zurich speech, Great Britain was not a founding member of the European Community. Even in 1957, the British still did not really feel that they were a part of Europe. For the British, Europe was the Continent, and when they crossed the English Channel, they considered that trip as "going to Europe." But by the 1960s Britain had changed its mind and—mainly out of economic necessity—applied for membership. France, under de Gaulle, feared for its own leadership position, and it twice vetoed the entry of Britain. It was only in 1973, when de Gaulle was out of office, that Britain was able to join. To this day, many British citizens have strong emotional reservations about the process of European integration. Denmark and the Republic of Ireland also joined in 1973; Greece followed in 1981; Spain and Portugal in 1986; Austria, Finland, and Sweden in 1995. After the breakdown of communism in 1989, it took until 2004 for the first formerly Communist countries to join the European Union: the Czech Republic, Hungary, Poland, Slovakia, Slovenia, and the three Baltic countries Estonia, Latvia, and Lithuania. At the same time the two Mediterranean islands of Cyprus and Malta joined the EU. Thus, currently the EU has 25 members.

To revitalize the EC, on February 18, 1986, its member countries signed the *Single European Act*. The act's goal was to set up a common market for goods, labor, capital, and services by the end of 1992. These goals were already contained in the Treaty of Rome, but with the Single European Act a fixed timetable was set up, and by January 1, 1993, the EC had, indeed, with a few exceptions, reached the goal of a common market. Profiting from the momentum of the project, in December 1991 at Maastricht in the Netherlands, the EC countries signed the *Treaty on European Union*. The goal of this ambitious Maastricht treaty is to strengthen the political and monetary ties in the community. It became effective on November 1, 1993, whereby the European Community became the European Union. For the remainder of the chapter, we will adhere to this latter usage, except when we refer to specific events before November 1993, for which we will still use the name *European Community*.

In addition to the Council of Europe and the European Union, some other organizations contribute to European integration. The *European Free Trade Association (EFTA)* was created by West European countries that did not wish to join the European Community. Great Britain was the most important founding member of EFTA, but, like most other founding members, it later changed its membership to the European Community. Currently, only four countries make up EFTA: Iceland, Liechtenstein, Norway, and Switzerland.

Then there is the *Western European Union (WEU)*. It has ten members, Belgium, France, Germany, Great Britain, Greece, Italy, Luxembourg, Netherlands, Portugal, and Spain. This organization is concerned mainly with defense issues and works closely with NATO. The close link between NATO and the Western European Union could be seen during the Yugoslav crisis, when ship traffic on the Adriatic Sea was controlled. This operation was done one week by NATO, the next week by the Western European Union. If, with the Treaty of Maastricht, the European Union increasingly takes on defense issues, the Western European Union may become redundant as a special organization.

Finally, there is the *Organization for Security and Cooperation in Europe (OSCE)*, which met for the first time from 1973 to 1975 in Helsinki and Geneva (initially under the name *Conference on Security and Cooperation in Europe*) and then met on a regular basis at different meeting places. This was the first institutional setting for Western and Central and Eastern European countries to meet. Also included in this institution were the United States, Canada, and the Soviet Union. After the breakup of the Soviet Union, its membership was taken over by Russia. In the Yugoslav conflict, the OSCE also played a role. When Croatia was internationally recognized, for example, the European Union referred, with regard to the rights of ethnic and national groups, to commitments subscribed to in the framework of the OSCE. In 1996 the OSCE supervised the elections in Bosnia.

If the multitude of European organizations sounds confusing, it indeed is. One must be a real expert to navigate the complex organizational network of European integration. A simplifying factor, however, is that the European Union is by far the most important organization. For the remainder of the chapter, we concentrate on the European Union and refer to the other organizations only when there is a special reason to do so.

Institutionally, the European Union is a hybrid of international and supranational organizations. In an *inter*national organization, each nation keeps its independence, whereas in a *supra*national organization, nations yield their sovereignty to the common organization. The hybrid character of the EU is best seen in its institutional structure. Its most powerful institutions, the Council of Ministers and the European Council, tend to act as though the European Union were an international organization. On the other hand, the behavior of the European Commission, which is also a powerful body, corresponds to a large extent to a supranational organization.

COUNCIL OF MINISTERS

When the European Community began to operate under the terms of the Treaty of Rome, the Council of Ministers, was considered the legislature, operating by the unanimity principle. The Council of Ministers still has important legislative functions, but increasingly it shares these functions with the European Parliament. The 25 member countries of what is now the European Union each send one minister to the meetings of the Council of Ministers. The particular minister sent depends on the issue under debate. The Council of Foreign Ministers, also called the General Affairs Council, is considered to be at the highest level. It deals not only with foreign policy issues but also with general matters, such as changes in the various treaties on which the European Union is based. For other matters, the corresponding ministers come together; for agricultural matters, for example, the ministers of agriculture would meet. Meetings also take place at the level of ministers for finance, social affairs, transport, and so on. This list illustrates the broad range of topics discussed by the Council of Ministers. We should remember that the main job of the ministers is in the governmental institutions of their home countries, however, they spend more and more of their time with their European Union colleagues.

How are decisions made in the Council of Ministers? Table 14.1 shows a series of selected statistics including the number of votes each country has in the Council of Ministers. This allocation of votes to each country is roughly proportional to the square root of its population, which obviously favors the smaller countries. On this basis the total number of votes is 321 and to reach a decision, a qualified majority of 232 votes is required. The votes in favor must also correspond to 62 percent of the total population of the European Union. Thus, one needs quite a bit of math to determine whether the Council of Ministers has made a positive decision.[6]

With the Single European Act, an attempt was made to give more importance to the majority principle. Although it was not possible to abolish the unanimity rule altogether, it was agreed to use majority voting on matters such as the internal market, the environment, and research and technological development. For politically more sensitive issues, however, such as taxation and rights of workers, each country still can claim its veto power, although it is more rarely used now. However, important exceptions exist, and countries do use their veto power. One such exception happened in 1996 when the European Union banned British beef as unsafe because of the so-called mad cow disease. When the European Union continued to delay the lifting of the ban, the British government reacted angrily, and for several weeks blocked all meetings of the Council of Ministers with its veto (Box 14.1).

Even when the majority principle is used, the requirement of a qualified majority of 232 votes out of 321 means that a small number of countries can block a decision of the Council of Ministers. With the accession of the 10 additional countries in 2004, is it possible that these new accession countries could block particular proposals? Why would they want to do that in the first place? Table 14.1, shows that they have much lower GDP per

---

Box 14.1 Furious Major Retaliates Against Beef Ban. British Pledge to Paralyze EU

John Major triggered Britain's biggest confrontation with Europe yesterday when, furious and feeling betrayed over its refusal to ease its beef ban, he declared that he was blocking all important progress in the European Union until further notice .... The first effect of the new policy will be that Britain will maintain its opposition—which it had been ready to drop—to Europol, the embryo European police force. A new convention on insolvency procedures, due to be sealed this week, will also be blocked. Britain will raise the beef ban at all meetings of European ministers, including those on unrelated issues such as social affairs and transport. EU officials accused Mr. Major of acting for domestic electoral reasons, but said his move could cause havoc.

Source: *The Times*, May 22, 1996.

TABLE 14.1 Member states of the European Union and selected statistics

Country	Population in 1,000	GDP per Capita in PPS*	Year of Joining the EU	Labor Productivity Per Hour Worked	Monthly Labor Costs†	Council of Ministers Votes	Seats in EU Parliament
Austria	8,067.30	121.9	1995	92.4	3,339.00	10	18
Belgium	10,355.80	118.2	1958	119	3,895.20	12	24
Cyprus	715.10	82	2004	n.a.	1,837.00	4	6
Czech Republic	10,203.30	70.3	2004	46.1	777.00	12	24
Denmark	5,383.50	122.6	1973	96.5	4,101.40	7	14
Estonia	1,356	50.6	2004	34.7	608.40	4	6
Finland	5,206.30	114.3	1995	92.2	3,489.30	7	14
France	59,630.10	110.2	1958	116	3,414.00	29	78
Germany	82,536.70	109.2	1958	102.5	3,726.00	29	99
Greece	11,018.40	81.7	1981	66.2	1,984.30	12	24
Hungary	10,142.40	61.1	2004	n.a.	763.70	12	24
Ireland	3,963.60	140.4	1973	113.4	n.a.	7	13
Italy	57,321.00	104.8	1958	89.9	2,904.00	29	78
Latvia	2,331.50	43	2004	30.5	357.30	4	9
Lithuania	3,462.60	48.2	2004	36.7	486.20	7	13
Luxembourg	448.30	221.9	1958	129.2	n.a.	4	6

(Continued)

TABLE 14.1 Continued

Country	Population in 1,000	GDP per Capita in PPS*	Year of Joining the EU	Labor productivity Per Hour Worked	Monthly Labor Costs[†]	Council of Ministers Votes	Seats in EU Parliament
Malta	397.30	70.5	2004	70	1,282.40	3	5
Netherlands	16,192.60	124.8	1958	111.2	3,714.00	13	27
Poland	38,218.50	46.7	2004	37.3	698.30	27	54
Portugal	10,407.50	76.4	1986	62	1,343.00	12	24
Slovenia	1,995	78.5	2004	59.7	1,496.70	4	7
Slovakia	5,379.20	52	2004	49.4	565.30	7	14
Spain	41,550.60	98.1	1986	88.3	2,017.00	27	54
Sweden	8,940.80	115.9	1995	94.3	4,312.70	10	19
United Kingdom	59,328.90	118.6	1973	94.3	3,642.40	29	78
Total:	454,552.30					321	732
United States	278,058.90	154.6		110.1			

Source: For population in 1,000 (2003), labor productivity per worker (2002), and monthly labor costs (2003), See Eurostat: http://epp.eurostat.cec.eu.int/.

* The GDP in PPS (purchasing power standards) and the labor productivity per hour worked is expressed as an index with the EU-15 set to 100.

† The monthly labor costs are expressed in euros in 2003 except for Italy, where the number refers to the year 2002, and for Austria, where the number refers to the year 2000. The source for the other data is on the EU Web site: http://europa.eu.int/.

capitas and much lower labor productivity than the EU-15 (the 15 original members). Economically they are less advanced than any of the EU-15. This economic divide might lead them to vote in a bloc to protect their interests. However, even if they did pool their votes they would have a total of only 84 votes in the Council of Ministers. Therefore, they could not stop a decision from taking place because there would still be a qualified majority of 237 votes left, six votes short of preventing a qualified majority.

EUROPEAN COUNCIL

The European Council brings together the chief executives of the 25 member countries. These are the most prominent political leaders in Europe. In the initial phase of the European Community, the European Council did not exist. It evolved from the practice, dating from 1974, of regularly organizing informal meetings of the chief executives. French President Valéry Giscard d'Estaing and German Chancellor Helmut Schmidt were instrumental in setting up this tradition. In the Single European Act, the European Council was formally established as an institution of the European Community. It meets at least twice a year for short sessions of a couple of days. The chair for these meetings rotates among all the member countries every six months, the same system as for the Council of Ministers. The president of the European Commission, which will be discussed in the next section, attends the meetings of the European Council in his own right. The foreign ministers are also in attendance at these meetings.

Compared with the United States, the European Council corresponds closely to the Governors' Conference. Imagine if the Governors' Conference were the most powerful political body in the United States! Each governor would probably feel responsible primarily for the interests of his or her own state. This is, indeed, the situation in the European Council. The power base for each participant is in his or her own respective country. To survive politically, the members of the European Council must, first of all, win elections at home. If they lose those elections, they are also out of the European Council. Thus, the members of the European Council naturally view a problem first from their own national perspective and not from an overall European view. Therefore, important decisions can be reached only if all national interests are more or less accommodated. Meetings of the European Council often resemble a "game of chicken," in which each participant tries to wait out all others before making concessions. This leads to hectic, late-night sessions in which some bargain is finally struck out of exhaustion. Quite often, however, such late-night agreements tend to obscure real differences, so that the issue must be taken up again at a later meeting. Observers have grown accustomed to an atmosphere of crisis at European Council meetings. But somehow the European Council muddles through to keep the European Union going. After all, the participants know that the demise of the European Union would leave every country worse off. Thus, a solution of some kind is always found, even if it is only to study the problem further. Overall, the European Council has become the most important institution of the European Union. It is here that the basic political compromises are worked out. They are usually prepared elsewhere, but the key issues are left to the chief executives. If their power base is weakened in their home countries, this also weakens decision making in the European Union.

EUROPEAN COMMISSION

The institution that brings continuity to the operations of the European Union is the European Commission. In contrast to the members of the Council of Ministers and the European Council, commissioners work full time for the European Union. There are 25 commissioners, one for each country. The members of the commission are nominated by their respective national governments and appointed by "common accord" of the governments of the member countries. Under the Maastricht treaty, their appointment has to be approved by the European Parliament. Even before the Maastricht treaty, the European Parliament could have forced the commission to resign *en bloc,* by a no-confidence vote. In fact, in March of 1999 in a scathing report issued by the European Parliament, the whole European commission resigned, amid charges of patronage, cronyism, and financial irregularities. This is quite instructive as it shows that the powers of the European Parliament and the European Commission are quite similar to those in the domestic realm of parliamentary systems.

The commission is headed by a president, who is chosen by agreement of the member countries. Once a president is appointed, the member countries appoint the other 24 members of the commission. The president of the European Commission is sometimes labeled by the American media as the "European president." Pictures are published entitled "Two Presidents," showing the American president and the president of the European Commission standing side by side. The power of the two offices, however, is quite different. Nevertheless, the 25 commissioners clearly are not to represent the interests of their national governments. In fact, they must take an oath swearing that they will represent the interests of the EU only and will not take any instruction from their national government or any other body. This is of course difficult in reality, as it is impossible to suddenly distance oneself from one's own national identity and interests. Still, the Commission is clearly the most supranational body of the EU.

In assessing the nature of the presidency of the European Commission, we see that there is an intriguing chicken-and-egg problem: What comes first, a powerful office or a powerful officeholder? Must the office be made powerful to attract powerful leaders, or is the first step appointing a powerful leader who can lend power to the office? At first, it was quite difficult to attract powerful leaders to head the commission. But recently, competition has increased among top politicians wishing to become president of the commission. When Jacques Delors resigned as president in 1994, the prime ministers of Belgium, the Netherlands, and Luxembourg all wanted the job. There was fierce bargaining in the European Council, and at the end, Jacques Santer, the prime minister of Luxembourg, was appointed. His predecessor, Jacques Delors, had served French president François Mitterrand as an influential economic minister but, at the time, had no immediate prospect of becoming president of France. Hence, he was willing to move to Brussels to head the commission. This pattern has not yet changed: To be the top leader in France and the other big countries is still preferable to being president of the commission. But as the appointment in 1994 demonstrated, top leaders in the smaller countries are increasingly eager to exchange their jobs for the position of president of the commission. The newest example is José Manuel Barroso, who in 2004 resigned as prime minister of Portugal to become president of the European Commission. It is still difficult, however, to recruit leading politicians to serve as ordinary commissioners. The public visibility of these positions is so low that many ambitious leaders fear dead-ending their careers in Brussels and prefer to stay in their national capitals.

The European Commission directs a large bureaucracy at the headquarters in Brussels. The commission meets at least once a week. Each commissioner is responsible for specific policy areas, such as external relations, agriculture, social affairs, energy, and transport. The commission is in charge of the European Union's routine day-to-day operations. It also has the authority to make certain policy decisions on its own, what Martin Shapiro and Alec Stone call "administrative rule making."[7] Sensitive policy decisions, however, are dealt with by the Council of Ministers and, if they are extremely sensitive, by the European Council. The main task of the commission is to prepare the meetings of the Council of Ministers and the European Council. The commission also has executive functions in the sense that it supervises the implementation of the decisions reached by the Council of Ministers, the European Council, and the European Parliament. In an official publication of the European Union, the responsibilities of the commission are presented as fourfold: (1) *Proposing* measures for the further development of European Community policy. (2) *Monitoring* observance and proper application of European Community law. (3) *Administering* and implementing European Community legislation. (4) *Representing* the European Community in international organizations.[8] In another official publication, the commission is seen "as the embryo of a European government" accountable to the European Parliament.[9]

EUROPEAN PARLIAMENT

In the Treaty of Rome, the European Parliament was called an "assembly," but in 1958, it gave itself its current name. Initially, the European Parliament consisted of delegates of the national parliaments, and it met for short sessions in Strasbourg. This led to useful contacts, but the European Parliament had virtually no decision-making power. It could approve nonbinding resolutions and submit questions to the Council of Ministers. Its only real decision power was to force the European Commission to resign with a no-confidence vote. But as we have seen earlier, this right was not used for a very long time, indeed not until 1999. Thus for a long time the European Parliament was not much more than a forum for an exchange of ideas among delegates from the national parliaments.

The real legislature was, as noted, the Council of Ministers, and this was increasingly seen as a democratic deficiency of the European Community. To be sure, the Council of Ministers had democratic legitimacy in the individual member countries in the sense that its members belonged to the respective national governments, and these national governments were selected by the national parliaments, which in turn were elected by the national electorates. But this was too long a chain to give to the Council of Ministers real democratic legitimacy. It was felt that the European voters should have a direct voice. Thus, on December 20, 1976, the Council of Ministers decided that the European Parliament should be directly elected by the European voters. The first direct elections took place in 1979. The term was five years, and further elections were held in 1984, 1989, 1994, 1999, and 2004. Voter turnout was 63 percent in 1979, 59 percent in 1984, 57 percent in 1989, 56 percent in 1994, 53 percent in 1999, and 45.5 percent in 2004. Compared to national European elections, these turnouts are rather low (Chapters 3 and 9). It is particularly disturbing that the trend is downward. This raises the question of the extent to which the European Parliament has been able to establish itself as a representative institution of the European voters.

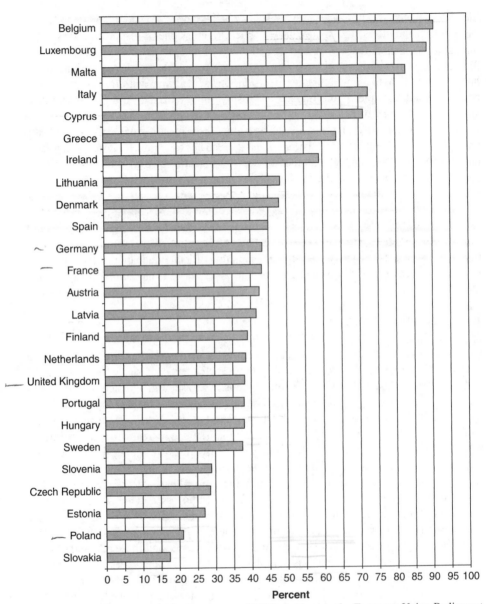

Figure 14.1 Voter turnout in the most recent (2004) elections to the European Union Parliament. (*Source:* http://www.euractiv.com.)

Inspection of Figure 14.1 shows that the "host" of the EU, Belgium, indicates the highest voter turnout to EU parliamentary elections, followed by Luxembourg. It also helps that in both countries, voting is mandatory. The third country that has mandatory voting is Greece, where over 60 percent of the population voted in the 2004 election. Somewhat surprising, and perhaps disappointing, is the very low turnout in the new accession countries. Of the ten new countries that joined the European Union, five (Slovenia, Czech Republic, Estonia, Poland, and Slovakia) rank at the bottom of that list, with only 17 percent of

Slovakians turning out. If voter turnout is a measure of the political involvement of the citizenry and their belief that by participating they can affect various outcomes, the declining turnout rates are disturbing, to say the least. It might very well be that citizens perceive politics in Brussels as too far removed to affect them and/or that their voice would not make a difference at all. The low turnout to elections for the European Parliament is one manifestation of the often cited "democracy deficit" that plagues the EU. This is paradoxical insofar as the impact of the EU on the daily lives of Europeans is increasing rather than decreasing.

What political parties are represented in the European Parliament? They are basically the same party families that can be found at the national levels: the Conservative (Christian Democratic) Party, which has about 36.6 percent of the seats; the Socialists, who control about 27 percent of the seats; and Liberal and Green parties, which have 12 and 5.3 percent of the seats, respectively (Figure 14.2).

Most interesting, two party groupings within the European Parliament are outspokenly against EU integration: the Independence-Democracy Party and the Union for Europe of the Nations. The latter states unmistakably that it favors a "Europe based on the freedom of nations to decide, where diversity is the first of all riches, and not a federal Europe which would subject sovereign nations and take away the identity of European peoples."[10] The Independence-Democracy Party was created specifically to prevent the establishment of a EU constitution and it "rejects the creation of a European superstate."[11] Together, the two parties have 64 parliamentary eats, which represents about 8.7 percent of all available seats. The MEPs (members of the European Parliament) sit in their chambers in Strasbourg and Brussels not according to their nationality but rather according to

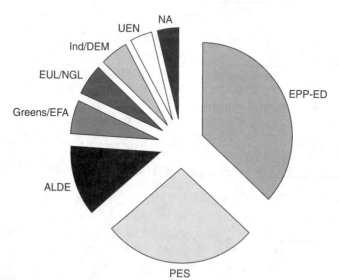

FIGURE 14.2 Parties represented in the European Parliament (2004). (*Source:* http://www. elections2004.eu.int.')

EPP-ED = European People's Party and European Democrats (Christian Democrats); Quark PES = Socialists; ALDE = Liberals; Greens/EFA = Greens and European Free Alliance; EUL/NGL = European United Left and Nordic Green Left; Ind/DEM = Independence-Democracy (a eurosceptic political group sometimes being quite outspoken against the very idea of European integration); UEN = Union for Europe of the Nations (a party favoring national sovereignty and only loose cooperation of European nations); NA = Nonattached.

their party affiliation. Just like in the national parliaments, party loyalty matters also in the European context, where MEPs who go against the party line may not be placed on particularly influential delegations or committees, or may even be fined, though this rarely happens.

The European Parliament has basically the same problem as the European Commission, in the sense that it is unclear whether a powerful office or powerful officeholders come first. In the first elections, some eminent leaders, such as Willy Brandt and François Mitterrand, were elected. But it soon turned out that, for many, their participation was mostly a symbolic gesture of goodwill. Brandt and Mitterrand, for example, gave up their seats in the European Parliament to continue their careers in Bonn and Paris. When the European Parliament was elected for the second time, relatively few prominent leaders entered the race. They considered a seat in the European Parliament an insufficiently powerful position. This still appears to be the case at the beginning of the third millennium.

How powerful has the European Parliament become since its direct election by the voters? A historical analysis of the development of national parliaments all over the world suggests that the crucial step has been gaining control over the budget. The U.S. Congress is powerful because it controls the purse. In this respect, the European Parliament still has little power. The budget does not originate in the European Parliament but in the European Commission. It then passes between the Council of Ministers and Parliament. The real budgetary power has remained with the Council of Ministers. Parliament can reject the budget but has no authority to draw up its own budget. Nevertheless, it has gained the right to make certain amendments to the budget in some limited areas. The power of the European Parliament ultimately will be determined in the battle over these budget questions. If Parliament can obtain significant control over both revenues and expenditures, it will be the crucial step in transforming the European Union into a truly supranational organization: Essential sovereign power will have been transferred from the member countries to the European level. But many politicians and voters—especially in Great Britain, but also elsewhere—fear such a development and will resist any effort to expand the European Parliament's budgetary power. Seen in this broader context, quarrels over the budgetary rights of the European Parliament are not at all technical in nature but go to the very heart of European integration.

In the parliamentary system of government to which Europeans are accustomed, it is crucial that parliament exercises power in the selection of the executive cabinet. In this respect, too, the European Parliament lacks power; it is not even clear who the executive is and whether the European Union has an executive at all. As we have seen in the preceding sections, the European Commission has executive functions for the day-to-day operations of the European Union. But for politically sensitive matters, the Council of Ministers makes executive decisions, although it also has legislative functions. Finally, there is the all-important European Council, which makes the most sensitive executive decisions.

The European Council does not depend on a vote of confidence of the European Parliament, nor does the Council of Ministers. For the European Commission, the situation is ambiguous. Legally, the European Parliament has the right, as we have seen in the last section, to dismiss the commission with a vote of no-confidence, which in fact, as noted, it did in the spring of 1999. But it has no right to select a new commission, so that the national governments could simply reappoint the old commission. With the Maastricht treaty, Parliament has received the additional right to approve the appointment of a new commission for its five-year term. It exercised this right in January 1995, when it confirmed the then 20 commissioners with an overwhelming vote of 416 to 103. Prior to the vote hearings were held with the individual commissioners. In 2004, a new commission president and 24 new commissioners needed to be installed for the 2004–2009 legislative period. The European Council nominated a new commission president, the already mentioned José Manuel Barroso, and the Council of Ministers nominated one commissioner from each country. This was followed by hearings by the European Parliament that voted on the whole body (the commission president and the 24 commissioners). The Barroso European Commission was approved by 449 member of Parliament, with 149 "no" votes, 82 abstentions, 12 who did not vote, and 38 absentees.[12] The European Parliament thus approved the commission body by a little over 61 percent. Thus, the approval by the European Parliament was not a formality at all. The increased power of the European Parliament was also shown when a right-wing Italian candidate, Rocco Butiglione, was withdrawn as commission candidate and other positions were reshuffled before the parliamentary vote was taken.

After approval by Parliament, the new "government of the EU" is appointed by the Council of Ministers. This process is similar to the process of *investiture*, the formal process of government formation that can be found in various national parliaments. Some discussion exists within the European Union concerning transforming the Council of Ministers into a second parliamentary chamber called the *Senate*. The institutional construction would be similar to that in Germany, where the Bundestag represents the people and the Bundesrat represents the Länder (states). Under this arrangement, the current European Parliament, as a first chamber, would represent the European voters; the renamed Council of Ministers, as a second chamber, would represent the individual countries. This would allow the European Commission to develop from an "embryo of a European government" (see previous section) into a real European government. As in a regular parliamentary system, it would derive its legitimacy from a vote of confidence in parliament. With such a development, the European Council would become redundant, because the European Commission clearly would be the executive. Such a construction would be in the interest of both the European Parliament and the European Commission, but certainly not of the political institutions in the national capitals. The strongest resistance against such a plan comes from the British House of Commons, which would be degraded to a local parliament, analogous to an American state legislature. There is also resistance from other national capitals, such as Copenhagen, the capital of Denmark. Thus, it is not likely that the European Union will receive clearly structured institutions of a parliamentary system any time soon. The ambiguous relationships among the current institutions will continue for some time. In the context of the present section, it is important to stress once more that the European Parliament is *not* a classical legislature. It shares this function in a complex way with the Council of Ministers. This ambivalence is expressed in the following description in an official publication of the European Union:

> The Council of Ministers, which represents the Member States, adopts Community legislation (regulations, directives and decisions). It is the Community's legislature, although in certain areas specified by the Single European Act and the Maastricht Treaty it shares this function with the European Parliament.[13]

This is typical, convoluted, bureaucratic language from Brussels, which makes it so difficult for Europeans to understand the institutions of the European Union. The fault, however, is not primarily with the bureaucrats in Brussels but with the unclear delimitation of the various European Union institutions.

If we look at the legislative process in detail, the European Parliament plays four different roles according to the issue at hand: (1) agreement of European Parliament required; (2) European Parliament has no say; (3) cooperation procedure between European Parliament and Council of Ministers; (4) co-decision procedure between European Parliament and Council of Ministers.

1. Based on the Single European Act and the Maastricht treaty, there are certain issue areas where the agreement of the European Parliament is required, such as the acceptance of new European Union members. The agreement of the European Parliament is also required for changes in the rules for the European parliamentary elections, for the introduction of a European citizenship, and for the organization of a European central bank.

2. There are other issue areas where the European Parliament has no say. This is the case for changes in the existing treaties of the European Union and the proposal and ratification of new treaties. Thus, the Maastricht treaty was ratified only by the member countries, but not by the European Parliament. This is a strong limitation on the power of the European Parliament because the various treaties form the constitution of the European Union. The European Parliament is also excluded from most foreign policy and security issues.

3. The cooperation procedure is described in Article 189c of the Maastricht treaty. It applies in particular to the issue areas of transport, environment, developing aid, workplace, and regional and social policies. For these issue areas, two readings in the Council of Ministers and two in the European Parliament are required, but ultimately the views of the council prevail.

4. The co-decision procedure was introduced with Article 189b of the Maastricht treaty. It applies in particular to the internal market, consumer protection, mutual recognition of diplomas, education, culture, and technology. In these areas, the European Parliament is able to block a proposal of the Council of Ministers. But Parliament is still not able to impose its own will. If, after its second reading, an absolute majority of Parliament rejects a proposal of the council, a conciliation procedure begins. If this procedure fails, Parliament can kill a proposal of the council if once again an absolute majority of the members of Parliament reject the proposal. Thus, the co-decision procedure gives the European Parliament a veto power in certain areas.

The European Parliament has its regular sessions in the French city of Strasbourg, and France very much insists that it continues to do so. Many committee meetings, however, and some extraordinary plenary sessions are held in Brussels, the seat of the European Commission. To make things even more complicated, the secretariat-general of the parliament is located in Luxembourg. Because the members of the European Parliament therefore travel a great deal, one sometimes speaks in this context of a "circus." Table 14.1 lists the number of seats held by each of the 25 member countries. The elections for the European Parliament are held within the individual countries. The election system in all countries is proportionality. Even Great Britain changed in 1999 to proportional representation, although for national elections to the House of Commons it kept the winner-take-all system (Chapter 3).

EUROPEAN COURT OF JUSTICE

The European Court of Justice (ECJ), located in Luxembourg, has 25 judges, who are appointed by "common accord" of the national governments of the member countries. We already referred to the ECJ in our coverage of the national coasts in Chapter 4, however, in the context of the current chapter we must come back in detail to the ECJ because it is such an important institution within the European Union.

The judges of the ECJ take an oath to decide cases independently of national loyalties. They are able to follow this oath to a large extent. Two aspects of the court's decision-making process help them to do so: first, the secrecy of their deliberations and, second, the absence of the recording of dissenting opinions in the court. As a consequence, to a large extent the judges can free themselves from accountability to their home governments.

A first landmark decision came in 1963 in *Van Gend & Loos v. Nederlandse Administratie der Belastingen.* A private Dutch importer invoked the common market provisions of the Treaty of Rome against the Dutch government, which attempted to impose customs duties on specified imports. The court proclaimed:

> The Community constitutes a new legal order . . . for the benefit of which the states have limited their sovereign rights, albeit within limited fields, and the subjects of which comprise not only Member States but also nationals. Independently of the legislation of the Member States, Community law therefore not only imposes obligations on individuals but it is also intended to confer upon them rights which become part of their legal heritage.[14]

With this ruling, the court established that individuals in the European Community have rights that they can enforce against their own national governments. The Dutch government had argued that the application of the Treaty of Rome over Dutch law was solely a question for the Dutch national courts. The ECJ ruled otherwise, so that "henceforth importers around the community who objected to paying customs duties on their imports could invoke the Treaty of Rome to force their governments to live up to their commitments to create a common market."[15]

A second landmark "constitutional" decision of the ECJ was *Costa v. ENEL,* which established that where a term of the Treaty of Rome conflicts with a national statute, the treaty must prevail. In a later publication, Judge Federico Mancini justified the decision with the argument that the supremacy clause "was not only an indispensable development, it was also a logical development."[16] His logic was that in a supranational organization, community law must prevail over member state law in cases of conflict. With the ratification of the Maastricht treaty, the ECJ even received the right to impose a penalty payment on a member country that fails to comply with its judgment. Box 14.2 shows how the ECJ ruled in two cases where individuals challenged decisions of their national governments. Both cases make clear that individuals can bring national governments to court and that European Union law prevails. In both cases the individuals were tobacco companies, and the issue involved health warnings on cigarette packs. European Community legislation had ordered that such warnings should cover at least 4 percent of the pack's surface. Subsequently, British law went further and ordered that 6 percent be covered; Italian law required that the health warning be printed twice on the same side of a cigarette package. The

---

**Box 14.2 EC Court Ruling Is Setback for U.K.
Cigarette Makers**

BRUSSELS—The European Court of Justice in Luxembourg ruled that Britain did-
n't breach European Community law by requiring larger health warnings on domestically produced cigarette packs than those called for by the EC. At the same
time, however, the EC court decided against Italy requiring two health warnings on
the same side of a cigarette package. The rulings were in response to two separate cases brought by the tobacco industry. The British case marked a setback for
British tobacco companies, which had argued that the U.K. government went too
far by requiring that health warnings and information on tar and nicotine levels
take up 6% of the surface they are printed on. A ruling adopted by the EC in 1989
calls for such warnings to cover at least 4% of the surface. The British law was challenged by Gallaher Ltd., a unit of American Brands; Imperial Tobacco Ltd., which
is part of the Hanson group; and Rothmans International Tobacco (UK) Ltd., a unit
of Rothmans International PLC.

Source: *Wall Street Journal,* June 23, 1993.

**Box 14.3 European Union Court Ruling Sets Affirmative
Action Limits**

BRUSSELS—The European Court of Justice, delivering a landmark ruling on sex discrimination, said today that governments could not impose affirmative action programs that give women absolute priority for jobs and promotions. In a case brought
by a male landscaper who works for the city of Bremen, in northern Germany, the
court ruled that such programs violated European Union equal opportunities law.

Source: *New York Times,* October 18, 1995.

ECJ ruled in the first case for the British government, and in the second case against the Italian government. These cases illustrate in how much detail the European Court intervenes in
national legislation. Box 14.3 shows how the ECJ, like the U.S. Supreme Court, delivers
landmark rulings with regard to sex discrimination and affirmative action at the workplace.

Overall, the ECJ has become very important in the legal system of the European
Union. Individuals, national governments, and the institutions of the Union must respect
the rulings of the court. Mary L. Volcansek makes this general point for Italy in writing that
"in the space of three decades, the Italian Constitutional Court accorded supremacy to
European Community law in the Italian legal system."[17] What holds for Italy also holds for
all other EU countries.

Do national governments bring each other to court in Luxembourg? On the basis of
Article 170 of the Treaty of Rome they can do so, but this article is rarely applied. The reason is that confrontations between member countries are potentially dangerous for the stability of the European Union. To prevent such inflammatory disputes, the court has actively
and successfully encouraged the increased use of Article 169 procedures, whereby it is the

European Commission that initiates action against a particular member country for not following community legal obligations. This device has a more objective character and allows a member country to more easily accept a ruling of the court than if it is directly confronted by another member country. To depoliticize its rulings even further, the ECJ often tries to settle an issue on the basis of Article 177, which allows it to define an issue not in terms of a dispute between national governments but between private parties of the respective countries. All this shows once again the great influence of the court for the internal life of the European Union. Lawyers in the member countries increasingly pay attention to the rulings in Luxembourg.

Even in areas such as criminal law, where national law has always been understood to reign supreme, European law is taking precedence over national law. In a far reaching decision in September 2005, the ECJ ruled that the EU has the power to introduce harmonized criminal law for its member states, creating for the first time a body of European criminal law that all members must adopt.[18] The reason why this is so crucial is that one of the last vestiges—namely, control over how to punish criminals and on what grounds—has largely moved from the national level to the supranational level. National authorities will continue to police particular offenses and national judges will still adjudicate whether a crime has been committed or not, but with this ruling, the European Commission gained the right to request member states to enforce various EU laws by using civil and criminal penalties.

This ruling was occasioned by a conflict between the Council of Ministers and the European Commission, which challenged the former about its interpretation of the "Framework Decision on the Protection of the Environment Through Criminal Law." The Council of Ministers, representing national interests, argued that, as EU law currently stands, member states cannot be forced to impose criminal penalties established by the EU. The European Commission, the most supranational institution in the EU, disputed this view and asked the ECJ to adjudicate this dispute, with the ECJ ultimately supporting the commission's stance.

This controversial ruling was fought mostly by the "older" members of the EU. Eleven governments opposed this ruling: Ireland, Denmark, Finland, Sweden, the Netherlands, Germany, France, the UK, Spain, Portugal, and Greece. The President of the European Commission welcomed the ruling, stating: "This is a watershed decision. It paves the way for more democratic and more efficient lawmaking at the EU level."[19] If this ruling passes through the European Parliament and a qualified majority of member states, it must be adopted by all 25 member states even if some may vehemently disagree with it. It is likely that it will pass, as the ruling will enhance the influence of MEPs.

There is no European national guard, such as the National Guard in the United States, to enforce European Union law, but the European Court of Justice can rely quite well on the member countries to enforce its rulings. To be sure, the national governments may sometimes protest over a particular ruling of the court, as seen with the ECJ decision about criminal law, but ultimately they will accept the legitimacy of the ruling. One of the most celebrated instances of a member country defying the court was the *Sheepmeat* case in 1979, in which the court ruled against the French government for imposing restrictions on the import of sheep meat from Great Britain. At first, France defied the ruling. But after losing in the first two instances, it accepted a third ruling of the court and asked merely for a delay in implementing its obligations.

EUROPEAN BUREAUCRACY

Perhaps the best guarantee of the European Union's continued existence is the many thousands of bureaucrats it employs. These "Eurocrats," as they are often called, have an obvious career interest in the continuation of European Union operations. In addition, many lobbyists working in Brussels have a personal professional interest in the survival of the Union. Over the years, all of these people, working directly or indirectly for the European Union, have developed some elements of a common cosmopolitan European culture. They tend to live in the same neighborhoods in Brussels, and they attend the same parties and share the same gossip. When the Eurocrats went on strike one day—without regard to nationality—it was said, of course as a joke, that this was the best sign yet that European integration was alive and well. A drawback to the development of this bureaucracy in Brussels is that ordinary European citizens increasingly see the European Union as a giant, anonymous organization over which they have no control. And yet, they sense that this distant bureaucracy has an important impact on their daily lives.

WHAT DOES THE EUROPEAN UNION DO?

What the EU can do depends very much on the resources it has. This raises a very important question: How is the EU financed? The EU is financed by essentially three elements: first, what is called *traditional own resources* (TOR). These are customs duties and agricultural duties levied on imports coming from countries outside the EU. A small amount is also contributed to the EU budget by sugar producers who pay levies for exporting sugar. That first element covers about 11.6 percent of total EU revenue. The second resource for the EU budget comes from levies based on the various member states' VAT (value added tax) levels, which accounts for about 14.4 percent of total EU revenue. Finally, the third and most important resource of EU budget are the contributions made by the various member states measured as a percentage of their GNI (gross national income). This third resource accounts for 73 percent of the EU budget. The total EU budget is currently capped at 1.24 percent of combined national GNIs.[20]

A glimpse at the expenditure side of the EU budget reveals that by far the largest amount is used up by agricultural policy and rural development, around 45 percent in 2003. This is followed by structural and cohesion funds (34 percent), internal policies (7 percent), external actions (5 percent), and, finally, pre-accession aid (3 percent).[21]

Agricultural Policy

In the 1970s the agricultural policies of the EU amounted to little more than subsidizing farmers. This often led to surpluses of "mountains of butter" and "lakes of milk" that were bought by the European Community and then destroyed in order to stabilize prices, while at the same time consumers paid relatively high prices for these goods. This overemphasis on food production had its roots in the postwar food shortages as well as the strong influence of farmers in the European Community. However, in 2003 the Common Agricultural Policy (CAP) moved to much broader goals: sustainable agricultural policies, which not only means increasing the competitiveness of European farmers but also achieving this with concerns for the ecological balance and the viability of farming as a respected profession.

But the CAP also is concerned about food quality and food safety in addition to animal welfare. There are now precise regulations as to how much space pigs, laying hens, and calves must have in their holding pens; light, temperature, and floor requirements; and how they must be treated during transport and prior to slaughter.[22]

A well-known point of contention between the United States and the EU is over genetically modified organisms (GMOs). The EU has been very suspicious of gene-spliced crops, termed "Frankenfood" in Europe, particularly in the wake of the outbreak of mad-cow disease in the United Kingdom and other European countries. The United States takes the view that the EU uses the health concerns of the European public as an excuse to impose nontariff barriers. Eventually the EU agreed that some GMOs can be sold in Europe, but only after they are labeled as such and when their traceability (where did they originate from?) is ensured. There is a healthy distrust among much of the European public for GMOs, seriously limiting the sales of such products.

Regional and Development Policy

The Structural and Cohesion Fund is designed to promote solidarity among EU countries by reducing developmental gaps among the regions and alleviating disparities among EU citizens. Among the most important elements of the Structural and Cohesion Fund are the development of infrastructure, such as roads, railroads, ports, bridges, airports, power lines, power generating plants, and others. The fund also provides support to prevent industrial decline, support the development of rural areas, provide training for workers, combat long-term unemployment, and promote research and development.

Since Ireland joined the EU in 1973, it received over 17 billion pounds in structural and cohesion funds. In the last ten years alone, the funds helped develop major road projects, rail systems, and the construction of seaports. In 1973, Ireland, Greece, Spain, and Portugal qualified for cohesion funds because their GNP per capita was less than 90 percent of the EU average. In 2003, Ireland did not qualify for the receipt of funds because it passed this threshold as a result of outstanding economic performance. However, as Table 14.1 shows, all of the ten new entrants to the EU do qualify for cohesion funds as a result of their GDP per capita being lower than 90 percent of the EU average.

As these short examples show, the two main goals of EU policy are agricultural and regional development policy. However, these are such broad definitions that it can be said that literally no policy area is left untouched by the EU. A remarkable feat occurred when, on January 1, 2002, the euro bills and coins were introduced in 12 out of the then 15 EU countries. Sweden, Denmark, and the United Kingdom still use their own national currencies. The European Central Bank described the establishment of the euro as "the biggest monetary changeover in history."[23] The ten new entrants will adopt the euro in the near future.

Common Currency—the Euro

Great efforts have been made by governments to persuade European publics to embrace the euro. As might be expected, it is not easy for any society to give up its currency, as it represents part of the identity as a nation. The economic advantages of having a unified currency across (most) of the EU area are evident. Anyone who has traveled in Europe before the euro knows the hassles connected with having to change currency (and paying transaction fees and commissions) every time one arrives in a different country. In addition, macroeconomic advantages of the euro range from eliminating exchange rate fluctuations, to price transparency that invigorates competition, to more opportunities for foreign investors. Also, because the economic area covered by the euro is so much larger than the previous individual economies with their own currencies, external shocks to the European economy will have much lower impacts on the euro area than they had when each nation had its own currency and was not economically integrated. Moreover, having a single currency in a market based on the four freedoms of movement (people, goods, capital, and services) and that encompasses over 450 million consumers makes the EU a powerful countervailing power to the economic hegemony of the United States and enhances its impact in international organizations such as the International Monetary Fund (IMF) and the World Bank.[24]

Though the introduction of the euro was an unqualified success, certain members of some EU countries' governments would like to rescind the euro and go back to their national currencies. Two Italian ministers, in a populist attempt to curry favor with voters who are dissatisfied with the economy have made the euro the scapegoat and have asked for a referendum to abolish the euro.[25] However, nobody in the Italian government is taking these suggestions seriously, as there are no procedures of how a country in fact could leave the euro.

More problematic for the public acceptance of the EU is the fashion by which France and Germany dealt with the "convergence criteria" connected to the establishment of the euro. Prior to the introduction of the euro in 1997, Germany insisted on the following two criteria: that governments must keep their deficits under 3 percent of their GDP and their national debts under 60 percent of GDP. Germany was concerned that with the introduction of the euro, member states might engage in lavish spending programs leading to inflation—an economic curse with which Germany had a particularly bitter experience in the 1920s. However, in the fall of 2003 both France and Germany experienced economic recessions, forcing them to exceed the 3 percent deficit rule of the convergence criteria. In theory, any member state exceeding one of these criteria would have to pay excessive fines. Alas, neither Germany nor France was punished, to the chagrin of many smaller European countries such as Ireland, Portugal, and Austria, which under heavy political and social costs stuck to the criteria. As a result, the existing rift between bigger and smaller EU members opened even further and a perception among the European publics grew that there were really two Europes: one for the big, powerful countries that could flaunt rules and another for the smaller ones that complied with them.

Continued Expansion: Where Does "Europe" End?

As Table 14.1 shows, ten new countries became members of the EU on May 1, 2004. In addition to Malta and Cyprus, eight countries belonged to the former Communist Central Eastern European bloc. The table also shows dramatic differences in per capita GDP, labor productivity, and labor costs between the "established" EU-15 countries and the ten newcomers. Incorporation of these eight relatively poor countries raises concerns about large numbers of cheap labor arriving in the "old" EU countries, that the more developed EU countries will have to pay for the reconstruction of the new Central and Eastern European members, and that investment capital from the richer EU countries will move towards the east, where labor costs are a fraction of those in the west. In fact, the Eastern European accession countries are already engaged in a "race to the bottom" in order to attract foreign direct investment from the rest of the EU.

In addition, some observers are concerned that the generous welfare systems in the "core" EU states such as Germany and Austria might act like a magnet and attract members of the accession countries. Just like countries are competing against each other in order to attract investment by lowering standards, so might welfare states have to begin lowering benefits to deter Central and Eastern Europeans to move to richer EU countries. Hans Werner Sinn, head of the Institute of Economics at the University of Munich, has argued that competition between states to reduce the generosity of their welfare systems in order to deter immigrants will lead to an erosion of the German welfare state, so that "in 50 years we'll have a situation like that in America."[26] Indeed, many countries imposed restrictions on the eligibility for welfare benefits to members of the accession countries: For example, members from the accession countries will have to be employed at least for two years before they can claim welfare benefits. In Germany and Austria, countries that directly border on the new accession countries, Central and Eastern Europeans will have to be employed for at least seven years before they can receive welfare benefits.

Though some of these concerns are well founded, similar arguments were heard when Spain, Greece, and Portugal were considered for membership. In the meantime, these countries have become trusted members of the EU, have seen dramatic economic development, and have upheld basic principles of democracy and human rights within their borders. The rationale for the 2004 expansion was that incorporating the ten countries would unite Europe in peace after a history of division and conflict, extending prosperity and stability to its member states, thus making Europe a safer place and stimulating economic and social reform in the new member states. It is very likely that these effects will occur in the long run.

The process of EU enlargement was negotiated through the treaty of Nice (signed in 2001), which laid the institutional groundwork for future enlargement. It was ratified in all the EU parliaments, except in Denmark and Ireland, which required referenda. The Irish people rejected the treaty in 2001 by 54 percent but in 2002 voted for it. The citizens in the ten accession countries all supported their respective accession treaty via referendum.

OUTLOOK

Expansion continues unabated. Next on the horizon of EU enlargement are Romania and Bulgaria, which are scheduled to join the EU on January 1, 2007. For countries to join the EU, they must meet the "Copenhagen criteria," which state that a prospective member must:

- be a stable democracy, respecting human rights, the rule of law, and the protection of minorities.
- have a functioning market economy .
- adopt the common rules, standards, and policies that make up the body of EU law.

Though both Romania and Bulgaria are on track for joining the EU, particular doubt is cast on Romania, which is often described as the "poorhouse" of Europe, with a GDP per capita that is less then 30 percent of the EU average. Both countries suffer from rampant corruption, weak public administration, and little regard for the rule of law. The EU has established a "safeguard clause" that comes into effect if the two countries do not make enough progress toward fulfilling the Copenhagen criteria. Employing the safeguard clause would mean that entry is postponed to 2008.

Undaunted, in November 2005, the European Commission presented an "enlargement package" that includes potential candidates for further enlargement in the Western Balkans, such as Albania, Bosnia and Herzegovina, Macedonia, Serbia and Montenegro, and Kosovo. These countries will be screened in terms of their progress toward fulfilling the Copenhagen criteria.

One of the most hotly debated countries considered for EU entry is Turkey. In October 2005, membership talks between the EU and Turkey began in earnest, thus securing Turkey's 40-year campaign to become a member of the EU. Though it could take ten years for Turkey to become an actual member, fierce resistance was put forth by many EU-15 countries, particularly France, Germany, and Austria. Austria had favored a solution that would grant Turkey "associate membership" status, but not full membership status. Austria finally gave in to full-membership talks with Turkey, after Croatia was also allowed to engage in membership talks with the EU. In a Eurobarometer opinion poll conducted in May/June 2005, only about 37 percent of the people in the current EU-25 favored EU membership for Turkey, with about 28 percent support from the Greeks, 21 percent support from Germans and the French, and 16 and 10 percent support from the Cypriots and Austrians, respectively.

There are three main concerns voiced against membership of Turkey in the EU: its size, poverty, and religion. First, if Turkey joined the EU in about ten years, it would have an expected population of around 80 million people. Given the drastic decline of Germany's population, which stands at around 82 million now. Turkey could easily be the most populous country in the EU ten years from now. With a population growth rate of 1.1 percent compared to .15 percent for the EU average, Turkey's population grows seven times faster than the EU average. This could mean that in terms of votes in the Council of Ministers and Seats in the EU Parliament, Turkey will have at least the same influence if not more than London, Berlin, or Paris.

The second concern voiced against Turkey's membership is its poverty level. In 2002, Turkey's GDP per capita was $6,408 in U.S. currency (measured in purchasing power parities), while in the EU-15 it was U.S. $26,019. In other words, the per capita value of all goods and services produced in Turkey is only about one-fourth of that produced on average in the EU-15. Education in Turkey also lags seriously behind all the EU-25 countries. The PISA scores (OECD's Program for International Student Assessment), which were designed to measure the effectiveness of school systems in providing young people with a solid foundation of knowledge and skills, show Turkey to be last compared to the EU-25 in terms of reading and science achievement. Thus, a serious developmental gap exists between Turkey and the EU-25, let alone between Turkey and the EU-15, which will require massive amounts of financial assistance over a long period of time. Most of this assistance will have to be provided for by the more well-to-do members of the EU.

The third issue, and for many observers the most intractable of all concerns, is the fact that Turkey is 99.8 percent Muslim. With the horrific attacks on 9/11/2001, the gruesome assassination of Theo van Gogh in the Netherlands by a radical Muslim, and the growing Islamophobia in Europe since the early 1990s triggered by increasing immigration of Muslims into relatively homogeneous European nations, many observers argue that European citizens will find it very difficult to accept Turkey as a partner in the EU on cultural grounds. One example of the cultural chasm separating Turkish and Western cultures can be found in the "honor killings" that have occurred in Berlin, Germany, where over a period of four months six Turkish women were murdered by their own family members, mostly their brothers or husbands, because they either wanted to end a relationship with

Box 14.4 The Death of a Muslim Woman

"THE WHORE LIVED LIKE A GERMAN"

In the past four months, six Muslim women living in Berlin have been brutally murdered by family members. Their crime? Trying to break free and live Western lifestyles. Within their communities, the killers are revered as heroes for preserving their family dignity. How can such a horrific and shockingly archaic practice be flourishing in the heart of Europe? The deaths have sparked momentary outrage, but will they change the grim reality for Muslim women? ... The shots came from nowhere and within minutes the young Turkish mother [Hatin Surucu] standing at the Berlin bus stop was dead.... Hatin Surucu, was not the victim of random violence, but likely died at the hands of her own family in what is known as an "honor killing." Hatin's crime, it appears, was the desire to lead a normal life in her family's adopted land. The vivacious 23-year-old beauty, who was raised in Berlin, divorced the Turkish cousin she was forced to marry at age 16. She also discarded her Islamic head scarf, enrolled in a technical school where she was training to become an electrician and began dating German men. For her family, such behavior represented the ultimate shame—the embrace of "corrupt" Western ways. Days after the crime, police arrested her three brothers, ages 25, 24 and 18. The youngest of the three allegedly bragged to his girlfriend about the Feb. 7 killing.... In many cases, fathers—and sometimes even mothers—single out their youngest son to do the killing.... In some cases, these boys are revered by their community and fellow inmates as "honor heroes"—a dementedly skewed status they carry with them for the rest of their lives.... Sometimes they are forced to kill their favorite sister.

Source: SPIEGEL ONLINE, March 2, 2005.http://www.spiegel.ed/international/0, 151,344374,00.html.
By Jody K. Biehl in Berlin

their Turkish partners, refused to wear the traditional *hijab*, (the Muslim headscarf), or, the ultimate shame, decided to adopt a Western lifestyle (see Box 14.4). Other observers raise the issue of geography: From a geographical perspective, only a very small part of Turkey is located on the European continent, which is separated from Asia Minor by the Bosporus strait. On which basis, they ask, can Turkey be admitted to the "European" Union?

To be sure, much of the negative reactions by European publics is based simply on racism and xenophobia, which cannot be tolerated, particularly given Europe's past. Yet in the case of Turkish accession and the relentless expansion by the EU, many Europeans are asking themselves the question, "What is Europe, and where does it end?" With accession of so many more countries, many of them increasingly diverging in cultures, economic capacities, and religions, on which grounds could a European identity emerge?

A CONSTITUTION FOR EUROPE: "NON" AND "NEE"

The purpose of creating a European constitution is to enshrine in one encompassing framework the multitude of complex treaties that have hitherto governed the EU. Moreover, the

Union's confusing three-pillar structure was to be streamlined into one body of law with a single legal personality. The EU constitution entailed a mechanism that would have enabled the EU to continue enlargements without having to establish separate treaties for each wave of expansion.

Ratifying the EU constitution could be achieved in two ways: by votes in the national parliaments or by the politically riskier method of referendum. For the constitutional treaty to come into effect, all 25 EU countries must ratify it. Before the French cast their ballots on the treaty, nine countries (Austria, Germany, Greece, Hungary, Italy, Lithuania, Slovakia, Slovenia, and Spain) had already endorsed the EU constitution. Spain did so in a referendum, with 77 percent of Spaniards supporting the document, although the voter turnout was barely over 42 percent.

The date for the French referendum on the EU treaty was set for May 29, 2005. That date was awaited with much anticipation as France was the first, large, founding member of the EU to hold such a referendum. Most remarkably, the French constitution did not necessitate a referendum on this issue. It could have been passed via votes in Parliament. However, a year prior to the 2005 referendum, French President Jacques Chirac decided to ratify the EU treaty via referendum, confident that it was winnable.

It was not. Election night brought a debacle for the French President and the "oui" supporters, as around 55 percent of the voters rejected the treaty. Voter turnout was a robust 70 percent. This result sent shockwaves across Europe as there was no "Plan B" in terms of what to do in case of a rejection of the treaty. Only three days after the French rejected the treaty, the Dutch held their referendum. The Dutch tend to be very loyal "Europeans," but there the treaty was shot down also, even more decisively—with 62 percent of the voters saying "nee" to the EU constitution and turnout of almost 63 percent. The people of two founding member states spoke, and they delivered a resounding slap in the face to the elites who favored passage of the treaty.

The shock of these two elections was so severe that the ratification schedule (ratification of the EU treaty in other countries) was suspended and replaced by an indefinite "period of reflection." The purpose of the suspension of the ratification schedule was to avoid further blows to the EU treaty and allow leaders of countries with wavering publics, such as Great Britain, to extract themselves from the process without having to face a referendum (see Photo 14.1).

Why did French and Dutch voters reject the EU constitution? It is fair to say that very few voters actually read the constitution before they made their decision. Few issues in the EU treaty were part of the public debate, which itself was cleverly orchestrated by the respective "yes" and "no" organizers. In France, section III of the treaty, which dealt with competition policy and market economy principles, became the focus of the "non" campaign, even though many of these principles date back to the Treaty of Rome signed in 1957! Critics of the document argued that section III would undermine social solidarity by favoring the well-to-do on the backs of the working class. In addition, with 10 percent unemployment, public fears were rampant that people from the new accession countries would come to France and take away jobs from the locals. The poster child of these fears was the imagined "Polish plumber" who would show up immediately to fix the sink and charge less than the French plumber, thereby driving French plumbers out of business.[27]

The most outspoken critics of the constitution were to be found on the either side of the political spectrum. The former socialist prime minister Laurent Fabius stirred up a very

PHOTO 14.1 Campaign poster of the revolutionary communist league imploring. Voters to vote "no" on the EU constitution and on Chira. The sign the protesters carry says: "Europe without borders—yes, Europe without jobs—no."

popular "non" campaign in his party, winning over many skeptics, even though the Socialist Party was officially a supporter of the EU constitution. Fabius feared that the constitution was too promarket, would undermine the French welfare state and leave insufficient protections for workers' interests. The communists, together with the Greens, unionists, and the antiglobalization movement made similar arguments about the undermining of the welfare state, the exploitation of the environment, and the loss of French identity should this referendum pass.

On the right of the political spectrum nationalists such as Jean Marie LePen were also against the EU constitution as he feared that this would allow even easier access of foreigners to come to France. Peasants and farmers remained unconvinced that supporting this document would be in their favor. In addition, the "no" vote on the constitution was as much a referendum on Jacques Chirac's policies as it was about the future of Europe as many parties and movements used this opportunity to strike a blow at the substance of Chirac's policies as well as his style of government.

In the Netherlands, the people voted "nee" for different reasons. Dutch "no" voters were concerned about "Europe" becoming too powerful and interfering with the traditionally very liberal Dutch policies on gay marriage and soft drugs. In addition, after the murder of filmmaker Theo van Gogh, the Dutch have become much more sensitive to immigration and the challenges associated with the growing heterogeneity of their society.

Overall, however, the rejection in both France and the Netherlands of the EU treaty highlighted the general disillusionment of the people with the highly elitist character of the EU. In these two referenda, people voted not only on the EU constitution, but on what they thought about the introduction of the euro, enlargement from 15 to 25 EU countries in 2004, the initiation of talks with Turkey to become a future member, and the general elitist way things are done in Brussels. It is well known that the EU suffers from a "democratic deficit," meaning that decisions are made at very high levels within the EU but also within the respective member states, and do not necessarily correspond to the desires of the citizens. There was remarkably little citizen input when the euro was introduced, and when the 2004 enlargement was decided. Once the voters finally had a chance to make their voices heard, they reflected on the totality of their concerns about the EU, and their verdict was a resounding "no." The rapid introduction of the euro and the zeal with which EU elites pushed through enlargement was too quick for many citizens, and with their vote they essentially called for a pause in the fast-paced changes.

The future of this EU constitution is indeed very bleak. It is highly unlikely that voters will change their minds in the near future on the same treaty. Not much will happen until the French general elections in 2007, from which new impulses might emerge to continue the push for a EU constitution. For the EU to go forward it needs a document that does essentially what is enshrined in the current document: streamlining the various treaties in one coherent treaty. Eventually, the EU will have a constitution, but it will take more time than anticipated by the Brussels elites. The EU will continue for now on the basis of a confusing patchwork of treaties, pillars, different competences, and so on that were established in the past. This complex arrangement, however, will not help endear the EU to the publics in Europe.[28]

Oftentimes critics of the EU integration process underestimate how far Europe has come. Only a little over 60 years ago, the bloodiest battles in the history of mankind occurred in Europe together with the most gruesome genocide ever conceived. Today, Europe, despite some undeniable challenges, is a flourishing, dynamic, modern single market encompassing over 450 million consumers who are at peace with one another. The EU project remains one of the most ambitious undertakings ever devised, in which countries voluntarily give up their sovereignty in order to reap the fruits that grow on common ground. The challenges that confront individual European democracies in the age of globalization are immense. European integration will ensure that European democracies can successfully compete against other economic superpowers such as the United States, Japan, and the future superpowers of India and China.

Discussion Questions

1. What does Europe gain/lose by establishing an "ever closer union"?
2. How would you define what "Europe" is?
3. Can you foresee a time when there is a "United States of Europe"? Yes/no, why?
4. What arguments favor/disfavor Turkey joining the EU?
5. Why is there a "democratic deficit" in the EU?
6. How would you suggest making the EU more responsive to the people?
7. In which policy areas do you think is the EU the strongest/the weakest?
8. What institutions account for the supranational/intergovernmental character of the EU?
9. Compare the EU institutions with those of the United States. What are the similarities/differences?

---

[1] BBC News. Q&A. GE's Failed Merger. July 4, 2001.

[2] *Neue Zürcher Zeitung*, April 24, 1996.

[3] *The Guardian*, April 2, 1996.

[4] Ibid.

[5] Philipp Büchler. *Die Entstehung der Sozialcharta des Europarates.* (Lizentiatsarbeit, Universität Bern, 1993).

[6] http://europa.eu.int/.

[7] Shapiro and Stone, "The New Constitutional Politics," 412.

[8] *The ABC of Community Law.* (Luxembourg: Office for Official Publications of the European Communities, 1991).

[9] *Europe in Ten Lessons.* (Luxembourg: Office for Official Publications of the European Communities, 1992).

[10] From UEN Party Platform: http://www.uengroup.org/home.html.

[11] From Independence-Democracy Party platform: http://www.europarl.eu.int/inddem/political%20program.htm.

[12] Giacomo Benedetto. 2004 European Parliament Election Briefing No. 22. (EPERN—European Parties Elections and Referendum Network).

[13] Ibid.

[14] Anne-Marie Burley and Walter Mattli. Europe Before the Court: A Political Theory of Legal Integration. *International Organization* 47, Winter 1993: 62–63.

[15] Ibid., 61.

[16] Ibid., 66.

[17] Mary L. Volcansek. Impact of Judicial Policies in the European Community: The Italian Constitutional Court and the European Community Law. *Western Political Quarterly* 42, December 1989: 580.

[18] Times OnLine. Europe Wins the Power to Jail British Citizens. September 14, 2005.

[19] Europa Rapid. Court of Justice Strengthens Democracy and Efficiency in European Community Lawmaking. http://www.europa.eu.int/rapid/pressreleases

[20] See the Europa Web site, http://www.europa.eu.int/budget/.

[21] Ibid.

[22] http://www. europa.eu.int/comm/food/animal/welfare/farm/.

[23] http://www.euro.ecb.int/.

[24]http://www.europa.eu.int/.

[25] BBC News. Italian Minister Seeks Lira Return. June 5, 2005.
http://news.bbc.co.uk/1/hi/world/europe/4615781.stm.

[26]Hans Wermer Sinn. "Den Sozials taat filt es zu schützen" *Netzeitung*, June 30, 2006.

[27]Cohen-Tanugi, Laurent. The End of Europe? *Foreign Affairs*, vol. 84, issue 5,
November/December 2005.

[28] Ibid.

CHAPTER 15

Globalization and European Democracies

Throughout this book, the central assumption is that countries are sovereign policymakers. Particularly in Chapter 9 on policy outcomes, we have argued that a whole host of outcomes, among them unemployment, economic growth, health, education, and environmental outcomes, are the result of idiosyncratic types of election systems, political parties, the processes of cabinet formation, the role of interest groups, and the specific historical experiences of modernization.

In the last chapter on the European Union, however, we highlighted the central trade-off that comes with joining the EU: In order to take advantage of a common market encompassing over 450 million consumers, the sovereignty of nations becomes restricted. How does joining the EU restrict sovereignty? If people can travel across intra-EU borders without any border controls; if goods, capital, and services can freely cross borders without the capacity of states to impose duties; if nations cannot shape exchange rate policies anymore because they all share the same currency (except the UK, Denmark, Sweden, and the new accession countries for now); if they are limited in the way they can engage in economic policy because they are not supposed to exceed budget deficits of 3 percent; if the quality of products must correspond to certain "harmonized" standards; if there are EU-wide regulations ranging from the environment to how to treat farm animals, to labor regulation; if the setting of interest rates is performed by a European-wide central bank; if EU law takes precedence over national law in increasing measure—if these and many other effects of the EU apply, one might say that the capacity of a country to engage in its "own" policies is restricted. These are just a few examples on how the EU limits the sovereignty of countries to engage in its own policymaking. This does not negate our claims in Chapter 9 that policy outcomes do reflect national idiosyncrasies; however, there is no doubt that the maneuvering room for national policymaking is becoming more tightly circumscribed.

But what does "Europeanization" have to do with "globalization"? Both of these concepts are in fact very much related, insofar as they both mean a reduction of sovereignty of nations. However, from the examples just given and from what we heard in Chapter 14, it is clear that Europeanization goes much further and deeper than globalization ever could, at least in the foreseeable future. The difference of globalization is that in the European context, the process is driven by clearly defined procedures, under the auspices of national elites, and ultimately, at least ideally, by the citizens of the various countries. Through referenda, a democratic process, they vote on whether or not to join the EU, notwithstanding the widespread observations that the EU suffers from a "democratic deficit." In addition, many other decisions are made by the people's representatives in the various nations' parliaments. What makes the EU such a unique historical process is precisely the fact that it unfolds against a detailed set of regulations, the so-called "acquis communautaire," a document that today encompasses about 80,000 pages. Once the people of a country have, through the democratic process of referendum, decided that they wanted to join the EU, this means that they are then obliged to accept and implement the "acquis," as it is known in short. The acquis, this common body of EU law, covers everything from free movement of people, to competition policy, to environmental issues, to the collection and use of statistics, to external relations, social policy and employment, and many other policy areas.

Thus, the difference between Europeanization and globalization is twofold: First, Europeanization is based, at least ideally, on a democratic process that involves either the citizens directly or their representatives. Second, it spells out in detail what it means for a country to join the EU. Globalization has no democratic impetus and there is no document that is comparable to the acquis that regulates in such detail every aspect of cross-border relations. Rather, globalization is a process that is "anarchic," that is, market driven without any regulation or oversight. Europeanization is driven by governments, whereas globalization is driven by markets.

WHAT IS GLOBALIZATION?

Globalization is a process whose origins are directly related to advances in technology, particularly transportation technologies. Globalization can be described as the "obliteration of distance" as a result of the development of sea-going ships; the invention of the locomotive, the airplane, and automobiles; and development of other transportation technologies such as the invention of the compass; and the utilization of motorways and containerization. In addition, large-scale transportation projects such as the opening of the Suez Canal and the completion of the Union Pacific Railroad in 1869—and, in more recent times, the Channel Tunnel connecting the United Kingdom with France—aid in the unfolding of globalization.

PHOTO 15.1 Container ships are a crucial link in global trade as they significantly reduce transportation costs.

There is a certain "hype" surrounding globalization, and the media portrays it as if it were a recent phenomenon. "Separate individuals have become more and more enslaved under a power alien to them . . . a power which has become more and more enormous and, in the last instance, turns out to be world market." This quote could have been gleaned from the sign of any antiglobalization protester who demonstrated at the latest G-8 meeting. Yet, these words were uttered over 150 years ago by Karl Marx as he penned *The German Ideology* in 1845/46![1]

In fact, in 1913, shortly before World War I, world merchandise exports as a percentage of GDP had reached such impressive levels that, after significant drops in the interwar period and also after 1950, it took the OECD until the late 1970s to reach similar levels of world trade. Trade, measured as the average of exports and imports as a percentage of GDP, in the United Kingdom was 27.7 percent in 1913; this level dropped to 13.1 percent in 1950, increased to 16.6 percent in 1970, and reached 21.1 percent in 1987, significantly short of the 27.7 percent the UK had achieved in 1913.[2] Thus, globalization is an uneven process marked by periods of rapid expansion of trade followed by contractions during the interwar years when many countries, but particularly the United States, took an isolationist stance and also during the immediate years after World War II.

It is true that the process of globalization accelerated in more recent years with the development of information and communication technologies. Advances in telecommunications, digital systems, satellite technology, fiber optics, and the Internet have dramatically reduced transportation and transaction costs, making products and services that were hitherto not tradeable ready to be exchanged in the global marketplace. Such products include perishable and seasonal fashion items, as well as the production and interpretation of information itself, such as management consultancy, films, television news, and others. A prime example of how globalization obliterates distance is today's capacity to outsource customer services for high-tech products to India or the Indian physician who interprets via the Internet a patient's x-ray taken in the United States or Europe. These technological advances are complemented by international organizations, such as the International Monetary Fund (IMF), the World Bank, and particularly the World Trade Organization (WTO), the latter of which zealously works towards a reduction of tariff and nontariff barriers in order to let the world market deal its "invisible hand" even more effectively.

The consequences of these technological developments and the impact of the WTO on the world economy are staggering: International trade has been growing at a much larger rate than economic output. Between 1950 and 1997 global economic growth increased by a factor of six while trade increased by a factor of 18 compared to 1950. Foreign direct investments increased from $12 billion in 1970 to $270 billion in 1995. One of the most direct effects of technological development on globalization is the capacity of capital markets to move international capital. Cross-border transactions of bonds and equities have grown by a factor of between 50 to 100 from 1980 to 1996, to the tune of over 1 trillion dollars a day.[3]

The consequences of globalization not only have an economic dimension, they also affect communities as international "cultural products" such as music, films, television, and others penetrate into hitherto local areas. For example, in 1996, the TV show, "Baywatch" was the most widely viewed show, with 1.1 billion viewers in 142 countries. It was shown on every continent except Antarctica.[4] By 2001, "Buffy the Vampire Slayer" had become the most popular TV show in the world, and today, the Chinese can watch the

foibles of "The Simpsons." In 2001, the share of U.S. films as a percentage of all films in Germany was 77 percent, and this share is 74 percent in the United Kingdom, 62 percent in Spain, 60 percent in Italy, and 47 percent in France. In all countries, except the United Kingdom, this percentage grew steadily between 1984 and 2001.[5]

Another form of cultural globalization can be observed in the various American traditions that have gained popularity in continental European countries, such as Halloween. Halloween originated with the Celts, is Pagan in tradition, and was transferred with Irish immigrants to the United States. Since only very recently, it is being celebrated in continental European countries such as Austria, with the exact same trappings of jack-o-lanterns, kids disguising themselves as ghosts, witches, or imps and demanding treats—except in Austria kids don't say "trick or treat" but rather "süss oder sauer" (sweet or sour). An Irish tradition thus was translated via migration to the United States, where it became widespread. Today, this tradition is making the trip back to Europe via satellite beams directly into households of Europeans who eagerly absorb American popular culture.

This little vignette demonstrates that along with technological development and cultural adaptation, migration is also a central element of globalization. Since the late 1950s, countries such as Germany and Austria have actively recruited so-called "guestworkers," first from Italy, then from former Yugoslavia and Turkey, to help in the reconstruction of their countries after World War II and during the years of the economic miracle of the 1960s and early 1970s. After the quadrupling of the oil prices in 1973/1974, however, labor immigration was curbed as economic activity came to a sudden stop. Nevertheless, incentives given to guestworkers to return home did not have the desired effects. In fact, despite a stop on labor migration, immigration into European countries continued on the basis of family reunification—the guestworkers brought in their wives and extended families, increasing the percentage of the foreign population.[6]

Figure 15.1 shows the foreign population across various European democracies over a ten-year gap. In most countries that percentage has increased over time, although it has decreased for Belgium, Sweden, and the Netherlands. Switzerland has by far the highest percentage of foreign population among its ranks, which is partly explained by the difficulty of becoming Swiss, followed by Austria and Germany. It is important to distinguish between *foreign population* and *foreign-born population*. The latter tends to generate higher percentages of the total resident population because it also includes subjects who are foreign born but have attained national citizenship. The OECD defines *foreign-born population* as follows: "The foreign-born population can be viewed as representing first-generation migrants, and may consist of both foreign and national citizens."[7] In some countries, the foreign-born population is significantly higher than the foreign population, such as in Sweden where that percentage makes up 11.5 percent of the population, in the Netherlands where it is 10.4 percent, and in Norway where it is 6.9 percent.

A second major development that led to further increases of migration from the East towards Western Europe was the fall of the Soviet Union. This unleashed waves of immigrants into Germany both as asylum-seekers as well migrants who, on the basis of their "ethnic German" status, were granted German citizenship immediately. Germany is one of the few countries, besides Israel, that allows its citizens who have emigrated to return to their homeland. People with papers indicating their German ethnic origins—regardless of how many generations they lived outside of Germany in Russia, or Kazakhstan, or other parts of Central and Eastern Europe—made use of their privilege and immigrated to Germany.

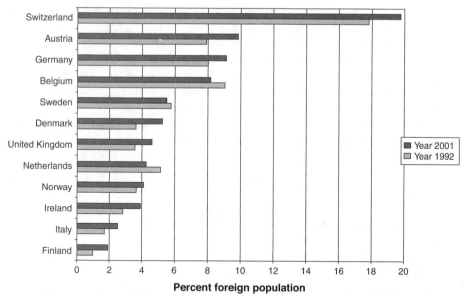

FIGURE 15.1 Foreign population in selected European democracies in 1992 and 2001. (*Source:* Trends in International Migration, 2003 [OECD].)

Between 1988 and 2004, over 3 million ethnic Germans immigrated to Germany, many of them ill-prepared in terms of the culture shock and lack of language and other skills. Ironically, the "ethnic Germans" prove to be much more difficult to integrate than the Turks and their descendants. The Turks have lived in Germany for decades, speak fluent German, have jobs and are well integrated, but yet have not been able to become Germans until recently.[8]

The clearest example of globalization, or, in other words, increasing interdependence, is probably the environment. For instance, while particular lifestyles are territorially bound (e.g., driving gas-guzzling vehicles in the United States or producing steel in Eastern Europe in the 1970s and early 1980s with coal-fired power plants), the effects of such behaviors or policies are not. The carbon dioxide from the SUVs traps heat and adds to the greenhouse effect, leading to global warming, while the sulphur emitted in the Czechoslovak steel mills came down as acid rain in Finland, destroying the aquatic life in thousands of Finnish lakes in addition to adding to the greenhouse effect. Polluted air does not recognize borders and will freely drift wherever the winds will carry it. Similarly, when the Chinese push forward with no-holds-barred economic development, this will manifest itself in a corresponding demand for oil; people all around the world will feel the effects of Chinese development in the form of higher oil prices and, again, in the form of increased pollution. As another example, the ancient tradition of cockfighting in Indonesia has led to the jumping of the avian flu virus from birds to humans. Though the avian flu virus has not mutated to the degree that it can be transmitted from human to human, if this does occur, modern transportation methods such as airliners will aid in the rapid dissemination of the virus, as they did in the case of AIDS. Meanwhile, the already infected birds take flight along their migration routes, carrying the bird flu virus with them to any country where they eventually settle down.

These examples highlight a central feature of both globalization and the environment: the interconnectedness of individuals and their lifestyles, regional and national policies, poverty, political development, diseases, wars, environmental outcomes, and many other aspects. Such interconnectedness decreases the capacity of nation-states to tackle such issues on their own while at the same time increases the importance of international organizations, leading some proponents of globalization to proclaim that national borders are becoming obsolete, while others decry this as "globaloney."

Globalization, then, can best be understood as a continuing process of integration and increasing interdependence between countries. In more practical terms, it means that more people worldwide:

- are most likely wearing a shirt made in China,
- have traveled abroad,
- are driving a foreign car and watching more foreign films,
- have jobs with international connections,
- are more aware of events abroad,
- count people from other countries among their friends,
- perhaps think of moving to another country,
- use modern communications technologies such as e-mail and the Internet,
- are affected by environmental outcomes not produced in your country,
- know more about other countries and cultures,
- are concerned about far-away diseases reaching their own country,
- work for an international company,
- are aware of other countries' traditions, consume products made abroad,
- invest in companies abroad,
- talk to people on the telephone or the Internet in another country, and/or
- use services generated in another country.

How should globalization be measured?

There is not one perfect measure to capture the elusive concept of globalization. But our discussion thus far has highlighted various dimensions of globalization, such as economic, cultural, technological, and political dimensions. The investment company A.T. Kearney together with *Foreign Policy Magazine* developed a globalization index essentially consisting of these four elements.[9] The economic dimension comprises two parts: trade as a percentage of GDP and foreign direct investment (FDI) as a percentage of GDP. The personal contact dimension is broken in three elements: international telephone traffic, international travel, and the amount of remittances and personal transfers of capital across borders. The technological dimension is also broken down into three elements: the number of Internet users per capita, the number of Internet hosts per capita, and the number of secure servers per capita. Finally, the political engagement dimension is subdivided into four elements: membership in international organizations, personnel and financial contributions to U.N. peacekeeping missions, the number of international treaties ratified, and governmental transfers.

According to this classification—which should be used with caution as two central elements of globalization are missing, migration and the production and distribution of

TABLE 15.1   Rankings of European democracies (with the United States for comparison purposes) in terms of globalization from highest to lowest (2005)

Country	Ranking 2005	Ranking 2004	Change 04/05
Ireland	1	1	0
Switzerland	2	2	0
United States	3	6	+3
Netherlands	4	3	−1
Denmark	5	8	+3
Sweden	6	9	+3
Austria	7	7	0
Finland	8	3	−5
United Kingdom	9	9	0
Norway	10	13	+3
Czech Republic	11	12	+1
Croatia	12	19	+7
France	13	10	−3
Slovenia	14	13	−1
Germany	15	12	−3
Portugal	16	22	+6
Hungary	17	20	+3
Spain	18	16	−2
Italy	19	17	−2
Greece	20	19	−1
Poland	21	21	0
Romania	22	26	+4

Source: A. T. Kearney and *Foreign Policy Magazine*. Globalization Index 2005. www.atkearney.com

cultural items such as films and TV shows—yields the rankings for 2004 and 2005 shown in Table 15.1.

Among European democracies, Ireland and Switzerland are the most "globalized" according to Table 15.1, followed by the United States, which moved up three ranks from 6 in 2004 to 3 in 2005. (These rankings do not include Singapore, which ranked the highest in 2005, nor countries such as Canada, Malaysia, New Zealand, or Australia. Only European countries and the United States are ranked.) It is interesting to note the great strides that Croatia and Romania made as trade flows and foreign direct investments dramatically increased in preparation for EU accession in Romania and eventually EU accession for Croatia. Countries such as Finland slipped as their predominant position in Internet use and Internet hosting has been undermined by the United States.

It is important to remind readers that this index is a composite index summing up the four elements. A central predictor for the degree to which a country is "globalized" is simply its size. For example, trade expressed as imports and exports as percentage of GDP in Luxembourg is almost 200, whereas in the United States that percentage is around 21.[10] This means that Luxembourg trades around twice as much as it produces while the United States trades only around a fifth of what it produces. The difference, of course, is that the United States has a gigantic internal market whereas Luxembourg, a very small country, is extremely exposed to the vagaries of international business cycles. Thus, by definition, the smaller a country is, the more "globalized" it has to be, at least in economic terms. This means the smaller a country is, the more its sovereignty is circumscribed by the forces of globalization. (I)t is this fact . . . which some consider troublesome—to which we now turn.

THE CHALLENGES OF GLOBALIZATION FOR EUROPEAN DEMOCRACIES

If it is true that globalization is driven by the logic of markets, many central elements of European politics should be affected. As a general rule, it is safe to say that governments are more interventionist in European democracies than in the United States, and thus should be more affected by the results of globalization. In addition, Europeans favor equality over liberty, again highlighting the central role of the state in achieving equality. For these reasons, European countries should be particularly affected by the process of globalization.

How do citizens feel about globalization? Globalization usually becomes an issue when there are violent street protests at World Economic Forum in Davos, Switzerland, or G-8 in Genova, Italy, and it appears that globalization is a widely disliked phenomenon. However, Figure 15.2 shows that this is not necessarily the case.

The graph in Figure 15.2 is ordered from the highest to lowest percentage of those who think that globalization is a "good thing." The Scandinavian countries and the Netherlands show a majority of people who believe that globalization is a good thing for their country, while Greece, France, and Spain are at the bottom of that list, with only around 30 percent of the people believing that globalization is a good thing. When it comes to the cultural dimension (i.e., when the question is asked whether people think that globalization "makes the world a duller and more uniform place"), few Europeans tend to disagree with that statement. In most European countries more respondents believe that globalization will make the world duller and more uniform. It is important to note, however, the very high percentages of "don't knows" in this survey (for ease of interpretation, not shown in Figure 15.2). For example, the average percentage of "don't know" for the question of whether globalization is a good thing is about 20, and that percentage rises to about 25 when it comes to the second question. This reflects a lack of reflection on this complex question and highlights the fact that many people are confused about the meaning of *globalization*, despite the fact that it has become such a buzzword during the last decade.

We now look at three challenges to European democracies that directly arise as a result of globalization: first, maintaining the generous European welfare state; second, the unprecedented levels of immigration into many of the "old" European countries; and third, the sense of loss of "community" across many of the same countries.

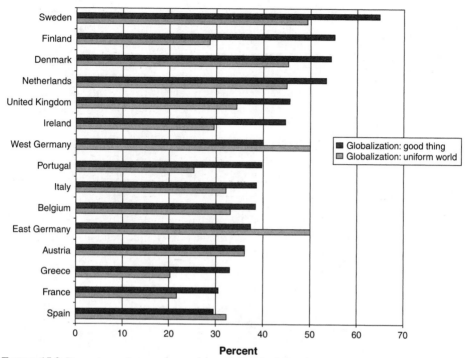

FIGURE 15.2 Percentage of respondents who agreed to the following question: "You may have heard of globalization, that is the general opening up of all economies, which leads to the creation of a worldwide market. Could you please tell me if you tend to agree or tend to disagree with the following statements: (1) Overall, globalization is a good thing for our country. (2) Globalization leads to a duller and more uniform world. (Graphs shows percentages who disagreed with these statements.) (*Source*: Eurobarometer [EB 61], European Commission 2004.)

The Welfare State and Globalization

Globalization's biggest challenge to national governments is dealing with the loss of control over domestic politics. As globalization unfolds and erodes the coveted principle of national sovereignty, who will address the demands of marginalized and dislocated citizens? Where is the locus of legitimate government if that very government is hamstrung by international market forces? To whom do citizens turn when there is mass unemployment, when they become sick, when there is an economic depression, when they get injured on the job, or when they lose their possessions in a natural catastrophe? Will they turn to their elected government for help or will they turn to the "world market"?

The world market has no address to which concerned citizens could send their petitions. There is no substitute for local politics, which can address the concerns of citizens. Nowhere is this more clearly visible than in the extent to which many European democracies have invested in social insurance schemes to ensure social harmony, provide equal opportunity, and other protection from unemployment or illness (see Figure 1.1 in Chapter 1). Denmark, Sweden, France, and Germany spend almost 30 percent of their GDP on such social expenditures, whereas the United States spends less than 15 percent.

In Chapter 1, we highlighted the presence of extensive welfare states as one of the distinguishing features of European democracies. Many observers, however, are concerned that globalization will undermine the capacity of European democracies to maintain their social protection schemes. What is the logic of their argument? In order to fund national health care, public pensions, stipends, unemployment insurance, and many other public programs, modern welfare states rely on tax revenues. Tax revenues depend largely on a vibrant business sector that invests in the domestic economy, thereby generating corporate taxes as well as personal taxes as a result of people employed by the company. These taxes, generated as a result of domestic economic activity, enable welfare states to fund their programs.

However, as we have noted, as a result of modern production and transportation technologies, many companies today have an "exit" opportunity, that is, an opportunity to leave their home country and produce in parts of the world where taxes are lower, wages are lower, and regulations such as environmental regulations are less stringent. Such "mobile asset holders" (mobile assets include capital, production facilities, and also highly qualified white-collar workers) will become "footloose," or able move to wherever the possibilities for higher profit are more promising, a process called *business process outsourcing*.

PHOTO 15.2 In the business world, few constraints for outsourcing are as compelling as this one.

It bears repeating that "outsourcing" is not a new phenomenon. It occurred already in the 1970s when the production of relatively simple products such as textiles, shoes, or assembly processes were moved off-shore.[11] In addition, companies have been moving their headquarters "off-shore" (i.e., to locations with much lower tax rates) for many decades. The point of off-shoring is to protect the company's "assets" by "mitigating" tax payments.

What is "new" is that nowadays even services, such as financial services, customer services, and software production and support are moved off-shore—these activities were previously believed to be very difficult to outsource. For example, New York parking tickets are sorted in Ghana; the data on unemployed New Jersey welfare recipients used to be handled in India.[12] This does not mean that more traditional forms of outsourcing have stopped. In a most ironic case, the uniforms of American border control agents are manufactured in Mexico.[13]

Nevertheless, the business sector that today shows a strong tendency for outsourcing is the information technology (IT) sector. In the summer of 2003, the board of the German high-tech giant Siemens announced that its software development division, which encompasses a workforce of 30,000, will no longer be able to keep these jobs in "expensive business locations" such as Germany, and is considering moving software development to India and China. Deloitte Consulting estimates that across Europe, 700,000 IT jobs will be moved to cheaper locations in the coming years. The situation is similar in the United States. According to Forrester Research, the American service sector will lose 3.3 million jobs by 2015. One out of four of the 500 biggest U.S. companies are outsourcing jobs off-shore.[14]

Capital appears to be greatly advantaged in this globalized world for two reasons: first, the owners of capital can put significant pressures on governments to provide inducements to the companies to stay by promising them lower taxes, fewer social services for their workers, and even help in reducing the influence of unions. Incumbents' reelection chances are seriously reduced if unemployment increases as a result of companies closing their doors and moving to another country. This puts governments in the worst possible position, insofar as they have to deal with rising unemployment on the one hand and at the same time face a reduced capacity to pay for unemployment benefits as a result of the shrinking tax base on the other hand. Consequently, incumbents have strong incentives to ensure that capital stays put by giving corporations tax breaks, by reducing the share of labor costs paid for by the employer, and through other economic incentives. For example, in many European democracies such as Germany, Austria, Belgium, and Finland, employers' contribution to social insurance is almost as high as the actual wage they pay their workers. The total labor costs per hour for an average American worker in 2003 consisted of about $18 for pay and $5 for social insurance, whereas in Germany the share of pay is almost the same as in America, around $19, but the social insurance element, in German called *Lohnnebenkosten*, comes out to about $15, for an hourly total of $34.[15]

The second major advantage owners of mobile assets have is when it comes to choosing a new location for production. For example, large multinational corporations will often play off one location against another, engaging the governments in a bidding war against each other. They will thus be compelled to offer better conditions than their competitor in terms of, again, lower taxes, less onerous regulation, and no costs for such facilities as roads, sewage systems, bridges, and so on that the company needs for production. This will lead to a continuous undercutting by countries of each other's bids to the point where companies will locate in the country with the lowest wages, least regulation, oftentimes unsafe working conditions, and where they have to pay the least amount of social services, a process known as "race to the bottom."

In the minds of many observers, these developments threaten the viability of the welfare state. If the tax base shrinks as a result of concessions given to holders of mobile capital to either stay put or to attract more of them, it is questionable whether the welfare state can continue to exist. These are legitimate concerns, yet, empirically, scholars have not been able to find a clear-cut connection between outsourcing and a reduction in the generosity of the welfare state.[16] Others have actually found that the more globalization is taking place, the more prominent the welfare state becomes, exactly the opposite of what the proponents of the globalization thesis assert. How can this be explained? The argument goes something like this: If it is true that modern Western nations cannot compete on the basis of price with less-developed societies, they must compete on the basis of quality. Producing high-quality products requires an extremely well-educated populace, which, in turn, can only be achieved through increased public investment into education (human capital) and infrastructure (physical capital). In other words, the more globalization proceeds, the more the welfare state is needed to counteract the adverse effects of globalization.[17] The verdict is still out on these academic issues, but there is no doubt that outsourcing is affecting the daily lives of millions of Europeans.

Immigration and Globalization

The second challenge to European democracies arises with increased immigration into Europe. The 19th century saw significant emigration *from* Europe, but since the early 1960s, Europe has become a destination for immigrants. Particularly Germany, but also Austria aggressively recruited so-called "guestworkers" from Turkey and former Yugoslavia to help in the reconstruction of their war-ravaged countries and during the economic boom, the so-called *Wirtschaftswunder* (economic miracle) that unfolded in the late 1950s until 1973/1974. In addition, as explained earlier, with the fall of the Berlin Wall, millions of asylum-seekers and ethnic Germans returned from far-flung corners of Central and Eastern Europe and Russia to Germany during the 1990s.

These were, of course, legal immigrants. However, over the last decade, Europe has been experiencing increasing illegal immigration, in the form of human trafficking organized by groups such as the Chinese "snakeheads" and the Italian and Russian Mafia in combination with poorly paid, corrupt border guards whose job is to supposedly secure the eastern borders of the EU. Countries with long sea borders such as Greece and Italy find it exceptionally difficult to patrol their waters and oftentimes, if they do encounter a ship smuggling illegal immigrants, are forced to aid women and children who were thrown overboard by the smugglers in order to escape. A second route of illegal immigration is from North Africa. Recently, the Italian government forcefully returned over 2,000 African migrants who had gathered on the small island of Lampedusa, Italy, who planned to continue their journey further north. They were returned in military aircraft to Libya, which has become a major staging ground for human traffickers wishing to smuggle Africans into Europe.[18] It is estimated that about 500,000 illegal immigrants make their way into Europe per year.[19]

A particular challenge for European governments is to deal with asylum-seekers, as it often is very difficult to ascertain their true motives. Asylum is generally granted if the asylum-seeker can show that he or she is politically persecuted at home. In many cases, however, people flee their homelands simply for economic reasons, but pretend to be in need of asylum protection. Over the past two decades, European democracies received about 9 million asylum applications, and only 3 million were granted. Germany, which until 1993 had one of the most liberal asylum laws in the world, processed over 438,000 asylum applications but granted asylum to only 4 percent in 1992, indicating that many applications were "bogus."[20] In other words, these were people hoping to find a better life with more economic opportunities by pretending to be politically persecuted.

In February of 2004, the Dutch government pushed through legislation that provided for the expulsion of more than 26,000 asylum-seekers, including Afghans, Somalis, and Chechens who are facing a civil war upon arrival in their country of origin. Under the new law, the first of its kind in Europe, children reared in the Netherlands and settled refugees with stable jobs will be uprooted and deported as the government attempts to clear a years-old asylum backlog in one "clean sweep." "If they are not expelled," said a spokesperson, "they will become illegal immigrants without any right to benefits."[21]

A large part of the illegal immigrants who make it into Europe are unskilled, do not speak the national language, and find it extremely difficult to adjust to the local culture. A large percentage of women are forced into prostitution in order to pay the smugglers who brought them into Europe. It is estimated that the business of human trafficking is second only to drug smuggling. Human trafficking is big business, with $7 billion generated by prostitution alone.[22]

European democracies face two separate yet related challenges: first, the political ramifications of legal and illegal immigration, and, second, how to integrate those who have been given legal status in a European country. Immigration into relatively homogeneous European societies is fueling resentment by natives—because the immigrants are "different" in race or religion, or they take jobs away from natives, or because natives believe they have come to exploit the cushy welfare state. These motives make for a volatile mix. Racial prejudices fueled the appalling attacks in 1992 and 1993 that involved the fire-bombing of Turkish families, Vietnamese foreign laborers, and asylum-seekers from Kosovo in the towns of Mölln, Hoyerswerda, Solingen, and Rostock.

People with such resentments are fodder for leaders of the radical right, who transform these sentiments of xenophobia into political support for their parties. Xenophobia has been an explosive political issue, and explains the electoral successes of Jean Marie Le Pen in France in 2002, Jörg Haider in Austria in 1999, and the 2004 electoral successes of two German radical right-wing parties in the Länder of Brandenburg and Saxony, located in former Eastern Germany. In Saxony, the NPD (*Nationaldemokratische Partei Deutschlands—* National Democratic Party of Germany) gained 9.2 percent of the popular vote and had 12 members in Saxony's parliament. In Brandenburg, another radical right-wing party, the DVU (*Deutsche Volksunion*—German People's Union) gained 6.1 percent of the popular vote, which translated into six seats.

The second challenge immigration presents is the integration of newcomers. Even if they have arrived legally, either as immigrants, asylum-seekers, or refugees, newcomers are often pushed to the margins of society, living in separate worlds oftentimes referred to as "parallel societies." They tend to gravitate toward larger cities and form ethnic enclaves such as in the Swedish city of Malmø, where almost 40 percent of the town of 250,000 is foreign born. Integration of newcomers who are racially, religiously, and ethnically "different" into the hitherto largely homogeneous European population is challenging enough, but is made even more difficult if "otherness" is reinforced by poverty—in other words, when almost all the poor are minorities and almost all the minorities are poor.

This toxic brew of discrimination, bad schools, prejudice, lack of opportunity, poor housing in ethnic ghettoes, poverty, and hopelessness exploded across France in the month of November 2005, when nightly riots occurred involving the burning of cars and property, perpetrated mostly by second- or third-generation Muslim immigrants of north or west African origin who constitute about 10 percent of the French population. One of the most potent origins of these riots is youth unemployment, which reaches a staggering 40 percent in those ethnic enclaves.[23] The riots revealed a wide chasm between the white, well-to-do French citizens and the marginalized citizens.

Though economic deprivation is certainly a major contributor to the French riots, they also point out the failings of the French Republican model of integration. This model essentially says that all French citizens have the same cultural identity—French. In fact, being French is the only acceptable identity. Everybody is supposed to be equal in this model insofar as all French citizens are the same "children of the Republic," as Jacques Chirac declared at the height of the riots.[24] The French model of integration is an assimilationist model requiring that everybody speak the same official language and go through a common curriculum in school. This model does not allow any other forms of identity, such as wearing the Muslim headscarf, as such outward symbols would threaten the identity of the nation. The *l'affaire du foulard*, the headscarf debate, has plagued France since 1989 when two schoolgirls, wearing the traditional Muslim headscarf *(hijab)*, were expelled from a public school. On March 15, 2004, French President Jacques Chirac signed a law banning the wearing of conspicuous religious symbols in schools on the basis that this would undermine the separation of church and state *(laïcité)* and national cohesion. Another element of the French Republican model is that the government does not keep official statistics on ethnicity, religion, or social class, as this would "violate the Republican tenet that France is 'one and indivisible.' "[25]

It is a bitter irony that this very model intended to create a sense of French identity based on common Republican principles did exactly the opposite: reveal dramatic differences in life chances between two classes of citizens—the "native" French with French-sounding names, addresses, and white skin color, and the second- or third-generation French citizens with dark skin, Muslim-sounding names, and addresses in the dilapidated suburbs.

The second strategy of incorporating new citizens is called *multiculturalism*, which represents the opposite of assimilation. The Netherlands has practiced multiculturalism for the last three decades, but this approach has also been found deficient. Multiculturalism means that the state recognizes the cultural differences of immigrants and actively assists them in maintaining their language—setting up schools for their children with a customized curriculum, exemptions from dress codes, affirmative action policies, or allowing dual citizenship.

In the Netherlands, too, "visible minorities," although being citizens, congregate in large numbers in big cities such as Rotterdam, where 50 percent of its inhabitants are foreign born. Even though multiculturalism is the polar opposite of assimilation, newcomers in multicultural societies are perhaps not living so much on the margins, but rather in "parallel societies," disconnected from the natives. This fact was not lost on the Dutch

Minister for Immigration and Integration, Rita Verdonk, who declared that "almost all EU member states are currently dealing with similar difficulties with regards to integration [of immigrants]: segregation of the housing market, educational and economic disadvantage among minority groups; social and religious tension, and a resultant breakdown in the social fabric."[26] A parliamentary report, released in early 2004, concluded that "the country's 30-year experiment in tolerant multiculturalism had been a failure, and has resulted in poor schools, violence, and ethnic ghettoes that shun intermarriage with the Dutch."[27]

The most drastic failure of integration is of course when visible minorities, even if they are citizens of a European country, use violence in the name of a different ideology or religion. Three of the four suicide bombers who killed 56 people and injured 700 others in London on July 7, 2005, were of Pakistani descent and one was of Jamaican descent, but they were all British citizens. In the wake of these bombings, carried out by radical Muslims, Tony Blair proposed strict antiterror measures, including surveillance of mosques, extremist Web sites, and bookstores, and deportation of radical Islamic leaders who incite anti-Western feelings among impressionable Muslim youths. British Prime Minister Tony Blair used strong language to defend his controversial deportation policy: "The rules of the game are changing. . . . We are angry. We are angry about extremism and about what they are doing to our country, angry about their abuse of our good nature. . . . We welcome people here *who share our values and our way of life*. But don't meddle in extremism because if you meddle in it . . . you are going back out again" (emphasis added).[28] This declaration is not consistent with British multiculturalism policies, and it is likely that political support for such policies, is waning in the wake of radical Muslim bombings. In addition to Britain, other nations have also engaged in the deportation of radical Muslim leaders. In the summer of 2005, Italy deported 8 radical Palestinian Imams and France ejected 12 so-called "Islamic preachers of hate."[29] The latest German immigration law includes explicit deportation measures for those who are preaching hatred, holy war, or violence (*geistige Brandstifter*).

These episodes demonstrate that incorporation of immigrants, particularly of Middle Eastern descent, is a significant challenge to European democracies, even if such immigrants have become citizens. There is no doubt that "Islamophobia" is spreading in European democracies. Europe, as opposed to the United States, does not have a "melting pot" identity. In fact, just the opposite is true. As we have seen in the French case, identity is connected to abstract Republican principles, or in the case of Germany, until recently, German identity was connected to blood relationships (*jus sanguinis*). These rigid forms of identity make it much more difficult for immigrants to find acceptance and equal life chances among their European host societies as compared to the United States, where upward social mobility among immigrants is more vigorous. Integration of immigrants is one of the biggest challenges European democracies will face in the near future because it raises a fundamental question: Who are we?

Nothing illustrates the political and cultural incompatibility between the west and Muslim countries more than the "cartoon controversy" which erupted in January of 2006. A Danish newspaper had published cartoons depicting the prophet Mohammed in September of 2005. One cartoon showed Mohammed wearing a bomb shaped turban whose fuse is on fire. Muslims around the world reacted angrily against these depictions and organized massive street demonstrations in Egypt, Pakistan, Malaysia, Thailand, Algeria, Afghanistan, and other Muslim countries as well as in many western nations with significant

Box 15.1 A Cartoon in 3 Dimensions; The Islam the Riots Drowned Out

CAMBRIDGE, MASS.-In a world of wrenching change, the Danish cartoon affair has widened a growing fissure between Islam and the West. The controversy comes at a time when many in the Islamic world view the war on terrorism as a war on Islam. They draw on memories of colonization and of the Crusades, when Western invaders ridiculed the Prophet Muhammad as an imposter.

Sadly, the recent polarization obscures a rich humanistic tradition with Islam—one in which cosmopolitanism, pluralism and a spirit of open-minded inquiry once constituted a dominant ethos. . . . Within the Muslim world, the cartoon Imbroglio has given ammunition to the two entrenched forces for censorship—namely, authoritarian regimes and their Islamic fundamentalist opposition. Both would prefer to silence their critics. By evincing outrage over the Danish cartoons, authoritarian regimes seek to divert attention from their own manifold failures and to bolster their religious credentials against the Islamists who seek to unseat them.

Ironies abound. Saudi Arabia leads the protests, yet is systematically destroying its Islamic heritage. The Wahhabis who dominate Saudi Arabia do not believe in honoring Islam's holy men and women or the Prophet Muhammad (they've proscribed the celebration of his birthday). Driven by sectarian zeal, the Saudi authorities have razed and dug up virtually every site in Mecca and Medina linked to Muhammad, members of his family and his companions.

But these acts of disrespect and desecration have failed to arouse any protest from those who now take to the streets to condemn the Danish cartoons.

Elsewhere, Sunni Muslim fundamentalist leaders express anger over the Danish cartoons, but no comparable indignation over suicide bombers who attacked Shiite Muslim mosques during Ramadan in Iraq. In Pakistan, blasphemy laws have been used by fundamentalists to attack Christians and Hindus. . . . The loudest and most murderous forces have chosen to forget the spirit of the Koran, which opens with an invocation of God's mercy and compassion and which repeatedly urges believers to practice patience and kindness. There is something very ugly about the power of the radicals, their recourse to violence, their anti-intellectualism and their ability to trample and blaspheme a more humanistic Islamic tradition. It is right and proper for Muslims to be offended, to be hurt, to protest. But we should be wary of the authoritarian voices that claim to speak and act in the name of Islam. The answer is not more violence and censorship, but rather peace, mercy and compassion.

Source: By EMRAN QURESHI, *New York Times*, February 12, 2006.

Muslim immigrants. The Danish, Norwegian, Italian, and other western embassies in many Muslim nations were attacked either by burning them down or damaging them otherwise. Many western nations recalled their ambassadors from Muslim countries for fear of their lives (Box 15.1).

Muslims consider depictions of Mohammed blasphemous and they are particularly offended by the degrading context in which their prophet is shown. Since the riots over the cartoon broke out, over 130 people lost their lives. The west reacted with claims that such depictions are protected by fundamental rights such as freedom of expression that finds its origin in western thought. Muslims, on the other hand argue that with the right of freedom of expression comes responsibility. This cartoon controversy highlighted that the nature of the conflict between Muslims and the west is cultural. While globalization facilitates contact with members of other cultures, it also highlights the differences between peoples, often with dire consequences. And yet, as long as immigration of Muslims into western countries continues, integration policies will be the only means to increase understanding between two potentially hostile group of peoples.

At the same time, Europe is in dire need of immigrants. The birthrate of most "old" European countries is declining, particularly in countries such as Germany and Italy. According to estimates by the Federal Statistical Office of Germany, by the year 2050, the German population will have shrunk to its 1963 level. This scenario assumes an average fertility rate of 1.4 children on average per woman, increases in life expectancy, *and* an inflow of 200,000 immigrants per year. During the last 30 years Germany's population shrank by 5.5 million, almost as many as those who have emigrated from Germany to the United States between 1815 and 1914. Estimates suggest that immigration would have to rise to 300,000 per year by 2020 and to half a million per year between 2030 and 2050 just to keep Germany's population at the current level.[30] This will present huge challenges to German politics and society. The task is to integrate immigrants in such a way that they feel accepted and part of the community—only then will the host society reap the benefits of their talents.

Globalization and the Fragility of Community

The previous section has highlighted challenges to community that are driven by people in motion. But globalization can affect communities even without "others" impinging on host societies. This is particularly an issue when economic interests clash with local cultures or traditions. The competitive pressures of globalization are often described as "inevitable," "natural," or "logical," and it is a common belief that one can do very little against the imperatives of the world market. The central claim here is that economic rationality clashes with deeply held moral or religious principles, and that, "inevitably," the "logic" of the market will undermine these moral and religious tenets, thereby destroying the very sense of community and identity of particular groups.

Two examples will illustrate this point. The first involves Austria. Austria is an overwhelmingly Catholic country, and in the past it required stores to be closed on Catholic holidays. One such Catholic holiday occurs in the middle of the busy Christmas shopping season, on December 8 (immaculate conception). In the neighboring country, Germany, the stores were open and thus many Austrians traveled to Germany to do their Christmas shopping. Pressure by the business lobby increased during the 1990s, and by the late 1990s Austrian politicians succumbed to these pressures of business and stores had to be opened on such holidays, to the dismay of the Catholic Church as well as the unions.

Similarly, in our second example, many American states still have so-called "blue laws" that do not allow the sale of alcohol on Sunday in grocery stores and supermarkets.

The idea is to regulate morality by protecting the sanctity of the Sabbath. People should honor their lord on this day, pray, and go to church rather than hitting the bottle. Blue laws specified penalties for such moral offenses as drinking on the Sabbath, playing cards, lying, swearing, and so on. In fact, the penalties could be quite severe—ranging from monetary fines, to whippings, to having body parts burned or cut-off, even to the death penalty. However, alcohol can still be consumed in restaurants and bars on Sundays, seriously undermining the original intent of regulating morality.

Both of these examples highlight what Benjamin Barber called the "market impera- tive": Markets know no morality.[31] When the rational market principle clashes with moral values, moral values almost always lose. After all, what is wrong with making money by selling beer on a Sunday in a grocery store? For critics of globalization, however, it is these very moral principles, oftentimes connected to religious traditions, that constitute the iden- tity of a community. It is these very markers that set nations, tribes, regions, and localities apart from one another and give them their sense of unique identity, of who they are, who and how they worship, what foods they eat, the language they speak, the movies they watch, the customes they have, the traditions they engage in, and a whole host of other activities. For these critics, however, markets work like a bulldozer, which, by flattening out these differences in the name of market logic, destroys these constitutive elements that are the very determinants of cultural identity and community and creates an Orwellian homogenized, standardized, and uniform world.

Food is a case in point. In August of 1999, a French farmer educated at the University of California, Berkeley, Jose Bové, together with some accomplices, wrecked a half-built McDonald's in the small French town of Millau, catapulting Bové to instant celebrity status. Bové is a sheep farmer who makes the famous French Roquefort cheese. The United States placed a tariff on Roquefort in retaliation for the French banning American hormone- treated beef. Bové's intent was to show how multinational agricultural companies standardize the production of agricultural products, impose standardized "taste," and, with the help of the World Trade Organization (WTO), undermine small, local agriculture based on "natural" production methods. Food for the French is not only an issue of sustenance, but it is a way of life, a manifestation of culture. McDonald's stands for the opposite of culture—it stands for homogeneity, standardization, sameness, and loss of color, texture, and local identity—at least in the eyes of globalization critics.

The French take "culture" seriously. There is such a thing called *l'exception culturelle Française* (French cultural exception), which means that "culture" is not something that can be bought and sold, that it is not a commodity. For the French, culture is not primarily entertainment, it is an artistic expression of what it means to be French. Given this wide- spread perception, it follows that culture in all its forms, but mostly in terms of films, mu- sic, fiction, and food needs to be protected from outside competition, particularly from the influence of Hollywood filmmakers who appeal to the lowest of human instincts. French elites believe that the market should not decide what becomes most popular—art needs to be supported for its own sake. Indeed, since the mid 1990s regulations are in effect stating that 40 percent of all films shown must be of French origin. In addition, for every ticket sold on a foreign film, a certain percentage goes to toward subsidizing the French film in- dustry. As a result, the French film industry is rather vibrant as compared to other Euro- pean countries.

However, it is not just France that jealously attempts to protect its culture from globalization. On October 20, 2005, the UNESCO (United Nations Educational, Scientific and Cultural Organization) approved a treaty, with an overwhelming majority of 148 to 2, allowing countries to protect movies, music, and other cultural treasures from foreign competition, known as the cultural diversity treaty. One of the countries that did not support that treaty was the United States. The treaty was sponsored by France and Canada, and wholeheartedly supported by the United Kingdom.[32] This came as a heavy blow to America, as films and music are some of its largest exports. American movies made $16 billion in 2004, and ensuring continued access to overseas markets had been one of the prime U.S. goals at the World Trade Organization.

IS GLOBALIZATION A THREAT OR AN OPPORTUNITY FOR EUROPEAN DEMOCRACIES?

Europe is "ready" for globalization for the simple reason that Europeanization has already integrated almost all of Europe to a remarkable extent—with free and open borders and unlimited exchange of goods, people, capital, and services. Europeanization is a process that goes much further and deeper than globalization. A thought experiment will help make the case. Take, for example, CAFTA, the Central American Free Trade Agreement: there are no "four freedoms" (free movement of people, commodities, services, and capital) between the United States and Central America, for example; there are no laws governed by CAFTA that take precedence over national laws; there is no common currency across CAFTA; there are no environmental, labor, or social regulations that apply to all CAFTA countries equally; there are no political institutions that give representation to the member states of CAFTA; there is no CAFTA passport; and so on. In fact, such developments seem unthinkable. Thus, what the EU has achieved in integrating 25 countries goes far beyond what even the most convinced proponent of globalization could hope for.

At the same time, globalization challenges the European welfare state, as noted earlier. This is clearly a threat, but also an opportunity: Because European democracies will not be able to compete on the basis of price, they will have to compete on the basis of quality. In order to produce high-quality products, Europe will need a highly educated workforce. Thus, globalization puts tremendous pressures on European education systems to be on the cutting edge. In addition, the welfare state may in fact function like a cushion, protecting the countries from the ups and downs of the international business cycle. It may even be the case that welfare states, for that very reason, will be able to better weather the challenges of globalization than less-developed welfare states. It is quite instructive that the populations of Sweden, Finland, Denmark, and the Netherlands, who embrace globalization the most, are also protected the most by very generous welfare states (see Figure 15.2).

Immigration and integration of newcomers represents another threat, but, again, another opportunity as well. Europe must open its borders for newcomers and integrate them in such a way that they have equal chances for social mobility. This will force European countries to move away from their parochial conceptions of identity based on Republican and/or ethnic principles. Europe is rapidly aging and will need the influx of newcomers to bolster population and maintain its social security systems. Germany understood these challenges and, in a historic act, changed its immigration law from *jus sanguinis* (where citizenship is based on blood relations) to *jus soli* (territorially based citizenship) in 2000.

The threat that "McDonaldization" will undermine European countries' identity, culture, and community is overdrawn. The very terms *identity* and *community* tend to have rather romantic connotations, and it is easy to get swept away by the warm and fuzzy feelings these terms convey. They suggest such emotions only if one belongs to the "in-group," but not to outsiders. However, what "community" is for one person may very well be intolerance, parochialism, and provincialism for another. To be sure, identity and community are essential for the self-image of a nation, region, or a local group, but without tolerance, they can also suggest stagnation, stasis, prejudice, and oppression. It also betrays a rather insular understanding of "culture," as if culture was not constantly shaped by interactions with other cultures. Other cultures might be viewed as threatening one's way of life, but just as equally they can be seen as enriching one's life.

It is ironic: Precisely because of the process of EU integration, each EU member country has a better chance to weather the assault of globalization than if they were exposed to it individually. This is possible for two reasons: First, EU integration is not anarchic. People and their representatives in the member countries do have a say about the most critical decisions the EU makes, despite claims about the elitist character of the EU. Second, the EU represents a mighty economic superpower that can impose itself and withstand pressures from other economic superpowers much more effectively than any individual EU country ever could, without the fear of retaliation. This can most clearly be seen in the recent decision by the EU to prevent Chinese textiles from flooding European markets by holding the shipments at European borders. Since January 1, 2005, Chinese textile products have saturated world markets as a WTO (World Trade Organization) restriction on quotas expired. The EU launched an investigation and concluded that certain types of Chinese imports need to be curbed to protect the European textile industry. It may very well be that in the future, the European Union will be able to shield Europeans from the less-desirable consequences of globalization while taking advantage of its benefits.

Discussion Questions

1. In what way is globalization affecting your personal life?

2. Is it possible to maintain one's sense of community and at the same time embrace globalization?

3. Why do immigrants in Europe seem to have more difficulty integrating into their host societies than in the United States?

4. Can you think of examples where the market imperative does not undermine one's sense of community, but rather fosters it?

5. Why might globalization affect Europe more than the United States?

6. What is the difference between "Europeanization" and globalization?

7. When did globalization begin?

8. What are the central factors that determine the extent of globalization?

9. What might the effects of business outsourcing be on your chance of finding a job?

10. What are the dangers that come with "obliteration of distance"?

[1]Karl Marx. *The German Ideology* (quoted in Robert Tucker. *The Marx/Engels Reader.* (New York, Norton and Company, 2nd ed., p. 163).

[2]Paul Krugman. Growing World Trade: Causes and Consequences. Brookings Papers on Economic Activity, 1995, 327–77.

[3]Markus M. L. Crepaz and Vicki Birchfield. Global Economics, Local Politics: Lijphart's Theory of Consensus Democracy and the Politics of Inclusion. In *Democracy and Institutions. The Life Work of Arend Lijphart.* (Ann Arbor, MI, the University of Michigan Press, 2000).

[4]*Guinness World Records Book.* 2001. http://www.guinnessworldrecords.com/.

[5]Human Development Report 2004. Globalization and Cultural Choice, p. 87.

[6]Markus M. L. Crepaz (forthcoming). *Trust Beyond Borders. Immigration, the Welfare State and Identity in Modern Societies.* (Ann Arbor: The University of Michigan Press).

[7]*Trends in International Migration, 2003.* OECD (Organization for Economic Cooperation and Development).—Paris

[8]Ibid.

[9]http://www.foreignpolicy.com/wwwboard/g-index.php.

[10]Markus M. L. Crepaz. Global, Constitutional, and Partisan Determinants of Redistribution in Fifteen OECD Countries" *Comparative Politics*, 2002, 34: 169–188.

[11]Fröbel Folker, Jürgen Heinrichs, and Otto Kreye. *The new International Division of Labour.* (Cambridge: Cambridge University Press, 1980).

[12]Wolfang Müller. Ihr seid einfach zu teuer. Eine Neue Welle der Globalisierung. *Freitag 04.* January 16, 2004.

[13]Lou Dobbs. CNN—America Tonight. November 28, 2005.

[14]Müller, ibid.

[15]Labour Costs. *The Economist*, June 26, 2004.

[16]Duane Swank. *Global Capital, Political Institutions and Policy Change in Developed Welfare States.* (Cambridge: Cambridge University Press, 2002). Another influential book is Geoffrey Garrett. *Partisan Politics in a Global Economy.* (New York. Cambridge University Press, 1998).

[17]Crepaz, 2002, ibid.

[18]Silvia Poggioli. National Public Radio. October 13, 2004.

[19]CNN. In-Depth Specials: Immigration, Europe on the Move. 2003.

[20]Crepaz, forthcoming, ibid.

[21]*London Daily Telegraph.* February 19, 2004.

[22]CNN, Immigration: Europe on the Move, ibid.

[23]An Underclass Rebellion. *The Economist*, November 12, 2005, p. 24.

[24]National Public Radio. France May Extend Government Emergency Powers. November 15, 2005.

[25]Alfred Stepan and Ezra Suleiman. French Republican Model Fuels Alienation Rather Than Integration. *Taipei Times*, November 18, 2005.

[26]Rita Verdonk, Dutch Minister for Immigration and Integration. Speech given on June 30, 2004, in The Hague at a meeting of the EU press.

[27]*London Daily Telegraph*, February 19, 2004.

[28]*Washington Post*. Blair Proposes Strict Anti-Terror Measures. August 6, 2005.

[29]Newstelegraph. Colin Randall. France Ejects 12 Islamic "Preachers of Hate." July 30, 2005.

[30]Reiner Klingholz. Demographie: Was Deutschland erwartet. *GEO Magazin* (April/May 2004).

[31]Benjamin Barber. Jihad vs. McWorld. *The Atlantic Monthly*, p. 53–63.

[32]Bridges. UNESCO Overwhelmingly Approves Cultural Diversity Treaty. *Weekly Trade News Digest*, Vol. 9, October 26, 2005: 36.

INDEX

311